Managerial Economics

Managerial Economics

Tools for Analyzing Business Strategy

Thomas J. Webster

LEXINGTON BOOKS
Lanham • Boulder • New York • London

Published by Lexington Books
An imprint of The Rowman & Littlefield Publishing Group, Inc.
4501 Forbes Boulevard, Suite 200, Lanham, Maryland 20706
www.rowman.com

Unit A, Whitacre Mews, 26–34 Stannary Street, London SE11 4AB

British Library Cataloguing in Publication Information Available

Library of Congress Cataloging-in-Publication Data

Webster, Thomas J.
Managerial economics : tools for analyzing business strategy / Thomas J. Webster.
    pages cm
Includes bibliographical references and index.
ISBN 978-1-4985-0793-6 (cloth : alk. paper) — ISBN 978-1-4985-0794-3 (electronic)
1. Managerial economics. 2. Economics, Mathematical. I. Title.
HD30.22.W433 2015
338.502′4658—dc23

                                                                2014043987

∞™ The paper used in this publication meets the minimum requirements of American
National Standard for Information Sciences—Permanence of Paper for Printed Library
Materials, ANSI/NISO Z39.48-1992.

Printed in the United States of America

Contents

Chapter 1

Managerial Economics and Strategy

For many of you reading these words, it is probably safe to say that life after university is just around the corner. If responsibility and leadership is what you are after, perhaps a corporate management position is in the cards—maybe even a business of your own. While being a successful manager or business owner depends on many factors, both tangible and intangible, the tools and techniques of analysis developed in these pages will help you along the way.

In an important study about the future of MBA programs, Srikant Datar, David Garvin and Patrick Cullen (2010) conducted interviews with dozens of deans from highly ranked business schools in the United States and Europe, and current and former senior business executives from the financial services, consulting, multinational organizations, and high technology industries. Several important insights emerged from these discussions.

According to these business leaders, business schools should train future managers "to reassess facts, frameworks, and theories" taught in the class-room. There are things that every business leader should know, such as the difference between assets and liabilities, the determinants of an industry's structure, the return on investment, and the four P's (product, price, place and promotion). Datar, Garvin and Cullen refer to this as the "knowing" component.

Business leaders also expressed the belief that business schools should also pay more attention "to developing the skills, capabilities, and techniques that lie at the heart of the practice of management"—what Datar, Garvin and Cullen refer to as the "doing" component. Finally, business schools should endeavor to instill in its students the values, attitudes, and beliefs that form manager's world views and professional identities—the "being" component.

The purpose of this text is to contribute to the "knowing" component. The analytical tools discussed in the pages that follow will help managers understand the limits of models and markets to effectively respond to a rapidly changing business environment to produce optimal "bottom line" results. By the time you turn the last page of this text, you should have a better understanding of how to effectively respond to the competitive challenges of the marketplace.

THE ROLE OF ECONOMICS IN BUSINESS MANAGEMENT

Unlike courses in accounting, finance, marketing, and management, some business students view courses in economics as too abstract to be of any practical value. Yet, each year, thousands of businesses file for bankruptcy protection because managers failed to efficiently organize the company's operations, misread market trends, allowed product quality to slip, or misinterpreted the activities and intentions of rival companies. Perhaps they failed to formulate optimal advertising or financing strategies, did not procure raw materials and components at least cost, or failed to provide adequate incentives to motivate workers to put forth their best efforts. These are just a few of the topics that will be discussed in this text. A course in managerial economics will not transform a budding entrepreneur into another Warren Buffet (Berkshire Hathaway), Bill Gates (Microsoft), or Mark Zuckerberg (Facebook), but it will help nascent managers identify optimal solutions to common business problems.

What is Economics?

Economics is the study of how individuals, institutions, commercial enterprises, countries, and governments allocate scarce resources amongst competing uses. By **scarcity** we mean that the output of goods and services is limited because the supply of productive inputs and other resources needed for their production is finite. The ability of managers to maximize shareholder value, for example, may be handicapped by insufficient operating budgets, limited access to finance capital, restrictive government regulations, labor shortages, high interest rates, and a host of other operating constraints.

Understanding the role of scarcity and the need to make choices is central to an understanding of economics and business. Because of scarcity, the decision to undertake a particular course of action is a simultaneous decision to forego alternative opportunities. Since resources are finite, every decision involves sacrifice. Scarcity necessitates trade-offs. The highest-valued alternative foregone whenever a choice is made called **opportunity cost**. In the marketplace, opportunity costs are reflected in the prices of goods and services. An understanding of economics is useful in business precisely because it helps managers identify profit opportunities in situations involving scarcity and tradeoffs.

What is Managerial Economics?

Managerial economics is the application of economic principles to topics of concern to managers. Managerial economics combines the various business disciplines (such as accounting, finance, marketing, and management) with quantitative methods (such as optimization analysis, game theory, statistics, and forecasting) to find optimal solutions to business problems. The manner in which a manager organizes the firm's operations depends on what the firm is trying to accomplish. We typically assumed that the goal of a firm is to maximize profit. The principles and tools of analysis developed in this book will help future managers optimally achieve a firm's organizational objectives, whatever they may be.

Managerial economics is concerned with developing a framework for predicting managerial responses to changes in the business environment. Many economists earn a living by advising businesses and government agencies on how best to reach its goals by bringing the "real world" closer to the ideal outcome hypothesized by economic theory.

Strategic Behavior

Economists assume that decision makers attempt to achieve the best possible outcome subject to scarce resources. Consumers to maximize their material and spiritual well-being given limited incomes and wealth. Firms maximize shareholder value subject to a fixed operating budget and finite human and non-human resources. Analyzing consumer and producer behavior is often simplified by assuming their actions have no effect on the behavior of others. In the real world, however, decisions are often mutually interdependent.

In business, decisions are rarely, if ever, made in a competitive vacuum. For this reason, an analysis of **strategic behavior** in which decisions made by an individual or group affect, and are affected by, the decisions of other individuals or groups, is central to the study of managerial economics. **Game theory** is the study of strategic behavior. Managers who are able to put themselves in the shoes of rival are more likely to successfully achieve the firm's objectives. Managers must be open to the idea that success does not always involve conflict, but may entail cooperation. Game theory is not a cookbook of recipes on how to deal with every strategic contingency. It is a tool kit for analyzing situations involving move and countermove.

Quantitative Methods

Quantitative methods include the mathematical tools and techniques of analysis, including optimization analysis, statistical methods, forecasting, and game theory. Managerial economics attempts to bring economic theory into the real world by quantifying business relationships by analyzing historical data to find optimal solutions to managerial decision-making problems. To see how this is done, suppose that a manager believes that the demand for a firm's good or service is given by the general expression

$$Q^d = f(P,M,P_y,A). \tag{1.1}$$

Eq. (1.1) says that the demand for a good or service (Q^d) is systematically related to variables such as price (P), per capita money income (M), the price of a competitor's good (P_y), and the advertising expenditures (A). If this relationship is linear, Eq. (1.1) may be written

$$Q^d = \beta_0 + \beta_1 P + \beta_2 M + \beta_3 P_y + \beta_4 A. \tag{1.2}$$

After collecting data on Q, P, M, and P_y, it should be possible to estimate the parameter values (β_i) using standard statistical techniques.[1] The resulting estimated equations can be used by managers to identify optimal pricing, advertising, and other strategies to achieve the firm's objectives.

THE ROLE OF A MANAGER

A manager is responsible for making the day-to-day, operational and long-run strategic decisions that determine a company's success or failure. Managers direct and coordinate the activities of workers, organize production processes, acquire raw materials and other inputs to produce goods and services for sale in the market. Managers make the non-routine decisions that move the firm closer to achieving its objectives, including identifying and exploiting emerging market opportunities, determining the optimal level of expenditures in research and development, product design and quality, formulating effective pricing and advertising strategies, and so on.

THE ROLE OF PROFIT

We generally assume that the objective of a firm is to maximize total profit (π), which may be defined as

$$\pi = TR - TC, \qquad (1.3)$$

where *TR* is the total quantity produced (*Q*) times the market price *(P)* and *TC* is the total cost of producing *Q* units of output. The importance of profit in market economies cannot be understated. In a competitive business environment, profit is the engine of maximum production and the efficient allocation of scarce productive resources. Increasing prices in some industries and falling prices in others reflect changes in societal preferences for goods and services. Above-normal profits attract investment into the production of those goods and services that are most demanded by the society. Declining or negative profits signal producers that society wants less of other goods and services. In the process, factors of production are reallocated from their lowest to their highest valued use. It is "invisible hand" of decentralized decision making in pursuit of profit that promotes economic growth and raises living standards. These benefits tend to be greatest in competitive market economies with minimum government interference.

The Objective of the Firm

A firm is an activity that transforms scarce factors of production into outputs of goods and services that are demanded by society. The manner in which productive resources are combined and organized depends of the objectives of the firm's owners, managers, or both. In some cases, the owner and manager are one and the same. In the case of publicly-owned companies, decisions are made by managers who are the designated agents of shareholders.

Although there are many possible organizational objectives, economists usually assume that the objective of the firm is to maximize profit. This behavioral assumption is central to the neoclassical theory of the firm, which posits that the firm is a profit maximizing "black box" that transforms inputs into outputs for sale in the market. While the precise contents are unknown, it contains the "secret formula" that gives the firm its competitive advantage. Neoclassical theory makes no attempt to explain what actually goes on inside this "black box," although the underlying **production function** is assumed to exhibit certain desirable mathematical properties, such as the **law of diminishing returns**, **returns to scale**, and substitutability between and among productive inputs. The appeal of the neoclassical model is its application to a wide range of profit-maximizing firms and market situations.

As intuitively appealing as the assumption of profit maximization may be, this simple behavioral assertion is too vague to be of any practical value. In fact, the objective of most publicly-held corporations is not to maximize profit, but to maximize shareholder value. If profits are received at the end of each period, this is equivalent to saying that the objective of the firm is to maximize the net present value (*NPV*) of the stream future net earnings, which is given by the equation

$$NPV(\pi) = \frac{\pi_1}{(1+i)} + \frac{\pi_2}{(1+i)^2} + \cdots + \frac{\pi_n}{(1+i)^n}, \tag{1.4}$$

where π is per period profit (net, after-tax, earnings), t is a time index, and i is the **interest rate** used to discount future cash flows.[2] The interest rate is the price paid for the use of borrowed funds.

The **discount rate**, which is given by the term $1/(1 + i)$, is used to determine the **present value** of some future amount. In Eq. (1.4), π_0 is the firm's current profit; π_1 is the expected profit at the end of year 1, and so on. Discounting is necessary a dollar received in the future is worth less than a dollar received today. The reason it is worth less is that a dollar received today can be reinvested at some interest rate to yield an even greater amount tomorrow. In fact, the market value of any asset is equal to its **net present value**, which is the difference between the present value of cash inflows and cash outflows.

Eqs. (1.3) and (1.4) explicitly recognize the importance of diverse managerial decisions to achieve the firm's organization objectives. The marketing department, for example, has primary responsibility for sales, which are reflected in the firm's **total revenue** (*TR*), which is equal to price times the number of units sold. The production department monitoring the production costs (*TC*), while finance is responsible for acquiring financing to support the firm's capital investment activities, for which the interest rate (i) is of critical importance. This more complete model of firm behavior also explicitly recognizes the difficulty of making decisions in which future outcomes are uncertain.

In the above discussion, it was assumed that profits and the discount rate in period t are known with certainty. In fact, this is never the case. On the other hand, suppose that management believes that the current discount rate remains unchanged and that profits are expected to grow at a constant rate of g percent per year. If $g < i$, the net present value of profits in perpetuity is

$$NPV(\pi) = \pi_0 + \frac{\pi_0(1+g)}{(1+i)} + \frac{\pi_0(1+g)^2}{(1+i)^2} + \cdots = \pi_0\left(\frac{1+i}{i-g}\right). \tag{1.5}$$

For given values of i and g, the term $(1 + i)/(i - g)$ is a constant. Thus, maximizing the net present value of profits in perpetuity is equivalent to maximizing the firm's current profits.

SOLVED EXERCISE

Suppose that a firm's current profits are $25 million. Management believes that the firm's profits are likely to grow at an annual rate of 5 percent. Calculate the net present value of the firm's stream of profits at a discount rate of 8 percent.

Solution

Substituting the above information into Eq. (1.5), the net present value of the stream of future profits is

$$NPV(\pi) = \pi_0 \left(\frac{1+i}{i-g} \right) = \$25 \left(\frac{1.08}{0.03} \right) = \$900. \qquad (1.6)$$

The net present value of the firm's stream of future profits is $900 million.

What's a Company Worth?

Economists generally assume that the objective of the firm is to maximize shareholder value. But, how do we define a company's worth? Is it the market value of the company's outstanding shares? The problem is that share prices are volatile as the stock market and mirror swings in the business cycle and changes in the mood of investors, which may have nothing whatsoever with the performance and value of individual companies.

Should we use a company's net worth as reported in its balance sheet? The problem here is that accounting standards differ from country to country. What is more, net worth does not fully reflect the value of such intangibles as brand-name recognition, goodwill, patents, and the talents and expertise of its human resources, which is the life's blood of any commercial enterprise, but especially high-technology companies.

In terms of Eq. (1.4), can we use a company's net income as an approximation of its expected future cash flows? This comes closer to our definition of a company's net worth, but even this might be improved upon. An alternative to this is a company's operating profit less than the rate of return on debt and equity capital. The data used to make these calculations, which includes operating cost, total revenue, and capital expenditure, are readily available from a firm's income statement. Not only is this a good way to measure changes in a company's value, it is an excellent benchmark against which to measure executive perks and bonuses.

Types of Profit

To say that goods and services that can be produced profitably will be, and those that cannot be produced profitably will not begs the question: What do we mean by the term profit? What is commonly thought of as profit to the business or lay person may not have the same meaning to an economist. Eq. (1.3) defines total profit as total revenue earned from the sale of a good or service sold minus the total cost incurred from its production. While there is little debate over the meaning of the term total revenue, the conventional notion of total cost differs from the meaning assigned to it by economists.

Accounting Profit versus Economic Profit

Most people think of the cost of doing business as consisting of only direct payments made to productive resources. **Explicit costs**, also called **accounting costs** and *out-of-pocket expenses*, include wages paid to workers and raw materials suppliers. By contrast, an economist's interpretation of costs goes back to the fundamental idea that resources are scarce and have alternative uses. All resources used in the production process involve foregone opportunities, including those for which no direct payment is made. These implicit sacrifices are just as important as out-of-pocket costs and must be considered whenever decisions are made that affect the value of the firm.

Total economic cost (*TC*) includes all relevant opportunity costs, which is the market value of all resources used in the production process—both explicit and implicit. An **implicit cost** represents the value of resources used in the production process for which no direct payment is made. An engineer who writes computer code for a large software company writer sacrifices his salary when he opens his own consulting firm. The engineer's salary is an example of an implicit cost. A landlord loses rental income if she opens a hobby shop in her own commercial building. The lost rental income is an implicit cost. A housewife who redeems a certificate of deposit and uses the proceeds to open a day-care center forgoes interest income. This lost interest income is an example of an implicit cost. A restaurant owner employs her teenage girls, but does not pay them a wage. The income they could have earned is an implicit cost.

When filing corporate tax returns, managers will report the firm's **accounting profit** (π_A), which is the difference between total revenue and total explicit (accounting) cost. But, when it comes to making decisions on behalf of potential investors, managers should consider the firm's **economic profit** (π), which is the difference between total revenue and total economic cost, which is the sum of total explicit costs ($TC_{explicit}$) and total implicit costs ($TC_{implicit}$).

$$\pi_A = TR - TC_{explicit} \tag{1.7}$$

$$\pi = TR - TC_{explicit} - TC_{implicit} = TR - TC_{economic} \tag{1.8}$$

SOLVED EXERCISE

Adam operates a small shop specializing in party favors. He owns the build-ing and supplies all of his own labor and money capital. Adam incurs no explicit rental or wage costs. Before starting his own business Adam earned $1,000 per month by renting out the store and earned $2,500 per month as a store manager for a large department store chain. Because Adam uses his own money capital, he also sacrificed $1,000 per month in interest earned on U.S. government treasury bonds. Adam's monthly revenues from operating his shop are $10,000 and his total monthly expenses for labor and supplies amounted to $6,000. Calculate Adam's monthly accounting and economic profits.

Solution

Adam's accounting profit appears to be a healthy of $10,000 − $6,000 = $4,000 per month. However, if we take into account Adam's implicit costs of $4,500, which consists of foregone rent, foregone salary, and foregone interest income, Adam's total economic profit is $10,000 − $6,000 − $4,500 = −$500 per month.

It is, of course, a simple matter to make accounting profit equivalent to economic profit by making explicit all relevant implicit costs. Suppose that a restaurant manager quits a $40,000 per year job to open her own restaurant. Since this is a sacrifice incurred by the budding restaurateur, the foregone salary is an implicit cost. On the other hand, this implicit cost can easily be made explicit by putting the restaurant owner "on the books" for a salary of $40,000. The distinction between explicit and implicit costs is further illus-trated in the following problem.

Normal Profit

Perhaps the most important opportunity cost to consider when evaluating a company's performance is the implicit cost of capital. One way to capture this is to include **normal profit** as a component of the firm's total economic cost. Normal profit is the minimum rate of return necessary to keep share-holders from pulling their investment in search of a higher rate of return elsewhere. Also known as a **normal rate of return**, it is the next best alterna-tive investment of equivalent **risk**. At any lower risk-adjusted rate of return, managers will find it difficult, if not impossible, to raise finance for capital investment.

Managers should view a normal rate of return normal as an implicit cost of doing business. A manager who does not earn at least a normal rate of return runs the risk of being replaced by shareholders with someone who can. The yield on short-term U.S. Treasury securities is typically used as a proxy for risk-free investments. A risk premium should be added to this interest rate to make investors indifferent between a risky and a risk-free investment. Alternatively, it could also be argued that the rate of return for an industry may also be used as an approximation of a representative firm's normal rate of return.

Operating Profit

A firm's **total operating cost** (TC_O) includes expenditures relating to a firm's ongoing operations. Total operating cost, which is also referred to as **total variable cost** (TVC), represents that portion of the firm's total cost that vary with the level of output. **Operating profit** (π_O), which is the difference between total revenue and total operating (variable) cost, is the firm's net income from its ongoing operations. Formally,

$$\pi_O = TR - TC_O = TR - TVC. \tag{1.9}$$

The important thing to note about Eq. (1.9) is that a firm that breaks even in an economic sense, it is still earning a positive operating profit that is equal to its normal rate of return. Alternatively, a firm earning zero economic profit is earning a rate of return that is equal to best alternative investment of equivalent risk, which is an amount just sufficient to keep shareholders happy. When economic profits are positive, the firm's profits exceed its normal rate of return. When this happens, new investment will be attracted into the industry. When economic profits are negative, investors will exit the industry in search of more attractive returns.

CONSTRAINTS ON THE OPERATIONS OF THE FIRM

Whatever the firm's goals, day-to-day managerial decisions are hamstrung by a myriad of operational constraints that make it difficult to achieve the best possible outcome. All firms, regardless of size, have a finite operating budget that makes it difficult to maximize shareholder value. Market constraints may include a shortage of skilled labor, a disruption in the flow of critical raw materials due to foreign social or political unrest, limited production capacity or warehouse space, or a shortage of finance capital. Minimum wage laws, pollution emission standards, government regulation, and proscriptions on certain types of business activities, and antitrust legislation may also inhibit the manager's ability to achieve the firm's goals.

Conflicts of Interest

Maximizing shareholder value profit is also complicated when responsibility for the day-to-day operations of the firm is delegated to mangers (agents) who act on behave of absentee owners (principals). Frequently, the self-interests of managers are in conflict with the self-interests of the shareholders. Even if a system of incentives is implemented that synchronize the self-interests of owners and managers, additional problems may arise if workers are not adequately motivated to put forth their best efforts on behalf of managers. It is not possible to maximize shareholder value if the company's stakeholders are not pulling in the same direction.

In addition to the intra-firm rivalries that limit the firm's earnings potential, managers must devise strategies to deal with conflicts of interest that inherent in all market transactions. To begin with, there is the obvious tension between buyers and sellers. The objective of consumers is to acquire goods and services at the lowest possible prices. The objective of producers is to supply these products at the highest possible price. Since market transactions are voluntary, the forces of supply and demand should result in mutually beneficial outcomes.

Managers must also devise strategies to effectively cope with inter-firm rivalries. In industries consisting of multiple firms competing for the right to sell their products, a gain in market share by one firm means a decrease in market share of rival firms. The discipline of the market guarantees that the winners in this competition are those firms that are able to provide the highest possible product at the lowest possible price. Unfortunately, the social welfare gains arising from market transactions are lessened when an industry is dominated by one or a few sells that enjoy **market power**.

The manager must also develop strategies to effectively exploit inter-buyer rivalrics in which consumers compete for the right to acquire available goods and services. When shortages develop for goods and services, buyers who are willing and able to pay a higher price will outbid rivals for the right to consume these products. This conflict highlights the **rationing function of prices**, and the roles of bargaining and auctions.

Other Players

A firm's operations and performance is closely linked to activities of other players in the marketplace. Investments in plant and equipment depends on the firm's access to external financing in financial markets. Government regulation and the legal system dictate the types of goods and services that may be produced and the activities that are legally permissible. In this section we will briefly review the roles of financial markets and government.

Financial Markets

Financial markets (stock, bond, and foreign-exchange markets) and financial intermediaries (commercial banks, savings banks, and insurance companies) perform the essential economic function of channeling funds from households, firms, and governments that have surplus funds and no productive uses for those funds, to those with a shortage of funds and productive investment opportunities. A breakdown in financial markets can lead to a sharp downturn in the economy and severe economic hardships, which could result in social and political instability.

Financial instruments are traded in financial markets. A **financial instrument** is a tradable claim on the issuer's future income or assets, such as common stock and bonds. **Common stock** represents a share of equity (ownership) in a publicly-owned corporation. It is a claim on the future earnings and assets of a corporation. A **bond** is a debt instrument that promises periodic interest payments for a specific period of time and principal repayment upon maturity. There are several ways of calculating interest rates. The most important of these is the **yield to maturity** (*YTM*), which is the interest rate that equates future payments received from a debt instrument with its value today. The *YTM* consists of the current market interest rate, which is determined by the supply and demand for savings, plus a risk premium. A **risk premium** is the additional return required to make an investor indifferent between a risky and a risk-free investment. The risk premium is the difference between the interest paid on bonds with default risk and default-free bonds. As a general rule, a manager will invest in plant equipment when the expected rate of return is greater than the cost of financing the investment. Unfettered access to capital markets is essential if a firm is to achieve its objective of maximizing shareholder value.

Government

Government participation in market economies can occur at both the micro and the macro levels. The goal of **macroeconomic policy** is to promote full employment, price stability, and economic growth. Macroeconomic policy consists of monetary, fiscal, and commercial policies. Monetary policy, which is conducted by the Federal Reserve System in the United States, is concerned with the regulation of the money supply and the availability of credit. Fiscal policy deals with regulating aggregate demand through government spending and taxation. In the United States, fiscal policy may be initiated by the President or the Congress, but only enacted by Congress. Commercial policy refers to the use of tariffs and other trade restrictions to improve a country's international competitiveness. **Microeconomic policy** involves government regulation to alter the composition of the output of goods and services to achieve socially desirable goals, such as a cleaner environment, improved access to education and health care, and increased medical and scientific research.

Social, political, and legal constraints can make it difficult, if not impossible, for managers to fully realize a firm's organizational objectives. Adam Smith (1776) argued forcefully that the actions of self-interested individuals are "led by an invisible hand" to promote the general public welfare. The interaction of self-interested buyers and sellers in perfectly competitive markets promotes **economic efficiency**. When economic efficiency is realized, all resources are employed in their highest-valued uses.

The concept of economic efficiency allows us to make an important conceptual distinction between the study of economics and business. Whereas economists interpret the inefficient allocation of resources as obstacles to be removed, businesses see inefficiencies as opportunities to be exploited. If the goal is to maximize shareholder value, managers should seek out and redirect undervalued resources to their higher valued uses. Undervalued resources represent potential wealth-creating opportunities.[3]

Since private transactions may result in socially inefficient outcomes, it is sometimes necessary for governments to intervene in the market to increase social welfare. Consumption and production efficiency requires that buyers and sellers make informed decisions. An important role for government is to ensure that market participants have equal access to as much information possible about the goods and services being transacted. To help consumers and investors make the best choices, governments require companies to print ingredients on product labels, provide health warnings on cigarettes packages, require that publicly traded companies make available to investors complete and accurate financial statements, and so on. In most developed economies, governments have mandated that new pharmaceuticals be tested and certified before being made available to the public, while members of certain professions, such as lawyers, doctors, nurses, and teachers, must be licensed or certified.

Another justification for government intervention in the marketplace is the existence of **externalities**. These third-party effects in market transactions can be either positive or negative. Economic efficiency requires that only those directly engaged in trade receive the corresponding benefits and incur the associated costs. When this occurs, the market price will fully reflect those benefits and costs. An externality is said to exist when an unwitting third party receives some of the costs or benefits from a market transaction.

Environment pollution is the best known example of a negative externality. To correct the inefficiencies that are introduced into the economy, the government frequently intervenes by regulating market activity. Government regulation can take two forms—economic and social. Economic regulation focuses the activities of a specific industry and can range from prescribing acceptable pricing and output practices to actually operating a business. Social regulation deals with industry-wide phenomena and involves such issues as health and safety standards in the workplace, consumer protection, environmental standards, and antitrust policy. The origins of antitrust regulation in the United States can be traced to the Sherman, Clayton and Federal Trade Commission Acts of the late-nineteenth and early-twentieth centuries. The focus of antitrust regulation is to protect consumers from the exercise of market power, especially by large firms.

THINKING AT THE MARGIN

We will conclude with a brief discussion of what it means to "think like an economist." Marginal analysis compares the costs and benefits of the next decision. Rather than looking behind to road already traveled, economists focus on the next step in the journey. If taking a step yields a positive net benefit, a manager should take one more step. It that step has a positive outcome, take another step, and so on. In this way, the firm moves ever closer to achieving its goal. On the other hand, if the next step leads to a negative outcome, the manager should step back and reevaluate.

In economics, the word marginal means "extra" or "additional" or "change." In a world of scarcity and tradeoffs, every decision involves marginal benefits and costs. To see what is involved, consider the situation in which the objective of a firm is to maximize profit. Table 1.1 summarizes the total benefits and total costs of producing up to 10 units of output (Q). If the manager of this firm were fortunate enough to have this information, the task

Table 1.1   Maximizing Profit

Q	TR (total revenue)	TC (total cost)	$\pi = TB - TC$ (total profit)	$MR = \Delta TR/\Delta Q$ (marginal revenue)	$MC = \Delta TC/\Delta Q$ (marginal cost)	$M\pi = MR - MC$ (marginal profit)
0	0	2	−2	—	—	—
1	19	1	18	19	−1	10
2	36	2	34	17	1	16
3	51	5	46	15	3	12
4	64	10	54	13	5	8
5	75	17	58	11	7	4
6	84	26	58	9	9	0
7	91	37	54	7	11	−4
8	96	50	46	5	13	−8
9	99	65	34	3	15	−12
10	100	82	18	1	17	−16

of determining how much to produce would be child's play. If units are indivisible, simply choose the level of output that maximizes profit. In this case, the manager would produce 6 units of output and earn a profit of $\pi = \$58$.

If the manager of the firm does not have access to the information provided in Table 1.1, there is another way to proceed. Before we do, however, let us define some basic terms:

- *Total revenue (TR)* is the firm's total benefit from the production and sale of a good or service. Specifically, *TR* equals the number of units sold times the price per unit.
- *Total cost (TC)* is the total cost of production. In the short run, total cost is the sum of total fixed cost and total variable cost. Total fixed costs do not vary with the firm's level of output. Total variable cost is the cost of procuring variable inputs, which increase with an increase in the level of output.
- *Total profit (π)* is the difference between total revenue and total cost.
- *Marginal revenue (MR)* is the change in total revenue from a unit change in total output. It is conventional to use the symbol "Δ" to denote a discrete change.
- *Marginal cost (MC)* is the change in the total cost from a unit change in total output.
- *Marginal profit (Mπ)* is the change in total profit from a unit change in total output.

According to the data in Table 1.1, the cost of producing nothing is $2, which represents the firm's fixed cost. If the firm produces and sells one unit, $19 is the added to total revenue. Total cost actually declines from $2 to $1. The firm's profit increases from −$2 to $18. It is clearly in the firm's best interest to increase production by one unit since the addition to total revenue *(MR)* exceeds the addition to total cost *(MC)*. Since $MR > MC$, the addition to total profit is positive $(M\pi > 0)$.

If producing one unit adds to the firm's profit, try producing another unit. By producing and selling a second unit, $MR = \$17$ and $MC = \$1$. Since this adds another $16 to total profit $(M\pi = \$16)$, the firm should consider producing and selling yet another unit of output, and so on. If marginal cost exceeds marginal revenue, marginal profit will be negative and total profit will fall. In this case, too many units have been produced, in which case output should be reduced.

A profit-maximizing firm should increase output whenever $MR > MC$. If $MC > MR$, the firm should decrease output. Profit will be maximized at the output level where $MR = MC$. At this output level, $M\pi = \$0$. In Table 1.1, this occurs when the firm produces 6 units of output and profit is maximized at $58.

Deriving Marginal from Total Values

In the above example, the firm's profit was maximized at the output level where $MR = MC$. It will frequently be the case that a firm's total revenue and total cost will be expressed in the form of an equation. To determine the firm's profit-maximizing level of output, it will be necessary to derive the firm's marginal revenue and marginal cost equations. This is a relatively simple procedure for students with a background in differential calculus since, for example, the marginal revenue equations is simply the first derivative of the total revenue equation, that is $MR = dTR/dQ$, where "*d*" is used to denote instantaneous change.

Fortunately, a course in calculus is not necessary to master the material presented in this text. For most of the equations representing total values presented in this course, a simple rule is sufficient to derive equations representing the corresponding marginal values. Suppose that you are given an equation of the form

$$Y = \beta_0 + \beta_1 X^1 + \beta_2 X^2 + \beta_3 X^3. \tag{1.10}$$

where Y is some "total" value of concern, such as total revenue (TR) or total cost (TC), the β's are known parameters, and X is an explanatory variable, such as units of output (Q). Eq. (1.10) may be written

$$Y = \beta_0 X^0 + \beta_1 X^1 + \beta_2 X^2 + \beta_3 X^3. \tag{1.11}$$

The corresponding equation for the marginal value of Y, such as marginal revenue (MR) or marginal cost (MC), may be obtained by bringing the exponent on X to the front of the term and subtracting one from the exponent, that is

$$MY = \frac{\Delta Y}{\Delta X} = 0\beta_0 X^{0-1} + 1\beta_1 X^{1-1} + 2\beta_2 X^{2-1} + 3\beta_3 X^{3-1}, \tag{1.12}$$

which simplifies to

$$MY = \beta_1 + 2\beta_2 X + 3\beta_3 X^2. \tag{1.13}$$

SOLVED EXERCISE

Suppose that a firm's total revenue and cost equations are given by the equations:

$$TR(Q) = 20Q - Q^2; \tag{1.14}$$

$$TC(Q) = 2 - 2Q + Q^2. \tag{1.15}$$

a. *Determine the marginal revenue (MR) and marginal cost (MC) equations.*
b. *At what output is total profit maximized?*
c. *What is this firm's total profit (π)?*

Solution

a. *From Eqs. (1.14) and (1.15) the marginal revenue and marginal cost equations are:*

$$MR(Q) = \frac{\Delta TR}{\Delta Q} = 20 - 2Q; \tag{1.16}$$

$$MC(Q) = \frac{\Delta TC}{\Delta Q} = -2 + 2Q. \tag{1.17}$$

b. *Total profit is maximized where MR(Q) = MC(Q). Setting Eq. (1.16) equal to Eq. (1.17) and solving, profit is maximized at Q = 5.5 units of output.*
c. *The firm's total profit equation is*

$$\pi(Q) = TR(Q) - TC(Q) = -2 + 22(5.5) - 2(5.5)^2 = \$58.50. \tag{1.18}$$

CHAPTER EXERCISES

1.1 Explain why an analysis of strategic behavior is critical for achieving success in business.
1.2 Explain what it means to "think strategically."
1.3 The Museum of Heroic Art (MOCHA) is a not-for-profit institution. For nearly a century, the mission of MOCHA has been to "extol and lionize the heroic human spirit." MOCHA's most recent exhibitions, which have featured such larger-than-life renditions of such pulp-fiction super heroes as Superman, Wolverine, Batman, Green Lantern, Flash, Spawn and Wonder Woman, have proven to be quite popular with the public. Art aficionados who wish to view the exhibit must purchase tickets six months in advance. The contract of MOCHA's managing director, Dr. Xavier, is currently being considered by the museum's board of trustees for renewal. Should theories of the firm based on the assumption of profit maximization play any role in the board's decision to renew Dr. Xavier's contract?

1.4   Many owners of small businesses do not pay themselves a salary. What effect will this practice have on the calculation of the firm's accounting profit? What effect will it have on the firm's economic profit? Explain.

1.5   It has been argued that profit maximization is an unrealistic description of the organizational behavior of large, publicly-held corporations. The modern corporation, so the argument goes, is too complex to admit to such a simple explanation of the managerial behavior. One alternative argument depicts the manager as an agent for the corporation's shareholders. Managers, so the argument goes, exhibit "satisficing" behavior in that they maximize something other than profit, such as market share or executive perquisites subject to the shareholders' minimum acceptable return on investment. Do you believe that this assessment of managerial behavior is realistic? Do you believe that the above description of shareholder expectations is essentially correct?

1.6   As a practical matter, how would you estimate the risk premium on an investment?

1.7   Discuss several reasons why a firm in a competitive industry might earn above-normal profits in the short run. Will these above-normal profits persist in the long run? Explain.

1.8   Firms that earn zero economic profit should close its doors and seek alternative investment opportunities. Do you agree? Explain.

1.9   Tillie's Trilbies estimates that revenues and expenditures for the next fiscal year are:

Total Revenue	$6,800,000
Cost of Materials	5,000,000
Cost of Labor	1,000,000
Advertising	100,000
Insurance	50,000
Rent	350,000
Miscellaneous Expenses	100,000

a. Calculate Tilly's accounting profit.

b. Suppose that in order to open her trilby business Tilly gave up a $250,000 per year job as a buyer at the exclusive Hammocker Shlumper department store. Calculate Tilly's economic profit.

c. Tilly is considering purchasing a building across the street and moving her company into that new location. The cost of the building is $5,000,000, which will be fully financed at a simple interest rate of 5 percent per year. Interest payments are paid annually on the last day of Tilly's fiscal year. The first interest payment will be due next year. Principal will be repaid in 10 equal installments beginning at the end of the fifth year. Calculate Tilly's accounting profit and economic profit for the next fiscal year.

d. Based upon your answer to part c, should Tilly buy the new building? Explain.

1.10 In the last fiscal year Neptune Hydroponics generated $150,000 in operating profits. Neptune's total revenues and total economic costs were $200,000 and $75,000, respectively. What is Neptune's normal profit?

1.11 The following table summarizes the net cash flows of two mutually exclusive capital investment projects. If cash flows are realized at the end of each period, which project should be adopted at an interest rate of 12 percent?

Period	Project A	Project B
1	100	350
2	200	300
3	250	200
4	300	200
5	350	100
Total	1,200	1,150

1.12 The total revenue and total cost equations of a firm are

$$TR = 25Q;$$

$$TC = 100 + 20Q + 0.025Q^2.$$

a. Graph total revenue, total cost, marginal revenue, marginal cost and total profit for output levels $Q = 0$ to $Q = 200$.

b. What is this firm's total profit equation?

c. Use marginal analysis to determine the level of output at which total profit is maximized.

d. Based on your answer to part c, what is the relationship between marginal revenue and marginal cost?

1.13 After twenty years, John Puller decided to retire and sell his business consulting firm for $12.5 million. Since the company's founding, profits have risen steadily at a rate of around 6 percent annually. Last year, the company generated after-tax profits of $250,000. At the current interest rate of 8 percent, is Puller's asking price realistic?

NOTES

1. A brief discussion of ordinary least squares regression analysis, which is used to generate parameter estimates of equations in linear form on the basis of historical data, is presented in the Appendix.

2. The time value of money recognizes that $1 received today is worth more than $1 received tomorrow. To see why, suppose that $1 received today can be invested at a 5 percent annual interest rate. A year from now, that $1 today will be worth $1.05. Alternatively, the present value of $1.05 a year from now is $1. The process of determining present value of some future amount is referred to as discounting.

3. An example of how the market reallocates economic resources to their highest valued use, consider the demise of the Beekman Theater, which was located in New York City's "fashionable" Upper East Side. Opened in 1952, the Beekman attracted large audiences until it was demolished in 2005. The Beekman was one of many stand-alone movie houses east of 5th Avenue between East 60th and East 96th Streets. Today, there are none. The reason was soaring real estate values. In 2014, the median list price per square foot was $1,350, compared with the city-wide average of just over $500 per square foot. The Beekman was replaced by a higher-valued breast cancer research facility operated by the Memorial Sloan-Kettering Cancer Center. While the Beekman's destruction was a bitter loss, it can be reasonably argued that society has been made better off by the economically more efficient use of the property upon which it once stood.

Chapter 2

Demand and Supply

All businesses perform essentially the same function—producing goods or services for sale in the market. Unfortunately, many businesses fail because managers sweat the day-to-day details while losing sight of the firm's primary objective—maximizing shareholder value. A manager who becomes mired in the firm's operational minutia and ignores market trends courts financial disaster.

In this chapter, we will examine how the interaction of buyers and sellers in competitive markets determine prices and availability of goods or services. The market mechanism discussed in this chapter makes several simplifying assumptions. We begin by assuming that the market consists of a large number of relatively small buyers and sellers with complete and symmetrical information. Since their respective contributions are very small, the decisions made by individual buyers or sellers have no effect on the market-determined price. In other words, individual buyers and sellers are said to be **price takers**.

DEMAND

A **market** is any arrangement that brings together buyers and sellers. The **market demand curve** is the horizontal summation of individual consumers' demand curves.[1] According to the **law of demand**, which pertains to market (not individual) demand, the *quantity demanded* of a good or service is inversely related to its price, *ceteris paribus*. This relationship is depicted as the downward-sloping demand curve in Figure 2.1. A decline in the market price of good x from P_1 to P_2, for example, results in an increase in quantity demanded from Q_1 to Q_2. This relationship is described as a *movement along* a stationary demand curve from point A to point B. At a basic level,

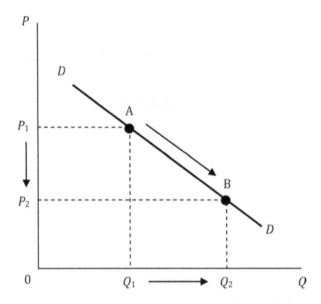

Figure 2.1

the law of demand can be justified on the basis of common sense and simple observation.

Income and Substitution Effects

At a more subtle level, the law of demand reflects the income and substitution effects of a buyer's purchasing decisions. The **income effect** says that as a product's price declines, a buyer's real purchasing power increases. By contrast, an increase in prices reduces a buyer's real income and purchasing power. We will have more to say about the relationship between changes in income and demand in the next section.

The **substitution effect** says that when there is no change in real purchasing power, an increase in the price of a good will cause buyers to unambiguously shift their purchases into a relatively less expensive substitutes. The substitution effect reflects changes in a consumer's **opportunity costs** from the price change.

The income and substitution effects usually complement and reinforce each other. A price decline, for example, will have both positive income and substitution effects, in which case there is no question that the ordinary demand curve will be downward sloping. In some cases, however, a price decline will result in a negative income effect. Fortunately, the positive substitution effect almost always dominates, which gives the demand curve its expected downward slope.

Demand Determinants

In addition to the price of the product, the market demand for a good or service depends on a variety of other factors, including money income, tastes and preferences, the prices of related goods, the number of consumer, price and income expectations, and so on. Factors other than the price of the good in question are collectively referred to as *demand determinants*.

Money Income

The most important limitation on a consumer's ability to purchase a good or service is money income. An increase in consumers' money income will increase the demand for most goods and services. This is shown in Figure 2.2 as a right-shift in the market demand curve from D_1 to D_2. Likewise, in most cases a decrease in money income, such as would occur during an economic downturn, results in fewer purchases and a left-shift of the demand curve (not shown). Such products are referred to as **normal goods**.

By contrast, the demand for an **inferior good** varies inversely with consumers' money income. During an economic expansion, rising incomes, sales and profits, the market demand for the services of bankruptcy lawyers and accountants declines. This decline is depicted as a shift to the left of the market demand curve. Conversely, the market demand curve for bankruptcy services will shift to the right during economic downturns. Other types of

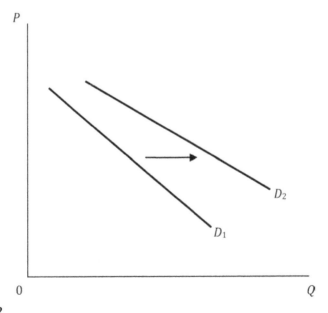

Figure 2.2

inferior goods include the demand for automobile repair services and used cars as consumers postpone purchases of new cars during recessions.

Tastes and Preferences

Changes in consumer tastes will also shift the market demand curve. Although changes in fads and fashions can be difficult to predict, there is an entire industry devoted to manipulating consumer tastes and preferences—marketing, but especially advertising. Advertising is generally of two types—informative and persuasive. **Informative advertising** provides prospective consumers with information about new or existing products, such as the seemingly ubiquitous advertisements for the iPad "tablet" during 2010. **Persuasive advertising** attempts to boost sales by creating an image that may have little or nothing to do with the product's physical characteristics. Persuasive advertising appeals to consumers' emotions.

An increase in advertising-inspired purchases is depicted as a right-shift in the market demand curve. If consumers have a negative opinion, the demand curve will shift to the left. In recent years, for example, consumers' concern about the health hazards of smoking has resulted in a dramatic decline in the demand for tobacco products in the United States. Many political candidates are notorious for running negative campaign ads against their opponents.

Prices of Related Goods

Changes in the prices of related goods also affect market demand. Related goods may be substitutes or complements. If two goods are **substitutes in consumption**, an increase in the price of good y will cause some consumers to shift their purchases into relatively less expensive good x. An increase in the price of Coca-Cola, for example, results in a decrease in the *quantity demanded* for Coca-Cola, but an increase in the *demand* by many consumers for relatively less expensive Pepsi Cola, Dr. Pepper, or fruit juices. Other examples of substitute goods include margarine and butter, coffee and tea, beer and ale, and laptop and tablet computers.

Figure 2.3 illustrates the effect of an increase in the price of good y on the demand for substitute good x. An increase in the price of good y results in a decrease in the quantity demand of good y, which is illustrated as a movement along the D curve from point A to point B. As the quantity demanded of good y falls, the demand for substitute good x increases. This is shown as a right-shift of the demand curve for good x from D_1 to D_2. Analogously, a decrease in the price of good y leads to an increase in the quantity demanded for good y and a left-shift of the demand curve for good x (not shown).

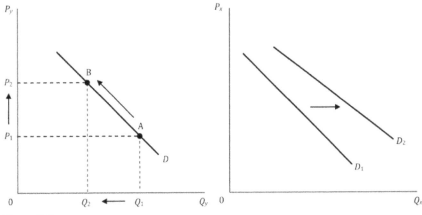

Figure 2.3

Goods are **complements in consumption** if they are consumed together, such as tennis rackets and tennis balls, skis and ski boots, kites and kite string, and computers and software. If goods x and y are complements, a decrease in the price of good y results in an increase in the *quantity demanded* of good y, and an increase in the *demand* for good x. The increase in the price of good y results in a decrease in the demand for complementary good x, which shifts the demand curve for good x to the left. Conversely, a decrease in the price of good y results in an increase in the quantity demanded of good y and an increase in the demand for good x, which shifts the demand function for good x to the right.

Sales Taxes

Sales taxes also affect the demand for a good or service. A *per-unit tax*, for example, is a fixed tax (t) per unit purchased. Suppose that the price is $10 and local authorities impose a $1 per-unit sales tax. This effectively raises the price to $11. A consumer who buys 100 units pays $1,100, of which $100 is collected by the government. If the price is $20 and the consumer buys 100 units, the amount going to the vendor doubles, but there is no change in government sales tax revenues.

In general, imposing a per-unit tax increases the price to the buyer to $P + t$. Suppose that the inverse demand equation with the per-unit tax is $P + t = a - bQ$. After subtracting t from both sides this becomes $P = (a - t) - bQ$. Increasing a per-unit sales tax lowers the P-intercept, but leaves the slope of the demand equation unchanged. In other words, there is a parallel left-shift of the demand curve. Conversely, removing or reducing the tax results in a parallel right-shift of the demand curve.

Alternatively, an *ad valorem tax* (from the Latin "according to value") is expressed as a percentage (τ) of the purchase price. Suppose that the price is $10 and there is a 10 percent ad valorem tax. A consumer who purchases 100 units at a price of $10 pays (1.1 × $10) × 100 = $1,100, of which $100 is collected by the government. A consumer who purchases 100 units at a price of $20 pays (1.1 × $20) × 100 = $2,200. In this case, the revenues going to the vendor and the government both double.

Imposing an ad valorem tax increases the price to the buyer to $(1 + \tau)P$. In this case, the inverse demand equation becomes $(1 + \tau)P = a - bQ$. After dividing both sides by $(1 + \tau)$ this becomes $P = a/(1 + \tau) - [b/(1 + \tau)]Q$. Increasing an ad valorem tax not only lowers the P-intercept, but the quantity demanded becomes more sensitive to a price change. In other words, the demand curve shifts to the left and becomes flatter. Reducing an ad valorem tax causes the demand curve to shift to the right and become steeper.

Number of Consumers

The market demand curve for a good or a service is the sum of the demand curves of the individual consumers. Thus, an increase in the number of buyers will increase the consumer purchases and shift the market demand curve to the right. The flood of Mexican immigrants since the 1980s, for example, increased the demand for Mexican cuisine in the Southwest. Conversely, economic recession in the Rust Belt lowered demand for real estate, home and auto repair services, and so on. Shifts in the market demand curve also reflect demographic changes, such as the significant increase in demand for health care and other senior citizen services as World War II "baby boomers" enter their retirement years.

Consumer Expectations

A change in consumer expectations regarding market conditions tomorrow can affect the demand for goods and services today. Suppose, for example, that pharmaceutical investors come to believe that a drug company's stock price is about to fall because of multimillion dollar law suit. To avoid getting caught "holding the bag," investors will act on those expectations, thereby turning their beliefs into a reality. If prospective new car buyers believe that prices for this year's models will be lowered in October as dealerships make room for next year's model, the demand curve for new cars in September will shift to the left.

Summarizing, a change in the *quantity demanded* for a good or service in response to a *change in its price* is illustrated as a *movement along* a stationary demand curve. A change in *demand* following a change in something *other than price* is depicted as a *shift* in the demand curve. Table 2.1 summarizes several of the demand shifts discussed in this section.

Table 2.1   Changes in Demand Determinants

Determinant	Change	Demand Curve Shift
Income		
Normal goods	↑ ↓	→ ←
Inferior goods	↑ ↓	← →
Tastes and preferences	↑ ↓	→ ←
Prices of related goods		
Substitutes	↑ ↓	→ ←
Complements	↑ ↓	← →
Sales taxes	↑ ↓	← →
Population	↑ ↓	→ ←

Estimating the Market Demand Equation

The relationships discussed in the preceding sections are of little practical value to managers unless the demand for a firm's good or service can be quantified. Suppose, for example, that the demand for good x (Q_x^d) depends on its price (P_x), per capita money income (M), and the price of a related good y (P_y). Although the precise manner in which these variables are related may never be known with complete certainty, a useful first step is to assume a linear relationship of the form

$$Q_x^d = \beta_0 + \beta_x P_x + \beta_M M + \beta_y P_y. \tag{2.1}$$

The hypothesized signs of the parameter values in Eq. (2.1) are $\beta_x < 0$ by the law of demand, $\beta_M > 0$ if x is normal, $\beta_M < 0$ if good x is an inferior, $\beta_y > 0$ if good y is a substitute, and $\beta_y < 0$ if good y is a complement.

Several statistical techniques are used to derive estimates of the coefficients on the basis of empirical data.[2] A statistical estimate of Eq. (2.1) will provide the manager with more precise information about how the company's unit sales will be affected by changes in each of these hypothesized explanatory variables. Expanding on ideas presented earlier, rewrite Eq. (2.1) as

$$Q_x^d = B + \beta_x P_x, \tag{2.2}$$

where $B = \beta_0 + \beta_M M + \beta_y P_y$. Solving for P_x we obtain the inverse demand equation

$$P_x = -\left(\frac{B}{\beta_x}\right) + \left(\frac{1}{\beta_x}\right)Q_x. \qquad (2.3)$$

Suppose an economic recession results in a decline in money income. If x is a normal good ($\beta_M > 0$), the result is a decline in the value of B and a shift to the left of the demand curve.

SOLVED EXERCISE

The estimated demand equation for a popular brand of fruit juice is given by the equation

$$Q_x = 10 - 5P_x + 0.001M + 10P_y, \qquad (2.4)$$

where Q_x is the per family monthly purchases in gallons, P_x is the price per gallon of the fruit drink ($2.00), M is the median annual family income ($20,000), and P_y is the price per gallon of a competing brand of fruit juice ($2.50).

a. *Interpret the parameter estimates of Eq. (2.4).*
b. *What are estimated monthly, per family purchases (sales) of this brand of fruit juice?*
c. *Rewrite the Eq. (2.4) to resemble Eq. (2.3).*
d. *Suppose that median annual family income increases to $30,000. How does this change your answers to parts b and c?*

Solution

a. *A $1 increase in the price of this brand of fruit juice will result in a 5-gallon, per-family decline monthly purchases. A $1,000 increase in median annual family income will result in a 1 gallon increase in per-family, monthly purchases. Since a $1 increase in the price of the competing brand results in a 10-gallon, per-family increase in monthly purchases of this brand, the two brands of fruit juices are substitute goods.*
b. *Substituting the indicated values into the demand equation yields*

$$Q_x = 10 - 5(2) + 0.001(20,000) + 10(2.5) = 45 \text{ gallons.} \qquad (2.5)$$

c. *Eq. (2.4) may be rewritten*

$$Q_x = 55 - 5P_x. \tag{2.6}$$

d. *The new monthly consumption of fruit drink is*

$$Q_x = 10 - 5(2) + 0.001(30,000) + 10(2.5) = 55 \text{ gallons.} \tag{2.7}$$

At the higher family income, Eq. (2.6) becomes

$$Q_x = 65 - 5P_x. \tag{2.8}$$

Since the value of the horizontal intercept has increased from 55 to 65, the demand curve for this brand of fruit juice shifts to the right.

Consumer Surplus

A detailed understanding of the market demand for a good or service has several important business applications. In the next chapter, for example, the estimated demand equation will be used to identify the effect of a price change on the firm's unit sales and total revenues. It can also be used to approximate the value that consumers receive from their purchases of goods and services. In Chapter 11 we will learn how managers can use this to formulate pricing strategies that enhance the firm's bottom line.

Consumer surplus is the value that buyers received from the purchase of a good or service in excess of the amount paid. In order to explain what we mean by this, consider the demand curve depicted in Figure 2.4, which illustrates the number of bottles of Gatorade that Joe will purchase after a game of softball on a hot summer day. Suppose in this thought experiment that Joe lives in a world populated only by truth tellers. After the game, Joe goes to his health club and orders a bottle of Gatorade. The health club does not have a menu of prices. Instead, each patron is asked to pay an amount equal to the value received from each bottle purchased. In keeping with this policy, Joe is asked how much a bottle is worth to him. Being very thirsty, Joe says that a bottle of Gatorade is worth $8, which is the amount that he pays.

After finishing his first bottle, Joe orders another. As before, Joe is asked how much the second bottle is worth to him. Not being as thirsty, Joe responds that he is willing to pay $6, $4 for the third bottle, and so on. If Joe stops after the third bottle, his total expenditures will be $18, which is precisely the value that Joe received from his purchases.

In a "perfect" world, a strategy of charging a price equal to the value of each unit consumed may be practical, but in the real world buyers have an incentive to understate the true value received so as to a lower price. For this

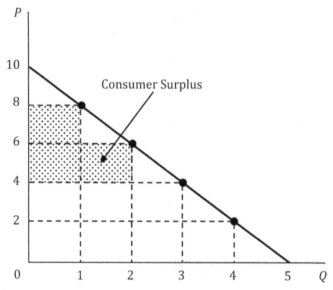

Figure 2.4

reason, firms typically publish a menu of fixed prices. The buyer knows precisely how much each unit will cost before deciding how many units to purchase. Suppose that a bottle of Gatorade is $4. How many bottles will Joe buy, and how much will he spend?

According to the information provided in Figure 2.4, Joe will certainly purchase the first bottle because the $4 paid is greater than the $8 of value received. Joe will also buy a second bottle since he will receive $2 of value in excess of the price paid. Joe will even buy a third bottle because the amount paid is equal to the value received. Joe will not purchase a fourth bottle, however, since he would lose $2 in value. Joe has spent 3 × $4 = $12 for total value received value of $8 + $6 + $4 = $18. Joe's consumer surplus of $18 – $12 = $6 is illustrated by the shaded area in Figure 2.4.

In the above example, we assumed that Joe's beer purchases were in discrete increments. Now, consider Figure 2.5, which represents the market demand for a good or service. If prices are infinitely divisible, consumer surplus is given by the shaded triangle P^*AE. At a price of P^*, the total value received from purchasing Q^* units consumed is given by the area $0P^*AEQ^*$. Total consumer expenditures is given by the area of the rectangle $0P^*EQ^*$. Thus, consumer surplus is $0P^*AEQ^* - 0P^*EQ^* = P^*AE$. For a linear demand equation, consumer surplus can be calculated using the equation

$$CS = \frac{1}{2}\left(A - P^*\right)Q^*.$$ (2.9)

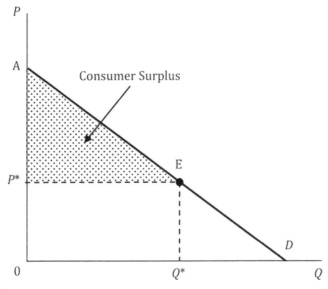

Figure 2.5

SOLVED EXERCISE

Suppose that a consumer's inverse demand equation is

$$P = 20 - 2Q. \tag{2.10}$$

a. *How many units will be purchased at a price is $6? What are the consumers' total expenditures?*
b. *Calculate the consumer surplus.*
c. *How much total value is received by this consumer?*

Solution

a. *From Eq. (2.10), at a price of $6, this consumer will purchase 7 units and spend $6(7) = $42.*
b. *From Eq. (2.9), consumer surplus is CS = 0.5(20 – 6)7 = $49.*
c. *The total value received is equal to the amount paid plus the value of consumer surplus, which is $42 + $49 = $91.*

SUPPLY

According to the **law of supply**, the quantity supplied of a good or service is directly related to a change in its market price, *ceteris paribus*. The *market*

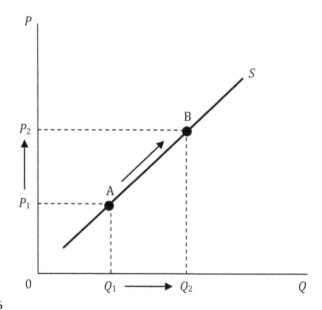

Figure 2.6

supply curve is the horizontal summation of the supply curves of the individual firms in an industry. This relationship is depicted in Figure 2.6. An increase in the market price of good x from P_1 to P_2 results in an increase in the *quantity supplied* from Q_1 to Q_2. This cause and effect relationship is depicted as a *movement along* the stationary supply curve from point A to point B. This is because an increase in the price of good x increases firms' expected revenues and profits from its sale. To exploit these profit opportunities, firms will increase the number of units offered for sale.

Supply Determinants

A change in any factor that affects a firm's bottom line will change the number of units offered for sale. An increase in the market price will result in an increase in the quantity supplied of a good or service. This is illustrated as a movement along a stationary market supply curve. A change in any other factor that affects the firm's profit will result in a shift in the market supply curve. These supply determinants include, among other things, input prices, production technology, taxes and government regulation, prices of related goods, and number of firms in the industry.

Input Prices

Other things being equal, a lower input price, such as might occur from a decline in energy prices, will reduce production costs and increase expected profit. Firms will respond by increasing output at each price, which will shift the market supply curve to the right. Conversely, an increase in employee wages and benefits from a new collective bargaining agreement will increase production costs, lower expected profit, and cause the market supply curve to shift to the left (not shown).

Production Technology

We typically think of a firm's production technology in terms of the economic capital (machinery, plant, equipment, and so on) used to inputs into outputs for sale in the market. In fact, production technology can also refer to the process by which managers organize production processes, such as improved inventory control and personnel management. Improved production technology implies that more output can be produced from given combination of inputs, or an unchanged amount of output can be produced using fewer inputs. In the first instance, this suggests an increase in revenues. In the second instance, this means a decrease in production costs. Either way, an improvement in production technology at fixed input and output prices suggests an increase in profits, which provided managers with an incentive to increase supply. This would be depicted as a right-shift of the supply curve.

Taxes and Government Regulation

The objective of the firm is to maximize shareholder value, which is related to after-tax profits. From a manager's perspective, higher corporate taxes and mandated government regulations increase the firm's cost of doing business and lower expected after-tax profit. Managers will respond by reducing output, causing the market supply curve to shift to the left. Conversely, lowering corporate taxes, receiving government subsidies, and removing costly regulations increase expected after-tax profits, encourage production and shift the market supply curve to the right.

Another type that affects industry supply is an *excise tax*, which is a tax on each unit sold. The difference between an excise tax and a sales tax is that an excise tax is levied on specific goods, whereas a sales tax is a general levy. Another difference is that excise taxes are collected from the supplier—not the consumer.

The manner in which excise taxes affect the supply curve depends on whether it is a per-unit tax or an ad valorem tax. Suppose, for example, that the government levies a $1 per-unit tax on a gallon of gasoline. This has the effect of shifting the supply curve up by the amount of the tax. This upward parallel shift results in a decline in supply. In a similar fashion, a reduction in a per-unit excise tax results in a downward parallel shift of the supply, which results in an increase in supply.

Alternatively, the government could levy an ad valorem excise tax. Since the amount of the tax is greater at higher prices than at lower prices, the supply curve not shifts up and becomes steeper. As in the case of a per-unit tax, the imposition of the ad valorem excise tax results in a decrease in supply. In an analogous fashion, the supply curve shifts down and becomes flatter following a reduction in an ad valorem excise tax resulting in an increase in supply.

Prices of Related Goods

Changes in the prices of goods sharing the same resources can also affect supply. These related goods are may be substitutes or complements in production. **Substitutes in production** involve trade-offs in the production of two or more goods or services using the same production facilities, such as the choice of producing halogen light bulbs or compact fluorescent light (CFL) bulbs on the same assembly line. Other things being equal, an increase in the price of halogen light bulbs will cause managers to devote a greater share of the firm's production capacity to its production, which reduce the assembly line time available to produce CFL bulbs. Thus, the higher price of halogen bulbs resulted in a decline in the supply of CFL bulbs.

Complements in production involve the joint production of two or more goods with the same production facilities. Cowhide, for example, is a by-product of beef production. An increase in the price of beef will result in an increase in the quantity supplied of beef and an increase in the supply of cowhide, even when there is no change in the price of cowhide leather.

Number of Firms

The market supply curve of a good or service is the sum of the supply curves of each individual firm in an industry. Thus, an increase in the number of firms will cause the market supply curve to shift to the right. In fact, any flow of new investment into the industry, perhaps because of the lure of above-normal profits, will increase market supply. Conversely, when investment flows out of an industry, the market supply curve will shift to the left.

Summary

A change in the *quantity supplied* of a product following a *change in its market price* is depicted as a *movement along* a stationary supply curve. A change in *supply* following a change in *something other than the market price* of the product is depicted as a *shift* in the entire supply curve. Table 2.2 summarizes the supply shifts discussed in this section.

Table 2.2 Changes in Supply Determinants

Determinant	Change	Supply Curve Shift
Input prices	↑	←
	↓	→
Technology	↑	→
Taxes	↑	←
	↓	→
Prices of related goods		
Substitutes	↑	←
	↓	→
Complements	↑	→
	↓	←
Number of firms	↑	→
	↓	←

Producer Surplus

The analytical supply counterpart to consumer surplus is **producer surplus**, which is the difference between total revenues received from the sale of a good or service and the minimum needed to produce it. A firm's supply curve reflects its marginal cost of production. A profit-maximizing firm will produce up to a level of output where marginal cost equals marginal revenue. A firm's total variable cost is equal to the sum of the marginal cost of producing each unit. Thus, producer surplus is equal to the firm's **operating profit**, which is the difference between the firm's total revenue and expenses relating to a firm's ongoing operations (total variable cost). This is not the same thing as the firm's total (economic) profit, which is the difference between total revenue and total (economic) cost. A firm's total cost is the sum of total variable and total fixed cost. On the other hand, if total fixed cost is "small," producer surplus is a good approximation of the firm's total profit.

Producer surplus for continuous prices is illustrated by the area of the shaded triangle in Figure 2.7. If the supply curve is linear, producer surplus equals

$$PS = \frac{1}{2}\left(P^* - \text{B}\right)Q^*. \tag{2.11}$$

A firm's producer surplus can be particularly valuable information for a manager. A profit maximizing firm will produce up to the level of output where marginal cost equals marginal revenue, which is the extra revenue received from the next unit sold. This occurs in Figure 2.7 at the output level Q^*. For every unit of output up to the last unit produced, $P^* = MR > MC$. Thus, the shaded area represents the extra revenue received in excess of what the firm would have been willing to produce each unit up to Q^*.

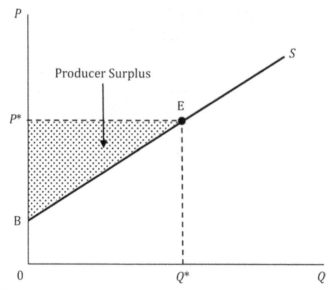

Figure 2.7

Producer surplus tells managers the maximum amount the firm can save by bargaining with resources suppliers over price. For example, suppose that the manager of a construction company is negotiating with a supplier over the price of steel rods. If the manager of the construction company knows the supplier's producer surplus, he or she also knows the minimum amount that the supplier would be willing to accept for the steel rods.

MARKET EQUILIBRIUM

We will now bring together the forces of demand and supply to explain how market price and output is determined. Figure 2.8 illustrates the concept of **market equilibrium**, which is the price (P^*) where the quantity demanded (Q^d) equals the quantity supplied (Q^s). At prices below the equilibrium price, a *shortage* exists since the quantity demanded exceeds the quantity supplied. At this low price, consumers compete amongst themselves to acquire the good or service that is in short supply. As consumers bid up the price, buyers who are unwilling or unable to pay the higher price will exit the market. At the same time, the higher price provides firms to an incentive to increase production. The increase in the quantity supplied coupled with the decrease in the quantity demanded as the price rises continues shortage is eliminated and a higher market-clearing price established.

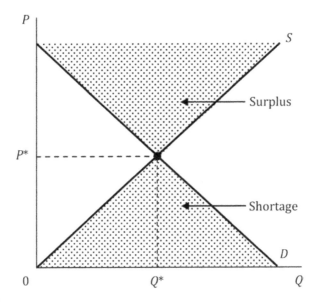

Figure 2.8

At prices above P^*, the quantity supplied exceeds the quantity demanded. Managers will respond to the unsold output and a build-up of inventories by lowering price and reducing production to more sustainable levels. This process will continue until the quantity supplied equals the quantity demand at a lower market-clearing price.

NET SOCIAL WELFARE

Consumer surplus is the value received by consumers from purchases of a product in excess of their expenditures. Producer surplus is the amount received by firms from sales of a product in excess of the minimum amount that they would have accepted to make the product available. The sum of consumer surplus and producer surpluses is referred to as **net social welfare**, which is depicted in Figure 2.9 for a purely competitive market.

The demand curve is a measure of the marginal social benefit (MSB) of consuming an additional unit. The supply curve measures the marginal social cost (MSC) of increasing output by another unit. As long as $MSB > MSC$ it pays for society to increase output. But, when $MSC > MSB$ it is in society's best interest to reduce output. Net national welfare is maximized at the level of output where $MSB = MSC$.

Net social welfare can be used as a measure of market efficiency. The greater the sum of consumer and producer surplus, the more socially beneficial

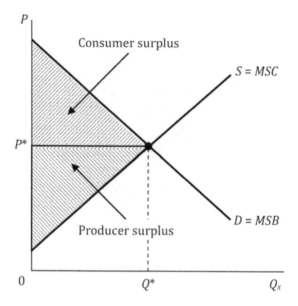

Figure 2.9

is the **market structure**. In this chapter, we have restricted out discussion to purely competitive market structures, which is considered the ideal way to organize commercial activity because it maximizes net social welfare.

SOLVED EXERCISE

Suppose that the inverse market demand and supply equations are

$$P = 9 - 2Q^d;$$ (2.12)

$$P = 6 + Q^s.$$ (2.13)

Calculate the value of net social welfare in this market.

Solution

Solving Eqs. (2.12) and (2.13), the market equilibrium price is P* = $7 and the equilibrium quantity is Q* = 1. The value of consumer surplus is CS = 0.5($9 − $7)1 = $1. The value of producer surplus is PS = 0.5($7 − $6) = $0.5. Thus, the value of net social welfare is NSW = CS + PS = $1.50. This solution is depicted in Figure 2.10.

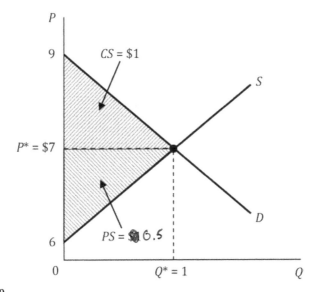

Figure 2.10

CHANGES IN DEMAND AND SUPPLY: PRICE AND OUTPUT DETERMINATION

We will now analyze the effects of a change in demand and supply conditions on the market-clearing price and equilibrium output. We will begin by first considering the effects of a change in market demand.

Demand Shifts

Suppose that medical research determines that eating cheeseburgers is healthy, which results in an increase in the demand for cheeseburgers. Other things being equal, this will cause the cheeseburger demand curve to shift to the right, as depicted in Figure 2.11. In a similar manner, if medical research demonstrates that cheeseburgers are unhealthy, the demand curve will shift to the left.

In general, a right-shift of the demand curve with no change in supply will result in an increase in both the equilibrium price and quantity. Conversely, a left-shift of the demand curve will cause the equilibrium price and quantity to fall.

Supply Shifts

Suppose that a decline in the price of cheese leads fast-food restaurants to expect higher profits from the sale of cheeseburgers. Other things being equal, profit-maximizing cheeseburger producers will increase output, which

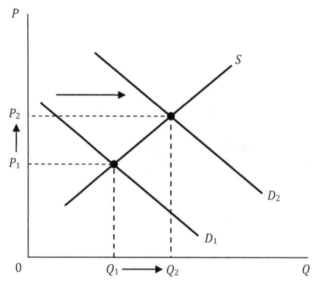

Figure 2.11

causes the supply curve to shift to the right, resulting in a decline in the equilibrium price and quantity. This is depicted in Figure 2.12.

Conversely, an increase in the price of cheese reduces expected profits resulting in a left-shift of the supply curve. This results in an increase in the equilibrium price and a decline in the equilibrium quantity. In general, a right-shift of the supply curve will result in a fall in the equilibrium price and an increase in the equilibrium quantity. Conversely, a left-shift of the supply curve will result in an increase in the equilibrium price and a decrease in the equilibrium quantity.

Demand and Supply Shifts

A shift in either the demand curve or the supply curve will result in an unambiguous change in both the equilibrium price and quantity. These predictable changes are summarized in the second column of Table 2.3. When both demand and supply change simultaneously, however, the effect on the market-clearing price and equilibrium quantity is more difficult to predict. The final outcome depends on how demand and supply change relative to each other. In the absence of such information, all we can say is that there will be an unambiguous change in either the equilibrium price or quantity, but an ambiguous change in the other.

To appreciate the difficulty associated with predicting equilibrium price and quantity changes when demand and supply changes, consider Case 1

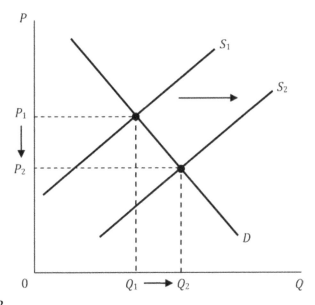

Figure 2.12

Table 2.3 Changes in Demand and Supply Determinants

Case	Separately	Together
1	$\Delta D\uparrow \rightarrow \Delta P\uparrow$ and $\Delta Q\uparrow$ $\Delta S\uparrow \rightarrow \Delta P\downarrow$ and $\Delta Q\uparrow$	ΔP? (ambiguous) $\Delta Q\uparrow$ (unambiguous)
2	$\Delta D\uparrow \rightarrow \Delta P\uparrow$ and $\Delta Q\uparrow$ $\Delta S\downarrow \rightarrow \Delta P\uparrow$ and $\Delta Q\downarrow$	$\Delta P\uparrow$ (unambiguous) ΔQ? (ambiguous)
3	$\Delta D\downarrow \rightarrow \Delta P\downarrow$ and $\Delta Q\downarrow$ $\Delta S\uparrow \rightarrow \Delta P\downarrow$ and $\Delta Q\uparrow$	$\Delta P\downarrow$ (unambiguous) ΔQ? (ambiguous)
4	$\Delta D\downarrow \rightarrow \Delta P\downarrow$ and $\Delta Q\downarrow$ $\Delta S\downarrow \rightarrow \Delta P\uparrow$ and $\Delta Q\downarrow$	ΔP? (ambiguous) $\Delta Q\downarrow$ (unambiguous)

in Table 2.3, which summarizes the effects of an increase in both demand ($\Delta D\uparrow$) and supply ($\Delta S\uparrow$). The second column of the table tells us what will happen when demand and supply change separately. An increase in demand alone results in an increase in both the equilibrium price and quantity, which is illustrated in Figure 2.11. An increase in supply alone results in a decrease in the equilibrium price and an increase in the equilibrium quantity, which is depicted in Figure 2.12. When demand and supply increase together, however, the analysis becomes a bit more complicated.

As we have seen, an increase in demand and supply both result in an unambiguous increase in the equilibrium quantity. On the other hand, an increase in demand causes the equilibrium price to rise while an increase in supply causes the equilibrium price to fall. In the first instance there is upward pressure on price, while in the second instance there is downward pressure on price. In the absence of additional information, it is not possible to know whether the demand-side or supply-side effect dominates, in which case the effect on the equilibrium price is ambiguous.

SOLVED EXERCISE

The marketing department of The Great Bombay Tea Company has estimated the weekly demand for its brand of gourmet pizza as

$$Q = 500 - 100P + 50I + 20P_y + 30A, \qquad (2.14)$$

where Q is the number of pizzas (000's), P is the market-determined price of Bombay's pizza, I is weekly per capita income, P_y is the price of the brand of pizza sold by Universal Foods, Inc., and A is Bombay's weekly advertising expenditures ($000's). The supply equation for Bombay's gourmet pizza is

$$Q = 1,800 + 450P. \qquad (2.15)$$

a. *What is the relationship between Bombay's pizza and Universal's pizza?*
b. *Suppose that I = $200, P_y = $20 and A = $100. What is the equilibrium price and quantity of Bombay pizza?*
c. *Suppose that Bombay's chief economist predicts that the current economic expansion will increase weekly per capita income to $255. What effect will this have on the equilibrium price and quantity?*
d. *Based on your answer to part c, how would you characterize Bombay's pizza?*

Solution

a. *Since a $1 increase in the price of Universal pizza results in a 20 thousand unit weekly increase in Bombay pizza sales, the two brands of pizza are substitutes.*
b. *Substituting these values into the demand equation yields*

$$Q = 13,900 - 100P. \qquad (2.16)$$

The equilibrium price and quantity are P* = $22 and Q* = 11,700.
c. *At the higher per capita income, the demand equation becomes*

$$Q = 16,650 - 100P. \tag{2.17}$$

Equating this new demand with supply, the equilibrium price and quantity are P* = \$27 and Q* = 13,950. The increase in per capita income has resulted in a higher market-clearing price and equilibrium quantity.

d. *An increase in per capita income resulted in an increase in the demand for Bombay's pizza. This was depicted as a right-shift of the demand curve. Bombay pizza can be characterized as a normal good.*

RATIONING FUNCTION OF PRICES

How realistic is the assumption of market equilibrium? Markets are continually buffeted by changes in demand and supply conditions. Temporary shortages and surpluses resulting from unexpected market disturbances are inevitable. The remarkable thing about unfettered markets is the speed at which market equilibrium is reestablished following a demand-side or supply-side shock. This fact should reinforce our faith in the underlying logic and stability of the free-market process.

When prices are "too low" and shortages result, competition among consumers will push up prices. Consumers who are unable or unwilling to pay the higher price drop out of the market. At the same time, higher prices are an incentive for firms to increase supply. Eventually, the shortage is eliminated and market equilibrium is reestablished. On the other hand, when prices are too high, there is a surplus of unsold goods. Firms will respond by lowering prices to dispose of excess inventory and reduce output to more sustainable levels. Consumers who were previously unwilling or unable to pay a higher price will be drawn into the market until the surplus is eliminated. This process by which changes in market-determined prices eliminate shortages and surpluses is referred to as the **rationing function of prices**. The essence of a decentralized free market is that impersonal changes in prices ultimately determines who gets what and how much.

The rationing function of prices underscores the notion of scarcity. Economically well-to-do consumers have a greater command over available goods and services than consumers of more modest means. This inevitably leads to complaints by some consumers who cannot afford to pay that the market-determined price is "unfair." The fact that an individual may not be able to afford a Bentley or a private island is not a problem of fairness, but a problem of limited resources. Still, this does not dissuade some individuals who believe that market outcomes are pernicious from seeking redress through other means, such as the political process.

Price Ceilings

While price rationing is fundamental to the market mechanism, it is not the only way to allocate scarce goods and services. At various times, and for various reasons, governments have short-circuited the price rationing function of markets by imposing a **price ceiling**, which is the maximum legal price that a firm can charge for its product.

To be effective, a price ceiling must be set below the market equilibrium price to prevent prices from rising. An example of a price ceiling is rent control. The political objective of rent control is to provide low-cost housing to low-income voters. The problem with price ceilings is that they create artificial shortages that are likely to persist and become worse over time. Moreover, price ceilings are socially inefficient because they result in a misallocation of resources. To understand what is involved, consider the situation depicted in Figure 2.13.

Suppose, initially, that the equilibrium price and quantity in Figure 2.13 is $P*$ and $Q*$, respectively. Net social welfare, which is a measure of market efficiency, is the sum of consumer surplus and producer surplus. Consumer surplus is the value of the area $a + b + c$. Producer surplus is given by the area $d + e + f$. Thus, net social welfare is given by the area $a + b + c + d + e + f$. Now, suppose that government imposes a price ceiling of P^c, which creates a shortage in the market of $Q^s - Q^d$. The imposition of the price ceiling reduces producer surplus to area f. Area d is the amount transferred from producers to consumers who are paying less than the full value of the last unit consumed (P^F).

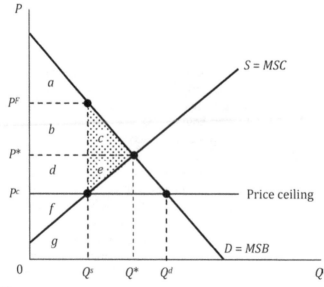

Figure 2.13

The total value received by consumers from Q^s units of output is given by the area $a + b + d + f + g$. Consumer expenditures are given by the area $f + g$. Thus, consumer surplus under the price ceiling is the area $a + b + d$. Net social welfare is now $a + b + d + f$. The change in net social welfare from the imposition of the price ceiling is $(a + b + d + f) - (a + b + c + d + e + f) = -c - e$. While consumers who have been able to acquire the product at a lower price have benefitted, the loss to consumers as a whole is $-c$, which is referred to as *consumer deadweight loss*. The loss to society as a whole from the misallocation of resources and a less than optimal amount of the product being supplied is given by the area $-e$, which is referred to as *producer deadweight loss*. The sum of consumer and producer deadweight loss, which is called *total deadweight loss*, is given by the shaded area in Figure 2.13. Total deadweight loss is a measure of the lost net social welfare that results from the price ceiling.

Alternatively, $MSB > MSC$ at the output level Q^s. In this market "too little" rental housing is supplied at the price ceiling. Society is made better off by allowing the market-clearing price to rise to P^*. Moreover, freed from the economic shackles of rent control, new construction will shift the supply curve to the right, which puts downward pressure on rents.

When the price rationing mechanism of the free market is not permitted to operate, some non-price rationing mechanism must be used to allocate products that are in short supply. The most common of these non-price rationing mechanisms is **queuing**. Standing line for sometimes hours on end was how gasoline was rationed after the U.S. Congress enacted a 57¢ per gallon price ceiling following the embargo of crude oil shipments to the U.S. in 1973–1974 by Organization of Petroleum Exporting Countries (OPEC).

Without the price ceiling, lines at gasoline stations would have disappeared overnight as higher prices would have equated the quantities demanded and supplied. Higher gasoline prices, however, would have jeopardized the reelection prospects of many members of Congress, and so the price at the pump was kept low. The full economic price of gasoline, which included the opportunity cost of waiting in line for hours on end, however, was much higher. In Figure 2.13, the full economic price is P_x^F, which is equal to the price ceiling plus the opportunity cost of waiting in line $P_x^F - P_x^C$. The difference between the full economic price and the price ceiling is the amount that consumers would be willing to pay to avoid waiting in line.

SOLVED EXERCISE

The market demand and supply equations for a product are

$$Q^d = 300 - 3P; \tag{2.18}$$

$$Q^s = -100 + 5P. \tag{2.19}$$

a. *Calculate the equilibrium price and quantity for this product?*
b. *Suppose that an increase in consumer income increases demand to*

$$Q^d = 420 - 3P. \tag{2.20}$$

  What are the new equilibrium price and quantity for this product? What is the value of net social welfare as a result of the increase in demand?
c. *What is the value of net social welfare as a result of the increase in demand?*
d. *Suppose that the government imposes a price ceiling that is equal to the original equilibrium price. What is the result of this legislation?*
e. *Calculate the change in the value of net social welfare after the imposition of the price ceiling.*

Solution

a. *Solving Eqs. (2.18) and (2.19), the equilibrium price is P* = $50. Substituting this price into the demand or supply equation and solving, the equilibrium quantity is Q* = 150 units of output.*
b. *Solving Eqs. (2.18) and (2.20), the new equilibrium price is P* = $65 and the equilibrium quantity is Q* = 225 units of output. This new situation is depicted in the following Figure 2.14.*

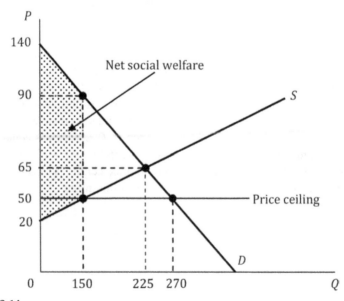

Figure 2.14

c. As a result of the increase in demand, consumer surplus is $CS = 0.5(140 - 65)225 = \$8,437.50$. The value of producer surplus is $PS = 0.5(65 - 20)225 = \$5,062.50$. Thus, the value of net social welfare before the price ceiling is $NSW = CS + PS = \$13,500$.

d. At the ceiling price of $P^c = \$50$, the quantity demanded is $Q^d = 270$ units and the quantity supplied is $Q^s = 150$ units. The price ceiling creates a shortage of $Q^d - Q^s = 120$ units of output.

e. After the imposition of the price ceiling, the value of consumer surplus is $CS = 0.5(140 - 90)150 + (90 - 50)150 = \$9,750$. The value of producer surplus after the price ceiling is $PS = 0.5(50 - 20)150 = \$2,250$. The value of net social welfare is $NSW = CS + PS = \$12,000$. This is given by the shaded area in Figure 2.14. The imposition of the price ceiling has reduced net national welfare by $\$1,500$.

Price Floors

The counterpart of a price ceiling is a **price floor**, which is the minimum legal price that a supplier can expect for its product. To be effective a price floor must be set above the market determined price of the product. Notable examples of prices floors are agricultural price supports and minimum wages.

An example of the social welfare effect of a price floor is depicted in Figure 2.15. Suppose that the market for cheese is initially in equilibrium at

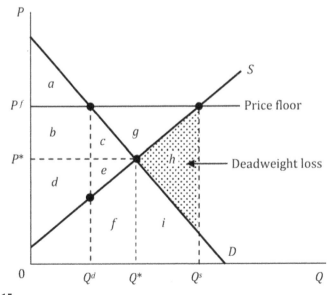

Figure 2.15

P^* and Q^*. Consumer surplus is the value of the area $a + b + c$. Producer surplus is given by the area $d + e$. Thus, net social welfare is given by the area $a + b + c + d + e$.

Now, suppose the government announces that it will guarantee cheese manufacturers a minimum price of P^f. The effect of the price floor is to create a market surplus of $Q^s - Q^d$. In the case, consumer surplus is given by area a. Producer surplus is given by the area $b + c + d + e + g$. Together, the sum of consumer and producer surplus is $a + b + c + d + e + g$. While it might appear that society has been made better off as a result of cheese price supports, this is not the end of the story.

There are several ways that federal government can administer an agricultural price support. One way is for the government to purchase the surplus at a cost to taxpayers of $c + e + f + g + h + i$. So far, net social welfare is $(a + b + c + d + e + g) - (c + e + f + g + h + i) = a + b + d - f - h - i$. The final outcome depends on what the government does with the surplus cheese. If the government distributes the cheese to low-income families free of charge, consumers receive value in the amount of the area $c + e + f + i$. Thus, the final outcome is net social welfare of $(a + b + d - e - f - h - i) + (c + e + f + h + i) = a + b + c + d + e - h$. National welfare is reduced by the area $-h$, which represents the amount of deadweight loss to society. Since the change in net social welfare is unambiguously negative, society has been made worse from the price floor.

Alternatively, $MSC > MSB$ at the output level Q^s. In this market, "too much" cheese is being supplied at the price floor. Society will be made better off by allowing prices to fall to its market-clearing P^*. Allowing the market mechanism to ration excess supply will eliminate the deadweight loss given by area h.

Another example of a price floor occurs in the labor market when the government enacts minimum-wage legislation, ostensibly to provide unskilled and uneducated workers with a "living wage." Although government can mandate a higher minimum wage, in a free market it cannot force employers to hire workers whose productivity is valued below the minimum wage. A profit-maximizing firm will not hire a worker if the addition to the firm's revenues is less than the minimum wage paid. The result is a surplus of unskilled and uneducated workers and a loss of social welfare. To make matters worse, a legal minimum wage makes it difficult for low-skilled workers to obtain work experience and on-the-job training that will enable them to command higher wages in the future. Society in general suffers because higher unemployment is associated with an increase in the crime rate. Taxpayers are made worse off because payroll taxes fund unemployment insurance and welfare payments.

SOLVED EXERCISE

Consider the following demand and supply equations for the product of a perfectly competitive industry:

$$Q^d = 25 - 3P; \qquad (2.21)$$

$$Q^s = 10 + 2P. \qquad (2.22)$$

a. *What is the equilibrium price and quantity in this market?*
b. *Suppose that government enacts a "price floor" on this product of P = $4. What is the result of this legislation?*

Solution

a. *Solving Eqs. (2.28) and (2.29), the equilibrium price and quantity are P* = $3 and Q* = 16 units of output.*
b. *At P = $4, the quantity demanded is Q^d = 13 units of output and the quantity supplied is Q^s = 18 units of output. As a result of the price floor there is a surplus of 5 units of output.*

ALLOCATING FUNCTION OF PRICES

An examination of the price-rationing mechanism of individual markets is called partial equilibrium analysis. By contrast, general equilibrium analysis is concerned with the simultaneous determination of equilibrium in all markets. General equilibrium analysis examines the process whereby a disturbance in one sector of a market economy is transmitted to other sectors of the economy and the resulting reallocation of productive resources.

The prices of final goods and services reflect changes in a variety of demand determinants, including consumer tastes and preferences. Since the demand for productive resources is derived from the demand for final goods and services, producers use price information to reallocate inputs from lower to higher valued uses. This process is referred to as the **allocating function of prices**. To see how this works, consider an increase in the demand for restaurant meals, which leads to an increase in prices and industry profits.[3] As a result, new capital investment flows into the restaurant and hospitality industry, which increases the demand for servers, chefs, and so on, thereby pushing up wages and benefits. This acts as a magnet for displaced workers, workers experiencing cuts in wages and benefits, and investment capital from contracting industries.

Benjamin Franklin warned the signers of the American Declaration of Independence from Great Britain that "We must all hang together, or assuredly we will all hang separately." In a way, this admonition underscores the important role of managers in identifying emerging market trends. It is often said that in economics everything hangs together. Changes in consumer demand for seemingly unrelated goods and services may produce ripple effects that could threaten a company's survival, or they may create new and promising profit opportunities.

CHAPTER EXERCISES

2.1   In recent years there has been a sharp increase in commercial and recreational fishing in the waters around Long Island. Illustrate the effect of "over fishing" on inflation-adjusted seafood prices at Long Island area restaurants.

2.2   New York City is a global financial center. In the late-1990s the financial and residential real estate markets reached record-high price levels. Are these markets related? Explain.

2.3   Large labor unions always support higher minimum-wage legislation even though no union maker earns just the minimum wage. Explain.

2.4   Discuss the effect of a frost in Florida, which damaged a significant portion of the orange crop, on each of the following.
a. Price of Florida oranges
b. Price of California oranges
c. Price of tangerines
d. Price of orange juice
e. Price of apple juice

2.5   What is consumer surplus and producer surplus? How can these concepts be used to evaluate changes in market efficiency?

2.6   Discuss the effect of an imposition of a wine import tariff on the price of California wine.

2.7   The market demand for Brand x has been estimated as:

$$Q_x^d = 1,500 - 3P_x - 0.05M - 2.5P_y + 7.5P_z,$$

where P_x is the price of Brand x, M per capita income, P_y the price of Brand y, and P_z the price of Brand z. Assume that $P_x = \$2$, $M = \$20,000$, $P_y = \$4$, and $P_z = \$4$.
a. With respect to changes in per capita income, what kind of good is Brand x?
b. How are Brands x and y related?

c. How are Brands x and z related?
d. How are Brands z and y related?
e. What is the market demand for Brand x?

2.8 Yell-O Yew-Boats, Ltd. produces Blue Meanies. Consider the demand and supply equations for Blue Meanies:

$$Q_x^d = 150 - 2P_x + 0.001M + 1.5P_y;$$

$$Q_x^s = 60 + 4P_x - 2.5W,$$

where Q_x is monthly per family consumption of Blue Meanies, P_x the price per unit of Blue Meanies, M median annual per family income ($25,000), P_y the price per unit of Apple Bonkers ($5.00) and W the hourly per worker wage rate ($8.60).
a. What type of good is Apple Bonkers?
b. What are the equilibrium price and quantity of Blue Meanies?
c. Suppose that median per family income increases by $6,000. What are the new equilibrium price and quantity of Blue Meanies?
d. Suppose that in addition to the increase in median per family income, collective bargaining by Blue Meanie Local # 1 results in a $2.40 hourly increase in the wage rate. What are the new equilibrium price and quantity?
e. In a same diagram, illustrate your answers to parts b, c, and d.

2.9 Consider the following demand and supply equations for sugar:

$$Q^d = 1,000 - 1,000P;$$

$$Q^s = 800 + 1,000P.$$

P is the price of sugar per pound and Q is the quantity of sugar in thousands of pounds.
a. What are the equilibrium price and quantity for sugar?
b. What is the value of net social welfare in this market?
c. Suppose that the government subsidizes sugar production by placing a price floor of $0.20 per pound. What is the relationship between the quantity supplied and quantity demand for sugar?
d. What is the effect on social welfare as a result of the price floor?

2.10 Occidental Pacific University is a large private university in California that is known for its strong athletics program, especially in football. At the request of the Dean of the College of Arts & Sciences, a professor from the economics department estimated that student demand for student enrollment at the university is

$$Q_x^d = 5,000 - 0.5P_x + 0.1M + 0.25P_y,$$

where Q_x is the number of full-time students, P_x tuition charged full-time students per semester, M national income (\$ billions), and P_y tuition charged full-time students per semester by Oriental Atlantic University in Maryland, Occidental's closest competitor on the grid iron.

a. Suppose that full-time enrollment at Occidental is 4,000 students. If M = \$7,500 and P_y = \$6,000, how much tuition is Occidental charging its full-time students?

b. The administration is considering a promotional campaign designed to bolster admissions and tuition revenues. The cost of the campaign will be \$750,000. The economics professor believes that the promotional campaign will increase demand to

$$Q_x^d = 5,100 - 0.45P_x + 0.1M + 0.25P_y.$$

If the economic professor is correct, forecast Occidental's full-time enrollment?

c. Assuming no change in real GDP or full-time tuition charged by Oriental, will the promotional campaign be effective? (*Hint*: Compare Occidental's tuition revenues before and after the promotional campaign.)

d. The director of Occidental's athletic department claims that the increase in enrollment resulted from the football team's NCAA Division I national championship. Is this claim reasonable? How would it show up in the new demand equation?

2.11 The market demand and supply equations for a good are:

$$Q^d = 50 - 10P;$$

$$Q^s = 20 + 2.5P.$$

a. What is the equilibrium price and equilibrium quantity?

b. What is the value of net social welfare?

c. What is the effect on net social welfare if the government imposes a price ceiling of \$3.00?

NOTES

1. The word "horizontal" indicates that the market quantity demanded is the sum of the quantities demanded by individual consumers along the horizontal axis.

2. A brief discussion of ordinary least squares regression analysis, which is used to generate parameter estimates of equations in linear form on the basis of historical data, is presented in the Appendix.

3. In 1970, Americans spent about $6 billion on fast food. By 2000, this had increased to more than $110 billion. The reason was principally economic. After peaking in 1973, the hourly wage in the U.S. declined steadily for the next twenty-five years. Housewives responded by entering the workforce in record numbers, which resulted in a dramatic increase in the demand for such services as cooking, cleaning, and child care. A generation earlier, three-quarters of the family budget allocated for food was used to prepare meals at home. By 2000, about half the family budget was spent dining out, mainly at fast-food restaurants. Americans now spend more money on fast food than on higher education, personal computers, computer software, or new cars, and more on movies, books, magazines, newspapers, videos, and recorded music combined.

Chapter 3

Elasticity

A firm's market performance depends on several factors, some of which are directly under a manager's control, while others are not. The individual firm cannot affect market interest rates, the pricing and advertising strategies of rivals, foreign-exchange rates that affect overseas sales or the cost of imports, business cycles, unemployment, or the rate of inflation. On the other hand, managers do control the firm's **organizational structure**, pricing, product design and packaging, marketing strategy, research and development expenditures, and so on. Changes in any of these factors can have a profound effect on the firm's bottom line.

In the previous chapter we examined how changes in price and other determinants affect the demand for goods and services. In this chapter we will explore these relationships in greater detail by introducing the important concept of elasticity, and how this measure can be used by managers to assess the effects of changes in the firm's pricing and advertising strategies, business cycle fluctuations, changes in the pricing and advertising strategies of rival firms, and other factors that affect the firm's bottom line. We will begin our discussion with the most important of these elasticity measures—the price elasticity of demand.

PRICE ELASTICITY OF DEMAND

In general, **elasticity** measures the percent change in the value of a dependent variable given a percent change in the value of an explanatory variable. Suppose, for example, the demand for a firm's product (Q_x^d) depends on its price (P_x), the consumer's money income (M), the price charge by rival firms (P_y), and the firm's advertising expenditures (A). This relationship may be written

$$Q_x^d = f\left(P_x, M, P_y, A\right). \tag{3.1}$$

On the basis of historical data, it should be possible for a firm to estimate the demand equation for its product, which may be used by a manager to improve the company's overall performance. Suppose, for example, that the demand for a firm's product x is given by the equation

$$Q_x = 127 - 50P_x. \tag{3.2}$$

This linear demand equation is depicted in Figure 3.1. The slope coefficient $\beta_x = -50$ tells us that the quantity demanded of good x increases (decreases) by 50 thousand units for every $1 decrease (increase) in its price.

The value of the slope may be calculated directly from the information provided in Figure 3.1. As we move along the demand curve from point A to point B, the value of the slope may be calculated as

$$\beta_x = \frac{\Delta Q_x}{\Delta P_x} = \frac{Q_2 - Q_1}{P_2 - P_1} = \frac{22 - 12}{2.10 - 2.30} = -50. \tag{3.3}$$

The value of the slope (β_x) measures the change in unit sales resulting from a change in the price of a good or service. How a consumer reacts to a $10 rebate on the purchase of an item selling for $100, however, can be quite different than the same rebate on an item that costs $1,000. A 10 percent rebate may be viewed as a real bargain; 1 percent rebate may be interpreted as a marketing ploy. On the other hand, if a firm offers a 10 percent rebate regardless of price, the consumer's reaction may be quite different. For the

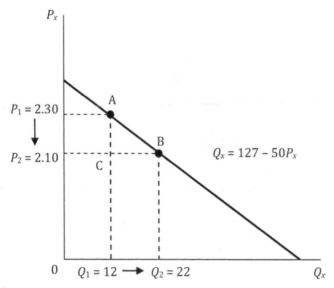

Figure 3.1

manager, the question is how will a 10 percent rebate affect the company's unit sales, revenues, and profits?

Another problem with the slope is that its numerical value depends on how we measure unit sales. Suppose, for example, that unit sales in Eq. (3.3) are measured in units instead of thousands of units. In this case, the value of the slope is $\beta_1 = -50,000$. Although we are dealing with the same relationship, changing the units of measurement changes the slope's numerical value. A related problem is comparing consumer sensitivity to similar price changes for different products, such as the demand for automobiles, yards of cloth, gallons of beer, and pounds of beef. To overcome these measurement problems, economists substitute the slope with the price elasticity of demand, which is a dimensionless measure of consumer sensitivity.

The **price elasticity of demand** measures the *percent* change in the quantity demanded of a good or service given a *percent* change in its price, that is

$$E_{x,x} = \frac{\%\Delta Q_x}{\%\Delta P_x}. \tag{3.4}$$

The first subscript of $E_{x,x}$ refers the quantity demanded of good x and the second subscript refers to the price of good x. In subsequent sections we will discuss several other elasticity measures that follow this convention.

SOLVED EXERCISE

Suppose that the price elasticity of demand for a product is −2. How will the quantity demanded of this product change is price is reduced by 5 percent?

Solution

Substituting these values into Eq. (3.4) we get

$$-2 = \frac{\%\Delta Q_x}{-5}. \tag{3.5}$$

Solving, the percent change in the quantity demanded is $\%\Delta Q_x = 10$. That is, a 5 percent reduction in price results in a 10 percent increase in quantity demanded.

Calculating the Price Elasticity of Demand

The price elasticity of demand is the percent change in the quantity demanded given a percent change in price. How we calculate the price elasticity of demand depends on the available information.

Midpoint Formula

Suppose you are given two price quantity combinations (P_1, Q_1) and (P_2, Q_2), such as points A and B in Figure 3.1. Calculating the price elasticity of demand using Eq. (3.4) is not as straightforward as it appears. This is because we normally calculate a percent change by subtracting the starting value from the ending value, and then divide by the starting value. For example, if price increases from P_1 to P_2, the percent change in price is would be calculated as

$$\%\Delta P_x = \left[\frac{P_2 - P_1}{P_1}\right]100 > 0. \tag{3.6}$$

On the other hand, if the price declines from P_2 to P_1, the percent change in price is

$$\%\Delta P_x = \left[\frac{P_2 - P_1}{P_2}\right]100 < 0. \tag{3.7}$$

Ignoring the sign change, Eqs. (3.6) and (3.7) are not equal because are the denominators are different. The same applies to calculating the percent change in quantity demanded. The effect on the calculated price elasticity of demand can be significant. For example, the price elasticity of demand when moving from point A to point B in Figure 3.1 is

$$E_{x,x} = \frac{\%\Delta Q_x}{\%\Delta P_x} = \frac{(22-12)/12}{(2.10-2.30)/2.30} = -9.58. \tag{3.8}$$

By contrast, the value of the price elasticity of demand when moving from point B to point A is

$$E_{x,x} = \frac{\%\Delta Q_x}{\%\Delta P_x} = \frac{(12-22)/22}{(2.30-2.10)/2.10} = -4.77. \tag{3.9}$$

What is needed is an elasticity measure that does not depend on whether we are moving from point A to point B, or from point B to point A. A convenient approximation of the price elasticity of demand is the **midpoint formula**, which is given by the equation

$$E_{x,x} = \left(\frac{Q_2 - Q_1}{P_2 - P_1}\right)\left(\frac{P_1 + P_2}{Q_1 + Q_2}\right) = \beta_x\left(\frac{P_1 + P_2}{Q_1 + Q_2}\right), \tag{3.10}$$

where $\beta_x = (Q_2 - Q_1)/(P_2 - P_1) = \Delta Q_x/\Delta P_x$ is the slope of the demand curve.

The midpoint formula allows us to calculate a price elasticity of demand that is invariant with respect to a price increase or decrease. Moving from point A to point B, the price elasticity of demand using Eq. (3.10) is

$$E_{x,x} = \left(\frac{22-12}{2.10-2.30}\right)\left(\frac{2.30+2.10}{12+22}\right) = -\frac{6.47}{1}. \qquad (3.11)$$

It is left as an exercise for the reader to show that this is the same value for the price elasticity of demand when moving from point B to point A. The interpretation of this result is that a one percent increase in price will result in a 6.47 percent decrease in the quantity demanded. Conversely, a one percent decrease in price will result in a 6.47 percent increase in the quantity demanded.

Point Price Elasticity of Demand

As we have seen, the price elasticity of demand has several advantages over the slope as a measure of consumer sensitivity. It is also easy to calculate and interpret. Unfortunately, the midpoint formula suffers from two weaknesses that reduce its usefulness. To begin with, the midpoint formula implicitly assumes that the underlying demand curve is linear. Since demand curves are more appropriately convex, the value $E_{x,x}$ is sometimes referred to as the **arc price elasticity of demand**.

Another weakness of the midpoint formula is that it produces a value that depends on the price-quantity combinations selected for its calculation. Care must be exercised when choosing (P_1, Q_1) and (P_2, Q_2). To see why, consider Figure 3.2. As we will soon discover, the percent change in the quantity

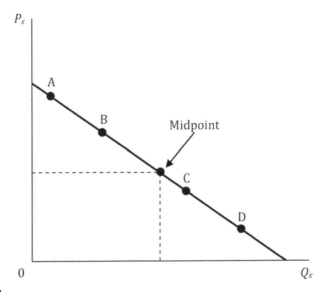

Figure 3.2

demanded is greater than the percent change in price for all price-quantity combinations above the midpoint, such as points A and B, and vice versa for price-quantity combinations below the midpoint, such as points C and D. At the midpoint, the percent change in the quantity demand equals the percent change in price.

It is important for a manager to know whether the quantity demanded for the firm's product is above or below the midpoint since a change in price will have predictable effects on a firm's revenues and profits. Unfortunately, a manager may know whether the price charged is above or below the midpoint. For this reason, it is important when using the midpoint formula for managers to choose price-quantity combinations that are "close" together. This will minimize the possibility of spanning the midpoint, which would make it difficult to identify consumer sensitivity to price changes.

An alternative to the midpoint formula is the **point price elasticity of demand** $(\varepsilon_{x,x})$, which is unique at each and every point along a demand curve. The point price elasticity of demand is given by the equation

$$\varepsilon_{x,x} = \left(\frac{\Delta Q_x}{\Delta P_x}\right)\left(\frac{P_x}{Q_x}\right) = \beta_x\left(\frac{P_x}{Q_x}\right),\tag{3.12}$$

where β_x is the slope of the demand curve.

Consider, for example, the demand curve given by Eq. (3.2). Using the midpoint formula, the price elasticity of demand over the line segment AB is $E_{x,x} = -6.47$. Since the slope of the demand curve is $\beta_x = -50$, the point price elasticity of demand at point A is

$$\varepsilon_{x,x}^A = \left(\frac{\Delta Q_x}{\Delta P_x}\right)\left(\frac{P_x}{Q_x}\right) = -50\left(\frac{2.30}{12}\right) = -9.58.\tag{3.13}$$

The point price elasticity of demand at point B is

$$\varepsilon_{x,x}^B = \left(\frac{\Delta Q_x^d}{\Delta P_x}\right)\left(\frac{P_x}{Q_x^d}\right) = -50\left(\frac{2.10}{22}\right) = -4.77.\tag{3.14}$$

The reader should note that the value of the price elasticity of demand using the midpoint formula is between the point price elasticity at points A and B. The reader is also cautioned that the price elasticity of demand using the midpoint formula is not a simple average of the point price elasticities.

SOLVED EXERCISE

Suppose that the demand for a good is given by the equation $Q_x = 50 - 2.25P_x$. Calculate the point price elasticity of demand when $P_x = \$2$.

Solution

$$\varepsilon_{x,x} = \left(\frac{\Delta Q_x}{\Delta P_x}\right)\left(\frac{P_x}{Q_x}\right) = -2.25\left(\frac{2}{50 - 2.25(2)}\right) = -0.099. \qquad (3.15)$$

Midpoint Formula versus the Point Price Elasticity

The main advantage of the midpoint formula is its minimal data require-ments. Only two price-quantity combinations are needed to calculate its value. This is particularly important for small and medium sized firms that lack the financial and technical resources to conduct sophisticated market and statistical research. All a manager needs to do is change the price of the firm's product by a small amount and use the resulting sales data to approximate the price elasticity of demand using the midpoint formula.

  Unfortunately, the midpoint formula may not be a particularly good mea-sure of consumer sensitivity to price changes. The midpoint formula intro-duces distortions that become more acute when price changes are large, or when the underlying demand curve is nonlinear. The point price elasticity is a superior measure of consumer sensitivity to price changes, although manag-ers should limit its application to small changes in price.

Definitions

According to the **law of demand**, there is an inverse relationship between a percent change in price and the percent change in the quantity demanded. For this reason, the price elasticity of demand is between zero and $-\infty$. It is sometimes convenient, however, to express the price elasticity of demand in absolute terms, which is always positive.

Price Elastic Demand

Demand is said to be **price elastic** when $|\varepsilon_{x,x}| > 1$ ($\varepsilon_{x,x} < -1$). In this case, the absolute value of the percent change in quantity demanded is greater than the absolute value of the percent change in price ($|\%\Delta Q_x| > |\%\Delta P_x|$). Suppose, for example, that a 2 percent increase in price results in a 4 percent decline in quantity demanded. The demand for this product is price elastic because $|\varepsilon_{x,x}| = |-4/2| = 2 > 1$. Demand is described as *perfectly elastic* when $|\varepsilon_{x,x}| = \infty$ ($\varepsilon_{x,x} = -\infty$). This occurs when $\Delta Q_x/\Delta P_x = -\infty$ or $P_x/Q_x = \infty$. These conditions are depicted for the linear demand curve in Figure 3.3.

Price Inelastic Demand

Demand is said to be **price inelastic** when $|\varepsilon_{x,x}| < 1$ ($-1 < \varepsilon_{x,x} < 0$). This occurs when $|\%\Delta Q_x^d| < |\%\Delta P_x|$. Suppose, for example, that a 2 percent increase in price leads to a 1 percent decline in quantity demanded. The demand for this product is price inelastic because $|\varepsilon_{x,x}| = |-1/2| < 1$. Demand is *perfectly inelastic* when $\varepsilon_{x,x} = 0$, which occurs when $\Delta Q_x/\Delta P_x = 0$ or $P_x/Q_x = 0$. These conditions are depicted in Figure 3.4.

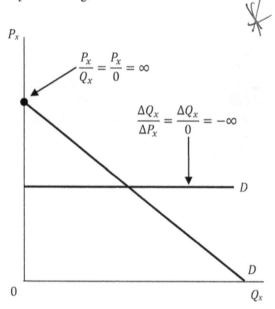

Figure 3.3

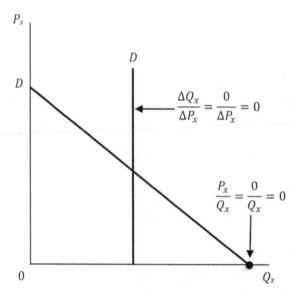

Figure 3.4

Unit Elastic Demand

Finally, demand is said to be **unit elastic** when $|\varepsilon_{x,x}| = 1$ ($\varepsilon_{x,x} = -1$), which occurs when $|\%\Delta Q_x^d| = |\%\Delta P_x|$. Suppose that a 2 percent increase in price leads to a 2 percent decline in quantity demanded. The demand for this product is unit elastic since $|\varepsilon_{x,x}| = |-2/2| = 1$.

Determinants of the Price Elasticity of Demand

Several factors that affect a consumer's sensitivity to a price change. In this section we will discuss three factors that affect the price elasticity of demand, including the number of close substitutes, the proportion of the consumer's income spent on the product, and the amount of time that a consumer has to adjust to the price change.

Substitutability

The price elasticity of demand is partly explained by the availability of close substitutes. Intuitively, the greater the number of close substitutes, the more price elastic is the demand for a product. This is because it is easier for buyers to find less expensive, albeit not perfect, alternatives. Conversely, the fewer the number of close substitutes, the less price elastic since substitutes are difficult to locate.

The price elasticity of demand also depends on how narrowly we define classes of products. The demand for Coca-Cola, for example, is more price elastic than the demand for soft drinks in general. When the price of Coca-Cola increases, consumers can switch to Pepsi-Cola, 7-Up, Dr. Pepper, Gatorade, and so on. On the other hand, there are fewer alternatives if there is an increase in the price of all soft drinks.

The demand curve for the product of a firm that has a large number of substitutes is "flatter" than the demand curve for a firm with few substitutes. The extreme case is when a firm has a large number of rivals that sell identically the same product. In this case, the demand for the firm's product is perfectly elastic ($|\varepsilon_{x,x}| = \infty$) and the demand curve horizontal. In this case, a manager that increases the price even slightly will discover that consumers will purchase nothing at all as they switch to the cheaper, identical products of rival firms. By contrast, when the demand for a firm's good is perfectly inelastic ($|\varepsilon_{x,x}| = 0$), consumers do not alter their purchases at all in response to a price change. In this case, demand curve is vertical.

Of course, the demand for a good or service is rarely perfectly elastic or perfectly inelastic. The demand curve for most goods and services is downward sloping. In the next section, we will learn about the important relationship between the price elasticity of demand and the firm's total revenue from sales of its product. In Chapter 11, we will discuss how this information can be used to formulate an optimal pricing strategy.

Proportion of Income

When the purchase of a good constitutes a relatively large proportion of a person's total expenditures increases, an increase in the price of a big-ticket item, such as a washer dryer or automobile, than an equivalent increase in the price of a good that constitutes a relatively small percentage of a family's income, such as an ounce of table salt. In 2013, the median per family income in the U.S was around $51,000. Members of this group will sit up and take notice of a 10 percent increase in the price of a $20,000 Honda Civic, will hardly bat an eyelash at an equivalent increase in the $1.40 price of a 2 liter bottle of Coke Classic.

Adjustment Period

In general, consumers tend to be less price sensitive in the short run than in the long run. For many goods and services it takes time for individuals and families to adjust their budgets expenditures to a price change. Consider, for example, an increase in the price of gasoline from, say, $3.50 to $5.00 per gallon. In the short run, many drivers have no choice but to pay the higher price since automobiles are essential to many aspects of a family's daily lives, such as getting the kids to school, driving to work, grocery shopping, and so on. In the short run, many drivers may be able to make modest adjustments in their driving patterns to reduce the number of miles driven, perhaps by combining trips to the super market with the daily commute to work. Over a longer period of time, however, some people will trade in their gas guzzlers for more fuel efficient substitutes. The fact that consumer purchases are sensitive to the adjustment period also helps to explain why airlines charge higher fares for tickets purchased the day before a scheduled flight than when a ticket is purchased two months in advance.

Total and Marginal Revenue

The price elasticity of demand is a valuable business tool because it enables a manager to predict how a price will affect unit sales and revenues. Suppose, for example, that a manager is contemplating a 10 percent price increase and the demand for the firm's product is price inelastic. If the price elasticity of demand is $\varepsilon_{x,x} = \%\Delta Q_x/\%\Delta P_x = -1/2$, the result will be a 5 percent decline in unit sales. The effect on total revenues can be can be decomposed into two effects. On the one hand, the price increase will push up revenues by about 10 percent. On the other hand, the decline in unit sales will push down revenues by about 5 percent. The net effect is an increase in total revenues of around 5 percent.

Suppose, on the other hand, that demand is price elastic and $\varepsilon_{x,x} = -2$. In this case, a 10 percent increase in price will increase revenues by about 10 percent, but the fall in sales will reduce revenues by about 20 percent. In this case, the net effect is a decline in total revenues of around 10 percent. Finally, if demand is unit elastic, a 10 percent increase in price will increase total revenues by about 10 percent, which will be exactly offset by a 10 percent decline in revenues from lost unit sales. The net effect is no change in total revenues.

To make the discussion more concrete, suppose that the demand for good x is given by the equation

$$Q_x = 80 - 10P_x. \tag{3.16}$$

Table 3.1 summarizes the price elasticity of demand and total revenue ($TR_x = P_x Q_x$) for alternative price quantity combinations. At a price of $6, for example, the quantity demanded is 20 units. At this price-quantity combination the point price elasticity of demand is −3 and the firm's total revenue is $6(20) = $120. The price elasticity of demand tells us that in the neighborhood of this price-quantity combination, a 1 percent decline in price will result in 3 percent increase in the quantity demanded and an increase in total revenue. Suppose that the firm lowers price to $5, which increases sales to 30 units and total revenue to $5(30) = $150. At this price-quantity combination the point price elasticity of demand is $\varepsilon_{x,x} = -1.67$. The price reduction from $6 to $5 results in a decline of total revenues of −$1 × 20 = −$20. The increase in sales at the lower price, however, results in increase in revenues of $5(10) = $50.

A $1 price reduction when demand is price elastic results in an increase in total revenue. What happens when price is reduced by $1 when demand is price inelastic? Suppose, for example, that the firm initially charges a price of $3 and sells 50 units. At this price-quantity combination the point price elasticity of demand is $\varepsilon_{x,x} = -0.6$ and total revenue is $3(50) = $150. If the firm cuts price to $2, sales will increases to 60 units. At this price-quantity

Table 3.1

P_x	Q_x	$\Delta Q_x/\Delta P_x$	P_x/Q_x^d	$\varepsilon_{x,x}$	Demand is	MR	TR
0	80	−10	0	0	Perfectly inelastic	−8	0
1	70	−10	0.014	−0.14	Inelastic	−6	70
2	60	−10	0.033	−0.33	Inelastic	−4	120
3	50	−10	0.060	−0.60	Inelastic	−2	150
4	40	−10	0.100	−1.00	Unit elastic	0	160
5	30	−10	0.167	−1.67	Elastic	2	150
6	20	−10	0.300	−3.00	Elastic	4	120
7	10	−10	0.700	−7.00	Elastic	6	70
8	0	−10	∞	$-\infty$	Perfectly elastic	8	0

combination the point price elasticity of demand is $\varepsilon_{x,x} = -0.33$ and total revenue is $2(60) = \$120$. Reducing price by \$1 causes total revenue to decline from \$150 to \$120. The price reduction lowers total revenue by $-\$1(50) = -\$50$ The increase in revenues from greater units sales is only $\$2(10) = \$20$. Lowering price by \$1 when demand is price elastic causes revenues to decline by \$30.

The above example highlights several important features that are common to all linear demand curves. Although the slope of this linear demand curve is the same at every price-quantity combination, the price elasticity of demand can take on any value between 0 and $-\infty$. Demand is perfectly inelastic ($\varepsilon_{x,x} = 0$) where the demand curve intersects the quantity (horizontal) axis. The demand curve is perfectly elastic ($\varepsilon_{x,x} = -\infty$) where the demand curve intersects the price (vertical) axis. At the midpoint of the demand curve, demand is unit elastic ($\varepsilon_{x,x} = -1$). Demand is price elastic for any price-quantity combination above the midpoint. Finally, demand is price inelastic for any price quantity combination below the midpoint.

The relationship between total revenues and price elasticity for a linear demand curve depicted is summarized in Figure 3.5 and Table 3.2. Total revenue is maximized when demand is unit elastic, which occurs at the midpoint of the demand curve. As price is lowered (raised) in the elastic region, the quantity demanded increases (falls) and total revenue increases (decreases). When the price is lowered (raised) in the inelastic region, the quantity demanded increases (decreases) and total revenue falls (rises).

Figure 3.5 summarizes the relationships among the price elasticity of demand, total revenue and **marginal revenue** (*MR*), which is the change in total revenue (ΔTR) from a change in the number of units sold. *MR* is positive for all price-quantity combinations along the elastic portion of the demand curve. Thus, lowering price will result in an increase in sales and revenues. *MR* is negative for all price-quantity combinations along the inelastic region of the demand curve. Reducing price in this region will result in an increase in sales, but a decrease in revenues.[2]

Formal Relationship between the Price Elasticity of Demand and Total Revenue

The tight relationship between price, the price elasticity of demand, total revenue and marginal revenue is summarized by the equation

$$MR = P_x\left(1 + \frac{1}{\varepsilon_{x,x}}\right) = P_x\left(\frac{1 + \varepsilon_{x,x}}{\varepsilon_{x,x}}\right). \tag{3.17}$$

We know that total revenue is maximized where $MR = 0$. Since $P_x > 0$, the term in the parenthesis of Eq. (3.17) must be equal to zero, which occurs

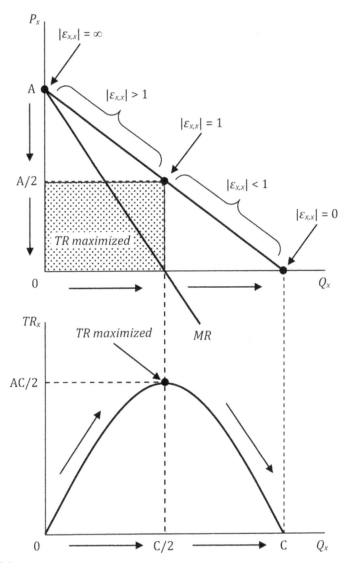

Figure 3.5

Table 3.2

$|\varepsilon_{x,x}|$	ΔP_x	ΔQ_x	$\Delta TR_x/\Delta Q = MR_x$
>1	−	+	+
>1	+	−	−
<1	−	+	−
<1	+	−	+
=1	−	+	−
=1	+	−	−

when $\varepsilon_{x,x} = -1$. When demand is elastic, $(\varepsilon_{x,x} < -1)$ the term in the parenthesis and marginal revenue must be positive. Thus, lowering price increases total revenue increases. When demand is inelastic $(-1 < \varepsilon_{x,x} < 0)$, the term in parenthesis and marginal revenue must be negative. Lowering price reduces total revenue. These relationships are also summarized in Figure 3.5 and Table 3.2.

SOLVED EXERCISE

Suppose that the demand for a firm's product is given by the equation

$$Q_x = 50 - 2.5 P_x. \tag{3.18}$$

Calculate the point price elasticity of demand and total revenue for $P_x = \$0$, $P_x = \$5$, $P_x = \$10$, $P_x = \$15$, and $P_x = \$20$. What can you conclude about the relationship between the price elasticity of demand and total revenue?

Solution

Total revenue is $TR = P_x Q_x$. From Eq. (3.18) we get

$$\varepsilon_{x,x} = -2.5 \left(\frac{P_x}{50 - 2.5 P_x} \right). \tag{3.19}$$

Eq. (3.19) can be used to calculate the price elasticity of demand for each price. These calculations are summarized in Table 3.3.

According to Table 3.3, total revenue is zero when demand is perfectly elastic or perfectly inelastic. When demand is inelastic, total revenue increases (decreases) when price is raised (lowered). When demand is elastic, total revenue increases (decreases) when price is lowered (raised). When demand is unit elastic, total revenue is maximized at $250.

Table 3.3

P_x	Q_x	TR	$\varepsilon_{x,x}$	Demand is
0	50	0	0	Perfectly inelastic
5	37.5	187.5	-0.33	Inelastic
10	25	250	-1.00	Unit elastic
15	12.5	187.5	-3.00	Elastic
20	0	0	$-\infty$	Perfectly elastic

INCOME ELASTICITY OF DEMAND

There are other important elasticity measures that are of concern to managers. The **income elasticity of demand** is a measure of consumer sensitivity to changes in money income, which reflects the ups and downs of the business cycle. The income elasticity of demand is the percent change in demand with respect to a percent change in money income, that is

$$E_{x,M} = \frac{\%\Delta Q_x}{\%\Delta M}. \tag{3.20}$$

As with the price elasticity of demand, how we estimate the income elasticity of demand depends on the information available. With pairs of values for income and quantity, the income elasticity of demand may be calculated as

$$E_{x,M} = \left(\frac{Q_2 - Q_1}{M_2 - M_1} \right)\left(\frac{M_1 + M_2}{Q_1 + Q_2} \right) = \left(\frac{\Delta Q_x}{\Delta M} \right)\left(\frac{M_1 + M_2}{Q_1 + Q_2} \right). \tag{3.21}$$

The corresponding point income elasticity of demand is

$$\varepsilon_{x,M} = \left(\frac{\Delta Q_x^d}{\Delta M} \right)\left(\frac{M}{Q_x^d} \right) = \beta_M \left(\frac{M}{Q_x^d} \right). \tag{3.22}$$

We learned that the demand for a **normal good** varies directly with consumers' money income, in which case the value of β_M is positive. Since money income and quantity must are also positive, for a normal good $\varepsilon_{x,M} > 0$, which says that a percent increase (decrease) in money income is accompanied by a percent increase (decrease) in demand. Normal goods may be further classified as necessities or luxuries. The demand for a **necessity** is relatively insensitive to income changes. The percent change in the demand for a good is less than the percent change in money income, that is, $0 < \varepsilon_{x,M} < 1$. Examples of necessities include electricity, rent, food, and health care. By contrast, the demand for luxuries tends to exaggerate swings consumers' money income. A good is a **luxury good** when the percent change in demand is greater than the percent change in money income, that is $\varepsilon_{x,M} > 1$. Examples of luxuries include foreign travel, restaurant meals, and foreign imports.

Since the demand for an **inferior good** is inversely related to a consumer's money income, the value of β_M in Eq. (2.1) is negative, thus $\varepsilon_{x,M} < 0$. Inferior goods are fairly common for individual consumers, but difficult to identify at the market level. An oft cited example of an inferior good at the market level is the demand for bankruptcy services, which tends to increase during recessions.

In Chapter 2 we discussed how a change in the price of a good affects a consumer's real income. The **income effect** for normal goods is closely related to the price elasticity of demand. Purchases of goods that are sensitive to price changes tend to be luxuries. Purchases of goods that are not sensitive to price changes tend to be necessities.

CROSS-PRICE ELASTICITY OF DEMAND

Another frequently used elasticity measure is the **cross-price elasticity of demand**, which measures the sensitivity of consumer purchases of a product with respect to a change in the price of a related good. Related goods in consumption may be complements or substitutes. The cross-price elasticity of demand measures the percent change in the demand for good x given a percent change in the price of related good y, that is

$$\varepsilon_{x,y} = \frac{\%\Delta Q_x}{\%\Delta P_y} = \left(\frac{\Delta Q_x}{\Delta P_y}\right)\left(\frac{P_y}{Q_x}\right) = \beta_y\left(\frac{P_y}{Q_x}\right). \tag{3.23}$$

The cross-price elasticity of demand takes its sign from the value of β_y. When $\varepsilon_{x,y} > 0$, goods x and y are substitutes. When $\varepsilon_{x,y} < 0$, the two goods are complements.

Up to this point, we have assumed that a firm produces a single product. Now, suppose that the firm produces multiple related products. What effect will a change in the price of one good have on a firm's total revenues? Suppose, for example, that a company sells two goods, x and y. The company's total revenue from the sale of these two products is

$$TR = TR_x + TR_y, \tag{3.24}$$

where $TR_x = P_x Q_x$ and $TR_y = P_y Q_y$. For very small changes in the price of good x, the change in the firm's total revenue given is given by the equation

$$\Delta TR = \left[TR_x\left(1+\varepsilon_{x,x}\right)+TR_y\left(\varepsilon_{y,x}\right)\right]\times\left(\frac{\%\Delta P_x}{100\%}\right). \tag{3.25}$$

SOLVED EXERCISE

Suppose that a firm earns $5,000 a month from the sale of good x and $3,000 from the sale of good y. The price-elasticity of demand for good x is $\varepsilon_{x,x} = -2$ and the cross-price elasticity of demand for good y is $\varepsilon_{y,x} = -4$. How will a one percent cut in the price of good x affect the firm's total revenue?

Solution

From Eq. (3.26) we obtain

$$\Delta TR = \left[\$5,000[1-2]+\$3,000(-4)\right](-0.01) = \$170. \qquad (3.26)$$

This result says that a one percent cut in the price of good x will result in a $170 increase in total revenues.

ADVERTISING ELASTICITY OF DEMAND

A very useful management tool is the **advertising elasticity of demand**, which measures the percent change in unit sales arising from a percent change in advertising expenditures. **Ceteris paribus**, we would expect that an increase in advertising expenditures will increase in unit sales and revenues. Symbolically, the advertising elasticity of demand is

$$\varepsilon_{x,A} = \frac{\%\Delta Q_x}{\%\Delta A} = \left(\frac{\Delta Q_x}{\Delta A}\right)\left(\frac{A}{Q_x}\right). \qquad (3.27)$$

SOLVED EXERCISE

A business consultant has estimated the following demand function for Rubicon & Styx's world-famous hot sauce "Sergeant Garcia's Revenge."

$$Q_x = 62 - 2P_x + 0.2M + 25A, \qquad (3.28)$$

where Q_x is the quantity demanded per month in thousands of units, P_x is the price per 6-oz. bottle, M is an index of consumer income, and A is the company's monthly advertising expenditures per month in thousands of dollars. Assume that P_x = $4, M = $150, and A = $4 (thousand).

a. *Calculate the number of bottles of "Sergeant Garcia's Revenge" demanded.*
b. *Calculate the price elasticity of demand. According to your calculations, is the demand for this product elastic, inelastic, or unit elastic? What, if anything, can you say about the demand for this product?*
c. *Calculate the income elasticity of demand. Is "Sergeant Garcia's Revenge" a normal good or an inferior good? Is it a luxury or a necessity?*
d. *Calculate the advertising elasticity of demand. Explain your result.*

Solution

a. *Substituting the given information into the demand function we get*

$$Q_x = 62 - 2(4) + 0.2(150) + 25(2) = 184 \, thousand. \qquad (3.29)$$

b. *The price elasticity of demand is*

$$\varepsilon_{x,x} = \left(\frac{\Delta Q_x}{\Delta P_x}\right)\left(\frac{P_x}{Q_x}\right) = -2\left(\frac{4}{184}\right) = -0.04. \qquad (3.30)$$

This result tells us that a 1 percent increase in the price of "Sergeant Garcia's Revenge" results in a 0.04 percent decrease in quantity demanded. Since $|\varepsilon_{x,x}| < 1$, the demand for this product is price inelastic. This might suggest that "Sergeant Garcia's Revenge" has no close substitutes.

c. *The income elasticity of demand is*

$$\varepsilon_{x,M} = \left(\frac{\Delta Q_x}{\Delta M}\right)\left(\frac{M}{Q_x}\right) = 0.2\left(\frac{150}{184}\right) = 0.16, \qquad (3.31)$$

which says that a 1 percent increase in consumer income results in a 0.16 percent increase in the demand. Since $0 < \varepsilon_{x,M} < 1$, this normal good is a necessity.

d. *The advertising elasticity of demand is given as*

$$\varepsilon_{x,A} = \left(\frac{\Delta Q_x}{\Delta A}\right)\left(\frac{A}{Q_x}\right) = 25\left(\frac{4}{184}\right) = 0.54. \qquad (3.32)$$

This result tells us that a 1 percent increase in Rubicon & Styx's advertising expenditures results in a 0.54 percent increase in unit sales.

CHAPTER EXERCISES

3.1 Suppose that you are a portfolio manager for a large, diversified mutual fund. The fund's chief economist is forecasting an economic slowdown. How will your knowledge of estimated income elasticities of demand to alter the composition of the portfolio?

3.2 Suppose that crime is positively related to profits from illegal drug sales and that the demand for drugs is price inelastic. The government's primary weapon in the war on drugs is the interdiction of illegal drugs flowing into the country from outside its borders. What is the likely effect of this policy on domestic crime rates? Can you suggest an alternative approach to the war on drugs?

3.3 Explain why a monopolist would never price its product along the inelastic portion of a linear demand curve.

3.4 A consortium of the world's leading oil producers form a cartel to control the supply of crude oil. The objective of the cartel is to raise price and increase revenues. What must be true about the demand for oil for this policy to be successful?

3.5 A consortium of the world's leading coffee bean producers form a cartel to the supply of coffee beans. The objective of the cartel is to lower prices and increase cartel revenues. What must be true about the demand for coffee beans for this policy to be successful?

3.6 The Sylvan Corporation produces wood sorrels. The price elasticity of demand is –0.25.
   a. What will happen to the quantity demanded if Sylvan raises its price by 10 percent?
   b. What will happen to Sylvan's revenues following this price increase?

3.7 Suppose that the cross-price elasticity of demand for good x is 2.5 and the price of good y increases by 25 percent.
   a. How would you characterize the relationship between goods x and y?
   b. How will the increase in the price of good y affect unit sales of good x?

3.8 Suppose that the cross-price elasticity of demand for good m is –1.75 and the price of good n falls by 10 percent.
   a. What is the relationship between goods m and good n?
   b. How will the fall in the price of good n affect sales of good m?

3.9 Suppose that the income elasticity of demand for a good is 3.5.
   a. How would you classify this good?
   b. What increase in income is required for demand to increase by 21 percent?

3.10 Suppose that the estimated demand equation for a firm's good is

$$Q_x = 100 - 10P_x - 2P_y + 0.1M + 0.2A,$$

where Q_x^d is unit sales of good x, P_x is the price of good x, P_y is the price of good y, M is per-family money income in thousands of dollars, and A is the level of advertising expenditures in thousands of dollars. Suppose that P_x = $2, P_y = $3, M = $50 (thousand), and A = $20 (thousand). Calculate the price elasticity of demand.

3.11 Silkwood Enterprises specializes in gardening supplies. The demand for its new brand of fertilizer is given by the equation

$$Q = 120 - 4P.$$

a. Silkwood is currently charging $10 a pound. What is the price elasticity of demand?
b. At this price, what is Silkwood's marginal revenue?
c. What price should Silkwood charge if it wants to maximize total revenue?
d. What is the price elasticity of demand at the revenue maximizing price?

3.12 Just-the-Fax, Max, Inc. has determined that the demand for its FAX machines is

$$Q = 3,000 - 1.5P.$$

a. Calculate the point price elasticity of demand when $P = \$600$.
b. At $P = \$600$ what is Max's marginal revenue?
c. Determine the total revenue maximizing price and quantity for the firm.

3.13 The market research department of Paradox Enterprises has determined that the demand for its product is

$$Q_x = 1,000 - 5P_x + 0.05M - 50P_z,$$

where P_x is the price, M median family income, and P_z is the price of bailiwicks. Suppose that $P_x = \$5$, $M = \$20,000$, and $P_z = \$15$.
a. What is the price elasticity of demand?
b. Is the firm maximizing its total revenue at $P_x = \$5$. If not, what price should Paradox charge?
c. Calculate the income elasticity of demand at $P_x = \$5$.
d. Calculate the cross-price elasticity of demand at $P_x = \$5$.

3.14 Suppose that the demand equation for a firm's product is

$$Q = 10 - 0.4P,$$

where Q is quantity and P is price.
a. Calculate the price elasticity of demand using the midpoint formula when $P_1 = \$13$ and $P_2 = \$12$.
b. Calculate the point price elasticity of demand at these prices. What, if anything, can you say about the relationship between the price elasticity of demand and total revenue at these prices?
c. What is the price elasticity of demand at the price that maximizes total revenue?

3.15 Suppose that the demand equation for widgets is

$$Q = 10,000 - 25P.$$

a. How many widgets will be sold for $100?
b. At what price will the demand for widgets zero?
c. What is the total revenue equation for widgets in terms of output? What is the marginal revenue equation in terms of output?
d. What is the price elasticity of demand when $P = \$200$? What is the firm's total and marginal revenue at this price?
e. What is the price elasticity of demand if the price of widgets falls to $P = \$150$? At this price what is the firm's total and marginal revenue? Explain your results.
f. What is the price elasticity of demand if the price of widgets rises to $P = \$250$? At this price what is the firm's total and marginal revenue? Explain your results.
g. Suppose that the supply of widgets is given by the equation

$$Q = -5,000 + 50P.$$

What is the equilibrium price and quantity?
h. What is the relationship between quantity supplied and quantity demanded at $P = \$300$?

3.16 The demand for a product is given by the equation

$$Q = 50 - 2P.$$

a. What is the point price elasticity of demand at $P = \$20$?
b. If the price falls to $P = \$15$, what happens to total revenues? What does this imply about the price elasticity of demand?
c. Verify your answer to part b by computing the arc price elasticity over this price interval.
d. What, if anything, can you say about the relationship between the point price-elasticities of demand calculated in parts a and b, and the arc price elasticity of demand calculated in part c?

Chapter 4

Production and Cost

All businesses perform essentially the same function—transforming inputs into outputs for sale in the market. The expectation of earning profit is the underlying incentive for most commercial activities in a market economy. In general, the objective of the firm is not just to turn a profit, but to make as much money as is legally, ethically, and socially permissible.

A necessary condition for maximizing profit is to minimize the firm's total cost of production. To accomplish this, managers must employ the correct types and combinations of labor, capital and other productive inputs, substitute higher-cost inputs with lower-cost substitutes, and adopt the most efficient production methods whenever possible. In short, a manager must have an intimate understanding of the firm's cost structure to achieve the goal of maximizing shareholder value. In this chapter, we will introduce several important production concepts and build upon those ideas to show that a firm's cost structure reflects its underlying production technology. We will conclude with discussions of the learning curve effect, optimal plant size, and multiproduct cost functions.

THE PRODUCTION FUNCTION

The mathematical statement that describes the process whereby productive inputs are efficiently transformed into outputs of goods and services is called a **production function**. To keep our discussion of the production function as manageable as possible, let us suppose that that the production of output (Q) requires the use of labor (L) and economic capital (K) inputs. This relationship may be written

$$Q = f(K,L). \tag{4.1}$$

Labor refers to the mental and physical talents and abilities of workers. Capital refers to mean manufactured inputs used for further production, such as tools, plant and equipment, storage facilities, and so on.

Eq. (4.1) describes the maximum output that can be produce from any combination of labor and capital inputs. The importance of understanding a firm's underlying production technology becomes readily apparent when we recall that the goal is to maximize profit. Inputs are used to produce goods and services, which are sold to generate revenue. Total revenue minus to cost of procuring inputs equals the firm's profit. In competitive markets, firms that do not produce at least cost will be pushed aside by rival firms that do. Understanding a firm's underlying production technology is important because it helps define the relationship between production, total cost, total revenue, and profit.

Production Relationships

Production functions reflect the unique relationship between inputs and outputs. Producing fertilizer, for example, is quite different from providing personal financial services. Three commonly encountered specifications are the linear, Leontief, and Cobb-Douglas production functions.

Linear Production Function

A **linear production function** with capital and labor input is given by the equation

$$Q = \alpha K + \beta L, \tag{4.2}$$

where α and β are positive constants. In Eq. (4.2), labor and capital are said to be *perfect substitutes* because a given amount of capital can always be substituted for a constant amount of labor to maintain a fixed level of output. For example, suppose that

$$Q = 3K + L. \tag{4.3}$$

According to Eq. (4.3), a unit of capital is always three times more productive than a unit of labor. To see this, suppose that a firm initially employs two units of capital and six units of labor to yield $Q = f(2, 6) = 3(2) + 6 = 12$ units of output. If the amount of capital employed is reduced from by one unit, total output will fall by 3 units. To compensate, the firm must should hire 3 additional units of labor to produce the same $Q = f(1, 9) = 3(1) + 9 = 12$ units of output. Since the values α and β are constants, three units of labor can be always be substituted for one unit of capital to maintain a given level of output.

Leontief Production Function

The **Leontief production function**, which is characterized by fixed factor proportions, is given by the expression

$$Q = \min[\alpha K, \beta L], \tag{4.4}$$

where α and β are positive constants. Because capital and labor are used in fixed proportions, they are said to be *perfect complements*. For example, to produce one bicycle you need one frame and two wheels. Two bicycles require two frames and four wheels, and so on. Frames and wheels must always be combined in the precise ratio of 1 to 2. Increasing the number of wheels without increasing the number of frames will not result in more bicycles. Both must be increased in fixed proportions.

The Leontief production function for bicycles may be written

$$Q = \min\left[F, \frac{1}{2}W\right], \tag{4.5}$$

where F is the number of frames and W is the number of wheels. Eq. (4.5) tells us that the maximum number of bicycles that can be produced from any given number of frames and wheels. Suppose, for example, that we have 10 frames and 12 wheels. It is not possible to produce 10 bicycles since this requires 20 wheels. We can, however, produce 6 bicycles with 12 wheels, and have 4 frames left over. Substituting these values into Eq. (4.5) we get

$$Q = \min\left[10, \frac{1}{2}(12)\right] = \min[10, 6] = 6. \tag{4.6}$$

Eq. (4.6) tells us that the maximum number of bicycles that can be produced with 10 frames and 12 wheels is the minimum of 10 or 6 bicycles.

Suppose that the manager of a bicycle store can purchase frames and wheels from a supplier for $50 and $25 respectively. The total cost of procuring 10 frames and 12 wheels is $800. If the manager can sell each bicycle for $500, the store will earn a profit of $2,200. Unfortunately, the manager did not maximize profit because too much was spent on frames. By purchasing 4 fewer frames, the manager could have increased the store's profit by $200.

Cobb-Douglas Production Function

The most versatile and empirically investigated algebraic specification is **Cobb-Douglas production function**, which is given by the equation

$$Q = AK^{\alpha}L^{\beta},$$ (4.7)

where A, α, and β are positive constants. Unlike the linear production function in which inputs are perfect substitutes, inputs in the Cobb-Douglas production function are *imperfect substitutes*. Depending on the values of α, and β, less capital must be replaced with ever-increasing amounts of labor, and *vice versa*, to maintain a constant level of output.

Consider, for example, the Cobb-Douglas production function

$$Q = 25K^{0.5}L^{0.5}.$$ (4.8)

Table 4.1 summarizes alternative output levels associated with alternative combinations of labor and capital. For example, 122 units of output can be produced with the labor and capital may combinations (3, 8), (4, 6), (6, 4), and (8, 3).

Table 4.1 also provides information about the substitutability of labor and capital. Suppose, for example, that the firm initially employs 3 hours of capital and 8 hours of labor to produce 122 units of output. If labor input is reduced from 8 to 6 hours, capital input must be increased from 3 to 4 hours to maintain output at 122 units. If labor is reduced by another 2 hours, capital input must be increased from 4 to 6 hours, or a trade off of 2 hours of capital for 2 hours of labor. In short, Eq. (4.8) says that increasing amounts of capital must be used to compensate for equal incremental reductions in labor input to produce a fixed amount of output.

The above discussion underscores the importance of efficiently combining productive resources to maximize profits. At fixed input and output prices,

Table 4.1

Capital	Labor							
	1	2	3	4	5	6	7	8
1	25	35	43	50	56	61	66	71
2	35	50	61	71	79	87	94	**100**
3	43	61	75	87	97	106	115	**122**
4	50	71	87	**100**	112	**122**	132	**141**
5	56	79	97	112	125	137	148	158
6	61	87	106	**122**	137	150	162	173
7	66	94	115	132	148	162	175	187
8	71	**100**	**122**	**141**	158	173	187	200

managers with a fixed operating budget must combine inputs to maximize output and revenues. Alternatively, to produce a fixed amount of output, managers must identify the input combination that minimizes cost. Table 4.1, for example, identifies four combinations of capital and labor input need to produce 122 units of output. Suppose that the firm can sell its output for $10 per unit and the price of capital and labor are $50 and $30 per hour, respectively. The reader should verify that to maximize profit, the firm should employ 3 hours of capital and 8 hours of labor.

PRODUCTIVITY MEASURES

Economists distinguish between production in the short run and production in the long run. The short run is that period of time during which at least one factor of production is fixed. All inputs are variable in the long run. Since there is always at least one factor that cannot be easily varied, it can be said that firms operate in the short run and plan it the long run. Three important short-run productivity measures for assessing the efficiency of a firm's operations are the total, average, and marginal products of a variable input.

Total Product of a Variable Input

Eq. (4.2) is the firm's **long-run production function** because both capital and labor are variable inputs. By contrast, suppose that the amount of capital available to the firm is fixed, while the firm is free to vary the amount of labor employed. In this case, the firm's **short-run production function** may be written

$$Q_L = f\left(K_0, L\right) = TP_L, \qquad (4.9)$$

where K_0 represents a fixed capital and L is variable labor. Since it is only possible to increase output by using more labor, Eq. (4.9) is sometimes referred to as the **total product of labor (TP_L)**. Similarly, if labor is fixed and capital is variable, the **total product of capital (TP_K)** becomes

$$Q_K = f\left(K, L_0\right) = TP_K. \qquad (4.10)$$

Average and Marginal Products of a Variable Input

The total product of a variable inputs and input prices define a firm's short-run total cost of production. At known output prices, it should be possible to identify the level of output that maximizes profit. Since operational decisions are made at the margin, a manager should understand how changes in output affect the firm's bottom line. For this reason, it is important to understand the relationship between average and marginal product of a variable input.

Average Product

The average product of labor (AP_L), which is a measure of per worker productivity, is given by the equation

$$AP_L = \frac{TP_L}{L}. \tag{4.11}$$

Similarly, the average product of capital (AP_K), which measures output per unit of capital, is

$$AP_K = \frac{TP_K}{K}. \tag{4.12}$$

Marginal Product

The marginal product of labor (MP_L) measures the change in total output resulting from an incremental change in labor input. The marginal product of labor is the first partial derivative (capital held constant) with respect to a change in labor input, that is

$$MP_L = \frac{\Delta TP_L}{\Delta L}. \tag{4.13}$$

Similarly, the marginal product of capital is the first partial derivative (labor input held constant) with respect to a change in capital input, that is

$$MP_K = \frac{\Delta TP_K}{\Delta K}. \tag{4.14}$$

The marginal products of labor and capital for the Cobb-Douglas production in Eq. (4.7) are

$$MP_L = \frac{\Delta Q_L}{\Delta L} = \beta AK^\alpha L^{\beta-1}; \tag{4.15}$$

$$MP_K = \frac{\Delta Q_K}{\Delta K} = \alpha AK^{\alpha-1}L^\beta. \tag{4.16}$$

LAW OF DIMINISHING RETURNS

The **law of diminishing returns** is a short-run production phenomenon. It asserts that as more of a variable input is added to one or more fixed inputs, at some point total output will increase, but at a decreasing rate. As labor is added to a fixed amount of capital, the positive incremental additions to total output get progressively smaller.

The law of diminishing returns—more accurately known as the *law of diminishing marginal product of a variable input*—can be seen in Table 4.1. Suppose, for example, that a unit of capital ($K_0 = 1$) is combined with increasing amounts of labor. As the number of units of labor employed is increased from $L = 1$ to $L = 6$, total output increases from 25 to 61 units. But, the incremental additions to output are 10, 8, 7, 6, and 5 units. In other words, total output increases at a decreasing rate.

While the data presented in Table 4.1 is peculiar to Eq. (4.8), this pattern is not atypical. To understand what is going on intuitively, consider the case of a small company produces crescent wrenches from sheet metal. Suppose that the company employs a single worker, and that there are five stages in the production process—cutting, grinding, drilling, polishing and finishing. Assume that while labor and sheet metal are variable inputs, the size of the factory and the number of work stations are fixed.

Suppose that a single worker can produce 100 wrenches per week by moving from work station to work station. What happens to total output if a second worker is hired? If we assume that that all workers are identical, we might expect output to double. But, this assumes that the second worker chases the first worker through each stage of the production process. This would be an inefficient way for the manager to organize the company's work force. A better approach would be to have the first worker specialize in, say, cutting and grinding, while the second worker specializes in drilling, polishing and finishing. Since specialization increases the productivity of each worker, we would expect output to more than double. We would expect even greater productivity gains by hiring a third, fourth and fifth worker. By exploiting the gains from specialization, we would expect output to increase at an increasing rate through at least the first five workers.

If we assume that per-unit input and output prices are constant, a profit-maximizing firm will hire at least five workers. This is because the cost of production increases at a constant rate, but output, revenues and total variable profit increases at an increasing rate. But what about hiring a sixth worker? An additional worker can perform tasks that are currently performed by the first five workers, but that does not directly contribute to the production process, such as waste disposal, transporting semi-finished product from work station to work station, storage, bookkeeping, marketing, and so on. By allowing assembly line workers to devote more time to producing wrenches, we would expect output to increase, but the marginal contribution to output to be less and less. In other words, the firm experiences diminishing marginal product starting with the sixth worker.

ISOQUANTS

In the next chapter we will develop optimality conditions that must be satisfied for a firm to maximize its profits. These optimality conditions summarize the interrelationships between product price, the marginal productivity of variable inputs and their prices. If the price of an input increases, managers may substitute the more expensive input with an input that is relatively less expensive to maximize profits. An example of this might occur a manufacturing operation replaces assembly line workers with industrial robots following negotiated higher wages and benefits by union representatives. The degree to which this may, or may not, be possible depends on the firm's production function.

In general, the combinations of capital and labor to produce a fixed level of output (Q_0) may be written

$$Q_0 = f(K,L). \tag{4.17}$$

The **marginal rate of technical substitution** is the rate at which capital must be substituted for labor to maintain a constant level of output, and vice versa. The degree of substitutability between variable inputs may be depicted as an **isoquant**, which is a diagram that summarizes the input combinations required to produce a given level of output. Suppose that output is a function of capital and labor input. The marginal rate of technical substitution is the slope of an isoquant.

For the linear production function in Eq. (4.2), $MRTS_{KL} = -\alpha/\beta$. In the case of Eq. (4.3) inputs are perfectly substitutable in the sense that labor and capital can be substituted at a constant rate of 1 unit of capital for three units of labor. Thus, the corresponding isoquants are linear. Examples of production processes in which the factors of production may be perfect substitutes include fuel oil versus natural gas for some heating furnaces, the use of energy to generate heat versus time and nature for some drying processes, and fish meal versus soybeans for protein in feed mix.

Capital and labor are perfect substitutes with linear production functions. By contrast, capital and labor in Leontief production functions must be used in fixed factor proportions, that is, $MRTS_{KL} = 0$. Capital and labor are said to be *perfect complements*. When inputs are perfect complements, it is not possible to substitute more expensive with less expensive inputs. Fixed factor proportions in Leontief production functions are depicted as L-shaped iso-quants. Examples of fixed-input production processes include some chemical products that require ingredients to be used in fixed proportions, such as fertilizer, automobile engines and body parts, wheels and frames for bicycles, and so on.

Table 4.1 summarizes values of total output from alternative combinations of capital and labor input for the Cobb-Douglas production in Eq. (4.8). We observed, for example, that it is possible for this firm to produce 122 units of output using the labor and capital input combinations (3, 8), (4, 6), (6, 4), and (8, 3). A representative collection of isoquants is called an **isoquant map**. The isoquants for 100, 122, and 141 units of output are depicted in Figure 4.1.

It turns out that the marginal rate of technical substitution is equal to the negative of the ratio of the marginal product of labor (MP_L) and the marginal product of capital (MP_K), that is,

$$\frac{\Delta K}{\Delta L} = MRTS_{KL} = -\frac{MP_L}{MP_K}. \tag{4.18}$$

To see why, consider Figure 4.2. Output remains unchanged as we move from point A to point B along isoquant Q_0. This movement can be decomposed into a movement from point A to point C, and then from point C to point B. As we move from point A to point C, total output declines by the

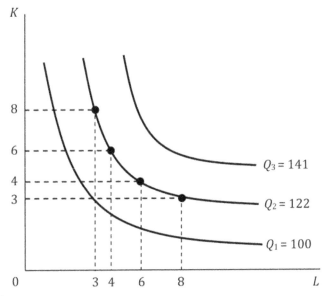

Figure 4.1

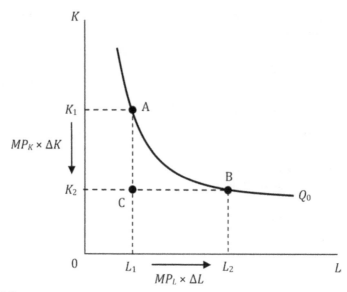

Figure 4.2

reduction in capital multiplied its incremental contribution to total output
($MP_K \times \Delta K$). In moving from point C to point B, output increases by an
amount equal to the addition of labor multiplied by its marginal contribution
to total output ($MP_L \times \Delta L$). For output to remain unchanged, the decline in
output must by moving from point A to point C must be offset by the increase
in output by going from point C to point B, that is,

$$MP_K \times -\Delta K = MP_L \times \Delta L. \tag{4.19}$$

Eq. (4.18) is found by rearranging Eq. (4.19).

The shape of the isoquant depends on the functional form of the production
function. For a Cobb-Douglas production function, isoquants are typically
convex with respect to the origin. For the production function in Eq. (4.7),
$MRTS_{KL} = -(\beta/\alpha)(K/L)$. That is, as we move from point A to point B in
Figure 4.2, for example, increasing amounts of labor must be substituted for
capital and the value (K/L) declines. Since (β/α) is constant, the slope of the
isoquant becomes less negative (flatter), and vice versa.

COST IN THE SHORT RUN

We have seen that it may be possible to produce a given level of output with
alternative combinations of inputs. We also learned that production in the

short run is subject to the law of diminishing returns, and that in the long run production may exhibit constant, increasing or decreasing returns to scale. Although an understanding of the firm's production function can provide the manager with many valuable insights regarding the nature of the relationship between inputs and outputs, it cannot by itself tell us the optimal combination of inputs or the level of output that will maximize the firm's profit. Something more is needed.

Throughout this text we assume that it is the role of managers to maximize shareholder value. In most cases, we will take this to mean that the objective of a firm is to maximize profit, which is the difference between total revenue and **total economic cost**. Output sold at market-determined prices defines the firm's total revenue. As we will learn in the next chapter, while alternative combinations of inputs that can be efficiently transformed into a given amount of output, not all of these input combinations carry the same price tag. While a manager may not know the precise mathematical specification of the firm's production function, a thorough understanding of the firm's cost structure is absolutely essential for achieving the firm's objective.

Total Cost

To maximize output, a firm must produce efficiently, which means obtaining the most output from a given combination of inputs. At fixed factor prices, producing efficiently means producing at least cost, which is a necessary condition for profit maximization. In general, managers should consider only the relevant costs of a particular decision. Deciding what costs are relevant to a decision can be tricky and frequently gives rise to confusion over such concepts as fixed cost, quasi-fixed cost, sunk cost, marginal cost, and incremental cost.

We will begin our discussion of the relevant costs of managerial decisions by assuming that the prices of labor and capital are known and determined in perfectly competitive factor markets. Thus, the firm's total economic cost of production may be written

$$TC(Q) = TFC + TVC(Q), \tag{4.20}$$

where TFC and TVC represent total fixed cost and total variable cost, respectively. **Short-run total cost** is the sum of total fixed cost and total variable cost.

Total Fixed Cost

Total fixed cost is the cost acquiring and maintaining inputs that do not vary with the level of output, and thus plays no role when determining the level of output that maximizes the firm's profit. Examples of fixed costs include ongoing expenses under a binding **contract**, such as rent paid under a lease for office space, general insurance premiums, legal retainers, and so on. Closely related to total fixed costs are **quasi-fixed costs**, which are payments that are incurred for quasi-fixed factors. For example, if a firm produces nothing, it is not necessary to incur the cost of electricity to provide lighting for its workers. These costs are only incurred once the firm begins to produce.

Related to fixed cost is **sunk cost**, which is an expense that cannot be recovered. Suppose, for example, that a new business venture rents office space. Lease rental payments are a fixed cost since they are ongoing and independent of the firm's day-to-day operations. By contrast, the one-time cost of the paint to refurbish the premises is a sunk cost that cannot be recovered. Another example is a textile manufacturer that leases a loom for $100,000 per year. These lease payments are a fixed cost since they remain unchanged regardless of whether the firm produces 5,000 or 100,000 yards of cloth. Suppose, on the other hand, that the manufacturer purchases a loom for $1 million. If the loom has a **salvage value** of $750,000, the firm has incurred a sunk cost of $250,000. If the loom has no resale or scrap value, the entire $1 million is a sunk cost. Fixed and sunk costs are overhead expenses are non-specific in that they are allocated across the firm's entire operations, but are irrelevant to specific managerial decisions.

Total Variable Cost

Total variable cost refers to expenses relating to a firm's ongoing operations. Total variable cost—also called **total operating cost**—includes the cost of acquiring variable inputs, such as labor, raw materials, components, and energy. Unlike total fixed cost, total variable cost varies directly with the firm's total output. Figure 4.3 depicts the relationships among TC, TVC and TFC for a production function that exhibits increasing then decreasing marginal product of labor.

The first thing to note about Figure 4.3 is that TFC is the same at all levels of output, even when the firm produces nothing at all. By contrast, TVC is zero when the firm produces nothing, but increases with the level of output. Moreover, TVC increases at an increasing rate when output exceeds Q_1 because of the law of diminishing returns. Finally, the TC curve lies above the TVC curve by precisely the amount of TFC.

Average and Marginal Costs

Managers of profit-maximizing firms make day-to-day production and pricing decisions based on how much the firm is earning on a per unit basis.

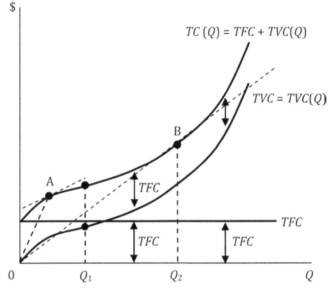

Figure 4.3

Before deciding how much to charge for a widget, a manager will want to know what a widget costs to produce. The manager also want to know how per-unit costs change as widget production increases. If total cost increases at a faster rate than the increase in production, per-unit widget costs will rise.

Average Total Cost

Average total cost is the firm's **per-unit cost** of production. It is the firm's total cost divided by the number of units produced. Dividing Eq. (4.20) by total output we get

$$ATC(Q) = \frac{TC(Q)}{Q} = AFC(Q) + AVC(Q). \tag{4.21}$$

Eq. (4.21) says that in the short run, average total cost is the sum of average fixed cost and average variable cost, which are both a function of total output.

Average Fixed Cost

Average fixed cost is the firm's per-unit total fixed cost of production. Average fixed cost is a short-run concept since it is a measure of the cost of the firm's fixed factor of production. Average fixed cost is given by the equation

$$AFC(Q) = \frac{TFC}{Q}. \tag{4.22}$$

Although total fixed cost is invariant with respect to the level of output, *AFC* asymptotically approaches zero as total output increases.

Average Variable Cost

Average variable cost, which is the firm's per-unit total variable cost of production, is given by the equation

$$AVC(Q) = \frac{TVC(Q)}{Q}. \tag{4.23}$$

If output is a function of fixed capital and variable labor, the relationship between *AVC* and total output depends on the relationship between the total output and the level of labor usage. Note that in Eq. (4.23), total variable cost varies with the level of output.

Marginal Cost

By definition, **marginal cost** is the change in the total cost resulting from unit increase in total output. This is not necessarily the same thing as the cost of producing the "last" unit. The cost of producing the last unit is the same as the cost of producing every other unit, which is the firm's per-unit cost. To illustrate this distinction, suppose that a firm hires a worker to increase its production of cuckoo clocks. If this worker is a skilled artisan who produces cuckoo clocks from start to finish then marginal cost is the cost of producing the last unit. On the other hand, if the firm hires an assembly line worker then marginal cost is the increase in total cost when one more cuckoo clock is produced since each worker depends on the contribution of every other worker. Since total fixed cost is invariant with respect to changes in total output, marginal cost measures the change in total variable cost given a change in total output. Thus, marginal cost is given by the equation

$$MC(Q) = \frac{\Delta TC(Q)}{\Delta Q} = \frac{\Delta[TFC + TVC(Q)]}{\Delta Q} = \frac{\Delta TVC(Q)}{\Delta Q}. \tag{4.24}$$

Incremental Cost

Related to marginal cost is the broader concept of **incremental cost**, which is the additional cost arising from the implementation of a managerial decision. Examples of incremental costs include the added labor and equipment costs required to introduce a new product line, the added expenses associated with servicing a new client, the increase in expenditures associated with a new investment or advertising strategy. These additional costs are incremental because they would not have been incurred otherwise.

Figure 4.4, which is derived from Figure 4.3, illustrates the relationships among *MC*, *ATC*, *AVC* and *AFC* for a production function that exhibits increasing and decreasing marginal returns to labor. Total cost and total variable cost initially increase at a decreasing rate. At constant factor prices, this indicates that the firm is experiencing increasing marginal returns so that marginal cost is positive but declining from zero to Q_1 level of output. For output levels greater than Q_1, total cost in Figure 4.3 increases at an increasing rate reflecting diminishing marginal product. In Figure 4.4, this relationship is depicted as a rising *MC* curve. While *MC* is positive throughout, it is minimized at output level Q_1, which corresponds to the inflection points on the *TC* and *TVC* curves in Figure 4.3.

We know from Eq. (4.21) that average total cost is the sum of average variable cost and average fixed cost. For this reason, the *ATC* curve must lie above the *AVC* curve. Since *AFC* declines as output increases, the vertical distance between *ATC* and *AVC*, becomes smaller. From Eq. (4.24), the value of *MC* is equal to the slopes of both the *TC* and *TVC* curves. Since the *TC* and *TVC* curves are upward sloping throughout, *MC* is always positive. As output increases from 0 to Q_1 in Figure 4.3, *TC* increases at a decreasing rate.

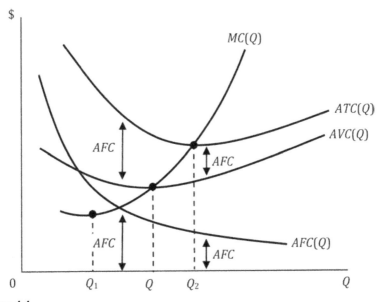

Figure 4.4

Beyond Q_1, however, output increases at an increasing rate. Thus, the *MC* curve in Figure 4.4 is U-shaped, with marginal cost minimized at the inflection point, which occurs at output level Q_1. Figure 4.4 highlights important relationships between the *MC*, *ATC* and *AVC* curves.

The U-shaped *AVC* and *ATC* curves are intersected from below at their minimum points by the MC curve. This reflects the general mathematical observation that when a marginal value is greater than its corresponding average value, the average value is pulled up. When the marginal value is less than its corresponding average value, the average value is pulled down. Finally, when the marginal value is equal to its corresponding average value, the average value is neither rising nor falling. That is, the average value is a local minimum or maximum.

SOLVED EXERCISE

Suppose that a firm's total cost function is

$$TC(Q) = 1,000 + 10Q^2. \tag{4.25}$$

a. *Determine the output level that minimizes average total cost. What is total cost, average total cost, and marginal cost at this output level? At this output level, what is the relationship between marginal cost and average total cost? Verify that ATC curve intersects the MC curve from below.*

b. *Determine the output level that minimizes average variable cost. At this output level, what is the relationship between marginal, average total, and average variable cost?*

Solution

a. *From Eq. (4.25) we obtain*

$$ATC(Q) = 1,000Q^{-1} + 10Q \tag{4.26}$$

$$\frac{\Delta ATC(Q)}{\Delta Q} = -1,000Q^{-2} + 10 = 0 \tag{4.27}$$

Solving Eq. (4.27), the output level that minimizes average total cost is Q = 10. At this output level, the firm's total cost is TC(Q) = 1,000 + 10(10)² = $2,000. Minimum average total cost is ATC(Q) = 1,000(10)⁻¹ + 10(10) = $200. Marginal cost at this output level is MC(Q) = 20(10) = $200. Thus, average total cost is minimized at the output level *where MC(Q) = ATC(Q). It is left as an exercise for the student to show that for MC to intersect ATC from below, ΔMC/ΔQ > 0 where Q = 10.*

b. *From Eq. (4.25), average variable cost is*

$$AVC(Q) = \frac{TVC(Q)}{Q} = 10Q. \tag{4.28}$$

Unlike the situation depicted in Figure 4.4, the AVC is not U-shaped but linear. This suggests the firm can only minimize AVC by producing nothing, that is, where Q = 0. At this level of output AVC(Q) = 10(0) = 0. TFC = 1,000 at all levels of output. Marginal cost is

$$MC(Q) = \frac{\Delta TC(Q)}{\Delta Q} = 20Q. \tag{4.29}$$

At Q = 0, MC(Q) = 20(0) = 0. Thus, at the output level that minimizes AVC, MC = AVC. This outcome is depicted in Figure 4.5.

Functional form of the Total Cost Equation

Figure 4.3 depicts the general shape of a short-run total cost function that exhibits increasing followed by decreasing marginal product of labor. As output is increased from 0 to Q_1, total cost increases at a decreasing rate.

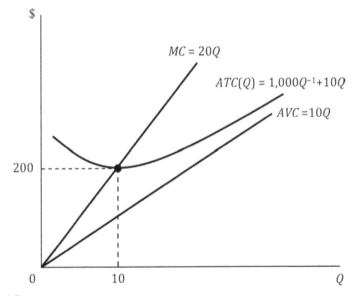

Figure 4.5

For output levels greater than Q_1, total cost increases at an increasing rate. At output level Q_1, marginal cost is minimized. This short-run total cost function may be characterized by the cubic equation

$$TC(Q) = \beta_0 + \beta_1 Q + \beta_2 Q^2 + \beta_3 Q^3, \qquad (4.30)$$

where $TFC = \beta_0$ and $TVC(Q) = \beta_1 Q + \beta_2 Q^2 + \beta_3 Q^3$.[1]

Eq. (4.30) is a general form of the total cost function because it reflects both increasing marginal product and diminishing marginal product. While the production may exhibit increasing marginal product at low levels of output, this is not guaranteed. The only thing that we can be certain of is that at some level of output, total cost will begin to increase at an increasing rate. For firms that experience diminishing marginal product at all output levels, the total cost equation is $TC(Q) = \beta_0 + \beta_1 Q + \beta_2 Q^2$ where $MC = \beta_1 + 2\beta_2 Q$ and $\Delta MC/\Delta Q = 2\beta_2$. For diminishing returns it must be that $MC > 0$ and $\Delta MC/\Delta Q = (\Delta TC/\Delta Q)/\Delta Q > 0$.

ISOCOST LINE

Suppose that the firm's operating budget (TC_0) is known and that market-determined rental prices of labor (P_L) and capital (P_K) are exogenous and fixed. For the production function $Q = f(K, L)$, the input combinations that the firm is able to procure is given by the

$$TC_0 = P_L L + P_K K, \qquad (4.31)$$

which can be more conveniently rewritten as

$$K = \frac{TC_0}{P_K} - \frac{P_L}{P_K} L. \qquad (4.32)$$

Eq. (4.31) is referred to as an **isocost line**, which is depicted in Figure 4.6. It will be used in conjunction with the firm's isoquant map to derive the optimality conditions for profit maximization in the next chapter. The vertical intercept (TC_0/P_K) and the horizontal intercept (TC_0/P_L) represent the maximum amounts of capital and labor that this firm can hire given its fixed operating budget. The slope of the isocost line, which is the ratio of the input prices (P_L/P_K), represents the rate at which the firm is able to substitute capital for labor, and vice versa. If we assume that capital and labor input are infinitely divisible, point A represents just one of an infinite number of input combinations that can be purchased or rented by the firm.

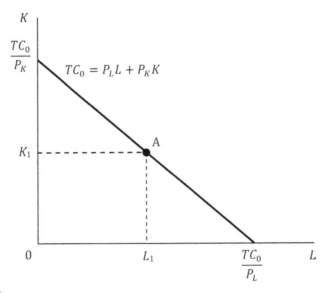

Figure 4.6

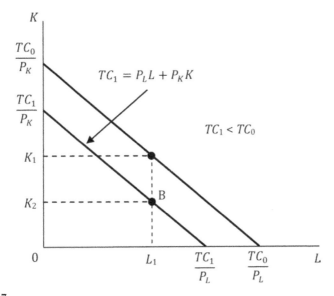

Figure 4.7

Suppose that the firm's operating budget is reduced from TC_0 to TC_1. If input prices are unchanged, the slope of the isocost line will be unaffected. On the other hand, the isocost line will experience a parallel shift to the left, which is depicted in Figure 4.7. The maximum amounts of capital and labor that the firm can employ are reduced to TC_1/P_K and TC_1/P_L.

The maximum combinations of capital and labor that the firm can purchase or rent are also reduced. Suppose, for example, that the firm continues to hire L_1 of labor. The maximum amount of capital that the firm can employ is reduced to K_2. The new input combination occurs at point B in Figure 4.7. Similarly, an increase in the firm's operating budget will cause the isocost line to parallel shift to the right, which increases the maximum combinations of capital and labor that the firm can be rented or purchased at fixed input prices.

Changes in the factor prices can also affect the position of the isocost line. Suppose, for example, that the rental price of labor increases from P_L to P_L'. This changes the slope of the isocost line from $-P_L/P_K$ to $-P_L'/P_K$, where $(-P_L'/P_K) < (-P_L/P_K)$. This is depicted in Figure 4.8 as a clockwise rotation of the isocost line around fixed point C.

Since the rental price of labor has increased, the maximum amount of labor that the firm can employ is reduced from TC_1/P_L to TC_1/P_L'. If we assume that the firm continues to employ the same amount of the more expensive labor as before, the maximum amount of capital that may now be rented or purchased must fall from K_1 to K_2. Similarly, a decrease in the rental price of labor will cause the isocost line to rotate in a counterclockwise direction around point C, which would enable the firm to procure more labor, more capital, or more of both.

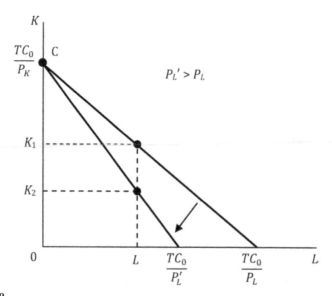

Figure 4.8

LEARNING CURVE EFFECT

It has sometimes been observed that firms that are first to market a new product are often the most successful. Standard Oil, Xerox, Microsoft, Amazon.com, Coca-Cola and Intel are examples of first movers that enjoy, or enjoyed, a competitive advantage because they were first to market a new product or innovation. In some cases, first movers were able to maintain their dominant market position by learning how to produce more efficiently. Other things being equal, the more a firm produces, the more efficient it gets at producing it. This ability to lower per-unit cost as a firm gains experience producing a good or service is called the **learning curve effect**. Consider the following numerical example. Suppose that a firm's per-unit cost for the first thousand units is $100, but can lower its per-unit cost by 25 percent by doubling output.[2] The firm's per-unit cost is $75 when it produces two thousand units, $56.25 when it produces four thousand units, $42.19 when it produces eight thousand units, and so on.

There are several explanations for the learning curve effect, including developing new or innovative production, organizational and managerial techniques, substituting lower-cost for higher-cost materials, improving existing product lines, creating innovative spin-offs of existing products, and so on. Learning curve effects may result from industry-wide and firm-specific factors. In the airline industry, for example, Boeing is using its years of experience in commercial aircraft production to develop it model 797 "blended wing body" commercial airliner that will have a reported payload of 1,000 passengers. If realized, the Boeing 797 could significantly reduce the company's per-passenger cost of production. By contrast, the per-unit cost of producing chickens was reduced by introducing industry-wide mass-production techniques.

The speed at which a firm "learns" may reflect the intelligence and creativity of managers, but may also have something to do with the nature of good itself or the underlying production technology. In general, the more standardized the product, such as cold-rolled steel, the more limited the possibility of lowering per-unit cost, no matter how much a firm produces. In some industries, improvements in production technology and product development tend to be evolutionary. By contrast, technological advancements in Apple's iPhone and iPhone "clones" have been breathtakingly rapid.

The experience gained over time can give firms with a significant competitive advantage and deter potential competitors from gaining a foothold in the market by passing cost savings along to customers in the form of lower prices. Consider, for example, the case of Aspartame—the low-calorie sweetener that was introduced to the public by G.D. Searle & Co. in 1983. In 1986,

Holland Sweetener Company entered into a **joint venture** with Tosoh Corporation of Japan and the Dutch State Mines to challenge Monsanto's hold on the European market.[3] Monsanto responded aggressively by slashing prices, which Holland could not match without suffering losses. Monsanto was able to pursue a **predatory pricing** strategy because it enjoyed significant cost and distribution advantages due to more than a decade of learning how to efficiently manufacture, market, and distribute its products. During that time, Monsanto was also able to establish, and ultimately exploit, significant brand-name (NutraSweet) recognition. According to Brandenburger, et al. (1997, p. 70), Monsanto had ". . . marched down its learning curve."

Learning curve effects have other important strategic implications. Suppose, for example, that a firm wants to purchase 4,000 units of a specialized component from a supplier with that exhibits the above learning curve effects. The supplier prefers a large order since this will allow it to "march down its learning curve" to earn an above-normal rate of return. If the output-producing firm knows the supplier's learning curve, however, it will offer $56.25 per unit, in which case the supplier will just break even. Even if the output-producing firm only suspects that supplier enjoys learning curve benefits, it could negotiate discounted prices on future purchases that are tied to the suppliers' profits on prior sales.

COST IN THE LONG RUN

For all practical purposes, there are always some factors that cannot be easily varied on short notice. In the long-run, however, managers are free to choose the optimal level of its fixed factors. For this reason, it is often said that managers operate in the short run, but plan in the long run. Of course, what constitutes the long run depends on the particular situation under consideration. If we assume that the fixed factor is the size of the firm's factory, the long run is the period of time it takes to expand its existing facilities, build a new plant, or both. Similarly, a firm's fixed cost could involve its contractual obligation obligations to resource suppliers, the wages and benefits paid to workers under a collective bargaining agreement, and so on. Moreover, a firm may still incur quasi-fixed costs in the long run.

Economies and Diseconomies of Scale

Returns to scale refers to the proportional change in total output resulting from an equiproportional change in all inputs. Consider, for example, Eq. (4.1). If output increases in direct proportion to the increase in all factors of production then the firm's production function exhibits **constant returns**

to scale. Consider the relationship between inputs and output in Table 4.1, which exhibits constant returns to scale. When $L = 2$ and $K = 3$, total output is $Q = f(2, 3) = 61$. When both capital and labor are doubled to $L = 4$ and $K = 6$, total output doubles to $Q = f(4, 6) = 122$. A firm experiences **increasing returns to scale** when a proportional increase in all inputs leads to a greater than proportional increase in total output. Finally, **decreasing returns to scale** occurs when a proportional increase in all inputs results in a less than proportional increase in output. Combined with quasi-fixed costs, returns to scale explain why a firm's long-run average total cost curve tends to be U-shaped, although this is not guaranteed.

To determine returns to scale, it is first necessary to estimate the firm's production function. The Cobb-Douglas production function is particularly well suited for empirical research because it is relatively easy to estimate using standard statistical techniques, and the estimated parameters tell us something about the degree of input substitutability, diminishing returns, and returns to scale. In the case of the Cobb-Douglas production function, returns to scale may be determined by examining the values of the exponents attached to the inputs, such as α and β in Eq. (4.7). The sum of these values is the proportional change in total output that results from an equal proportional change in all inputs. Returns to scale for Eq. (4.7) are summarized in Table 4.2.

Returns to scale in production are important because this has a direct effect on the firm's long-run per-unit cost. For any given level of output, there is an optimal plant size. Since the firm's short-run average total cost must be greater than or equal to long-run average total cost, the firm's **long-run average total cost curve** can be drawn as the lower "envelope" of the firm's short-run average total cost curves. If the firm's production technology exhibits increasing returns to scale at low levels of output, increasing the firm's scale of operations will lower its per-unit cost. To see why, suppose factor usage is doubled. At fixed factor prices, the firm's total cost of production will double as well. Since output more than doubles, the firm's per-unit cost must decrease. This happy state of affairs, which is referred to as **economies of scale**, which is depicted in Figure 4.9 as the downward sloping portion of the long-run average total cost ($LRATC$) curve for increasing output levels up to, but not including, Q_3.

By contrast, **diseconomies of scale** reflect an increase in per-unit cost at fixed factor prices as a firm expands the scale of its operations. This is

Table 4.2

$\alpha + \beta$	Returns to scale
= 1	Constant
> 1	Increasing
$0 < \alpha + \beta < 1$	Decreasing

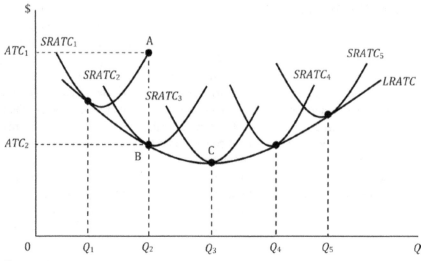

Figure 4.9

because the firm's total cost rises proportionately with an increase in total factor usage, but total output increases less than proportionately. In Figure 4.9, diseconomies of scale are depicted as the upward sloping portion of the long-run average total cost for output levels greater than Q_3. Finally, per-unit cost is unchanged when the firm experiences constant returns to scale. This is because at fixed factor prices, the firm's total cost increases proportionately with the increase in total output. In Figure 4.9, this occurs at output level Q_3 where long-run per-unit costs are neither rising nor falling.

Figure 4.9 depicts the relationship between a firm's short-run and long-run average total cost curves. Suppose initially that the firm is producing Q_1 units of output along the short-run average total cost curve $SRATC_1$. Now, suppose that the firm experiences a permanent increase in the demand for its product to Q_2. The manager of this firm has the choice of sticking with its current plant and incurring a per-unit cost of ATC_1 (point A), or expanding its facilities to lower its per-unit cost to ATC_2 (point B). The optimally efficient scale of operations is consistent with $SRATC_2$. If the demand for the firm's product increases to Q_3, this firm again faces the choice of sticking with its current factory or expanding, which lowers its short-run average total cost curve to $SRATC_3$.

Note that for output levels greater than Q_3 in Figure 4.9, building a new plant shifts the firm's short-run average total cost curves up and to the right. Expanding the firm's scale of operations increases its per-unit cost. Thus, the most efficient (least cost) scale of operations for this firm is represented by the short-run average total cost curve $SRATC_3$. The minimum point (point C) on the long-run average total cost curves is (somewhat unfortunately) referred to as the firm's **minimum efficient scale of production**.[4]

Unlike the short-run average total cost curves that derive their shape from the law of diminishing returns, the long-run average total cost curve derives its shape from returns to scale in the presence of quasi-fixed costs. In Figure 4.9, the firm enjoys economies of scale over the range of output from 0 to Q_3 because of increasing returns to scale. Output levels greater than Q_3 exhibit diseconomies of scale because of decreasing returns to scale. We have already seen that the firm's long-run average total cost curve is the lower "envelope" of its short-run average total costs curves. What does this tell us about the firm's long-run marginal cost curve?

We know that the firm's short-run marginal cost curve intersects the minimum point of the short-run average total cost curve from below. Thus, the firm's long-run marginal cost equals the firm's short-run marginal cost evaluated at each optimal level of output. In Figure 4.10 this occurs at point A for output level Q_1, point B for output level Q_2, and so on. The long-run marginal cost curve will intersect the long-run average total cost curve at point C for output level Q_3, which is the firm's minimum efficient scale of production.

Sources of Economies of Scale

Economies of scale were the most important reasons for the rise of mega-corporations in the twentieth century, and continue to be the motivating force behind many mergers and acquisitions to this day. The early growth and success

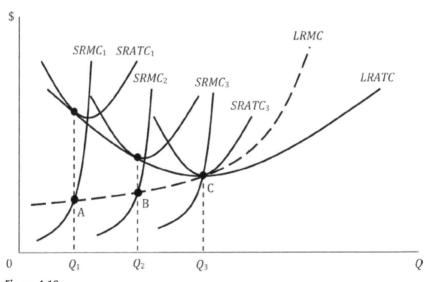

Figure 4.10

of the Ford Motor Company, for example, was due to the dramatic decline in the per-unit automobile cost following the introduction of the assembly line production.

Economies of scale can emerge from of the firm's activities. Large companies, for example, are better able to support sophisticated research and development (R&D) than smaller companies. R&D in the pharmaceuticals industry is critical, but the cost of discovering the next, new wonder drug is prohibitive and increasing. As a result, horizontal mergers in the pharmaceuticals industry, which are to spread R&D expenditures across a greater volume of sales, are commonplace. Economies of scale have been traced to several sources, including indivisible up-front costs, specialization, inventories, and the cube-square rule.

Indivisible Up-Front Costs

The most common source of economies of scale has to do with production processes in which indivisible, up-front costs can be reduced on a per unit basis as output is increased. These up-front costs are indivisible if they cannot be scaled down below some minimum level. It has been estimated, for example, that it cost 20th Century Fox between $230 million and $500 million to produce James Cameron's epic movie *Avatar*. By early-2010, worldwide ticket sales approached $2 billion. At an average ticket price of $8, this translates to around 250 million tickets. If the actual cost of producing *Avatar* was somewhere near the lower end of these estimates, total tickets sales in the neighborhood of 30 million tickets would have been necessary for 20th Century Fox to break even. This phenomenon is also typical of high-technology products that require high per unit sales to justify significant, up-front outlays for research and development.

Specialization

As firms become larger, economies of scale may be realized from specialization in production, sales, marketing, research and development, and other areas. Specialization tends to increase the firm's productivity in greater proportion than the increase in operating cost associated with greater size. Some types of machinery, such as large electrical-power generators and large blast furnaces, operate more efficiently at greater levels of output. Moreover, large companies are able to reduce operating costs because they are able to negotiate lower prices from suppliers and more favorable financing terms from creditors.

Inventories

Firms that are required to carry inventories may also experience economies of scale. Firms that do not carry adequate inventories to meet unanticipated increases in customer demand run the risk of losing market share to more reliable suppliers. Manufacturers that do not maintain adequate inventories of important components can production delays and sales backlogs.

Unfortunately, the cost of carrying inventories drives up the cost of each unit sold. Inventory costs may include the interest on short-term operating loans, insurance costs, warehousing costs, the risk of inventory depreciation, such as might occur due to technological or fashion obsolescence, and so on. Firms with high sales volume of sales can enjoy economies of scale because they are able to maintain a lower inventory to sales ratio.

Cube-Square Rule

Another source of economies of scale is the cube-square rule. In physics, this relationship states that as the surface of a container (such as the circumference of a pipe line, oil tanker, size of a warehouse, vats used for brewing beer, and so on) expands by some factor, its capacity increases by a multiple of that factor. The cube-square rule derives its name from the fact that doubling the diameter of a hollow sphere increases its volume eightfold, that is, by a factor of $2 \times 2 \times 2$.

The cube-square rule is important source of economies of scale in situations where the total cost of producing at capacity is proportional to surface area, whereas production capacity is proportional to volume. An example of this are the economies of scale associated with oil pipelines. The cost of pumping oil through a pipeline is proportional to its circumference and the distance travelled. By contrast, the amount of oil that can be pumped depends on the pipeline's volume. Since volume increases faster than circumference, per gallon pumping costs decline.

Sources of Diseconomies of Scale

Economies of scale can also have a darker side. As companies grow larger to reap the benefits of economies of scale, it becomes more difficult to efficiently coordinate production processes. The resulting increase in the proportion of the firm's work force made up of middle managers leads to a rapid increase in personnel and **transaction costs**, at which point economies of scale become exhausted and diseconomies of scale being to set in.

An increase in the size of a company is frequently accompanied by rising per-unit production costs. These diseconomies of scale can frequently result in a greater than proportional increase in employment costs. There are several explanations for this, including labor unions, compensation differentials, the principle-agent problem, and bloated middle management.

Labor Unions

Workers in large firms are often unionized. While workers at smaller firm in the U.S. economy discuss wages, benefits and working conditions with employers on a one-to-one basis, union workers engage in collective bargaining. If union and management do not come to terms, the workers may go out on strike, which results in lost output, lower sales and profits. The pressure to come to terms results in union workers receiving 10 to 20 percent better wages and benefits than nonunionized workers. In addition, workers at smaller firms are generally expected to work longer hours, which increases per worker productivity and lowers per worker compensation.

Compensating Differentials

As firms expand and diversify, it becomes necessary to recruit workers from a much wider geographic area. To attract high quality workers, large firms pay higher wages (compensating differentials) to attract a better pool of applicants, which increases the quality of its workforce. Firms must also pay compensating differentials to offset higher employee transportation and relocation costs. Compensating differentials may also be necessary to retain highly trained workers who would otherwise sell their services to competitors. This is particularly true when the firm has incurred substantial recruitment and training costs.

Principle-Agent Problem

A company's success is tied to the effort that is put forth by managers on behalf of owners, and by workers on behalf of managers. Unless properly motivated, managers and workers tend to engage in activities that are in their own best interest, but which are not in the best interest of the company. This is situation, which is known as the **principle-agent problem**, will be discussed at greater length in the next chapter. One way to motivate workers and managers to put forth their best efforts on behalf of shareholders is to provide incentives that tie compensation to the company's performance, including opportunities for advancement, perquisites, **performance bonuses**, **profit sharing**, **stock options**, and so on. As a firm gets larger, these incentives tend to become more important and more expensive, which results in greater per-unit production cost.

Bloated Middle Management

Another source of diseconomies of scale has to do with changes in a company's bureaucratic structure. As the scale and scope of a company's operations expand, it becomes increasingly more difficult to coordinate the activities of the firm's various organizational components. It also becomes more difficult to monitor worker performance. As a result company growth is often accompanied by greater than proportional increase in the use of middle managers to regulate the firm's activities, which pushes up per-unit costs. In fact, one of the reasons why large companies downsize their operations or divide into smaller **profit centers** is to reduce or eliminate the added expense associated with a bloated tier of middle managers.

MULTIPRODUCT COST FUNCTIONS

Up to this point we have only considered firm that produce a single product involving multiple inputs. Yet, many firms produce a variety of goods using the same production facilities. Toyota, for example, produces a family of cars and trucks. Pharmaceutical companies such as GlaxoSmithKline manufacture a variety of medicines and vaccines to treat asthma, diabetes, digestive problems, and so on. Sony produces a wide range of consumer goods ranging from personal computers, high-definition TVs and video games to music CDs big-screen entertainment. Thus, for many firms, total cost is a function of many products, not just one. In this section we will consider some important issues relating to multiproduct cost functions.

A **multiproduct cost function** summarizes the cost of efficiently producing two or more products using the same production facilities. To keep matters simple, suppose that a firm produces just two products, Q_1 and Q_2. In this case, the firm's total cost function is given by the relationship

$$TC = TC(Q_1, Q_2).$$ (4.33)

A multiproduct cost function has the same basic interpretation as a single-product cost function. The difference depends upon the nature of the relationship between and among the goods produced. There are two important multiproduct cost relationships: economies of scope and cost complementarities.

Economies of Scope

Related to economies of scale is the concept of **economies of scope**, which says that the total cost of producing two or more goods together is less than the cost of producing each good separately. Whereas economies of scale involves changes in the firm's total cost as its scale of operations increases, economies of scope is a phenomenon that involves changes in total cost as the firm increases number and/or variety of goods and services produced, such

as chicken farms that produce poultry and eggs; automobile companies produce cars and trucks; computer companies produce computers and monitors.
These cost savings can be traced to the production of multiple products that
require the same skills and resources, or when the output of one division is
used as an input for the output of another division.

For a firm producing two goods, a production process exhibits economies
of scope when

$$TC(Q_1,0) + TC(0,Q_2) > TC(Q_1,Q_2). \qquad (4.34)$$

This inequality says that it is less expensive for, say, Toyota to produce
cars and light trucks by more intensively utilizing a single assembly plant
than by using a separate (underutilized) assembly plant for each. It is cheaper
for Olive Garden to produce both pasta and parmesan meals using the same
ovens, tables, refrigerators, etc., than it is to produce these meals in separate
restaurants. It is more economical for Comcast to jointly provide internet
services and instant messaging than it is to provide these services separately.

Economies of scope may result from the joint use of production facilities. In the case of Olive Garden, joint production of pasta and parmesan
meals avoids duplicating expenses for such factors as chairs, tables, ovens,
refrigerators, etc. Economies of scope may result from joint marketing programs, or the cost savings associated with using the same management team
to direct multiple operations. In some cases, the production of one good is a
by-product of the production of a related good. Sheet metal manufactures, for
example, also produce scrap metal and shaving that can also be sold.

Economies of scope have been used to justify **conglomerate mergers**,
which involves the merger of firms from unrelated industries. Economies of
scope were the driving force behind the creation of many large international
conglomerates in the 1970s and 1980s, including Mitsubishi in Japan, BTR
and Hanson in Britain, and Raytheon and ITT in the U.S. The logic behind
these mergers was the potential cost savings from leveraging financial skills
across a diversified range of industries. Several conglomerates that were
formed in 1990s were justified on the basis that the same people and systems
could be used to market many different products. This was the logic underlying the merger of Travelers Group (financial services) and Citicorp (banking)
in 1998. In 2002, Citicorp spun off Travelers Property and Casualty because
of the insurance unit's drag on company earnings.

Cost Complementarities

Cost complementarities exist when the marginal cost of producing good 1 in
Eq. (4.33) declines with an increase in the production of good 2. Examples of

cost complementarities include the simultaneous production of beef and leather, and donuts and donut holes. Slaughtering cattle for beef without considering the potential usefulness of leather by-products, and vice versa, is not only poor business but wasteful. The added cost of producing beef and leather from the same herd is lower than producing beef and leather from separate herds. The added cost of making donuts or donut "holes" (Dunkin Donut's "munchkins") in the same vat of oil is lower than when making donuts and the holes separately.

SOLVED EXERCISE

The total cost equation of a firm that produces two goods is given by the equation

$$TC(Q_1, Q_2) = 100 - Q_1 Q_2 + Q_1^2 + Q_2^2. \tag{4.35}$$

a. *Do economies of scope exist if the firm produces 2 units of Q_1 and 4 units of Q_2?*
b. *Does this total cost equation exhibit cost complementarities?*

Solution

a. *For economies of scope to exist then Inequality (4.34) must be satisfied.*

$$TC(Q_1, 0) = 100 - 2(0) + 2^2 + 0^2 = 104 \tag{4.36}$$

$$TC(0, Q_2) = 100 - (0)4 + 0^2 + 4^2 = 116 \tag{4.37}$$

$$TC(Q_1, Q_2) = 100 - (2)(4) + 2^2 + 4^2 = 112 \tag{4.38}$$

Economies of scope exist since 104 + 116 = 220 > 112.
b. *Yes, since*

$$\frac{\Delta MC_1}{\Delta Q_2} = \frac{\Delta MC_2}{\Delta Q_1} = -1 < 0. \tag{4.39}$$

The above Solved Exercise illustrates two aspects of corporate mergers and divestitures when multiproduct cost functions are involved. In the presence of economies of scope, a merger of two firms could result in significant cost reductions. Conversely, a firm that divests itself of an unprofitable subsidiary might enjoy significant cost savings.

CHAPTER EXERCISES

4.1 Suppose that the production function of a firm is given by the equation

$$Q = 2K^{0.5}L^{0.5},$$

where Q represents units of output, K units of capital, and L units of labor.
a. What is the marginal product of labor and the marginal product of capital when $K = 40$ and $L = 10$?
b. What kind of returns to scale does this production function exhibit?

4.2 Suppose that a firm's production function is

$$Q = 5K^{0.5}L^{0.5},$$

where Q is units of output, K and L are machine and labor hours, respectively. Suppose that the amount of K available to the firm is fixed at 100 machine hours.
a. What is the firm's total product of labor equation? Graph the total product of labor equation for values $L = 0$ to $L = 200$.
b. What is the firm's marginal product of labor equation? Graph the marginal product of labor equation for values $L = 0$ to $L = 200$.
c. What is the firm's average product of labor equation? Graph the average product of labor equation for values $L = 0$ to $L = 200$.
d. What are the returns to scale for this production function?

4.3 Suppose that a firm's short-run production is

$$Q = 2L + 0.4L^2 - 0.002L^3,$$

where Q is units of output and L is labor hours.
a. Graph the production function for values $L = 0$ to $L = 200$.
b. What is the firm's marginal product of labor equation? Graph the marginal product of labor equation for values $L = 0$ to $L = 200$.
c. What is the firm's average product of labor equation? Graph the average product of labor equation for values $L = 0$ to $L = 200$.
d. Does this production function exhibit constant, increasing, or decreasing returns to scales when labor usage is increased from $L = 2$ to $L = 4$?

4.4 Suppose that the average product of labor is given by the equation

$$AP_L = 600 + 200L - L^2.$$

a. What is the equation for the total product of labor?
b. What is the equation for the marginal product of labor?

c. At what level of labor usage is $AP_L = MP_L$?
d. Does this production function exhibit constant, increasing, or decreasing returns to scale capital and labor usage is $L = 25$ to $L = 100$?

4.5 The total cost equation of a firm is

$$TC(Q) = 5,000 + 2,000Q - 10Q^2 + 0.25Q^3,$$

where Q is the level of output.
a. What is the firm's total fixed cost?
b. What is the equation for the firm's total variable cost?
c. What is the equation for the firm's average total cost?
d. What is the equation for the firm's marginal cost?

4.6 Suppose that a firm's average total cost can be described by the equation

$$ATC(Q) = 10(0.8)^{(logQ/log3)},$$

where output (Q) is in hundreds of units. What does this equation imply about the firm's learning curve effect?

4.7 Suppose that the total cost of producing goods 1 and 2 is given by the equation

$$TC(Q_1, Q_2) = aQ_1^2 - bQ_1Q_2 + cQ_2^2,$$

where a, b and c are positive constants. Verify that Q_1 and Q_2 are cost complements.

NOTES

1. This relationship can be estimated using ordinary least squares regression analysis in which the dependent variable is total cost and the explanatory variables are Q, Q^2, and Q^3. A brief discussion of this estimation procedure is presented in the Appendix.

2. The per-unit cost equation used in this example is

$$ATC(Q) = 100(0.75)^{(logQ/log2)}.$$

3. Better known by Monsanto's brand name NutraSweet, Aspartame was accidentally discovered by G.D. Searle chemist James Schlatter, who was trying to develop an anti-ulcer drug. Searle, which was acquired by Monsanto in 1985, was granted a patent for Aspartame in 1970, which expired in 1987.

4. This is someone unfortunate description since the firm is producing *most* efficiently at this scale of production.

Chapter 5

Profit Maximization

In the preceding chapter we saw how a firm's cost structure is defined by its underlying **production function**. We are now in a position to explain how a firm goes about achieving its objective of maximizing profit. It is possible to approach this topic from either of the two directions. Given input and output prices, profit maximization can be viewed as a constrained optimization problem in which the firm's objective is to maximize output subject to a fixed operating budget. Alternatively, profit maximization may involve minimizing the total cost of producing a predetermined level of output. As it turns out, the necessary conditions for profit maximization are the same in both cases.

In the first part of this chapter we will derive general conditions that must be satisfied for a firm to maximize profit. We will then explore some real-world complications that make it difficult, if not impossible, to apply these optimality conditions in practice. We will examine alternative methods for purchasing factors of production at least cost and explore several techniques that are used to encourage managers and workers to put forth their best efforts for the benefit of all the firm's stakeholders.

PROFIT MAXIMIZATION

We generally assume that objective of a firm is to maximize shareholder value. This fundamental idea applies to both for-profit and not-for-profit activities. The purpose of a charitable organization, university, or a Fortune 500 company is to produce a good or service that has greater value than the inputs used in its production. Consider, for example, the case of City Harvest.

For more than a quarter decade, the mission of City Harvest has been to feed the hungry in New York City. City Harvest does this by collecting more than 20 million pounds of excess food from restaurants, grocers, corporate cafeterias, manufacturing concerns and farms, which is then delivered free of charge to more than 600 food programs using a fleet of trucks and bicycles. Each week, City Harvest feeds over a quarter million hungry New Yorkers. As a charitable organization, City Harvest does not earn revenues from the sale of a product. Rather, it funds its activities from donations by individuals and companies who derive satisfaction from the services that City Harvest provides to the community. While the activities of City Harvest do not benefit shareholders, New York City stakeholders are made better off because the value of services rendered exceeds the cost of resources used in its production.

The objective of any commercial enterprise is to add value. There should be no other rationale for its existence. In the long run, businesses that do not maximize shareholder value will not survive. In a competitive market place, firms that are inefficiently run with be pushed aside by more efficient rivals.

What is the relationship between maximizing profits and maximizing share prices? A quick glance at the earnings of the top-performing companies listed on the New York Stock Exchange reveal that in any given year, some stock prices have performed better than the industry average, while others have performed worse. Since share prices reflect the **present value** of expected future profits, the answer to this seeming contradiction has to do with the difference between a company's short-run and long-run performance. When a company performs above expectations, share prices rise. When a company performs below expectations, share prices fall.

In the 1990s, Cisco System recorded substantial net earnings, which was reflected in high share prices. Market analysts came to expect continued stellar earnings gains. The problem for Cisco was that is difficult to live up to inflated expectations. When, in 2000, earnings reports came in at below expectations, Cisco's share prices fell from a high of $80 per share in March to $50 per share in June, even though the company continued to register profits that were growing faster than the market average.

Why focus on **economic profit**? In spite of the day-to-day fluctuations in share prices, stock market valuations are related to a company's net earnings. For this reason, it is important for managers to keep a close eye on the firm's bottom line. In this chapter, we will develop the general conditions that must be satisfied if a manager is to maximize the firm's net earnings. This will be followed by a brief discussion of several real-world concerns that must be dealt with to transform theory into performance.

Optimal Input Combinations

Given fixed input prices and a known production function, what is the optimal combination of labor and capital? Optimality can be considered from two perspectives. It may refer to maximizing output subject to a fixed budget constraint. Alternatively, it may refer to minimizing total cost subject to a given level of output. Depending on the circumstances, either situation may be encountered in practice.

Consider a large multinational firm comprising several **profit centers** that are responsible for the production and sale of a different product. Suppose that the firm's senior managers determine each division's operating budget or production targets. In the first instance, maximizing profit at given product prices involves maximizing output and revenues. In the second instance, maximizing profit involves minimizing total cost.

We will begin by considering the situation in which a division's operating budget is known. In this case, the optimal input combination is depicted in Figure 5.1, which combines the **isoquant map** of imperfect input substitutability in Figure 4.1 with the isocost line in Figure 4.6.[1]

To maximize profit, the objective is to reach the highest **isoquant** (produce the most output) possible given the division's fixed cost (operating budget). In Figure 5.1, this occurs at point B at the output level Q_1. Moving away from point B along the isocost line involves moving to a lower level of output and revenues. At either point C or point A the firm produces $Q_0 < Q_1$.

To understand what is going on, consider the marginal rate of technical substitution from Chapter 4, which is reproduced in Eq. (5.1).

$$\frac{\Delta K}{\Delta L} = -\frac{MP_L}{MP_K} = MRTS_{KL}. \qquad (5.1)$$

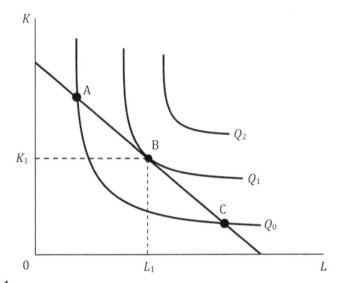

Figure 5.1

The slope of the isocost line is

$$\frac{\Delta K}{\Delta L} = -\frac{P_L}{P_K}.$$
(5.2)

At point C in Figure 5.1, the isocost line is steeper than the isoquant, that is,

$$-\frac{MP_L}{MP_K} > -\frac{P_L}{P_K}.$$
(5.3)

Rearranging Inequality (5.3) we obtain

$$\frac{MP_L}{P_L} < \frac{MP_K}{P_K}.$$
(5.4)

Inequality (5.4) says that the marginal product of labor per dollar spent on labor is less than the marginal product of capital per dollar spent on capital. The firm can increase its output by reallocating its fixed budget dollars away from labor and into capital. Analogously, at point A we have

$$\frac{MP_L}{P_L} > \frac{MP_K}{P_K}.$$
(5.5)

Inequality (5.5) says that the firm can increase its output by reallocating budget dollars away from capital and into labor. Reallocating budget dollars will continue until the firm maximizes output at point B where the isocost line is tangent to isoquant, that is,

$$\frac{MP_L}{P_L} = \frac{MP_K}{P_K}.$$
(5.6)

Eq. (5.6) says that for the firm to maximize profit, the marginal product per last dollar spent on each input must be equal. For the *n*-input case, this optimality condition may be generalize to

$$\frac{MP_1}{P_1} = \frac{MP_2}{P_2} = \cdots = \frac{MP_n}{P_n}.$$
(5.7)

Alternatively, the optimality conditions of Eqs. (5.6) and (5.7) may be viewed as a cost minimization problem. In this case, the objective of the firm is to minimize the total cost of producing a fixed amount of output. This situation is depicted in Figure 5.2. The profit-maximizing level of output occurs using the cost-minimizing input mix at point B. Although the firm can also produce Q_1 at either point A or point C, only point B represents a least-cost combination of capital and labor.

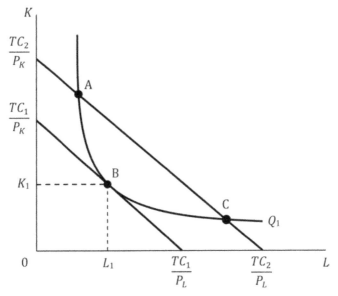

Figure 5.2

In general, when minimizing total operating costs subject to a fixed level of output, or when maximizing total output subject to a fixed operating budget, the marginal product per last dollar spent on each input must be the same for all inputs.

SOLVED EXERCISE

A firm produces at an output level where the marginal product of labor (MP_L) is 50 units and the marginal product of capital (MP_K) is 100 units. Suppose that the wage rate (P_L) is \$25 and the rental price of capital (P_K) is \$40.

a. *Is this firm maximizing profit?*
b. *What should the firm do if it is not allocating its budget efficiently?*

Solution

a. *Optimal input usage is given by Eq. (5.6). Substituting we get*

$$\frac{50}{\$25} = \frac{2}{\$1} < \frac{2.5}{\$1} = \frac{100}{\$40}. \tag{5.8}$$

Since Eq. (5.6) is not satisfied, this profit-maximizing firm is not allocating its budget efficiently.

b. *This firm is currently adding 2 units of output for the last dollar spent on labor and 2.5 units of output for the last dollar spent on capital. This firm can get greater output bang for the buck by reallocating its fixed budget away from labor and into capital. As more labor is hired, MP_L falls. As less capital is used, MP_K rises. The manager of this firm should continue to reallocate the budget until Eq. (5.6) is satisfied.*

Maximizing Profit in Practice

Assuming that production is efficient and resources are procured at the least cost, satisfying Eq. (5.6) guarantees that a profit-maximizing firm rents or purchases the correct combination of labor and capital. But, how is this optimality condition satisfied in practice? In fact, the process of determining the optimal mix of variable inputs is a relatively straightforward affair. To see how, assume that a firm can sell its output for $5 per unit and the wage rate (P_L) is $50. Suppose that the firm is currently employing three workers. Is the manager of this firm using the correct number of workers, or can the firm increase its profit by changing the size of its workforce? To answer this question, we need to compare the net contribution of each worker to the firm's bottom line.

The increase in the firm's total output from an incremental increase in the number of workers is the marginal product of labor of labor. To determine whether hiring another worker will increase the firm's profit, it is necessary to compare the additional revenues from the sale of the extra output with the additional cost per worker. This extra revenue generated is called the **value marginal product of labor** (VMP_L), and is given by the equation

$$VMP_L = P \times MP_L. \tag{5.9}$$

Similarly, the extra revenue earned from the sale the additional output from purchasing another unit of capital is the **value marginal product of capital** (VMP_K), which is

$$VMP_K = P \times MP_K. \tag{5.10}$$

To maximize profit, a manager should always hire another worker provided that the marginal contribution to the firm's revenues (VMP_L) is greater than the wage rate, which is referred to as the **marginal resource cost of labor** (MRC_L). (The rental price of an additional unit of capital is the **marginal resource cost of capital** (MRC_K)). Should this firm hire another worker? To answer this question, consider information provided in Table 5.1 Adding a fourth worker will increase total output by 12 units, which can be sold in the market for VMP_L = $60. Since the MRC_L is P_L = $50, hiring another worker

Table 5.1

L	P	$MP_L = \Delta Q/\Delta L$	$VMP_L = P \times MP_L$	$MRC_L = P_L$	$VMP_L - MRC_L$
0	$5	–	–	$50	–
1	$5	5	$25	$50	–$25
2	$5	8	$40	$50	–$10
3	$5	11	$55	$50	$5
4	$5	12	$60	$50	$10
5	$5	13	$65	$50	$15
6	$5	12	$60	$50	$10
7	$5	11	$55	$50	$5
8	$5	8	$40	$50	–$10
9	$5	5	$25	$50	–$20
10	$5	0	0	$50	–$50

adds $10 to the firm's bottom line. Thus, it will be in the firm's best interest to hire a fourth worker. In fact, the firm should hire up to seven workers since the marginal contribution to the firm's bottom line is positive. It would be a mistake to hire an eighth worker since to added wage cost is greater than the marginal addition to the firm's revenues.

In general, a manager of a profit-maximizing firm should continue to hire infinitely divisible variable inputs up to the point where its value marginal product of an input is equal to its marginal resource cost, and no further. It is interesting to note that hiring or purchasing variable inputs in this manner is perfectly consistent Eq. (5.6). To see this, recall that a manager should continue to hire variable labor and capital up to the point where:

$$VMP_L = P \times MP_L = P_L = MRC_L; \tag{5.11}$$

$$VMP_K = P \times MP_K = P_K = MRC_K. \tag{5.12}$$

Dividing Eq. (5.11) by Eq. (5.12) gives us Eq. (5.6). Note that the price plays no role when determining the mix of variable inputs that maximizes a firm's profit (Why?).

SOLVED EXERCISE

Suppose that a firm is maximizing profit.

a. *If the rental price of capital is $80 and the marginal product of capital is 20 units, what is the market price of the output of this firm?*
b. *If the wage rate is $100, what is the marginal product of labor?*

Solution

a. *If the firm is producing efficiently then,*

$$VMP_K = P \times 20 = \$80 = MRC_K. \tag{5.13}$$

Solving, the market price of this firm's product is P = \$4.
b. *From Eq. (5.11)*

$$VMP_L = \$4 \times MP_L = \$100 = MRC_K. \tag{5.14}$$

Solving, MP_L = 25 units of output.

Optimal Input Substitution

Consider, again, the situation depicted in Figure 5.1 in which the profit-maximizing combination of capital and labor are K_1 and L_1, respectively. How will a change in the price of an input affect the optimal mix of factors? Suppose, for example, that the price of a unit of labor increases from P_L to P_L'. This new situation is depicted in Figure 5.3.

If the firm's operating budget remains unchanged, the increase in the price of labor causes the firm's isocost line to become steeper by rotating clockwise from DE to DF. The profit-maximizing firm will not be able to sustain

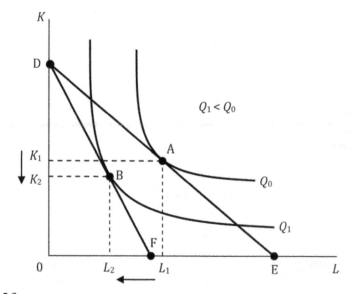

Figure 5.3

the same level of output. In Figure 5.3, the point at which the isocost line is tangent to the isoquant moves from point A to point B. In all cases, the firm will definitely use less of the more expensive labor, but could employ more or less capital depending on the shapes of the isoquants. In the situation depicted in Figure 5.3, the firm uses less of both capital and labor.

HOW TO PROCURE INPUTS

So far, we have learned that to maximize profit, managers must allocate the firm's operating budget such that the marginal product per last dollar spent on each input must is equal. While this tangency condition is easy to assert, it is difficult to achieve in practice. This is because at least two conditions must be satisfied. To begin with, the firm must produce efficiently. This requires that capital, raw materials and other non-human factors of production inputs be employed in their first, best use and that the firm's human resources are putting forth their best efforts. In addition to producing efficiently, maximizing shareholder value requires that factors of production be procured at least cost. The most cost-effective method depends on several considerations, including transaction costs and the importance of specialized investments.

One of the most important considerations when procuring inputs is to minimize the total **opportunity costs** of the transaction, which include the price paid for the resource and any related expenses. **Transaction costs** refer to payments that are required to facilitate the exchange, including search costs, brokerage fees, inspection costs, commissions, expenses related to identifying profitable marketing opportunities, shipping costs, the cost of education and training, legal fees, and the cost of preparing and enforcing contracts (North, 1985). Reducing transaction costs increases profitable business opportunities and promotes investment in physical and human capital.

Transaction costs typically begin with search costs, which involve the opportunity cost of gathering information, out-of-pocket travel and other expenses associated with finding a suitable supplier. Once a supplier has been located, the output-producing firm may incur negotiating costs to determine price, input quality, and the obligations of the contracting parties. Transaction costs also include expenditures incurred to deliver inputs for further processing, such as when an oil company leases a tanker to transport crude petroleum to a refinery.

There are several possibilities for procuring inputs when attempting to minimize transaction costs. One way is to purchase the inputs in the spot market. Alternatively, minimizing transaction costs may involve signing a long-term contract with an input supplier. A third method is to bypass external suppliers by producing the input internally. Identifying the most cost-effective method for procuring inputs is critical when attempting to satisfy the optimality conditions summarized by Eqs. (5.10) to (5.12).

Spot Exchange

An off-the-shelf purchase of a good or service constitutes a **spot exchange**. In the absence of specialized investments (to be discussed in the next section), a spot exchange involves negligible transaction costs. There is no legally binding relationship between buyer and seller. Once the transaction is consummated, both parties go their own way. Transactions that occur "on the spot" are the most direct and least complicated way for a firm to acquire an input.

The primary advantage of a spot exchange is that the output-producing firm and the input-supplying firm specialize in what they do best. Spot exchanges work best when there are a large number of firms supplying a standardized input in which specialized investments are not required. When transaction costs become very high it may be in the output-producing firm's best interest to produce an input internally, which could divert resources away from the firm's core activities. This could prevent the firm from realizing cost savings from specialization.

The main disadvantage of purchasing inputs in the spot market is that there is little or no quality control and where the legal doctrine of *caveat emptor* (buyer beware) frequently applies. Suppliers are under no legal obligation to replace defective components (although they may choose to do so to maintain customer good will). If the input does not measure up to specifications, the buyer may have no recourse but to duplicate its purchase, which could significantly drive up production costs. To make matters worse, the seller may suffer a loss of customer good from selling a faulty product, which could jeopardize the firm's existence.

Contracts

A possible solution to the problems associated with a spot exchange is to purchase inputs under a **contract**. A contract is a legally binding agreement that obligates the buyer and seller to perform, or refrain from performing, a specified act in exchange for something of value. Unlike a spot exchange, contracts extend the relationship between buyer and seller into the future.

Contracts are used to guarantee that inputs meet buyer specifications. Contracts are also used by firms to guarantee future delivery of an important input. A **futures contract** is an agreement to buy or sell real or financial assets at a predetermined price for future delivery. The timely delivery of crude petroleum, for example, is absolutely essential if a refinery is to satisfy its customers' refined oil and gas requirements. A disruption in these deliveries would adversely affect a refinery's production schedule, which could severely damage its customer relationships.

As with a spot exchange, the main advantage of a contract is that the buyer and seller enjoy the benefits of specialization. Under a contract, the buyer has legal recourse if inputs do not measure up to specifications. In general, contracts are easy to write, and work well, when the obligations of both parties are clear cut.

The main disadvantage of contracts is that they are costly to write. The more complicated the relationship or transaction, the more difficult it is to write a contract that covers every contingency. The input-buying firm may also incur additional costs from unforeseen difficulties not covered under the terms of the contract. Incomplete contracts open the door to future litigation, which gives rise to unanticipated legal costs. This problem becomes more severe the longer the life of the contract.

Optimal Contract Life

Suppose that a manager has determined that purchasing an input under contract is more cost effective than purchasing in the spot market or producing the input internally. Although contracts are expensive to write, they offer several benefits. Contracts specify input prices and quality before specialized investments are undertaken, thereby avoiding possible hold-up problems. Contracts define the obligations of the output-producing and input-supplying firms with respect to price, delivery schedules, input specifications, and so on.

Having decided to procure an input under contract, the manager must then decide on an optimal contract life? Establishing a long-term relationship with a supplier involves both benefits and costs. The marginal cost of writing a contract tends to increase at an increasing rate as its life is extended. This is because the future is uncertain and becomes increasingly more so the further out you go. As a result, it becomes increasingly more difficult, and costly, to write a contract that covers every possible contingency. Specifying a mutually acceptable price for a transaction that is consummated a week from now is a reasonably simple matter, but can become very contentious for a contract that specifies deliveries two years hence. Inputs that are highly specialized today may be standardized in the future. Buyers who are locked into a long-term contract can incur significant opportunity costs because they are not able to take advantage of lower future prices. For these reasons, the marginal cost of preparing a contract tends to increase at an increasing rate as the length of the contract is extended. This relationship is depicted in Figure 5.4.

The marginal benefit of extending the life of a contract include the increased certainty guaranteed future delivery, eliminating potential hold-up problems, and avoiding bargaining and other transaction costs associated

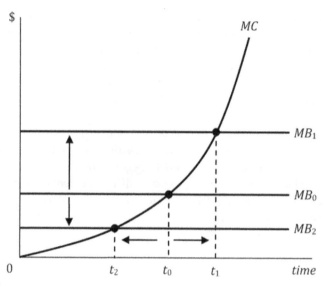

Figure 5.4

with renegotiating new agreements. For simplicity we will assume that the marginal benefit of a contract remains constant over time. This is depicted as the horizontal line labeled MB_0 in Figure 5.4. The optimal contract life occurs where the marginal cost and marginal benefit of extending the contract's life are equal. In Figure 5.4, this occurs at a contract life of t_0 periods.

Suppose that the marginal benefit of having a contract increases, perhaps because of an increase in transaction costs, perhaps because specialized investments become more expensive, important, or both. This is depicted as an up shift in the marginal benefit curve, say from MB_0 to MB_1. In Figure 5.4, these added costs can be mitigated or avoided by extending the life of the contract from t_0 to t_1. On the other hand, if an input becomes more standardized, or specialized investments and the hold-up problem become less important, the marginal benefit of being locked into a long-term contract declines, which results in a down shift of the marginal benefit curve from MB_0 to MB_2. This shortens the optimal contract life from t_0 to t_2.

The optimal contract life is also affected by a change in the marginal cost of writing a longer-term contract. This can occur when there is an increase in legal fees, specialized investments become more important, or when the future becomes more uncertain, which makes it more difficult to write a contract that covers every possible contingency. This depicted in Figure 5.5 as an up shift of the marginal cost curve from MC_0 to MC_1, which shortens the optimal contract life t_0 to t_1. Alternatively, the marginal cost of writing longer term contracts declines as the contracting environment becomes less complicated or

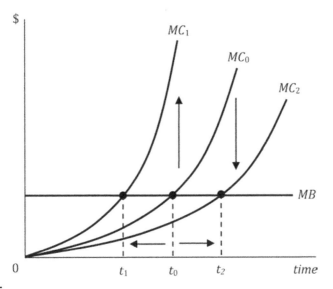

Figure 5.5

the future less uncertain. This is depicted as a down shift of the marginal cost curve from MC_0 to MC_2, which extends the optimal contract life from t_0 to t_2.

Vertical Integration

When it is very difficult and costly to write a contract, a firm may choose to produce the input internally, otherwise known as **vertical integration**, which is typically accomplished by merging with an existing supplier. The main advantage of producing inputs internally is that the firm has complete control over input quality. Unlike spot exchanges and the use of contracts, however, vertical integration involves the diversion of scarce resources away from the firm's core activities. The firm will also incur increased management costs associated with running a more complex operation.

SPECIALIZED INVESTMENTS

A **specialized investment** is a human or physical capital expenditure that must be incurred by either the output-producing firm or the input-supplying firm before a transaction can take place. An example of a specialized investment is when a computer manufacturer invests in a device to test the reliability of microprocessors purchased from an outside vendor. This investment may involve a **sunk cost** if it has little or no value in an alternative use. Specialized investments lead to a **relationship-specific exchange** because the transaction establishes a long-term relationship between the buyer and seller. Since specialized investment involve transaction costs, it is necessary to identify the optimal (least costly) method of procuring inputs.

Types of Specialized Investment

The nature of specialized investment depends on any of a number of factors. A specialized investment may reflect the geographic location of the output-producing and input-supplying firms. It may have something to do with the underlying production process. It may even have something to do with the relationship between a producer of a final good or service and the end user. In general, specialized investments fall into several categories, including site-specific investments, physical-asset-specific investment, investments in dedicated assets, and specialized investment in human capital.

Site-Specific Specialized Investment

A **site-specific specialized investment** occurs when the buyer and seller locate in physical proximity to more efficiently facilitate an exchange and reduce transaction costs. For example, an aluminum plant that is located near a bauxite mine to reduce shipping costs is an example of a site-specific specialized investment. A petroleum refinery that is situated near a port facility to accommodate oil tankers is another example of a site-specific specialized investment. These investments are more valuable because buyer and supplier are located in close proximity.

Physical-Asset-Specific Specialized Investment

A **physical-asset-specific specialized investment** refers to expenditures incurred by input-supplying firm to meet precise specifications of the output-producing firm. An example of this occurs when Rolls Royce invests in a specialized machine tool to produce a jet engine to meet precise specifications for Airbus. This investment is specialized because it has little or no value in producing engines for, say, Boeing.

Investment in Dedicated Assets

A **dedicated asset** is a general investment in plant and equipment that is required to satisfy a specific order, such as when Electro-Motive Diesel (a subsidiary of General Motors) and Land Systems (a subsidiary of General Dynamics) built an assembly plant to produce Stryker armored vehicles for the U.S. Army, or when International Systems invested in an assembly line to produce integrated circuits for IBM. These are examples of investments in dedicated assets because the expenditures would not have incurred without a contract with the buyer.

Another type of specialized investment occurs when workers are required to obtain skills, know-how or information that is more to one employer than it is to some other employer. These specialized investments in human capital include tangible skills, such as how to use firm-specific inventory control software. Specialized investment in human capital also includes such intangible skills as understanding of unwritten rules of corporate behavior, standard operating procedures, and the **corporate culture**. A manager who has developed skills to effectively operate within a one corporate environment may be less effective in another organization with a different culture and routines. Specialized investments increase transaction costs because they often involve bargaining costs, may lead to underinvestment, or cause either party to the transaction to engage in opportunism.

Bargaining Costs

When inputs are standardized, quality uniform, transaction costs are low, and input market competitive, input prices will be determined by the forces of supply and demand. Under these conditions, little or no time will be spent negotiating input prices. On the other hand, when inputs are not standardized, specialized investment is involved, or the market is imperfectly competitive, prices are likely to be negotiated.

Negotiations over price and input specifications take time. Employing lawyers or other intermediaries to negotiate favorable contract terms can be time consuming and expensive. Complicating the process is when either side adopts strategies to extract price and other concessions. For example, a buyer might refuse to take delivery unless the supplier reduces price. The supplier might counter by lowering product quality to restore profit margins. Either side may then seek legal redress, which results in unbudgeted attorney's fees and court costs. These additional factors will further inflate transaction costs.

Underinvestment

In addition to bargaining costs, specialized investments may be less than optimal. Since specialized investments have little or no value in an alternative use, there is an incentive to under invest. Underinvestment can lead to increased replacement, legal and other costs due to input product quality. An example of this is when a firm requires workers to obtain specialized training. If the worker is required to pick up the tab, there is an incentive to obtain the training from a low-cost provider, or spend as little time training as possible.

A related problem is when an employer under-invests in the training and education of its workers because these skills can command higher wages and benefits from rival firms. An example of this is when a firm offers tuition reimbursement to its employees. While this benefit lures higher quality job applicants, it also undermines the employer-employee relationship by making better-trained workers more attractive to other firms. As a result, employers often attach strings to these benefits, such as requiring workers to pay a pro-rated portion of the tuition, such as offering 100 percent tuition reimbursement for a grade of A, 75 percent for a B, and nothing for a grade of C and below. Alternatively, employers frequently ask workers who receive tuition reimbursement to sign a performance contract requiring that the worker remains with the company for a specified period of time. If the employee accepts another job offer before that time, he or she is required to repay the full amount of reimbursed tuition.

The same line of reasoning applies to investment in nonhuman capital as well. Suppose a supplier invests in specialized equipment to produce a component for a particular customer. If this equipment has little or no value in an alternative use, there is an incentive to purchase a less expensive, more unreliable model. As in the case of a worker who under invests in his or her human capital, the result can be significantly higher transaction costs.

Opportunism

An interesting problem arises when one party to a transaction takes advantage of the sunk costs of a specialized investment incurred by the other party. To understand the nature of **opportunism**, which also referred to as the **hold-up problem**, consider the situation depicted in Figure 5.6 in which the manager of a construction company purchases steel rods used to reinforce concrete from an outside supplier. Suppose that the market for steel rods is competitive and that the market-determined price is $50 per steel rod.

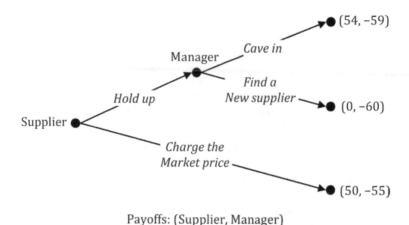

Payoffs: (Supplier, Manager)

Figure 5.6

Suppose that the manager randomly chooses a supplier from the telephone book. Before taking delivery, the construction company is required by local building codes to inspect the steel rods at a cost of $5 each. After inspecting the steel rods, the supplier decides to "hold up" the buyer by charging $54. The manager has two choices: Either cave in to the supplier's attempt to extort a higher price, or find a different supplier and duplicate inspection costs. If the manager agrees to the supplier's demand, the cost per steel rod is $59. If the manager finds another supplier and duplicates inspection, the cost per steel rod is $60. Other things being equal, it is in the manager's best interest to pay the extorted price.

There are several possible solutions to the hold-up problem. One possibility is for the manager to enter into a legally-binding contract with the supplier that specifies the sales price before inspecting the steel rods. Such contracts may also include product specifications to ensure quality, as well as dispute resolution procedures. Another way to deal with the problem of opportunism is to require that the supplier post a **performance bond** that guarantees delivery at an agreed price. Still another factor that that might mitigate or eliminate the hold-up problem is a possible loss of reputation. A supplier that repeatedly extorts customers will not only lose any repeat business, but will also be shunned by prospective customers.

Of course, problem of opportunism can be a two-way street. Suppose that the steel rods are not standardized but must be manufactured to precise specifications. In order to make the sale, the input supplier must invest in specialized equipment. If the input supplier does not sell the steel rods to the construction company, this specialized investment becomes worthless. In the absence of a contract, the construction company can hold up the supplier for a lower price after the specialized investment expense has been incurred. Unfortunately, this approach to avoiding transaction costs associated with the hold-up problem replaced with the added legal expense of preparing a contract.

PROCURING INPUTS INVOLVING
SPECIALIZED INVESTMENTS

As we have seen, there are three basic ways for a firm to procure inputs—buy in the spot market, purchase under contract, or produce internally. A profit-maximizing firm should select the method that minimizes transactions cost. The method chosen may depend on the exchange-specific nature of the relationship between output producer and input supplier.

A spot exchange is usually the most cost-effective method of procuring a standardized input. When specialized investments are not involved, transaction costs are low, and there are multiple suppliers, the discipline of the market tends to result in competitive prices of high quality inputs. Price negotiations and contracts to guarantee that inputs meet precise specifications are unnecessary. Attempts by individual suppliers of near or perfect substitutes to extract more favorable terms will be unsuccessful.

When specialized investments require price negotiations, input quality is important or must meet precise specifications, a spot exchange will not be the most cost-effective method for obtaining an input. Even when inputs are standardized, but require specialized investments, contracts are useful for guaranteeing future delivery or avoiding supplier opportunism.

Although contracts may require substantial up-front transaction costs in the form of legal fees, and negotiation costs, they reduce unforeseen expenses down the road. They are an effective means of overcoming the hold-up problem by fixing an input price prior to undertaking a specialized investment. Contracts also avoid duplicate expenditures and damaged customer relationships when inputs do not meet minimum quality standards or there is a disruption in delivery of the final product.

Contracts reduce problems of underinvestment by extending the relationship between output producer and input supplier. An input supplier is less likely to invest in inferior equipment to produce an input if its future relationship with the output-producing firm is at stake. Similarly, a firm is more willing to fully invest in worker training if it believes that the worker will be around for a few years.

Determining the most cost-efficient method of procuring inputs when specialized investments are involved depends on the relative importance of transaction costs associated with specialized investments, and the efficiency losses and internal control problems arising from vertical integration. When transaction costs are less than contracting costs, it will be in the output-producing firm's best interest to purchase inputs in the spot market. When this is not the case, the firm should consider procuring inputs under contract. When transaction costs are very high, it may be in the firm's best interest to produce the input internally. The basic considerations in the make-or-buy decision-making process are summarized in Figure 5.7.

Producing inputs internally mitigates or eliminates the problem of opportunism by bringing previously independent production processes under one roof. Perhaps the most serious drawback to vertical integration is resources away from the firm's core activities, that is, the firm no longer specializes in what it does best.

Another serious drawback is that the discipline of the market, which encourages the production of a quality inputs at least cost, must be replaced with system of strict internal controls. Moreover, since the input is produced internally by an "upstream" division, it is up to the firm's accountants to

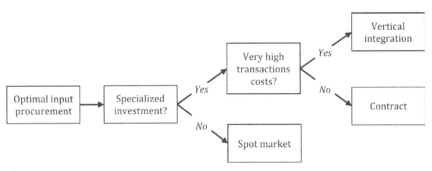

Figure 5.7

determine the correct "price" that will be paid by the "downstream" division. This is known as the **transfer pricing** problem. Determining the correct price of the internally produced input is critical if a firm is to avoid the problem of **double marginalization**, which occurs when the upstream and downstream divisions operate as separate profit centers rather than integral parts of a single firm. If the internally produced input is not correctly priced, the result is lower profits and reduced shareholder value.

PROMOTING MAXIMUM EFFORT: THE PRINCIPAL-AGENT PROBLEM

The tangency conditions of Eqs. (5.6) to (5.8) require that the firm's operating budget be efficiently allocated to maximize profit. To accomplish this, inputs must be procured at least cost and the marginal product of each input is maximized. Nonhuman resources be efficiently employed and the firm's human resources (managers and workers) must put forth their best efforts. Unfortunately, the **organizational structure** of many firms gives rise to the **principal-agent problem** in which one group of individuals (agents) fails to represent the best interests of another group of individuals (principals) because their interests are not properly aligned. This problem arises because principals and agents are responding to different incentives.

There are at least two levels of the principal-agent problem in business. The owner-manager principal-agent problem arises at the upper levels of the corporate hierarchy when managers fail to represent the best interests of absentee owners (shareholders). At lower levels of the corporate hierarchy is the manager-worker principal-agent problem, which occurs when workers do not put forth their best efforts for managers. At the heart of the principal-agent problem is the fundamental trade-off between effort and leisure. To induce managers and workers to forgo some leisure (that is, to put forth greater effort), some form of compensation must be linked to the company's performance, which is of greatest concern to shareholders.

Owner-Manager Principal-Agent Problem

A distinguishing feature of modern large corporations is that they are not owner-operated. Responsibility for the firm's day-to-day operations is delegated to managers who are supposed to represent the best interests of absentee owners. Theories of economic behavior are based on the assumption of rational self-interest. Managers receive utility from leisure. Owners want to maximize profit, which depends on the level of effort put forth by managers. When a manager's compensation is not linked to the company's performance, a fundamental incentive problem emerges. The **owner-manager principal-agent problem** arises when the interests of owners and managers are not properly aligned. If a company underperforms, was this the result of factors beyond the manager's control, or was it because managers did not put forth their best efforts? How can absentee owners be assured that managers are putting forth their best efforts to maximize shareholder value?

Suppose, for example, that a manager is paid a fixed annual salary of, say, $200,000, regardless of the amount of effort put into the job. Unless properly motivated, a fundamental conflict may arise between owners who value profit, and managers who derive utility from the non-pecuniary perquisites that come with the job. Fixed compensation alone will not promote diligence by managers. In the absence of constant monitoring, managers have an incentive to engage in activities that are personally beneficial, but which are detrimental to shareholder value. Golf outings, bloated expense accounts, three-hour lunches, and a general lack of attention to the firm's day-to-day operations could adversely affect the company's bottom line. The resulting decline in shareholder value is a result of these **agency costs**.

Will an increase in a manager's fixed compensation solve this problem? If there is no penalty for negligence, managers will continue to substitute diligence for leisure. To overcome the owner-manager principal-agent problem, managers must be made to care as much about profit as do the shareholders. One way to accomplish this is structure a contract with *internal incentives* that aligns the interests of the owners and the managers. Such contracts may include provisions for **profit sharing**, **stock options**, **performance bonuses**, and other rewards that link a manager's compensation to the company's performance. Suppose, for example, that a manager is offered a share of the company's profits in addition to a modest base salary. If hard work results in greater profit, the manager and the shareholders benefit. Of course, the extra effort put forth by the manager depends on the marginal utility of an additional dollar of income. Owners must take care not to offer a base salary that is too generous; otherwise the added income may not provide the intended incentive.

The principal-agent problem also helps to explain why managers might not put forth their best efforts even when there is no provision for internal incentives. *External incentives*, such as a manager's *reputation* may also compel managers to put forth their best efforts. This is because managers with proven supervisory and organizational skills will be much in demand by other firms.

Another example of an external incentive is *job security*. Shareholders who believe that the firm is underperforming may move to replace senior managers. Closely related to a **shareholder revolt** is the threat of a **hostile takeover**. Firms that underperform become the target of corporate raiders who attempt to wrest control of the shareholders. Once a takeover is complete, the new owners often install a more effective management team to increase earnings and raise shareholder value. This latent threat gives incumbent managers with a strong incentive to put forth their best efforts on behalf of the current owners.

Asymmetric Information

Incentive contracts are an effective means for ensuring that agents act in the best interest of principals, but only if both parties have complete information. **Asymmetric information** is at the heart of the principal-agent problem. Asymmetric information describes a situation in which one party in a transaction has more, or better, information than the other party to the same transaction. The owner must decide which manager to hire, but only the manager knows whether he or she is qualified for the job. The dilemma confronting the owner, which arises before a job offer is made, is referred to as **adverse selection**.

Another problem that may arise in the presence of asymmetric information is **moral hazard**, in which the manager behaves in a way that is detrimental to the owner after accepting an employment contract. The owner must then decide on the best way to motivate a manager to put forth his or her best effort. One way to accomplish this is with the use of an **incentive contract**, which aligns the interests of owner and manager. A flawed or improperly structured incentive contract, however, can impose substantial agency costs. An example of this is when an owner uses stock options to promote diligence, but the manager engages in unethical or illegal activities to temporarily increase shareholder value, which is ultimately detrimental to the company and its owners.

A classic example of moral hazard is when a fully insured driver is less careful because there are no monetary consequences from an accident. For this reason, insurance companies typically require drivers to pay a portion of the accident costs (a deductible payment) before the insurance coverage kicks in. Incentive contracts can be similarly structured to ensure that managers share in both the gains and losses resulting from the performance of their duties. The fact that this appears to be the exception rather than the rule explains why senior executives of some large financial institutions are awarded multimillion dollar bonuses, sometimes at taxpayer expense, in spite of the fact that their decisions resulted in billions of dollars in shareholder losses and, in some cases, insolvency.

According to a survey published in 2007 by the U.S. Bureau of Labor Statistics, the average weekly compensation of investment bankers is ten times the national average. In the wake of the financial meltdown in 2008, many critics began questioning whether Wall Street's system of compensation was responsible. These critics argue that because the interests of bankers, shareholders and the public were not properly aligned, managers of financial institutions have there is a strong incentive put investors and depositors money at risk because the possibility of substantial short-term gains.

Most proposals for reforming the current system involve shifting compensation away from an individual's performance towards bonuses in the form of stock options. Proponents argue that this will more closely align the interests of all of the stakeholders. An alternative approach would to stagger bonuses over several years, which would give individual employees a vested interest in the company's long-term performance. On the other hand, skeptics argue that even these remedies may not work.

Share-based compensation was already commonplace at the time of the financial collapse. Employees of Bear Sterns, for example, owned a third of the company's shares. Yet, only a relatively small number of the company's employees were involved in risky hedge-fund activities that brought the fabled global investment bank to its knees. Bear Sterns was subsequently absorbed in a fire sale by JPMorgan Chase.

One of the problems with changing the current system of compensation is that financial institutions are under intense pressure to keep and retain so-called "rainmakers," and better pay attracts more talented people. If investment banks hold the line on bonuses, private-equity firms and hedge funds will quickly snatch up disgruntled traders.

Compounding the problem of misaligned interests is the moral hazard problem of too-big-to-fail, which many critics argue was the root cause of the shake-out in the financial industry and ensuing economic recession in 2007–2008.[2] Operating under the belief that the federal government would bail out troubled investment and commercial banks, hedge fund managers were encouraged to gamble with their clients' money. Compounding the problem, government regulators also failed in their oversight responsibilities, such as in the mortgage-backed **financial derivatives** market. In spite of the public outcry in the months and years following the financial collapse, meaningful reform has failed to materialize.

Manager-Worker Principal-Agent Problem

Once the owner-manager principal-agent problem is resolved, it is necessary to move down corporate hierarchy and consider the relationship between managers and workers. As with managers, workers that do not have a stake in the company's performance will substitute work for leisure. This conflict of interest is called the **manager-worker principal-agent problem**. One way to get workers to put forth their best efforts is to closely monitor performance, but the increase in worker performance tends to be outweighed by the cost. What is more, monitoring tends to negatively affect worker morale and productivity. The trick is to get workers to want to perform to the best of their abilities. Only if all of the company's stakeholders are pulling in the same direction will it be possible to maximize shareholder value.

Under a system of fixed compensation, workers have a utility-maximizing incentive to shirk. But, as with managers, workers can be encouraged to put for their best efforts by linking compensation to performance. There are several examples of such "positive" incentives, such as profit sharing, revenue sharing, and piece work.

Profit sharing works the same way with workers as it does with managers. Workers are likely to work hard if the fruits of their labors are reflected in their paychecks. Another approach to enhancing worker productivity is to tie compensation to the revenues. This method of compensation is appropriate when worker performance directly impact's a firm's revenues. Perhaps the best known form of revenue sharing is sales commissions. We tend to associate revenue-based incentive schemes with insurance agents, real estate brokers, automobile sales persons, and so on, but gratuities (tips) received by bartenders and restaurant servers also constitute a revenue-based incentive scheme.

One problem with revenue sharing, however, is that it tends to lead to unethical behavior. This is especially problematic in situations involving one-time or impersonal customer contact where the salesperson is unconcerned with the negative consequence of misrepresentation in order to close a deal. The negative stereotypes associated with such professions as telephone marketers and used-car salespeople attest to the potential dangers of linking compensation to revenues.

Another problem with revenue sharing is that there is no incentive to minimize cost. Corporate executives who pay expense accounts to curry favor with clients to obtain lucrative contracts, and bartenders and restaurant servers who give free drinks and food to inflate tips attest to some of the problems associated with revenue-based incentive schemes.

Another "positive" incentive scheme is **piece work**, which links worker compensation to the number of units produced. Piece work, which is common in such labor-intensive industries as textile and footwear manufacturing, often engender a "sweat shop" working environment. The main problem with this type of performance-based incentive scheme is that quantity is achieved at the expense of quality. This could result in the firm developing a reputation for shoddy workmanship, customer dissatisfaction, lost sales, and less-than-optimal profits.

Positive performance-based incentives schemes encourage workers to put forth greater effort. By contrast, "negative" incentives are based on threats and intimidation. Two examples of negative incentive schemes are the use of *time clocks* and *spot checks*.

Many firms require workers to "punch in" on a time clock when they arrive at work, and "punch out" when the leave for the day. The purpose of time clocks is to ensure that workers do not show up late and leave early. Repeat offenders are typically subject to punitive measures, such as loss of pay or outright dismissal. While time clocks are useful for monitoring a worker's presence, they do not monitor performance. In fact, the use of time clocks connotes a lack of trust by managers in the integrity workers, which could lead to morale problems and lower productivity.

A more effective method is to perform spot checks, which monitor both presence and performance. There are two distinct problems with spot checks. To be effective, spot checks must be random; otherwise workers will know when to work hard and when to goof off. Spot checks must also be frequent enough to raise the expected penalty from being caught shirking. Frequent spot checks, however, are costly and reduce the firm's profitability. As with time clocks, spot checks also lower worker morale. As a general rule, incentives based on threats and intimidations are inferior to positive, compensation-based solutions.

CHAPTER EXERCISES

5.1 WordBoss, Inc. uses 4 word processors and 2 desk-top computers to generate reports. The marginal product of word processor is 50 pages per day and the marginal product of a desk-top computer is 500 pages per hour. If the rental price of a word processor is $1 per hour and the rental price of a desk-top computer is $10 per hour, is WordBoss utilizing word processors and desk-top computers efficiently?

5.2 Numeric Calculators produces a line of abaci. Its production function is

$$Q(L,K) = 2L^{0.6}K^{0.4}.$$

Numeric has a weekly budget of $400,000 and has estimated the unit cost of capital is $5.

a. Numeric is maximizing profit. If the cost of labor is $10 per hour, what is the Numeric's output level?

b. The labor union is presently demanding a wage increase that will raise the cost of labor to $12.50 per hour. If the budget and capital cost remain constant, what effect with this have on the size of Numeric's labor force it continues to maximize profit?

c. At the new cost of labor, what is Numeric's new output level?

5.3 A firm produces at an output level where the marginal products of labor and capital are both 25 units. Suppose that the rental price of labor and capital are $12.50 and $25, respectively.

a. Is this firm maximizing profit?

b. If the firm is not producing efficiently, how might it do so?

5.4 MagnaBox installs automobile CD players. Its production function is

$$Q(L,K) = K^{0.5}L^{0.5},$$

where Q represents the number of CD players installed, L the number of labor hours, and K the number hours of leased installation equipment, which is fixed at 250 hours. The rental price of labor and capital are $10 and $50 per hour, respectively. MagnaBox has received an offer from Cheap Rides to install 1,500 CD players in its fleet of rental cars for $15,000. If Magna Box maximizes profit, should it accept this offer?

5.5 The production function of an online retailer that hires unskilled (U) and semiskilled (S) workers in its distribution division is given by the equation

$$Q(U,S) = 2U + 4S.$$

a. What is the marginal product of unskilled labor?

b. What is the marginal product of semiskilled labor?

c. Unskilled workers earn the minimum wage of $7.25 per hour and semiskilled workers are paid $10 per hour. Both worker types work 40 hours a week. If the weekly operating budget is $12,000, how many skilled and unskilled workers should the distribution division hire?

5.6 The W. V. Whipple Corporation specializes in the production of whirly-gigs. W. V. Whipple, the company's founder, president, and chief executive officer, has decided to replace 50 percent of his work force of 100 workers with industrial robots. Whipple's current capital requirements are 30 units. Whipple's current production function is given by the equation

$$Q(L,K) = 25L^{0.3}K^{0.7}.$$

After automation, Whipple's production function will be

$$Q(L,K) = 100L^{0.2}K^{0.8}.$$

Under the terms of Whipple's current collective bargaining agreement with United Whirly-Gig Workers Local 666, the cost of labor is $12 per worker. The cost of capital is $93.33 per unit.
a. Was Whipple maximizing profit before automation?
b. After automation, how much capital should Whipple employ?
c. By how much will Whipple's total cost of production change as a result of automation?
d. What was Whipple's total output before automation? What is total output after automation?
e. If market price of whirly-gigs is $4, how were Whipple's profits affected by automation?

5.7 Fairway Chemicals manufactures fertilizer for golf courses. The production function for a particular brand of fertilizer is

$$Q = \min[3P, N],$$

where Q is pounds of fertilizer, P pounds of phosphate, and N pounds of nitrogen.
a. What is the marginal product of phosphate?
b. What is the marginal product of nitrogen?
c. Suppose that the prices of phosphate and nitrogen are $1.50 and $4.50, respectively. Suppose that Fairway has budgeted $90,000 to produce this brand. How much phosphate and nitrogen will Fairway purchase to maximize total output?
d. How much of this brand of fertilizer should Fairway produce?
e. What is Fairway's profit from this brand of fertilizer if the price is $5 per pound?

5.8 Stay Fresh is a profit-maximizing company that produces filters for air conditioners. Stay Fresh can sell all the filters that it produces in this highly competitive market for $6 each. The company's total cost equation is

$$TC(Q) = 25 - 2Q + 0.5Q^2.$$

Determine Stay Fresh's profit-maximizing level of output, total revenue, total fixed cost, total variable cost, total cost, and total profit.

NOTES

1. The optimal input combination depends of the degree of input substitutability. For a linear production functions (perfect input substitutability), one input combination is just as good as any another when $MP_L/MP_K = P_L/P_K$. Diagrammatically, the linear isoquant lies on top of the linear isocost line. More likely is the case when $MP_L/MP_K \neq P_L/P_K$, which the result is a "corner solution." When the linear isocost line is steeper than the linear isoquant, the firm will use all capital. When the linear isoquant is steeper than the linear isocost line, the firm will use all capital. In the case of a Leontief production function (perfect input complements), the corner of the L-shaped isoquant touches the linear isocost line at a single point. A change in an input price that is accompanied by an offsetting change in the firm's budget leaves the optimal input combination unchanged. This will rotate the isocost line around a fixed point at the corner of the isoquant.

2. The idea behind "too big to fail" is that certain businesses, particularly large financial institutions, are such an integral part of the fabric of the economic system that the government cannot allow them to fail because this would have dire consequences for the entire country.

Chapter 6

Corporate Structure and Culture

We have thus far developed general economic principles for maximizing shareholder value, but have said nothing about the firm's administrative structure and corporate culture within which employees go about their daily routines. A company's organizational structure and culture can be a source of competitive advantage if it results in a more cost efficient and flexible operation. In fact, many firms have failed because they were unable to adapt to a rapidly changing competitive environment because of a rigid and hidebound corporate hierarchy. Still other businesses have been torn apart from within because of a divisive corporate culture that failed to imbue its managers and workers with a shared vision and a sense of common purpose.

THE SUPPLY CHAIN

We will begin our discussion of corporate structure and culture by briefly reviewing the process whereby raw materials and components are transformed into final goods and services. The **supply chain** summarizes the process whereby production moves from the procurement of raw materials and components to the distribution and sale of the final good or service. The activity performed at each link in the supply chain may be performed by several firms in the same industry, each with its own organizational structure. The activities of two or more links in the value chain may even be performed by a single firm. The left-hand side of Figure 6.1, for example, illustrates the supply chain for the final production and distribution of a generic consumer good.

The oval on the right-hand side of Figure 6.1 is the U-form organizational structure (discussed below) of Firm I, which may be one of several firms that occupy the intermediate goods processing link in this supply chain.

139

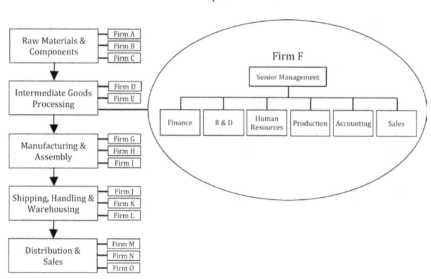

Figure 6.1

This organizational structure lists several support services that are performed in house. In some cases, many of these functions are out-sourced to independent contractors. Automatic Data Processing, Inc., for example, provides payroll, human resource management, and benefits administration services to many large corporations. Many firms that are known for their functional expertise also provide support services to other companies. Pepsi and Nike, for example, are well known for their marketing expertise; Merck and Dow Corning are expert in financial planning; UPS in logistics; General Electric in strategic planning; Toyota in human resource management. The challenge for managers is how best to organize these activities to lower cost and increase shareholder value.

Transaction Costs

When should different firms perform the activities at each link in the supply chain? When should these activities be consolidated? As we saw in the last chapter, minimizing an transaction costs is an important consideration when deciding the most cost-effective method of procuring raw materials and components. Recall that **transaction costs** refer to payments that are required to facilitate the exchange, inspection costs, commissions, shipping costs, and so on.

In general, it will be in the firm's best interest to buy in the spot market when intermediate goods and services are standardized and transaction costs low. With an off-the-shelf purchase, there is no legally binding relationship between buyer and seller. Once the transaction is consummated, buyers and sellers go their separate ways. Purchasing inputs "on the spot" is the most direct and least complicated way to procure an input.

The main advantage of a **spot exchange** is that the output-producing firm and the input-supplying firm specialize in their respective core activities. The main disadvantage is that if the input does not measure up to specifications, the buyer may have no recourse but to duplicate the purchase with another supplier. More importantly, firms selling defective products because of faulty components may suffer a loss of customer good will, which can hurt future sales and jeopardize the firm's existence. A possible solution to the problems associated with a spot exchange is to procure inputs under **contract**.

Contracts overcome many of the problems associated with spot transactions by extending the relationship between the output-producing firm and the input supplying firm beyond the actual transaction. As we saw in the last chapter, contracts specify price and input specifications, which overcome problems of **opportunism**. There is legal recourse if either party fails to live up to the terms of the contract. Contracts can also be used to guarantee future delivery. This is important because supply disruptions could damage a firm's relations with end users. In general, contracts work well when the obligations of buyer and seller parties are clear cut.

The main disadvantage of contract is that they are costly to write, monitor, and enforce. The more complicated the underlying transaction or contracting environment, the more difficult and costly it will be to write a contract that covers every contingency. Incomplete contracts open the door to future litigation, which gives rise to unanticipated legal costs.

Finally, when it is difficult to write a contract that covers every contingency and transaction costs are very high, a firm may decide to produce to input or support activity internally. The main advantage of vertical integration is that the firm has greater control over input quality and price. The main disadvantage is that producing inputs internally involves the diversion of scarce resources away from the firm's core activities. The firm will also incurs increased management costs associated with running a more complex organization.

VERTICAL INTEGRATION

We saw in Chapter 5 that there are several ways in which a firm can procure inputs. The most cost-efficient method of procuring inputs depends on transaction costs, the role of **specialized investments**, and the efficiency losses and internal control problems associated with vertical integration. When transaction costs are low, markets competitive, inputs standardized, and

specialized investments are not involved, it will be in the firm's best interest
to purchase in the spot market. When these conditions are not satisfied, it may
be in the firm's best interest to procure inputs under contract. When contracts
become prohibitively expensive, however, it may be in the best interest of a
firm to produce inputs internally.

Vertical integration is the merger of two or more firms or activities from
different links in the same supply chain. In Figure 6.1, for example, this
would involve the merger of, say, firms B, I and M. Vertical integration is
the up-and-down combination of two or more firms from different stages of
production. Scott Paper, for example, harvests its own timber, which it processes at its own mills, transforms into paper products at its own factories,
which it then distributes using its own delivery fleet. Fisher Body, which is
owned by General Motors, manufactures automobile frames. By contrast,
Nike and Benetton outsource most stages of the production process to independent contractors. Many companies even prefer to outsource services that
their customers prefer, such as maintenance and repair. How a company
organizes the various stages of production depends on factors that are unique
to its operations.

The main advantage of vertical integration is that the firm has complete
control over input quality and delivery. Unlike spot exchanges and the use of
contracts, however, vertical integration diverts of scarce resources away from
the firm's core activities. The advantages and disadvantages of producing an
input internally are peculiar to each industry. It also has much to do with the
firm's location in supply chain.

The decision to make or buy hinges on which method involves the lowest
transaction costs. It also depends on where the firm is located in the supply
chain. A firm's relationship with another firm in the supply chain can be
described as *upstream* or *downstream*. Earlier stages in the supply chain,
such as the production of raw materials and components, are said to be
upstream, while the later stages, such as distribution and final sales are said
to be downstream. In the 1920s, for example, aluminum supplier Alcoa integrated forward by producing aluminum foil. More recently, HBO integrated
backward when it began producing its own programming. Pixar Animated
Studios produces computer-generated animated films for the Walt Disney
Company, which are distributed to AMC, United Artists, and other theater
chains. Disney is downstream from Pixar, but upstream from AMC.

The decision to vertically integrate and use outside suppliers is referred to
as **tapered integration**. A frequently cited example of tapered integration
is Coca-Cola and Pepsi-Cola, which operate their own bottling subsidiaries,
but also use independent contractors to bottle and distribute their soft drinks.
This procurement strategy has several advantages. Tapered integration allows
a firm to expand its input and output channels without incurring substantial

capital outlays. The firm can also threaten to use its own production capacity more intensively to extract favorable terms from outside suppliers. Conversely, a firm can threaten to use independent contractors to pressure in-house suppliers to produce more efficiently. ExxonMobil, for example, produces and refines crude oil. Its refining capacity is significantly greater than its crude oil production. Substantial external purchases of crude oil exert significant pressure on internal producers to remain competitive.

Tapered integration also has potential drawbacks. It may not be possible, for example, for the firm or its supplier to produce at levels sufficient to exploit economies of scale. In addition, coordination problems may arise with production runs, product specifications, delivery times, internal and external monitoring and control, and so on. Finally, the firm may sacrifice economies of scope if duplicate production facilities are not used to capacity. This problem may be exacerbated if managers fail to shut down money-losing operations.

HORIZONTAL INTEGRATION

Horizontal integration refers the merger of two or more firms occupying the same link in the supply chain. In Figure 6.1, for example, this would involve the merger of, say, firms H and I. It is to the side-to-side combination of two or more competing firms producing near or perfect substitutes. These firms produce goods and services that are close substitutes, that is, they have a high **cross-price elasticity of demand**. As with vertical integration, the objective of a horizontal merger should be to increase shareholder value, which may result from several factors. A larger firm, for example, may be able to extract greater discounts from suppliers. A horizontal merger may also make it possible for the firm to exploit economies of scale or scope. A horizontal merger that results in a significantly larger share of the market may also increase the firm's **market power** to earn above-normal rates of return.

Economies of Scale

A firm experiences **economies of scale** when per-unit cost of production falls following a proportional increase in the use of all factors of production. The most common source of economies of scale is the per-unit reduction of up-front costs that cannot be scaled down below some minimum level. Firms may also be able to realize costs savings from increased specialization in production, sales, marketing, research and development, and other areas. If productivity increases faster than a firm's operating cost as the firm gets larger, per-unit costs will fall. Related to this is that some types of equipment, such as large electrical-power generators and blast furnaces, operate more efficiently at greater levels of output.

Another source of economies of scales has to do with optimal inventory levels. Holding inadequate inventories can result in production delays, sales backlogs and lost market share. Firms with high sales volume may be able to lower their inventory to sales ratio, which reduces per-unit inventory costs, including interest expense on short-term operating loans, insurance, warehousing expense, and inventory depreciation.

Economies of Scope

Another potential source of savings from a horizontal merger is **economies of scope**, which arise when the total cost of producing two or more goods using the same production facilities is less than the total cost of producing each good using separately. Economies of scope, which has been described as leveraging a company's core competencies, may be realized at any link in the supply chain. When a company sells a variety of related products or sells in multiple markets, economies of scope may be realized in such areas as transportation and distribution, advertising, research and development, and so on.

Economies of scope are common in industries where a firm's product is routed through several markets. In the commercial airline industry, for example, passengers typically travel along a hub-and-spoke **network**. A passenger travelling on Delta Airlines from Tucson to New York City, for example, will first fly along a "spoke" to the world's largest "hub" at Hartsfield-Jackson Atlanta International Airport. The passenger will then fly the final leg of the journey along another spoke to John F. Kennedy International Airport. By offering hub connections in Atlanta, Delta is able to transport passengers less expensively than by offering direct flights. This is because the marginal cost of increasing an airplane's "load factor" (ratio of passengers to available seats) is negligible. Since, say, doubling the number of passengers does not require doubling the size of the flight crew or amount of fuel consumed, the airline is able to spread its fixed cost over greater traffic volume.

DIVERSIFICATION

Since around the middle of the last century, many companies expanded into areas that were outside their core competencies. Mitsubishi Heavy Industries of Japan, for example, began as a shipbuilding operation. Today, Mitsubishi produces everything from automobiles to air conditions; oil tankers to wind turbines; cruise ships to rocket ships. New York-based General Electric produces a broad spectrum of products, including consumer appliances, turbine generators, jet engines, medical imaging equipment. TRW Inc., which was founded in 1901 as the Cleveland Screw Cap Company, diversified into aerospace, automotive and credit reporting business before being acquired by the aerospace giant Northup-Grumman in 2002. Firms that diversify into unrelated businesses are referred to as **conglomerates**.

Diversification is the process of reducing nonsystematic risk by undertaking a variety of investments or investing in a variety of assets. One way to achieve this is by means of a **conglomerate merger**, which is the joining of two or more firms from links in different supply chains. It is the side-to-side merger of firms from unrelated industries. Several reasons have been put forward to justify diversification, including economies of scale and scope, lower transaction costs, smoother cash flows, access to internal capital markets, diversified shareholders' investment, and realized gains from acquired undervalued firms.

Economies of Scale and Scope

As with horizontal mergers, diversification is often justified on the grounds of economies of scale and economies of scope. There is some evidence (Brush, 1996) that some firms realize significant gains in market share and operational **synergy** from conglomerate mergers. The sources of these gains, however, are unclear. It has been argued that economies of scope from diversification result when firms focus on a narrow segment of the market in which production of unrelated products shares a common technology. The evidence for this, however, is unconvincing. One study (Nathanson and Cassano, 1982) found that while this happens occasionally, as in the case of Schlitz, Maytag and Zenith, there were at least as many firms (Union Carbide, Allis-Chalmers, and Gulf and Western) that sold products using technology with almost nothing common.

Economies of scope may be realized when a firm is able to expand its underutilized organizational skills and resources into unrelated lines of business (Penrose, 1959; Prahalad and Bettis, 1986). The idea is that some organizational skills, such as product development, distribution, advertising, information systems, human resource management and finance, are common to most business enterprises. While this may be true in some cases, many managers mistakenly believe that skills developed specifically for one type of business can be seamlessly transferred to a completely unrelated activity. Unfortunately, many conglomerate mergers cannot be justified on the basis increased shareholder value and are little more than an expression of managerial hubris. Managers may come to believe that a company's success is a reflection of their own superior talents, rather than on a thorough understanding of the businesses involved in a diversification initiative.

Lower Transaction Costs

Transaction costs are payments in excess of the price paid to supplies, such as commissions and contracting costs. Transaction costs can be significant, especially when specialized investments are involved, which can exacerbate coordination problems between output-producing and input-supplying firms. When this occurs, a vertically integrated firm producing multiple products may be preferred to multiple independent firms.

Smoother Cash Flows

One possible benefit from diversification is **cross subsidization**. In some cases, the demands for the products of a diversified company are countercyclical. When this occurs, cash flows from the sale of one product line may be used to subsidize the working capital requirements of another product line. Cross subsidization lowers a company's financing costs because it is easier and less expensive for a division to obtain working capital during periods of slack demand.

Internal Financing

A variation of cross subsidization occurs when the resources of a cash-rich business can be used to underwrite profitable business ventures by the cash-poor business. If the investment would not otherwise have occurred, funding this profitable investment internally will increase shareholder value.

A counter argument to this rationale for a conglomerate merger is that even a cash-poor company should be able to locate financing for profitable investments from external sources. While this may be the case, funding internally reduces financing and transaction costs (Stein, 2003). To begin with, a cash-poor company has more and better information about its willingness and ability to nominally service its debt obligations. In the presence **asymmetric information**, lenders will require a greater interest premium to compensate for the added risk. This problem will be exacerbated if the new debt is subordinate to the firm's existing debt. Finally, external debt requires more due diligence, which increases monitoring and other transaction costs.

Diversifying Shareholder Investment

An interesting rationale for a conglomerate merger is that it diversifies the investments of the firm's shareholders. A broadly diversified company, so the argument goes, is in a better position to weather reversals in any one of its product lines. Thus, company shareholders receive some measure of protection against risk.

One of the criticisms of this line of reasoning is that shareholders do not need the firm's managers to diversify their risk. They can do so on their own by building a portfolio of financial instruments representing claims on a broad range of companies. On the other hand, if a company is owned by a relatively small number of large shareholders, conglomerate mergers may be the best hedge against risk.

Undervalued Firms

Yet another justification for diversification is acquiring undervalued firms to increase shareholder value. This line of reasoning is highly suspect since it is difficult to believe that a firm's manager is able to identify undervalued companies that have been overlooked by professional portfolio managers, investment bankers, and other finance professionals. Moreover, once a take-over target has been identified and publicized, competitive bidding among potential buyers will drive up share prices, thus eliminating the underlying rationale for the proposed acquisition.

STRATEGIC ALLIANCES

In some cases, firms may enter into a **strategic alliance** by collaborating on projects, exchanging information, or sharing production facilities. Strategic alliances allow participating firms to economize on cost without sacrificing autonomy.

Strategic alliances may be vertical, horizontal or conglomerate. *Vertical alliances* involve collaboration between firms occupying different links in the supply chain, such as occurred when Texas Instruments and ACER entered into a partnership to build a microprocessor manufacturing plant in Taiwan. By contrast, a *horizontal alliance* involves a partnership between two or more firms producing close substitutes, such as when Electro-Motive Diesel teamed up with Land Systems to produce the Stryker-armored vehicle for the U.S. Army. Lastly, a conglomerate merger involves the union of two or more firms producing unrelated products, such as when McDonald's agreed to install restaurants in Japanese Toys "R" Us stores.

A particular form of strategic alliance is the **joint venture**, which occurs when two or more firms create and jointly operate an entirely new business. An example of a joint venture is when Merck and Johnson & Johnson joined forces to create Johnson & Johnson-Merck Pharmaceuticals Company. This joint venture manufactures over-the-counter heartburn relief treatments as Pepcid Complete and Mylanta. It also produces Pepcid AC, which is the over-the-counter version of Mercks's prescription ulcer drug Pepcid.

Alliances represent a middle ground between make and buy arrangements. When a firm decides to purchase an input or activity in the market, both the buyer and the supplier maintain their independence. By contrast, an alliance is akin to a marriage in which cooperation, coordination, and information sharing is the norm. For alliances to be successful, relationships must be based on mutual trust and respect, rather than rely on contracts. Disputes must be resolved through negotiation rather than litigation.

Although alliances combine many of the best features of buy and make, they also suffer from many of the same weaknesses. Independent firms that collaborate run the risk of losing control over proprietary information that gives one or both companies their competitive edge. In addition, a loose governance structure can lead to coordination problems between parent companies. In many cases there is no formal mechanism for making decisions and resolving disputes, such as occurred when IBM and Apple Computer attempted to develop a new operating system in the early 1990s.

FIRM ARCHITECTURE

The term **firm architecture** refers to the stakeholder's shared vision of what a company is and how it should operate. It is not just a formal description of the company's administration—its "wiring diagram"—but also the informal relationships that expedite the intramural flow of information and define the decision-making process. A firm's architecture can be an important source of competitive advantage if it reduces transaction costs by improving operational efficiency.

Following a brief discussion of the evolution of the modern corporation, we will examine the interrelated problems of departmentalization and coordination and control in large enterprises. This will be followed by a discussion of several organizational prototypes that describe the administration of many large corporations. The chapter concludes with a discussion of the shared values, beliefs, traditions, philosophy, and norms of behavior that define the character and *esprit de corps* of a modern corporation. A company's corporate culture shapes its goals and defines its social responsibilities.

Evolution of the Modern Corporation

Until the mid-nineteenth century, most businesses were family owned and operated. This was due in part to underdeveloped transportation and communications networks, which consisted primarily of wind-powered sea and river voyages, mule-drawn canal barges, and horse-drawn wagons over pitted, uneven, and muddy dirt roads. Since these transportation networks carried news as well as cargo, communications was equally slow and inefficient, which severely limited the geographic scope of the markets served by family enterprises.

The fundamental nature of free-market capitalism began to change with the onset of the Industrial Revolution in England around 1840 with the development of the steam engine, which dramatically improved transportation, communications, and production. By the 1870s, the steam engine replaced water power as the most important source of energy in factories in United States. Construction of a network of railroads in the decades immediately following the Civil War was a major factor in stimulating economic growth and development.[1] The virus-like growth of the country's transportation network resulted in improved and more reliable service. It also made it easier and cheaper for companies to acquire raw materials and to distribute finished products. Along with the rapid dissemination of information concerning new production technologies, this enabled firms to lower per-unit costs by taking advantage of economies of scale and scope. Mass production also led to an explosion in the range and variety of consumer products.

In addition to inadequate transportation and communication systems, firms were also limited in size and scope by an inability to raise finance capital for investment. Acquiring funds by "going public" and issuing shares of stock was virtually unheard of, and debt financing was limited to small, private loans. As finance capital became easier to procure with the development of a sophisticated financial system, opportunities for starting new businesses and expanding existing ones flourished. Many local businesses soon expanded into regional, national, and international markets.

As business became more diverse, a firm's architecture became more complicated. Organizational structures began to reflect increased specialization in functional responsibilities, including purchasing, manufacturing, distribution and sales, finance, public relations, research and development, and so on. This required a cadre of professional managers responsible for integrating and coordinating the day-to-day activities of the various functional components of a modern, large industrial or commercial enterprise. It did not take long for owners to recognize that an organization's administrative structure was a key to a business's success or failure.

Corporations began to be organized into semiautonomous divisions responsible for day-to-day operations, such as meeting production quotas set by senior management. Headquarters was responsible for determining overall goals and strategy, and for making decisions on matters with company-wide implications, such as research and development, corporate finance, government and shareholder relations. By the mid-twentieth century, multinational corporations such as Exxon, Citibank, Coca-Cola, and Dow Corning were reorganized along geographic, product and functional lines.

As the operations and range of activities of the modern large corporation expanded, it became increasing more difficult to coordinate production processes across different markets, product lines, and customer groups. In many cases, the solution involved reorganizing the company's administrative structure, which required a cadre of professional middle managers to facilitate communications and coordination between and among a growing number of diverse functional departments. Unfortunately, this often led to a bloated tier of middle managers that led overlapping responsibilities resulting in **diseconomies of scale** and declining shareholder value.

By the late-twentieth century, many large corporations began to address some of these problems by flattening its hierarchical structure and refocusing on their core competencies. In addition, many in-house activities, such as marketing, payroll, logistics, and human resource management, were outsourced. Networks and alliances between and among related businesses were forged, expanded and cultivated. By reducing the firm's scale of operations and pruning middle management, leaner and more profitable operations often emerged. Yet, in spite of this trend in down-sizing, by the turn of the twenty-first century, horizontal, vertical, and conglomerate mergers reached an all-time high.

ORGANIZATIONAL STRUCTURE

Organizational structure describes the way in which a company organizes its human resources. It represents management's solution to internal and external coordination and control problems to achieve a firm's objectives, such as maximizing shareholder value.

Chain of command refers to a managerial hierarchy in which authority and accountability flows from senior to junior echelons within an organization. There are at least two interrelated problems in a chain of command that must be addressed as the size of the organization increases: departmentalization, and coordination and control.

Departmentalization involves the division of labor into groups and subgroups according to some organizing principle, such as function, product lines, location, or time. A company that is organized around function might include human resources, finance, research and development, manufacturing, purchasing and sales departments. A company may be organized along product lines, such as a clothing manufacturer with separate divisions for men's, women's, and children's wear. A location-based administrative structure may be organized along regional or international lines. Time-based businesses include airport limousines and private security firms that provide 24-hour service in which workers are organized into 8-hour shifts.

In general, managers should organize the firm's human and non-human resources to lower transaction costs. For example, a company may organize its product lines to avoid duplicating specialized investments, shipping and warehousing, and input procurement costs. Another rationale for departmentalizing is to exploit economies of scale and scope. Pharmaceutical companies such as Pfizer and Eli Lilly, for example, produce a family of products. Economies of scope exist when the production facilities can be used to produce more than one type of pharmaceutical, or when people trained to perform one task can use their skills to perform related tasks, such as advertising different product lines for arranging financing for unrelated capital projects. Related to this is departmentalization to exploit economies of scale, such as might occur when research and development is concentrated in a single department instead of being dispersed throughout the company.

Departmentalization also has implications for the **principal-agent problem**. Recall that agency problems arise with managers or workers (agents) do not act in the best interest of the owners or managers (principals). Randomly monitoring an agent's performance is one solution to this problem. Evaluating and rewarding performance in some departments, such as finance or accounting, may be difficult and could result in higher agency costs.

Once a company's organizational hierarchy has been established, managers may then have to contend with **coordination and control** problems. Coordination refers to managing information flows between and among departments. Control refers to the allocation of decision-making authority within the organization. Coordination and control are interrelated because managers require timely and critical information to make efficient decisions about the firm's operations. For example, poor coordination between the marketing and manufacturing divisions could result in inventory and delivery problems that result in lost sales and lower profits.

There are two approaches for resolving coordination and control problems. The first approach emphasizes departmental autonomy. The second approach stresses the importance of developing strong inter departmental relations. In the case of departmental autonomy, the inter departmental flow of information is minimal. Department managers make independent decisions and report directly to senior management. This approach is typical of diversified companies that organize into semiautonomous **profit centers**. Managers' compensation depends on whether they meet or surpass targets established by senior management.

An alternative to semiautonomy are departments with strong lateral ties. This makes sense when economies of scale and scope require close cooperation across functional areas. Lateral relations can be informal, as might occur when groups are organized on a temporary or *ad hoc* basis. They can also be formal, such as with a matrix organizational structure in which team members are drawn from different functional departments to work on particular project. As we will see in the next section, a potential source of friction is overlapping loyalties. Team members are responsible not only to the project manager, but also to their own department managers.

TYPES OF ORGANIZATIONAL STRUCTURE

A large company's chain of command may be centralized or decentralized. Long-run, strategic decisions are typically centralized at the senior management level. Operational decisions, which are made at lower levels of the corporate hierarchy, may be centralized or decentralized. While department and division managers have varying degrees of operational latitude on day-to-day matters, but are subject to oversight and review by senior managers.

There are many ways to organize a company's human resources, but the most common organizational structures include the unitary (functional) form (U-form), the multidivisional form (M-form), a U-form/M-form hybrid, the project matrix, and the contractual network. These organizational structures reflect the centralized or decentralized nature of a company's chain of command and a company's response to strategic and operational market challenges.

Unitary (Functional) Form (U-Form)

Before the turn of the last century, most large firms were a loose confederation of formerly independent companies in which coordination and control was the responsibility of the company's founder. The onset of the industrial revolution, however, created opportunities for achieving significant economies of scale and scope. Firms invested in large-scale production facilities and internalized activities previously outsourced to independent contractors, such as sales and distribution. The organizational structure that emerged was the **unitary (functional) form**, or simply the **U-form**.

The U-form is a centralized multifunctional organizational structure in which individual departments perform specific functions, such as production (the manufacture of a good or service), marketing (promotion and sales), human resources (attracting and retaining qualified personnel), finance (managing the firm's financial resources), research and development (creating new and improved product lines), and accounting (financial reporting). The firm's human resources are organized according to expertise, skills, and activities. Figure 6.2 depicts a simplified U-form organizational structure in which department vice presidents, or their equivalent, report to the president, who may then report to the chief executive officer (CEO) in the case of a publicly-held corporation, who reports to the board of directors.

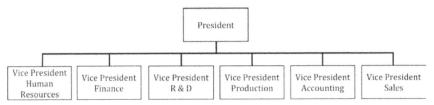

Figure 6.2

Advantages of the U-Form

Firms that adopted the U-form in the early twentieth century enjoyed a competitive advantage in the marketplace. Organizing the firm's operations around functional areas promotes employee technical expertise. Specialization leads to well-defined career tracks, which can boost morale and worker productivity. The U-form also leads to a more efficient use of human resources since it is easier to reallocate personnel as needed within a functional area.

In addition to reducing transaction costs, the U-form makes it easier to exploit economies of scale since increase employee expertise and specialized equipment make it possible to more efficiently manage large workloads. Lower transaction costs may also be realized because of improve coordination since activities within functional areas are related. Finally, specialization improves technical competencies that can be a source of competitive advantage over rival firms. As a result of these advantages, this early organizational structure was quickly mimicked by other firms, but there were disadvantages to the U-form as well.

Disadvantages of the U-Form

As a company grows and its product line, geographic reach, and customer base becomes more diverse, the U-form gives rise to a number of problems. Department managers find it increasingly more difficult to process the massive volumes of information that characterize large corporations. Coordination across functions that is required to resolve complex problems becomes increasingly difficult as interdepartmental conflicts are passed up the chain of command for resolution.

As companies become larger and more complex, principal-agent problems tend to become more serious as the organization's goals become subordinate to the parochial interests of managers and functional specialists. Managers become less concerned with the company's bottom line than with their own salaries, perquisites, **stock options**, and other benefits. Finally, the advantages of employee specialization in exploiting economies of scale and reducing transaction costs can also be a source of weakness. The functional form limits the opportunity for managers to develop an understanding of other departments and of the overall operations of the organization.

When to Adopt the U-Form

The U-form is most effective for small- and medium-sized companies that require a simple hierarchal administrative structure to operate more efficiently, but are not so large as to make coordination and control problematic. Such companies have limited product offerings, sell in local or regional markets, and have a relatively homogeneous clientele. The U-form may also be appropriate for larger corporations that operate in a relatively stable business environment. Domino's Pizza, for example, sells pizza and related food items. It is the second-largest pizza chain in the United States. Although it operates more than 9,700 corporate and franchised outlets in about 70 countries, the company has a U-form organizational structure in which operations, distribution, finance, and administration are the major functional areas.

Multidivisional Form (M-Form)

The U-form hierarchical structure is effective in exploiting economies of scale for small- and medium-sized businesses with a relatively homogenous product line, narrow market and customer base. This organizational structure is unwieldy and inefficient for companies with diversified product lines, operate in diverse geographic markets, or have a heterogeneous clientele. The primary reason for this is information overload.

As a company broadens its business activities (product lines and services), moves into new geographic regions (regional and international), or diversifies its customer base (households, businesses, and government), it becomes increasingly difficult for senior management to monitor the company's multivariate activities and interests. This increases transaction costs and administrative expenses as the tier of middle managers is expanded to process the flow of information, and coordinate programs involving multiple departments. The subsequent erosion of company profits requires a new organizational structure.

Ideally, an organization's structure should minimize transaction costs (Chandler, 1977; Williamson, 1967, 1975). For companies with multiple product lines, a diverse clientele, and that operate widely separate geographic locations, the **multidivisional form (M-form)** is superior to the older, more traditional, U-form. The M-form consists of two or more quasi-independent divisions with their own functional structure that pursue their own goals and have little or no connection with other divisions. Unlike the U-form, which is organized according to function, the M-form is organized according to product line, geographic regions, customer type, related business activities, and so on. Each division operates as a separate company, has its own U-form, and is ultimately responsible to senior management of the corporation. Figure 6.3 illustrates a typical "wiring diagram" for an M-form organizational structure.

The three most common divisions of the M-form are along product, geographic, and customer lines. Product divisions are typically responsible for individual or closely related product lines. A classic example of this occurred in the early 1900s when General Motors CEO, Alfred Sloan, Jr., reorganized the company around separate divisions (Buick, Cadillac, Chevrolet, Oldsmobile, and Pontiac). Each division represented a distinct, self-contained business with its own functional hierarchy. Day-to-day operational duties were delegated to division managers, while senior management retained responsibility for overall corporate strategy and financial control. Each division was responsible for making business-level strategic decisions, which would feed into the corporation's overall strategy.

Geographic divisions are organized according to location. For example, Time Warner Cable, the New York City-based cable telecommunications company that operates in 28 states, is organized into West Coast, Midwest, Northeast, New York, Carolina, and Texas regions. Finally, companies that

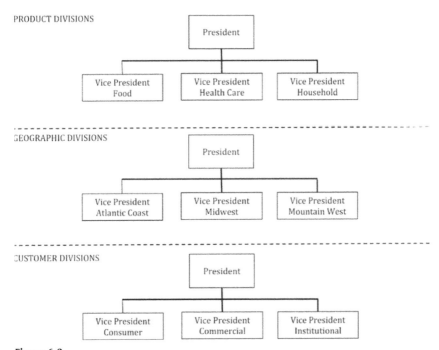

Figure 6.3

are organized into customer divisions provide specialized services to customers of diverse characteristics and needs, such as businesses, government, and consumers.

Advantages of the M-Form

The M-form has several advantages over the U-form. Divisions are able to react more swiftly to changes in the business environment because it is not necessary to coordinate with other divisions. The M-form tends to be more customer-oriented, especially when divisions are organized according to customer type. The M-form also simplifies command and control since it is easier for senior management to monitor the performance of divisions with dedicated responsibilities. This leads to a more efficient allocation of company resources. It is also easier to identify and exploit potential synergies involving two or more divisions.

A multidivisional corporate structure also engenders a spirit of competition between and among divisions, which can improve the overall company performance and increase the value of the firm. This can lead division managers to aggressively pursue emerging market opportunities. Finally, the multidivisional form provides managers with greater opportunities to develop their managerial skills since they interact more frequently with multiple functional areas.

Disadvantages of the M-Form

There are several potential disadvantages of the M-form. Divisions may be forced to complete for scarce resources, such as financing. Moreover, interdivisional rivalry may lead to a failure to coordinate activities, which can result can be a duplication of effort and an inefficient use of company resources. Division managers also have a tendency to pursue their own parochial interests at the expense of overall corporate goals. The benefits of the M-form may also be dissipated if senior managers assume control when divisions experience operating difficulties. This can exacerbate internecine rivalries if the division under senior management control does not have to compete for scarce company resources. The company's bottom line may also suffer since there is less pressure on senior managers to perform.

When to Adopt the M-Form

The multidivisional form is most likely to be adopted by large corporations characterized by significant differences in products and services, geographic locations, and clientele. In spite of these differences, the M-form may not be appropriate if a company enjoys significant economies of scale from shared resources across functional areas of different divisions.

U-Form/M-Form Hybrid

As the name suggests, a **U-form/M-form hybrid** combines functional and multidivisional corporate structures to exploit the best features of both organizational structures. This hybrid organizational structure is characteristic of large firms with diverse product lines, clientele, or geographic markets, but centralize key functions to lower transaction costs, efficiently utilize company resources, and exploit economies of scale and scope. Proctor & Gamble's (P&G) simplified hybrid structure is depicted in Figure 6.4.

P&G corporate structure includes the usual corporate functions of human resources, global business services (including finance, information technology and research and development), and external relations. Divisions are organized into product lines (global beauty, household, and health & well being) and global markets. Functional departments within a hybrid structure often have staff authority, whereas divisions are typically characterized by top-to-bottom line authority (chain-of-command).

Advantages of a Hybrid Structure

Organizations that that adopt a hybrid structure may be able to benefit from economies of scale. They may also be in a position to efficiently utilize its physical and human resources in functional areas. The hybrid structure may

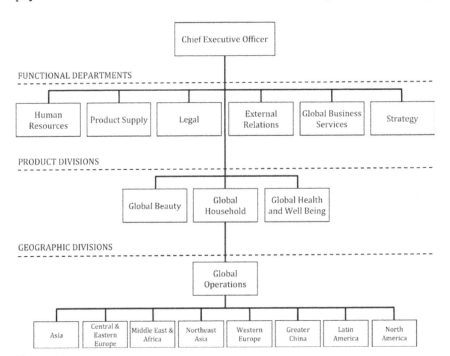

Figure 6.4

also make it possible for product, geographic, and customer divisions to adapt quickly to changes in the business environment. A hybrid structure may also make it possible to avoid the interdivisional rivalries that sometimes occur with the multidivisional form by more closely aligning divisional and corporate goals.

Disadvantages of the Hybrid Structure

Because of its more complex nature, the functional departments of corporations that adopt the hybrid structure tend to become bloated at the staff management level. To make matters worse, managers of functional departments may attempt to exercise authority over the company's divisions, which could lead to internecine conflicts. Finally, although divisions are generally able to flexibly respond to changes in the business environment, it may be difficult for the organization to respond rapidly to situations that require coordination between divisions and functional departments.

When to Adopt a Hybrid Structure

The hybrid structure is best suited for large corporations that face considerable business uncertainty that is best handled with a multidivisional structure requiring functional expertise and is in a position to benefit from economies of scale and the more intensive use of its human and physical resources. Organizing a company by divisions and functional departments is expensive. For this reason, a hybrid organizational structure is most appropriate for large firms with substantial resources.

Matrix Structure

The M-form was more successful at generating above-normal rates of return because it streamlined the flow of information, improved coordination and control, and lowered transaction costs. In business, as in almost everything else, imitation is the sincerest form of flattery. Before long, firms that adopted the M-form began to lose their competitive edge. Beginning in the 1970s, a new organizational arrangement emerged—the matrix structure.

The **matrix structure** superimposes horizontal divisional reporting onto a heirarchical functional structure involving semiautonomous projects. Projects may be organized around a company's product line, geographic regions, or customer types. One of the first companies to adopt a matrix management approach occurred just after World War II by Koninklijke Philips Electronics N.V. (more commonly known as Philips), the Amsterdam-based electronics company that organized its operations around national organizations and product divisions.

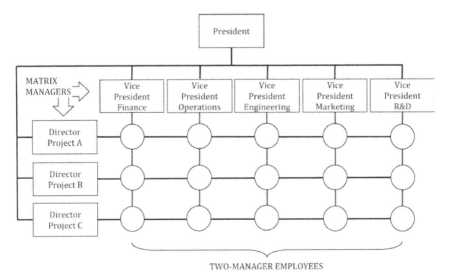

Figure 6.5

An example of the matrix structure is depicted in Figure 6.5. The vice presidents of five functional departments make up the vertical structure of this firm. Three project directors of divisional units make up horizontal structure. Department vice presidents and project directors are the matrix managers of this organizational structure. Project directors organize teams of employees drawn from the various functional departments according to specialized skills and the needs of the project. In this case, project directors, who are ultimately responsible for the success of the project, report directly to the president of the company.

Advantages of the Matrix Structure

Proponents of the matrix structure argue that the team approach encourages cross-fertilization and the flow of ideas across organizational lines. Decentralized decision also makes it possible for a company to react more quickly to changes in the business environment since more decisions are made at the division and department levels. This frees senior management to focus on long-term business strategy. The matrix structure also adds a degree of flexibility to the company's operations by making it possible to allocate human and capital resources more efficiently, which reduces capital outlays and associated transaction costs. Functional specialists, for example, can be reassigned to projects where their skills are most needed.

Disadvantages of the Matrix Structure

Opponents argue that the matrix structure can lead to conflicts between department and division managers, which can adversely affect company performance. Overlapping responsibilities often requires an added layer of managers and support staff to make the system work, which increase overhead and related expenses. It also increases the amount of time that it takes to process information and reach decisions. Even relatively minor decisions tend to be made by groups in the matrix structure. Moreover, if teams are granted too much independence, it may be difficult for senior management to monitor project performance.

A potentially more serious problem has to do with divided loyalties of team members. Team members effectively have two bosses—department and project (division) managers. Functional department managers, not project (division) managers, are responsible for promotions and career advancement of team members. As a result, team members may be more concerned with maintaining good departmental relations than with the needs of clients or project goals.

When to Adopt a Matrix Structure

To justify the use of a matrix organizational structure, the benefits of horizontal coordination across divisions must outweigh the corresponding administrative complexity. In general, a matrix structure may be justified when three conditions exist. First, the business environment makes it necessary to focus on both the functional and divisional aspects of the company's operations. Such a situation might arise when a company has a diverse, high-technology product line that calls for a multidivisional approach, but also requires a strong engineering department. Second, an uncertain and rapidly changing business environment requires an organizational structure that is capable of processing large amounts of information and coordinating activities quickly. Finally, the matrix structure may be appropriate when there is pressing financial need to share human and physical resources across departments, such as would occur in high competitive markets.

Contractual Network

In some businesses economies of scale and cost efficiencies exist for some activities, but not in others. When this is the case, a top-to-bottom hierarchy in which all functional departments are organized under the same roof may not be an effective way to utilize a company's limited resources. Instead, it may make more sense for the core company to outsource any activity that can be performed more efficiently by an independent contractor, such as payroll, benefits administration, manufacturing, distribution and security. This affiliation of independent companies, such as the one depicted in Figure 6.6, is referred to as a **contractual network**.

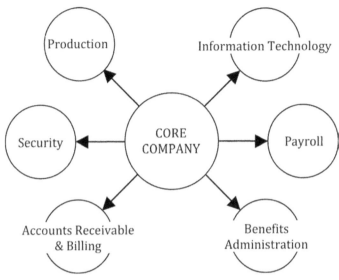

Figure 6.6

Businesses that utilize networks of subcontractors outsource any activity that can be done more cheaply and efficiently by other companies. The role of managers at the center of the network is to coordinate activities between and among subcontractors to achieve the organizations goals. An example of a successful contractual network is the Swedish clothing company H&M (Hennes & Mauritz). Founded in 1947, H&M operates retail outlets in several countries, including Austria, Belgium, Canada, Finland, France, Hong Kong, Japan, the Netherlands, Portugal, Russia, South Korea, Spain, Sweden, and the United States. The company also does not own any clothing factories. Instead, it outsources production to a network of more than 700 suppliers around the world, two-thirds of which are located in low-cost Asian nations. As a result, H&M has greater cost flexibility and is better able to respond to shifting fashion trends.

Advantages of a Contractual Network

The primary advantage of a contractual network is that it allows small- and medium-size companies to enjoy economies of scale and cost efficiencies that would not be possible if functional departments were internalized. Contractual networks also make it possible for an organization to avoid significant fixed costs that would result if these activities were brought under one roof. Outsourcing day-to-day operations also makes it possible for management to focus on what the core business does best, such as product design, innovation and marketing.

Disadvantages of a Contractual Network

The main disadvantage is the nebulous nature of a network often creates confusion, such as when two or more managers issue conflicting directives to company and satellite employees at different locations. An extra layer of oversight to manage company-related activities to avoid project delays and production backlog, which increases operational and transaction costs.

While this organizational structure provides flexibility and reduces overhead and costs, contractual network structure may introduce supply uncertainties as company managers are forced to rely on contractual workers to perform important tasks. In addition, since the core company does not have all of the usual functional departments, it may be necessary for skilled in-house workers to perform multiple tasks. This can lead to unfriendly competition among managers and supervisors to secure the services of the most skilled employees. What is more, product quality and customer relations may suffer if workers with multiple assignments find it difficult to focus on individual assignments.

When to Adopt a Contractual Network

Contractual networks are best suited for small- and medium-sized companies that do not have sufficiently large production runs to exploit economies of scale. This organizational structure may also be appropriate for organizations with limited human and physical resources that require flexibility to adapt to an uncertain and rapidly changing business environment.

STRATEGY OR STRUCTURE: CHICKEN OR EGG?

The age-old causality dilemma of which came first, the chicken or the egg, has also been applied to the relationship between corporate strategy and structure. To answer this question, noted business historian Alfred Chandler (1962) examined the origins of several leading U.S. firms, including Du Pont, General Motors, Sear & Roebuck, and Standard Oil. He found that each of these companies exhibited a similar pattern of development. Namely, changes in strategy created management problems that necessitated a change in its organizational structure to more efficiently utilize company resources to fuel growth.

More recently, however, some researchers (Frederickson, 1986) have begun to question this view arguing that an organization's structure may be influenced by a corporation's strategy. Eastman Kodak, for example, suffered $3.5 billion in lost sales between 1981 and 1985 to competitors such as Fiji Film because its inefficient functional structure was not appropriate for its diverse product line. Kodak was subsequently reorganized into 34 divisions ranging, which operated as quasi-independent businesses. Within 2 years, almost every product experienced an increase in its domestic market share and registered significant export gains. Clearly, this was a case of structure following strategy. But, the switch to a multidivisional structure led to changers in its corporate strategy. In short, there is no clear-cut directional causality. In the matter of the linkage between strategy and structure, if the chicken lays an egg, an offspring with somewhat different personality traits is likely to follow.

CORPORATE CULTURE

Up to this point we have discussed some of the ways in which a business may be organized—a company's superstructure. We now turn our attention to the community of people who determine the success or failure of the enterprise. In particular, we will discuss **corporate culture**, which refers to the shared values, beliefs, traditions, philosophy, and norms of behavior of a corporation—a company's personality. Corporate culture influences the way employees dress and behave. Along with an employee's worker's on-the-job performance, corporate culture influences a company's system of rewards and punishments. It determines the boundaries of the interoffice relationships—its customs, rituals, and taboos.

Corporate culture is more than a company's unwritten code of conduct and behavior. Corporate culture can directly affect its bottom line since it encompasses a set of unwritten rules that dictate the way things get people to behave and the manner in which things get done. Corporate culture can be a source of competitive advantage if it reduces transaction costs by speeding up information processing by employees and lowers the cost of monitor worker behavior. Corporate culture is also important in shaping a company's goals and defining its social responsibilities.

Corporate culture can be a source of competitive advantage if it reduces transaction costs. It can also create problems when different corporate cultures clash, such as might occur when a company with an informal management style merges with another company with a strict hierarchical structure. Employees of the more casual firm might feel that their creativity is being stifled. Employees of the strict hierarchy who are used to being told what to do may feel rudderless. An example of this occurred in 1984 when IBM acquired Rolm Corporation, a Silicon Valley–based producer of computerized phone systems, for $1.3 billion. The resulting odd-couple marriage was problematic from the start. IBM's rigid management style was incompatible with Rolm's laid-back corporate culture. Divorce was a foregone conclusion. In 1998, IBM sold Rolm to the German engineering conglomerate Siemens for $333 million.

Unwritten Rules

The idea that corporate culture involves a set of unwritten rules and codes of conduct, which lowers monitoring, information-processing and transaction costs, is illustrated by a scene in the 1992 Academy Award–nominated film, *A Few Good Men*. In this courtroom drama, Navy lawyer Lieutenant Junior Grade Daniel Kaffee (portrayed by Tom Cruise) defends two Marines accused of murdering Private First Class William Santiago at Guantanamo Bay Naval Base (Gitmo), Cuba.

Kaffee's defense is that it was an accidental death caused by an extrajudicial disciplinary action known as a "code red," which the two Marines on trial were ordered to enforce after Santiago failed to follow the chain of command. To demonstrate to the court that their action was not officially sanctioned, prosecuting attorney Captain Jack Ross (Kevin Bacon) asks another Marine, Corporal Jeffrey Barnes (Noah Wyle), to turn to the section in the U.S. Marine Corps Standard Operating Procedures that deals with code reds. Confused, Barnes replies that "code red is a term that we use." Ross replies: "Is there no book. No pamphlet or manual, no regulation or set of written orders or instructions that lets me know that, as a Marine, one of my duties is to perform code reds?" "No sir." Replies Barnes. "No book, sir."

On re-direct examination, Kaffee hands Barnes the same manual and asks: "Corporal, would you open this book up to the part that says were the mess hall is." "Well, Lieutenant Kaffee," says Barnes, "that's not in the book either, sir." Feigning confusion, Kaffee asks: "Well, I don't understand. How did you know where the mess hall was if it wasn't in this book?" Barnes's reply: "I guess I just followed the crowd at chow time, sir."

When conventional wisdom guides an employee's actions, it is not necessary to incur the cost of formally codifying these rules or of hiring managers to monitor an employee's behavior. Thus, the flow of information and the decision-making process is more efficient, which reduces transaction costs and contributes to a firm's competitive advantage.

Creating a Corporate Culture

How does a company create or shape its corporate culture? A corporate culture embodies a company's goals and priorities. Sometimes these goals can be made explicit in the form of a published mission statement. Sometimes it is defined in terms of the manner in which power and control is distributed within the organization. Sometimes it evolves as a set of core beliefs and unwritten rules, such as when a manager tells a new employee that "this is the way we do things around here." Corporate culture is the way a company's employees behave when someone is not looking over their shoulders.

There are several factors that define a corporation's culture. A new employee, for example, typically learns the corporate culture by observing the behavior of others. This may involve dress codes, standard operating procedures, working hours, and so on. In most businesses, for example, the official work day is from 9:00 a.m. to 5:00 p.m. In reality, however, the corporate culture may dictate something quite different. A 10 to 12 hour work day for investment bankers, for example, is the norm.

Many companies seek to reinforce the existing corporate culture by recruiting a certain type of employee. Some high-technology companies, for example, take pride in recruiting the brightest, albeit somewhat eccentric, candidates possible. Others companies base their selections on family background. Some companies only recruit from Ivy League universities. Still others have a preference for candidates that are over six feet tall. The purpose of these hiring practices is to reinforce a kind of tribal bonding that is consistent with the prevailing corporate culture.

Firms in certain industries also have similar corporate cultures. The corporate culture of JP Morgan Chase is not dissimilar from that of Citibank. Firms in the entertainment industry are likely to exhibit similar attitudes and modes of behavior. The corporate culture of start-up high-technology firms is often influenced by the Silicon Valley way of doing things. Corporate culture will also reflect the society in which the firm operates. The corporate culture of a Brazilian subsidiary of an American multinational firm will be quite different from that of its sister Japanese subsidiary.

CHAPTER EXERCISES

6.1 How can a firm's organizational structure be a source of competitive advantage?

6.2 What is a specialized investment and how can it affect the manner in which a company procures its inputs?

6.3 Why would a company choose to produce an input under contract as opposed to purchasing the input in the spot market?

6.4 Under what circumstances would a firm choose to vertically integrate instead of procuring an input from an independent supplier under a contract?

6.5 Explain the importance of economies of scale and economies of scope in company's merger and acquisition decisions?

6.6 What is the difference between a conglomerate merger, strategic alliance, and joint venture?

6.7 What is the role of economies of scale in a company's decision to choose a network organizational structure?

6.8 What organizational structure is most appropriate when employees from different functional departments are organized into teams according to product types, geographic regions, customer types, and so on?

6.9 Is there a link between corporate strategy and structure?

6.10 Explain what is meant by corporate culture. How can a company's culture be a source of competitive advantage?

6.11 How can a clash of cultures following a merger affect a firm's performance?

6.12 In what ways do you believe that the opening quotation by Harold S. Geneen relates to topics discussed in this chapter?

6.13 Suppose that a company outsources finance, production, sales, distribution, marketing, and human resources to outside contractors. The company also employs the services of an independent consulting firm to help coordinate the activities of the marketing and sales contractors. Finally, the company uses the services of another firm to handle government relations and contracts. Prepare a network "wiring diagram" summarizing these relationships.

6.14 Grip Right, Inc. manufactures made-to-order hand tools specializing in crescent wrenches. Production is organized around teams of 30 workers with a daily production quota of 100 wrenches. Once the high quality sheet metal is procured by the purchasing department and the company takes delivery, the manufacturing process involves six stages: cutting, grinding, drilling, polishing, finishing and packaging. A separate department is responsible for shipping.
   a. What organizational structure would you propose for this company?
   b. How would you organize each team?
   c. Suppose that Grip Right were to expand its operations overseas? What modifications to the company's organizational structure would you suggest?

6.15 Suppose that a firm manufactures multiple lines of household appliances. This company enjoys economies of scale because many of these products are made with similar electronic components. In your opinion, should this company be organized along multidivisional lines according to product, or along functional lines (manufacturing, sales, research and development, etc.)?

6.16 Electronic Communications and Control (EComCon) Corporation produces cell phones. The company outsources its marketing (MKT), payroll (PAY), health care and retirement (HCR) benefits programs. EComCon also outsources its production to firms A, B, and C, which are located in three different geographic locations. These production contractors are also responsible final delivery to local retail outlets. Since these manufacturers do not maintain their own fleet of trucks, this task is further outsourced to several delivery subcontractors (DEL). Construct the "wiring diagram" for this contractual network.

NOTE

1. In the 1840s, railroad mileage in the United States tripled, and tripled again in the 1850s. In 1850, there were about 9,000 miles of railroad track. In the first eight years following the Civil War, the country's network of railroads doubled in size, and then doubled again in the next 14 years. By 1890, the railroad system had exploded to about 130,000 miles. By 1915, railroad mileage peaked at around 254,000 miles.

Chapter 7

Industry Organization

The primary responsibility of managers is to direct the firm's activities to maximize shareholder value. In a competitive business environment, managers who do not doggedly pursue this objective will not survive. Managers who do not efficiently organize the firm's resources will be replaced by those who can. The success of a firm, however, is often determined by forces that are beyond a manager's control. Managerial decisions are not made in a competitive vacuum. Decisions about pricing, production, marketing, research and development, and so on, frequently affect, and are affected by, decisions made by rival firms. In the previous chapter, we examined the firm's internal environment and developed general principles for efficiently organizing the firm's resources. In this chapter, we will explore the firm's external environment—the nature and structure of the industry within which the firm operates.

MARKET STRUCTURE

There is no set of principles that can tell managers how best to navigate the shifting currents of business competition. Effective management, however, depends on a thorough understanding of **market structure**, which is business environment within which the firm operates. Market structure determines whether a firm has **market power**, which is the ability to price a product above marginal cost and earn a positive **economic profit**. A firm in an industry consisting of a large number of equivalently-sized rivals producing a homogeneous product has little to no market power. This is because the contribution of any single firm to industry supply, and therefore its ability to influence the market-determined price of its product, is negligible. In this case, output, and not price, is the manager's critical decision variable.

By contrast, price is an important decision when a firm accounts for significant proportion of market supply, or when the firm is able to carve out a market niche by differentiating its product from those of its rivals.

There are many ways to characterize the structure of an industry. A useful starting point is to identify the external and internal factors that contribute to an understanding of a firm's market power including: the number, size, and distribution of rival firms; the number, size, and distribution of buyers; product differentiation; and the conditions of entry into, and exit from, the industry.

Number, Size, and Distribution of Rival Firms

The ability of a firm to set the price of its product frequently depends on the number and size (in terms of total output) of rival firms in the same industry that produce a similar product. In general, the greater the number of similarly sized small firms in an industry, the less market power of any individual firm. By contrast, a firm that dominates industry output is in a better position to push the market-clearing price in a direction that is most favorable to its bottom line.

Number, Size, and Distribution of Buyers

Markets may also be categorized by the number and size distribution of buyers. A single buyer in a market comprising many small buyers does not have the ability to influence the market-determined price. On the other hand, a buyer that accounts for a significant proportion of purchases from an industry may be able to extract significant price and other concessions from producers. The extreme case of this is a market that consists of a single buyer, which is referred to as a **monopsony**. A market comprising a few large buyers is referred to as an **oligopsony**, such as government expenditures on space exploration.

Product Differentiation

Product differentiation refers to the degree to which the product of a firm differs from those of its rivals. Other things being equal, when products are perfect substitutes, buyers will purchase from the firm that charges the lowest price. Many raw materials and agricultural commodities producers fall into this category. On the other hand, firms that produce goods or services with distinctive characteristics may be able to exercise a measure of control over price. Automobile producers, for example, charge different prices for different models. These prices reflect differences in styling, gas mileage, horsepower, drivetrains, audio systems, visual displays, warranties and so on.

Entry and Exit Conditions

The ease with which investment flows into and out of an industry can affect a firm's market power. If entry by new firms is unimpeded, above-normal returns will attract new investment into the industry, which increases supply and puts downward pressure on prices and squeezes profits of incumbent firms. On the other hand, when it is difficult for firms to enter an industry, incumbent firms with market power will continue to exercise a degree of control over price to earn positive economic profits. A pharmaceutical firm that enjoys patent protection, for example, is in a better position to charge what the market will bear for its product.

The ease with which productive resources can be transferred to some other use will also influence the managerial decision-making process. Industry output, prices and profits are more sensitive to changes in market conditions when resources are easily transferred to some other activity, such as the use of migrant farmers in agriculture. By contrast, the structure of an industry is likely to be more stable when resources used in the production process are highly specialized, such as highly trained doctors and medical technicians in the health care industry.

THE FIVE FORCES

It is the obligation of a manager to maximize and sustain shareholder value. Although a firm may be able to earn positive economic profits in the short term, there is no guarantee that it will continue to do so in the long run given the competitive pressures of the market place. Michael Porter (1980) identified five "forces" that affect an industry's ability to sustain profitability and attract new investment.

Three of Porter's five forces come from external sources (horizontal competitors), including *the threat of entry* by potential rivals, *the threat of substitutes*, and the nature of *competitive rivalry*. The other two forces involve threats from internal sources (vertical competitors), including *the bargaining power of buyers* and *suppliers*. Porter's five forces can be used as a framework for evaluating the effects on shareholder value from changes in a firm's competitive environment. It can also be used to help formulate a firm's business strategy. Figure 7.1 summarizes the interrelationships of Porter's five forces.

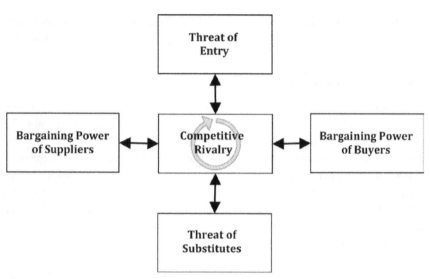

Figure 7.1

Threat of Entry

Above-normal returns attract new firms into an industry, which increase total output, depress prices and squeeze profits. Thus, the ability of incumbent firms to sustain profits depends on their ability to block entry by newcomers. There are several possible **barriers to entry**, including **economies of scale**, high **sunk costs**, reputation, brand-name loyalty, patents, licenses and copyrights, trade and environmental legislation, switching costs, and so on. If incumbents are not able to restrict entry, economic profit may evaporate, in which case the flow of investment will dry up. In this extreme case, which is referred to as perfect competition, individual firms lack market power and become price takers.

Threat of Substitutes

The demand for the output of an industry tends to be more price elastic the greater the number of close substitutes. The existence of close substitutes erodes profitability, which reduces the amount of new investment flowing into the industry.

Competitive Rivalry

Competitive rivalry is the main driver in Porter's five forces model. For most industries, the intensity of competitive rivalry can have a profound effect on the ability of firms to sustain long-run profits. Competitive tensions, which tend to be greatest in industries that are not highly concentrated, exert downward pressure on profits. Other factors that contribute to nature and intensity of rivalry among firms include the degree of product differentiation, switching costs, technological innovations and government legislation.

Bargaining Power of Buyers

Buyers that are able to extract discounts and other more favorable terms reduce a firm's ability to extract and sustain profits. The ability to extract concessions tends to be greatest in industries that sell to a relatively few "high volume" buyers; where the cost of switching to other products is low; or when there is a large number of close substitutes.

Bargaining Power of Suppliers

Profits also tend to be lower in industries where suppliers of raw materials, components, labor services, and so on have the power to negotiate more favorable terms. This bargaining power tends to be greatest when transactions require **specialized investments**, input markets are highly concentrated, or when there are few close substitutes.

INDUSTRY TYPES

Standard textbook discussions of market structure typically assigned firms to one of four distinct industry types, which differ in terms of the degree of competition. From the most to least competitive, these market structures include perfect competition, imperfect competition (monopolistic competition and oligopoly) and monopoly. Table 7.1 summarizes the main features of these market structures.

Perfect Competition

Perfect competition is an industry characterized by a very large number of small firms (in terms of output) producing a homogeneous output. Entry into, and exit from, this industry is easy. In spite of conventional wisdom, perfect competition is a comparatively rare market structure since there are very few industries in which firms produce identically the same product. Perfect competition is a reasonably good description of industries that produce commodities, such as wheat or corn.

A distinguishing feature of perfect competition is that firms have no control over the price of their product. This is because each firm's contribution

Table 7.1 Market Structures

		Market Structure		
		Imperfect Competition		
Characteristic	Perfect Competition	Monopolistic Competition	Oligopoly	Monopoly
Number of firms	Very many	Many	Few	One
Type of product	Homogeneous	Differentiated. Many close substitutes	Homogeneous or differentiated.	Unique. No close substitutes.
Market power	None; firms are "price takers"	Some; limited by the availability of close substitutes	Limited; pricing decisions characterized by strategic behavior	Considerable; firms are "price makers."
Barriers to entry and exit.	Few to none; easy entry and exit	Few; easy entry and exit	Considerable	Entry impossible.
Non-price competition	None	Considerable; advertising, brand-name recognition, and trademarks to promote customer loyalty	Considerable; especially with respect to differentiated products	None since there is only one firm; monopolies frequently advertise for other reasons

to industry output is small. Perfectly competitive firms lack market power because changes in output are too small to shift the industry supply curve and affect the market-determined price. Because entry to and exit from the industry is easy, each firm earns zero economic profit in the long run.

Imperfect Competition

Unlike perfect competition, firms in imperfectly competitive industries can exercise a degree of discretion of the price charged for their products. This market power may be the by-product of an industry consisting of a few large firms in which there are significant barriers to entry, or because individual firms have carved out a market niche of loyal customers by differentiating their products. The two industry types that fall into this category are monopolistic competition and oligopoly.

Monopolistic Competition

Monopolistic competition is also characterized by large number of firms in which entry and exit is unimpeded. The difference between this and perfect competition is that each firm attempts to carve out its own market niche by distinguishing its product on the basis of design, workmanship, customer service, and so on. By segmenting the market, each firm has some degree some market power, although its ability to set price is limited by the availability of many close substitutes. Non-price competition, such as advertising, brand-name identification, and trademarks to promote customer loyalty, is another distinguishing feature of this market structure. Industries that fall into this category include fast-food restaurants, soft drinks, and cosmetics, to name just a few.

Oligopoly

The textbook definition of an **oligopoly** is that it is an industry that consists of a few firms producing a standardized or a differentiated product. The word "few" in this context is a bit slippery. In fact, oligopolies are better described in terms of industrial concentration, which is the percentage of total industry output accounted for by the largest firms. Examples of oligopolistic industries include steel, automobiles, household appliances, telecommunications equipment, and so on.

The distinguishing feature of oligopoly is **strategic behavior**. Pricing, output, marketing, financing, research and development, and other decisions made by managers affect, and are affected by, the decisions made by managers of rival firms. In Chapters 9 and 10 we will examine some of the tools and techniques for analyzing strategic behavior.

An important feature of imperfectly competitive industries is the importance of non-price competition in the form of advertising expenditures to reinforce customer loyalty through product differentiation, which entails emphasizing real or perceived differences in a firm's product relative to those of rival firms. The goal is to carve out a market niche of loyal customers. Within its subset of total market demand, an individual firm may be able to exercise a degree of market power.

There is considerable variation across industries in terms of the resources devoted to advertising. Advertising generally serves one of two purposes. **Informative advertising** occurs when a firm attempts to boost sales by providing consumers with information about the physical attributes of its product. Informative advertising promotes competition by making it possible for consumers to make more informed choices. Informative advertising is used to announce modifications to existing products or the introduction of an entirely new product line. By contrast, **persuasive advertising** attempts to boost sales by creating an image that may have little or nothing to do with the product's physical characteristics, such as when a group of elegantly dressed socialites are shown drinking a particular brand of scotch.

Informative advertising may be positive or negative. *Positive advertising* extols the virtues of a firm's product by comparing it with products offered by rival firms, such as "our toothpaste brightens your smile better than other leading brands." *Negative advertising* emphasizes the less desirable aspects of a competitor's product, such as "their brand of laundry detergent leaves your wash looking dull." Negative advertising is frequently used by politicians to tear down their opponents to garner votes.

Sometimes an increase in the demand for a firm's product arising from its advertising expenditures comes at the expense of lost sales by competing firms. At other times, advertising expenditures by one firm increased demand for the output of the entire industry. The importance of advertising in some industries can be seen in Table 7.2, which summarizes advertising expenditures in 2007 as a percentage of sales for 28 of the top 200 industries in this category.

Table 7.2   Industry Advertising to Sales Ratios (2007)

Industry	*Advertising/Sales*
Transportation services	0.169
Distilled and blended liquor	0.157
Perfumes, cosmetics, toiletries	0.137
Rubber and plastic footwear	0.119
Book publishing and printing	0.117
Educational services	0.113
Games, toys and children's vehicles	0.107
Dolls and stuffed toys	0.102
Food and related products	0.100
Communications services	0.085
Motion pictures, video tape production	0.084
Cable and other pay TV services	0.074
Radio broadcasting stations	0.059
Chemicals and allied products	0.057
Sporting goods	0.056
Apparel	0.051
Amusement and recreation services	0.048
Computer peripherals	0.029
Motor vehicles and car bodies	0.025
Advertising	0.011
Computers and office equipment	0.007
Farm machinery and equipment	0.007
Business services	0.004
Hospital and medical services plans	0.004
Metal mining	0.004
Computer storage devices	0.003
Construction machinery and equipment	0.002
Drugs and proprietary—wholesale	0.000

Source: Industry estimates.

Monopoly

A **monopoly** is an industry that consists of a single firm that produces a unique product with no close substitutes. Entry by new firms is assumed to be impossible (otherwise it would cease to be a monopoly). Since the output of a single firm is the output for the entire industry, monopolies exercise a considerable degree of market power. Increasing or decreasing output shifts the industry supply curve to the right or left, which raises or lowers price. Unlike perfectly competitive firms, which are described as price takers, monopolies are referred to as **price makers**. Examples of monopolies include public utilities and companies that enjoy patent protection for some of their products, such as pharmaceutical companies.

INDUSTRIAL CONCENTRATION

The industry types discussed in the above paragraphs lie along a competitive continuum. At one extreme where business rivalry is most intense is perfect competition. At the other extreme is a pure monopoly, which has no competitors. In between are the two intermediate cases of imperfect competition—monopolistic competition (which somewhat less competitive than perfect competition) and oligopoly (which is less competitive than monopolistic competition). The intensity of business competition tends to reflect the degree of **industrial concentration**, which refers to the proportion of total industry sales that is accounted for by the largest firms. Industrial concentration in perfectly competitive industries is low because total output is diffused across a very large number of small firms. In the case of monopoly, total industry output is accounted for by a single firm. Intermediate cases of industrial concentration include monopolistic competition and oligopoly.

Industrial concentration can be an important source of market power and profits. As a general rule, the larger a firm's share of the market, the greater its ability to charge a price that is above marginal cost to earn above-normal rates of return. The most profitable firms tend to be those that dominate its industry. When we think of the most successful U.S. commercial aircraft industry, for example, The Boeing Company immediately comes to mind. J. P. Morgan Chase, Bank of America, and Citibank are the largest and among the most profitable U.S. bank holding companies. Industry leaders Exxon Mobil and Chevron rank among the world's most profitable oil and gas companies. Microsoft and Oracle dominate with the computer software industry.

Concentration Ratios

The two most commonly used measures of industrial concentration are the various concentration ratios and the Herfindahl-Hirschman Index, both of which are published Census Bureau of the U.S. Department of Commerce, which can be readily accessed on the Internet. **Concentration ratios** measure the percentage of total industry sales accounted for by the largest n firms, that is

$$C_n = \omega_1 + \omega_2 + \cdots + \omega_n, \qquad (7.1)$$

where $\omega_i = 100(S_i/S_T)$, S_i the sales of the ith firm, and S_T the sales for the entire industry. The U.S. Census Bureau calculates concentration ratios for the largest 4, 8, 20, and 50 companies in an industry. Industries with a large number of small firms have concentration ratios are closer to zero percent, which indicates low concentration. Industries that are dominated by a few very large firms have concentration ratios closer to 100 percent. Table 7.3 summarizes the 4-firm concentration ratios (CR) and Herfindahl-Hirschman indices (HHI) for 32 industries in the Unites States in 1992 according to their four-digit Standard Industrial Classification (SIC) code.[1] A four digit number assigned to identify a business based on the type of business or trade and manufacturing.

Another problem with concentration ratios is that they are sensitive to how narrowly an industry is defined. Concentration ratios are calculated using standard industrial classifications published by the U.S. Department of Commerce, which are based on the similarity of production processes. These classification, however, ignore substitutability across products, such as glass versus plastic containers, which have a high **cross-price elasticity of demand**.

Still another problem is that U.S. census data used to calculate concentration ratios are based on domestically produced goods and do not include import competing products. Table 7.3 indicates, for example, that the eight largest motor vehicles and car bodies companies account for 84 percent of industry output. This statistic clearly overstates the actual market share of U.S. automobile companies when foreign automobile manufacturers are included.

Finally, concentration ratios are calculated using national statistics. As such, they ignore the regional distribution of industry sales. Suppose, for example, that an industry has a 4-firm concentration ratio of 0.5, which suggests that the industry is not highly concentrated. But, suppose that these firms sell their products in different parts of the country. Regionally, this industry may be highly concentrated, but this fact is masked by the 4-firm concentration ratio that is calculated using national data.

SOLVED EXERCISE

An industry consists of 10 firms. The first two firms have sales of $5 million each, the next two firms have sales of $3 million each, and the remaining six

Table 7.3   Measures of Industrial Concentration (1992)

SIC	Industry	Number of Firms	Value of Shipments ($million)	4-Firm CR (percent)	HHI (percent)
2021	Creamery butter	31	1,034	49	874
2024	Ice cream and frozen desserts	411	5,291	24	293
2037	Frozen fruits and vegetables	182	7,528	28	313
2041	Flour and grain mill products	230	6,294	56	972
2043	Cereal breakfast foods	42	9,799	85'	2,253
2046	Wet corn milling	28	7,045	73	1,521
2047	Dog and cat food	102	7,024	58	1,229
2273	Carpets and rugs	383	9,831	40	854
2296	Tire cord and fabrics	12	976	75	2,682'
2411	Logging	12,985	13,879	19'	158'
2511	Wood household furniture	2,636	8,743	20'	167 '
2731	Book publishing	2,504	16,753	23	251
2771	Greeting cards	157	4,196	84'	2,922'
2812	Alkalis and chlorine	34	2,787	75	1,994
2833	Medicines and botanicals	208	6,439	76	2,999'
2841	Soap and other detergents	635	14,762	63	1,584
2911	Petroleum refining	131	136,579	30	414
3221	Glass containers	16	4,860	84'	2,162
3274	Lime	57	904	46	693
3312	Blast furnaces and steel mills	135	16,565	37	551
3334	Primary aluminum	30	5,849	59	1,456
3411	Metal cans	132	12,112	56	1,042
3484	Small arms	177	1,384	43	679
3511	Turbines and turbine generators	64	5,843	79	2,549
3562	Ball and roller bearings	123	4,290	51	852
3565	Packaging machinery	590	3,127	16 '	154'
3581	Automatic vending machines	105	816	52	844
3641	Electric lamps	76	3,001	86'	2,702'
3711	Motor vehicles and car bodies	398	151,712	84	2,676
3823	Process control instruments	822	6,469	27	256
3931	Musical instruments	437	982	25	304
3993	Signs and advertising specialties	4,468	5,424	6'	24'

Source: Concentration ratios in manufacturing, *1992 Census of Manufacturers Report MC92-S-2*, Washington, DC: U.S. Department of Commerce, Economics and Statistics Administration, Bureau of the Census, 1997.

firms have sales of $2 million each. Calculate the 4-firm and 8-firm concentration ratios for this industry.

Solution

Total industry sales are S_T = $28 million. From Eq. (7.1), C_4 = 18 + 18 + 11 + 11 = 58 percent and C_8 = 18 + 18 + 11 + 11 + 7 + 7 + 7 + 7 = 86 percent. The largest eight firms account for 58 percent of total industry sales. The largest eight firms account for 86 percent of total industry sales.

Herfindahl-Hirschman Index

An alternative measure of industrial concentration is the **Herfindahl-Hirschman Index** (HHI), which is calculated as

$$HHI = \omega_1^2 + \omega_2^2 + \cdots + \omega_n^2, \qquad (7.2)$$

where n is the total number of firms in the industry and ω_i is firm i's percent share of total industry. HHI is superior to concentration ratios because it used data for the entire industry instead of just a few large firms. Moreover, by squaring individual market shares, HHI assigns a greater weight to larger firms. The Herfindahl-Hirschman Index ranges in value from zero to 10,000. An HHI close to zero is typical of an industry consisting of a very a large number of very small firms that is not very concentrated. By contrast, an HHI of 10,000 is an industry consisting of a single firm. Unfortunately, HHI suffers from many of the same shortcomings as concentration ratios since it is also calculated using U.S. census data.

While HHI is a better measure of industrial concentration, it suffers from the other shortcomings of concentration ratios. Both measures are sensitive to how broadly or how narrowly industries are classified. Since both measures ignore domestic penetration by foreign firms they tend to overstate the degree of industrial concentration. Lastly, both measures are calculated using data for the entire country and tell us nothing about the degree of local and regional industrial concentration.

The practical significance of the HHI stems from its role in the enforcement of U.S. antitrust legislation. The belief that increased industrial concentration was detrimental to consumers was initially addressed in the U.S. with the passage of the Clayton Act (1914). This legislation proscribed several business practices that "substantially lessen competition in an industry." The Clayton Act also gave the U.S. Department of Justice (DOJ) the authority to monitor and, if necessary, prohibit **horizontal integration** (the merger of two or more firms from the same industry producing near or perfect substitutes). The Celler-Kefauver Act (1950) closed this loophole by extending this mandate to include **vertical integration** (the merger of upstream and downstream firms in the **supply chain**) and **conglomerate mergers** (the merger of two or more firms from different supply chains).

Although the Clayton and Celler-Kefauver Acts gave the federal government the authority to take legal action to block mergers, it was not until 1968 that the Antitrust Division of DOJ published guidelines to reduce uncertainty about proposed mergers that it found unacceptable. Until then, firms might devote substantial financial resources to structure a merger, only to have these efforts undermined by a DOJ lawsuit. Initially, these guidelines specified that if an industry's 4-firm concentration ratio was equal to or greater than 75 percent, the merger of a firm with a 15 percent or more market share with another firm controlling as little as 1 percent market share would be challenged in the courts. These guidelines, which were amended in 1984, replaced the 4-firm concentration ratio with the Herfindahl-Hirschman Index.

According to the revised guidelines, a proposed merger between two firms in an industry with a HHI of 1,000 or less will not be challenged since it is not a threat to social welfare. If HHI is between 1,000 and 1,800, proposed mergers within the same industry will be reviewed if the resulting index rises by more than 100 points. Finally, an industry with an HHI greater than 1,800 would be considered highly concentrated. In this case, proposed mergers that raise the index by more than 50 points will be challenged. A recent example of this was the proposed takeover of T-Mobile by the American Telephone and Telegraph Company (AT&T).

In March, 2011, AT&T announced its intention to acquire T-Mobile, the American subsidiary of T-Mobile International AG, a division of Deutsche Telekom. The following August, the DOJ filed a lawsuit in federal court to block the proposed merger. In November, the Federal Communication Commission announced that it opposed the proposed $39 billion takeover on the grounds that it was not in the public interest. Less than a month later, AT&T withdrew its tender offer and would write off $4 billion in the current quarter to cover breakup fees owed to T-Mobile's parent company. Had the proposed merger been approved, it would have catapulted AT&T, the second-largest mobile phone provider in the U.S., into the number one spot, ahead of industry leader Verizon Wireless.

DOJ opposition to the proposed merger came as no surprise. From the beginning, the takeover faced a storm of criticism from smaller wireless network competitors. More importantly, the DOJ found that the merger would have raised the Herfindahl-Hirschman Index by 368 points to 3,216—well above the trigger of 50 and 1,800 required for DOJ review under the revised antitrust guidelines. According to the DOJ complaint, AT&T and T-Mobile competed in 97 of the nation's largest 100 consumer markets. They also competed nationwide for business and government customers. AT&T's acquisition of T-Mobile would result in higher prices, poorer quality services, fewer choices and fewer innovative products for the millions of American consumers who rely on mobile wireless services.

SOLVED EXERCISE

Two industries consist of 10 firms. Both industries have total sales of $28 million. The two largest firms in industry A have sales of $5 million, the next two firms have sales of $3 million, and the remaining six firms have sales of $2 million. In industry B, the largest firm has sales of $10 million, the next two firms have sales of $4 million each, the next three firms have sales of $2 million each, and the remaining four firms have sales of $1 million each. Based on the Herfindahl-Hirschman Index, which industry is more concentrated?

Solution

From Eq. (7.2), $HHI_A = 2(18)^2 + 2(11)^2 + 6(7)^2 = 1,184$ and $HHI_B = (36)^2 + 2(14)^2 + 3(7)^2 + 4(3.5)^2 = 1,184$. Industry B is more concentrated than industry A because the largest firm in industry B accounts for 36 percent of total industry sales, whereas the largest firm industry A accounts for just 18 percent.

MARKET POWER AND PRICING

The greater a firm's market power, the greater is its ability to charge a price greater than marginal cost to earn positive economic profits in the long run. Large firms have market power because they account for a significant portion of total industry output. Such firms are said to be "price makers." By contrast, perfectly competitive firms that produce a homogeneous product lack market power because their contribution to industry supply is small. Since price is not a decision variable, these firms are said to be **price takers**.

Lerner Index

A measure of a firm's ability to charge above marginal cost is the **Lerner Index**, which is given by equation

$$L = \frac{P - MC}{P} = -\frac{1}{\varepsilon_{x,\,x}}. \tag{7.3}$$

Rearranging Eq. (7.3) we obtain

$$P = \left(\frac{1}{1-L}\right)MC = \left(\frac{\varepsilon_{x,x}}{1+\varepsilon_{x,x}}\right)MC. \tag{7.4}$$

The terms $1/(1-L)$ and $\varepsilon_{x,x}/(1+\varepsilon_{x,x})$ in Eq. (7.4) are referred to as the firm's mark-up factor. A firm in a perfectly competitive industry has no market power since the demand for its product is infinitely elastic ($\varepsilon_{x,x} = -\infty$). To maximize profit, it sets price, which is the firm's marginal revenue, equal to marginal cost. In this case, the Lerner index is equal to zero and the mark-up factor is equal to 1. By contrast, a firm with market power will only produce along the elastic portion of the demand curve for its product (why?). Thus, the value of the Lerner index for a profit-maximizing firm with market power must lie in the internal $0 < L \leq 1$. Thus, the value of the Lerner index lies between zero and unity. For example, if the price elasticity of demand for a firm's product is $\varepsilon_{x,x} = -2$, the corresponding Lerner index is 0.5. In this case, a profit-maximizing firm will mark up its price by 50 percent over marginal cost.

SOLVED EXERCISE

Suppose that the demand equation for the product sold by a monopolist is

$$P(Q) = 12 - 7Q. \tag{7.5}$$

The total cost equation is

$$TC(Q) = 100 + 4Q + Q^2. \tag{7.6}$$

a. *Calculate the Lerner Index and the price elasticity of demand.*
b. *What is the firm's mark-up factor?*

Solution

a. *The firm's marginal revenue equation is*

$$MR(Q) = 12 - 14Q. \tag{7.7}$$

Equating marginal cost with marginal revenue, the profit-maximizing level of output is 0.5 units of output. At this level of output, P = \$8.50 and MC = 5. From Eq. (7.4), L = 0.41 and $\varepsilon_{x,x} = -1/0.41 = -2.43$ (price elastic).
b. *This firm's mark-up factor is*

$$\frac{1}{1-L} = \frac{1}{1-0.41} = 1.69. \tag{7.8}$$

This firm will charge a price that is 69 percent greater than its marginal cost.

Rothschild Index

Another useful indicator of market power is the **Rothschild Index**, which measures the demand sensitivity of a change in the price of the output of an entire industry relative to that for an individual firm. The Rothschild Index is the ratio of the **price elasticity of demand** for the output of an entire industry (ε_i) to the price elasticity of demand for the output of an individual firm (ε_f), that is

$$R = \frac{\varepsilon_i}{\varepsilon_f}. \tag{7.9}$$

Since the price elasticity of demand for output of the entire industry is less than or equal to the price elasticity of demand for the output of an individual firm, the Rothschild Index varies between zero and one. In the case of a monopoly, the price elasticity of demand for the product of the firm and industry are the same $(\varepsilon_i = \varepsilon_f)$ in which case the Rothschild Index is equal to one. At the other extreme is the demand for the product of a perfectly competitive firm, which is infinitely elastic $(\varepsilon_f = -\infty)$. In this case, the Rothschild Index equals zero.

SOLVED EXERCISE

Suppose that the price elasticity of demand for the output of an individual firm is −4 while the price elasticity of demand for the output of the entire industry is −2.

a. *Calculate the Rothschild index for this industry.*
b. *What is the relative impact on firm and industry sales from a 10 percent increase in price?*

Solution

a. *From Eq. (7.14), the Rothschild Index for this industry is R = 0.5.*
b. *A 10 percent increase in price will reduce industry demand by 20 percent, whereas demand for the output of the firm declines by 40 percent. The change in demand for the output of the entire industry is half as sensitive as that for the firm.*

PROFITABILITY

It is tempting to conclude that companies in highly concentrated industries earn significantly higher rates of return. In fact, this is not always the case. A cursory examination of the data in Table 7.4, which summarizes the profits of selected U.S. companies as a percent of total returns, total assets, and shareholder equity in 2011, suggests that the correlation between a company's profit

Table 7.4 Selected Company Ratios of Returns on Revenues, Assets, and Equity (2011)

Company	Industry	Return on Revenues	Return on Assets	Return on Equity
Ford	Automotive	0.148	0.109	1.070
GlaxoSmithKline	Pharmaceuticals	0.199	0.137	0.789
IBM	Computers	0.148	0.137	0.732
Boeing	Aerospace	0.058	0.048	0.523
McDonald's	Restaurants	0.204	0.163	0.396
Apple	Consumer electronics	0.267	0.237	0.353
Dell	Computer hardware	0.056	0.077	0.342
Unilever	Consumer goods	0.099	0.101	0.335
PepsiCo	Beverages	0.097	0.087	0.299
Microsoft	Computer software	0.230	0.139	0.247
ExxonMobil	Oil and gas	0.084	0.122	0.238
General Mills	Food processing	0.095	0.069	0.221
Home Depot	Retailing	0.055	0.093	0.219
Time Warner Cable	Mass media	0.085	0.033	0.219
Raytheon	Aerospace	0.075	0.073	0.202
Wal-Mart	Retailing	0.035	0.076	0.200
United Technologies	Conglomerate	0.086	0.054	0.191
Panera Bread	Restaurants	0.075	0.113	0.173
Procter & Gamble	Consumer goods	0.125	0.077	0.162
Anheuser-Busch	Beverages	0.150	0.052	0.156
Cisco Systems	Telecom. Equipment	0.175	0.087	0.153
Johnson & Johnson	Pharmaceuticals	0.149	0.081	0.152
Walt Disney	Mass media	0.134	0.076	0.135
Pfizer	Pharmaceuticals	0.148	0.055	0.122
Merck	Pharmaceuticals	0.131	0.059	0.119
Dow Chemical	Chemicals	0.040	0.035	0.096
Comcast	Mass media	0.074	0.026	0.084
Coca-Cola	Beverages	0.187	0.027	0.069
Citigroup	Financial services	0.108	0.001	0.059
AT&T	Telecommunications	0.031	0.015	0.039
Macy's	Retailing	0.024	0.007	0.026
Verizon	Telecommunications	0.022	0.010	0.026
Bank of America	Financial services	0.007	0.000	0.004

Source: Annual reports.

and the degree of industrial concentration is not tight. The Ford Motor Company, for example, recorded rates of return on revenues, assets, and shareholder equity of 15, 11, and 107 percent, respectively. This is seemingly consistent with a Herfindahl-Hirschman Index (in parentheses) for the U.S. automobile industry in 2002 was 2,754. By contrast, the rates of return on revenues, assets, and shareholder equity for Verizon Communications were a mere 2, 1, and 3 percent, respectively, in spite of the fact that the HHI for this industry was 2,873. At the other extreme is PepsiCo, exhibited admirable rates of return on revenues, assets, and shareholder equity for 10, 9, and 30 percent, respectively. Yet, the HHI for the soft drink industry was a mere 710. Although industrial

concentration may be important is explaining a firm's ability to price its product above marginal cost to earn above-normal rates of return, clearly there may
be other factors that can positively impact a firm's bottom line.

Variations in Profits Across Firms and Industries

In market economies, price changes signal resource owners and entrepreneurs
where goods and services are in greatest demand by society. This would suggest that risk-adjusted rates of return tend to be equal across industries and
among firms. Established industries, such as food production, chemicals and
basic metals generate a lower rate of return on assets than the pharmaceuticals
and telecommunications, aerospace and defense, and healthcare industries.
There are several theories that help to explain these differences.

Frictional Theory of Profit

According to the *frictional theory of profit*, differences in risk-adjusted rates of
return depend on whether the industry is in short-run or long-run competitive
equilibrium. A firm is in short-run competitive equilibrium if it earns above or
below normal rates of return. If firms are earning positive economic profits then
new firms enter the industry, which increases output, lowers prices and will
eventually squeeze profit margins. On the other hand, if the industry is earning
below normal rates of return, some investors will liquidate their holdings and
search for a better rate of return. As firms exit the industry, total output declines,
prices rise, and profits recover to more normal levels. An industry is said to be
in long-run competitive equilibrium when firms are just earning a normal rate
of return. When this occurs, investors will have neither an incentive to enter
or exit the industry. In this case, output levels and prices are relatively stable.

   In fact, industries are rarely in long-run competitive equilibrium because of
recurring supply-side and demand-side disturbances. Supply-side shocks may
occur when the development of a new production technology reduces a firm's
operating costs or when an increase in energy prices, such as might occur
when the Organization of Petroleum Exporting Countries (OPEC) reduces
production quotas, which has the opposite effect. Demand-side shocks may
result from the introduction of new products, such as when Apple introduced
its iPad, or from shifting consumer tastes and preferences.

Risk-Bearing Theory of Profit

The *risk-bearing theory of profit* suggests that above-normal profits are
required to attract productive resources into industries with above-average
risk, such as pharmaceuticals, and petroleum exploration. This line of reasoning is analogous to the idea that the rate of return on corporate equities

should be higher than that for corporate bonds in to compensate investors for the increased uncertainty associated with the returns on these financial assets.

Sometimes a firm will earn above-normal profits because it is in a position to exercise market power, which is the ability to influence the market-determined price of its product. As we have seen, a firm's market power may be positively related to its share of industry sales. If a firm has many competitors with each having about the same market share then its market power will be proportionately reduced. Any attempt to increase price in the face of stiff competition would result in a significant decline in sales. At the other extreme, a monopolist, which is the sole supplier of that good or service that has no close substitutes, has considerable discretion over its selling price. As we will explore in Chapter 8, there are several sources of monopoly power, including **government franchises**, patent protection, economies of scale, and control over an essential factor of production.

Marginal Efficiency Theory of Profit

An extension to the competitive theory of firm behavior is the *marginal efficiency theory of profit*. According to this theory, a firm's ability to extract above-normal profits in the long run may be due to its ability to produce more efficiently than its rivals. Perhaps the firm has proprietary access to superior production technology or uses more cost-effective management techniques. If this results in economies of scale then a firm may emerge as a natural monopoly, which will be discussed in the next chapter.

Innovation Theory of Profit

The *innovation theory of profit* postulates that a firm's ability to generate above-normal rates of return is the result of being the first to market a new product or technology. Steve Jobs, the founder of Apple Inc., became a multimillionaire by pioneering the desktop, personal computer. In 2010, Apple surpassed software giant Microsoft as the world's largest technology company in terms market capitalization—second only to ExxonMobil as the largest company in the United States—through such market innovations as the iPhone, iPod and iPad. Historically, above-normal profits due to product innovation have proven to be short lived as they tend to invite a host of imitators.

OTHER CRITERIA FOR CLASSIFYING INDUSTRIES

It should not be surprising that industrial concentration, market power and profitability are the most frequently used criteria for judging the social desirability of alternative market structures. This is because the behavior of firms in highly concentrated industries is frequently, and justifiably, interpreted as being antithetical to the best interests of consumers who pay higher prices for less variety of goods and services than is typically the case with more competitive market structures.

Although industrial concentration and market power are important organizing criteria, especially for public-policy purposes, they are not the only criteria that may be used for classifying industries. Depending on its ultimate application, other criteria for classifying industries include similarity of production technologies, the nature of market demand, degree of industrial integration, importance of research and development, level of advertising, and the contribution of an industry to overall social welfare.

Production Technology

Some industries are noteworthy in terms of the composition of the inputs used in the production process. Industries that use a great deal of labor relative to capital and other factors of production are said to be *labor intensive*. This is typical of the textile and footwear industries where highly specialized skills are not generally required. Industries that require relatively large amounts of investment in plant, equipment, machinery, research and development, are described as *capital intensive*. Examples of capital intensive industries include petroleum exploration, development and refining, computers, telecommunications, aerospace and automobile industries.

Firms in industries that are similar in terms of factor intensity, or which have access to similar or standardized production technologies, will have similar cost structures. Such firms are not likely to enjoy a competitive advantage in the market place. If a firm does have a competitive edge, it must come from some other source, such as proprietary access to a superior production technology that enables it to produce at lower per-unit cost. If this competitive advantage is significant and sustainable, the firm may eventually come to dominate the industry.

Nature of Market Demand

The structure of an industry may also reflect market demand. Industries that produce goods and services for which consumer demand is relatively thin may only be able to support a few, relatively small, firms. By contrast, when consumer demand is robust and no single firm enjoys a competitive advantage, a large number of firms may be required.

Another factor that may determine the structure of an industry has is the ease with which consumers are able to acquire information about price and other details of a particular good or service. An individual shopping for a vacation package to Disney World need only have access to a personal computer with an Internet connection to such travel websites as Expedia, Travelocity, and Orbitz. Since product information is easy to obtain, price differentials will be small or nonexistent, and not generally subject to negotiation. For the managers of firms in which product information is easy to obtain, formulating optimal pricing strategies is a relatively simple and straightforward affair.

At the other extreme, suppose that one side of a transaction has more or better information about the good or service than the other side. This problem of **asymmetric information** gives rise to several problems. Consider the situation in which a buyer is in the market for a used car. Only the seller knows whether the used car is "lemon" or a "plum." For the transaction to take place, the buyer must first incur transaction costs to determine the quality of the used car. Once this is done, a transaction price must be negotiated. If the cost to the buyer of acquiring information about the quality of the used car is too high, the transaction may not take place.

In some cases it is the buyer, and not the seller, that enjoys the benefits of asymmetric information. A classic example of this is the sale of automobile insurance. In this case, only the buyer of automobile insurance knows if he or she is a safe driver. The challenge confronting the seller of automobile insurance is to distinguish between high-risk and low-risk drivers before determining optimal premium and deductible payments.

Another way to distinguish between industries is the price elasticity of demand. Some industries produce goods or services that are relatively insensitive to price changes, such as the demand transportation, food, pharmaceuticals, and clothing. By contrast, the demand for other goods and services, such as restaurant meals and foreign travel, are quite sensitive to price fluctuations. These differences can have a profound effect on a firm's pricing strategy.

To further complicate matters, firms in a given industry may produce several versions of the same product. In the soft drink industry, for example, Coca-Cola and Pepsi Cola are close, but not perfect substitutes. While producers of Dr. Pepper and Seven Up compete for the same soft drink dollar, these products are not close substitutes. Another example is Toyota and Ford. Both produce automobiles, but each has a loyal customer base.

Degree of Industrial Integration

Another way to explain the structure of an industry is in terms of the number of stand-alone businesses that have been brought under one roof, a process known as *industrial integration*. Some industries are more conducive to integration than others, and there are several ways of accomplishing this, including friendly mergers and hostile takeovers.

The reasons why different businesses are brought together are many and varied. A firm may become the target of a hostile takeover when its market value is depressed because of mismanagement. When this occurs, corporate raiders will attempt to wrest control of the business, after which a management team is installed to increase earnings and shareholder value. Alternatively, integration can occur at the time of the firm's inception.

Business mergers can take several forms, including horizontal integration, vertical integration, and by forming a conglomerate. Managers of large and diversified businesses may enjoy several competitive advantages, including lower transaction costs, economies of scale, increased market power, the ability to extract supplier discounts, access to low-cost capital financing, and so on.

Vertical Integration

Vertical integration, which was discussed at length in the previous chapter, refers to the merger of one or more links in the same supply chain. A computer manufacturer that also produces silicon that is used to produce microprocessors, which are then to produce computers, is an example of a vertically integrated business. Producing inputs internally reduces transaction costs by eliminating the middleman. It also mitigates or eliminates the problem of **opportunism**. The main disadvantage of vertical integration is that the firm sacrifices cost efficiencies by diverting resources away from its core activities.

Horizontal Integration

Horizontal integration refers to the side-to-side combination of one or more competing firms producing near or perfect substitutes. In other words, horizontal integration involves merging two or more firms that occupy the same line in the supply chain. A merger between, say, Dell and Gateway into a single personal computer company would constitute a horizontal merger. The benefits of a horizontal merger come from economies of scale and scope, and from increased market power. On the flip side, consumers may be made worse off from an increase in industrial concentration.

Diversification

A conglomerate merger combines two or more firms from unrelated industries. A series of mergers in the 1960s transformed American Can Company into a multiproduct **conglomerate** selling containers, clothing and financial services.[2] In the 1970s and 1980s, the American tobacco company Phillip Morris bought 7-Up, General Foods, and Kraft.

It is difficult to generalize the benefits of diversification. In addition to lower **transaction costs** from economies of scale and scope, diversification may make it possible for firm to practice **cross subsidization** or smooth its cash flows by merging countercyclical product lines. This makes it easier and less expensive for a division to obtain working capital during periods of slack demand. Conglomerate mergers also suffer from many of the same weaknesses as vertical mergers in that resources may be diverted away from the firm's core activities. This can be especially problematic if specialized managerial talent is in short supply.

Research and Development

Research and development (R&D) is the creation of new knowledge and its practical applications. It was once believed that technological progress and product innovation was a by-product of a highly competitive business environment. Barriers to entry that shielded highly concentrated industries from intense competition resulted in lackluster product development. This belief underwent a serious reevaluation following the publication of the seminal works of Joseph A. Schumpeter (1942) and John Kenneth Galbraith (1952) who argued that industrial concentration was a wellspring of technological change. The reason for this was that only large firms possessed the resources to invest in significant amounts of research and development. While this argument is supported by empirical evidence, R&D expenditures also reflect the level of technology that characterizes an industry's output.

The Organization of Economic Cooperation and Development (OECD, 1999, 2001) classify technological intensity according to an industry's R&D expenditures as a percentage of the value of total production. High-tech industries such as aerospace (12.7 percent) and pharmaceuticals (11.3 percent) devote significantly more resources to R&D than do medium-high technology industries, such as electrical machinery and apparatus (3.8 percent) and motor vehicles (3.5) percent. Medium-low technology industries, such as rubber and plastic products (0.9 percent) and basic metals (0.7 percent) spend only marginally more on R&D than do such low-technology industries as food products, tobacco and beverages (0.4 percent) and textiles, textile products, leather, and footwear (0.3 percent).

CHAPTER EXERCISES

7.1 In what way is the Herfindahl-Hirschman Index is superior to concentration ratios? How does the U.S. Justice Department use the Herfindahl-Hirschman Index to monitor suspected violations of antitrust legislation?

7.2 Consider an industry that consists of 12 firms. Total annual sales of the largest firm are $10 million. Total annual sales of the next three firms average $7.5 million each. Total annual sales of the next four firms in the industry average $2 million each. Finally, total annual sales of the remaining firms in the industry average $500 thousand. Calculate the 4-firm and 8-firm concentration ratios for this industry.

7.3 An industry consists of five firms with annual sales of $1.2 million, $250,000, $100,000, $75,000 and $50,000.

  a. Calculate the Herfindahl-Hirschman Index for this industry.

  b. Calculate the 4-firm concentration ratio for this industry.

  c. In your opinion, would the U.S. Justice Department approve a merger between the two largest firms in this industry? Explain.

  d. Would the U.S. Justice Department approve a merger between the third and the fourth largest firms? Explain.

7.4 The market-determined price of a product produced in a perfectly-competitive industry is $5. The total cost equation of a firm in that industry is

$$TC(Q) = 25 - 5Q + 0.5Q^2.$$

Calculate the Lerner Index and price elasticity of demand.

7.5 The inverse demand equation for the product sold by a monopolist is

$$P(Q) = 6 - Q.$$

The monopolist's total cost equation is

$$TC(Q) = 5 + 0.5Q^2.$$

Calculate the Lerner Index and price elasticity of demand?

7.6 The price elasticity of demand for the output of a firm is −2 and the price elasticity of demand for the output of the entire industry is −0.5.

  a. Calculate the Rothschild Index for this industry.

  b. Suppose that firm and industry prices increase by 5 percent. What is the relative impact on firm and industry sales?

NOTES

1. The Standard Industrial Classification (SIC) code is four digit industrial classification system prepared by the U.S. Census Bureau. First introduced in 1937, SIC codes are being replaced by North American Industry Classification System (NAICS) codes, which are six-digit numbers first published in 1997. Certain U.S. government agencies, however, still use SIC codes, including the U.S. Securities and Exchange Commission.

2. In 1986, the American Can Company divested itself of its packaging operations to become the financial conglomerate Primerica.

Chapter 8

Perfect Competition and Monopoly

In economics we assume that decision makers attempt to maximize some objective function subject to one or more binding constraints. In the theory of the firm, for example, we typically assume that managers maximize profit, or some other rational objective, such as maximizing market share, subject to a given operating budget and resources prices, market structure, and so on. In this chapter we will examine the market extremes of perfect competition and monopoly. In each case, we will begin with a brief review of the standard models of price and output setting behavior.

PERFECT COMPETITION

The necessary conditions for the existence of **perfect competition** are rarely encountered in the real world. The term perfect competition is used to describe a market consisting of a very large number of small firms producing an identical product in which entry into, and exit from, the industry is unimpeded. Because its relative contribution to total industry supply is negligible, the ability of any individual firm to shift the market supply curve, thereby affecting the market-clearing price, is negligible. Since perfectly competitive firms lack **market power**, they are said to be **price takers**. Although the market demand curve is downward sloping, the demand for the output of an individual firm is perfectly elastic since it can produce and sell as much of its product at a constant price. The term perfect competition is somewhat of a misnomer since it implies a level of strategic interaction that does not exist.

Although rare, perfectly competitive industries do exist and can be found in markets for agricultural commodities, basic metals, foreign exchange, and financial securities. An analysis of this **market structure** is nonetheless important since it yields important insights into real world phenomena. As Milton Friedman (1962, p. 120) observed: "I have become increasingly impressed with how wide is the range of problems and industries for which it is appropriate to treat the economy as if it were competitive."

An important assumption about perfect competition is that all market participants possess complete and perfect information. Unlike imperfectly competitive markets, advertising and other marketing strategies designed to influence consumer purchases play no role since it is common knowledge that the products of perfectly competitive firms are identical. The only demand determinant that matters is price. Thus, individual firms that charge above the market-determined price will experience a total loss in sales as buyers shift to lower-price suppliers. Conversely, undercutting rival firms will result in an economic loss since perfectly competitive firms can sell everything they produce at the higher, market-clearing price.

Short-Run Perfectly Competitive Equilibrium

In the standard model of perfect competition, the collective output decisions of individual firms determine industry supply. The equilibrium price and quantity are determined at the intersection of the market demand and supply curves. Since a perfectly competitive firm cannot by itself affect the market-determined price of its product by shifting the supply curve, the total number of units produced is the manager's only decision variable.

To maximize profit, a perfectly competitive firm will produce up to the output level where marginal revenue equals marginal cost ($MR = MC$). Since a perfectly competitive firm does not have market power, marginal revenue equals the market-determined price ($MR = P$). Thus, the necessary condition for profit maximization in the short run is for a perfectly competitive firm to produce at an output level where price equals marginal cost ($P = MC$).

Figure 8.1 depicts a perfectly competitive firm that maximizes its short-run profit by producing Q_1 units of output where $P_1 = MC$. At output Q_1, the firm's total revenue ($TR = P_1 Q_1$) is given by the area of the rectangle $0P_1AQ_1$. The firm's total cost ($TC = ATC_1 Q_1$) is given by the area of the rectangle $0ATC_1BQ_1$. Since $TR > TC$, this firm earns an **economic profit** equal to the area of the shaded rectangle ATC_1P_1AB. In general, a firm will earn a positive economic profit whenever $P > ATC$.

The situation depicted in Figure 8.1 represents a short-run perfectly competitive equilibrium because above-normal rates of return will attract new firms and investment into the industry. As industry output increases, the market-clearing price will decline. This is depicted in Figure 8.2 as a shift to the right of the market supply curve from S_1 to S_2, which causes the

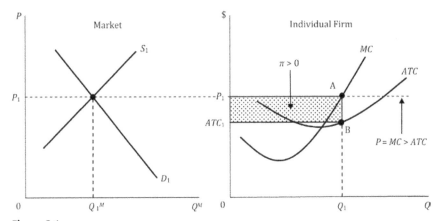

Figure 8.1

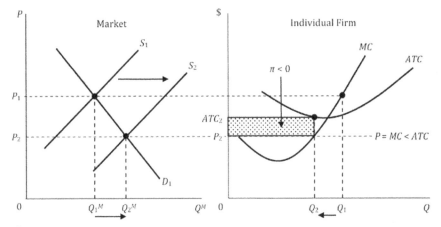

Figure 8.2

market-clearing price to fall from P_1 to P_2 and the market equilibrium quantity to increase from Q_1^M to Q_2^M.

The situation depicted in Figure 8.2 also represents a short-run perfectly competitive equilibrium because the decline in price resulting from the entrance of new firms into the industry has transformed economic profits for the typical firm into economic losses. The firm depicted in Figure 8.2 maximizes profit by producing Q_2 units of output where $P_2 = MC$. At this output level, total cost ($TC = ATC_2Q_2$) is greater than total revenue ($TR = P_2Q_2$). The resulting economic loss is given by shaded rectangle in Figure 8.2. Below-normal rates of return will cause some firms and investors to exit the industry. As industry supply declines, the market-clearing price rebounds. When will this adjustment process come to an end?

SOLVED EXERCISE

Suppose that the total cost equation of a perfectly competitive firm is

$$TC = 1,000 + 2Q + 0.01Q^2. \qquad (8.1)$$

If the market-determined price is $10, what is the firm's profit-maximizing level of output and profit?

Solution

From Eq. (8.1), the marginal cost equation is

$$MC = 2 + 0.02Q. \qquad (8.2)$$

For a perfectly competitive firm, P = MR. Equating marginal cost and price, the profit-maximizing level of output Q = 400 units. Total economic profit is $\pi = TR - TC = \$600$.

Economic Losses and Shutdown

Figure 8.2 depicts a typical firm in a perfectly competitive industry earning a below-normal rate of return. When this occurs, some firms will to exit the industry, which causes industry output to fall and the market-clearing price to rise. But, which will exit the industry—and why? To answer this question, consider the situation depicted in Figure 8.3, which replicates the right-hand side of Figure 8.2, but includes the firm's total variable cost curve.

A firm's decision to shut down depends on the relationship between the firm's economic loss and its total fixed cost. In Figure 8.3, the firm's economic loss is given by the area P_2ATC_2AB. If the firm shuts down, it is still obligated to pay its fixed costs. In Figure 8.3, the firm's total fixed cost ($TFC = AFC_2Q_2$) is given by the area AVC_2ATC_2AC. Since the firm's total fixed cost is greater than its economic loss, it will pay for the firm to continue to produce, at least until it is no longer obligated to pay these fixed costs.

Consider, for example, a firm that has fixed costs consisting primarily of lease rental payments on office space. The firm is obligated to pay rent regardless of whether the business is doing well or poorly. If the firm losses are less than these rental payments, the firm will continue to produce, or at least until the lease expires. Since the leases of all such firm's do not expire on the same date, some firm will shut down soon than later. In fact, the departure of some firms may make it possible for other firm to survive the shakeout in the industry resulting from initially low prices.

Another way to interpret the situation depicted in Figure 8.3 is to compare the firm's **operating profit** ($\pi_0 = TR - TVC$), which is given by the area AVC_2P_2BC, with its total fixed cost. Although this firm is earning a negative economic profit, it is earning a positive operating profit. Since this firm is able to pay at least a portion of its total fixed cost it will continue to operate in the short run.

Finally, suppose that the market clearing price falls to P_3 in Figure 8.4. In this case, the firm's operating loss equals its economic loss, in which case the firm

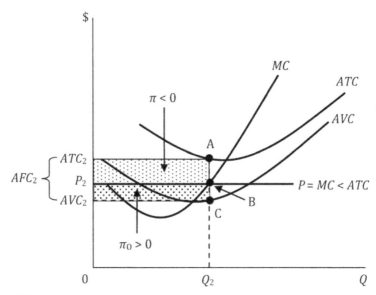

Figure 8.3

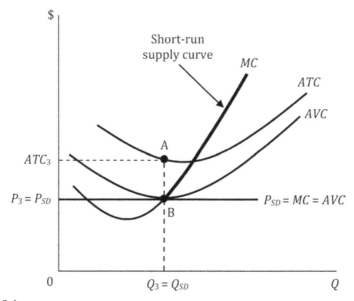

Figure 8.4

is indifferent between operating and shutting down. This is because the firm's economic loss and total fixed cost are the same. If it continues to operate, it will lose the area P_3ATC_3AB. If it shuts down, it will lose the same amount. One thing is certain. If the market-clearing price falls below P_3, the firm will shut down since its total fixed cost, which it is still obligated to pay, is less than its economic loss by continuing to operate. Alternatively, at the output level Q_3, this firm is earning zero operating profit, which means that the firm is just able to pay is variable costs. There is nothing left over to pay some of its fixed cost.

Although the firm depicted in Figure 8.4 is indifferent between continuing to operate and shutting down at a price of P_3, it most certainly will shut down if the price falls below P_3. For this reason, a price that is equal to a profit-maximizing firm's minimum average variable cost is called the firm's shut-down price (P_{SD}).

Figure 8.4 also allows us to define a perfectly competitive firm's short-run supply curve as that portion of its marginal cost curve that lies above its average variable cost curve. Recall that a profit-maximizing, perfectly competitive firm will produce where $P = MC$. As the market-clearing price rises above average variable cost, it traces out the firm's supply curve. As noted in Chapter 2, the market supply curve is the horizontal summation of the supply curves of the individual firms in an industry. In fact, the industry supply curve represents the industry's short-run marginal cost of production.

Long-Run Perfectly Competitive Equilibrium

Firms will continue to enter and exit a perfectly competitive industry until they earn zero economic profit. This occurs at the output level where the market-clearing price equals minimum average total cost. This is referred to as the firm's break-even level of output (Q_{BE}), which occurs at Q_3 in Figure 8.5.

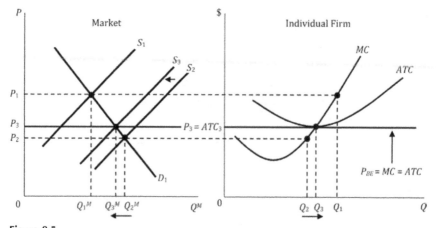

Figure 8.5

The corresponding price is called the break-even price (P_{BE}). At this output level, total revenue ($TR = P_3 Q_3$) equals total cost ($TC = ATC_3 Q_3$) resulting in zero economic profit ($\pi = 0$). Since the typical firm in this industry is just earning a normal rate of return, there is longer any incentive for new investment to flow into, or out of, the industry.

Optimal Plant Size

Our analysis of an industry's adjustment to long-run perfectly competitive equilibrium is almost complete. The situation depicted in Figure 8.5 constitutes a long-run competitive equilibrium provided that incumbent firms are firms operating at their **minimum efficient scale of production**, which was discussed in Chapter 4. If not, it will pay for a profit-maximizing firm experiencing economies of scale to expand its scale of operations until it minimizes its short-run and long-run per-unit costs. If this is not the case, it will be in the firm's best interest to expand or contract the scale of its operations until it is producing at point C in Figure 4.10.

This final situation is depicted in Figure 8.6. The lure of positive economic profits will attract new firms and investment into the industry causing output to increase, prices to fall, and profits to be squeezed. When firms are earning a negative economic profits, some firms will exit the industry or go out of business causing output to decline, prices to rise, and profits to recover. Only when firms of an optimal plant size are earning zero economic profits is there no longer any incentive for firms and investment to enter or exit the industry.

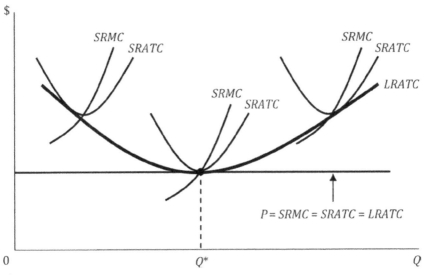

Figure 8.6

A firm is in long-run competitive equilibrium when it produces a level of output where the market clearing price not only equals short-run marginal cost (SRMC) and minimum short-run average total cost (SRATC), but equals minimum long-run average total cost (LRATC) as well.

SOLVED EXERCISE

Suppose that price charge by a perfectly competitive firm is $20, and its total cost equation is

$$TC = 125 + 4Q + 0.05Q^2. \tag{8.3}$$

a. *What is the firm's profit maximizing level of output?*
b. *What is the firm's average total cost?*
c. *Is this firm in short-run or long-run competitive equilibrium?*
d. *Suppose that an influx of new firms lowers the market-determined price from $20 to $9. What is average total cost? Is this firm in short-run or long-run competitive equilibrium?*

Solution

a. *From Eq. (8.3), the marginal cost equation is*

$$MC = 4 + 0.1Q. \tag{8.4}$$

   Since this firm is a price taker then P = MC = $20. Equating marginal revenue with marginal cost, the profit-maximizing level of output is Q = 160 units.
b. *Substituting Q = 160 into Eq. (8.3), the firm's total cost is TC = $2,045. Average total cost is ATC = $2,045/160 = $12.78.*
c. *Since P > ATC, this firm must be earning a positive economic profit. The firm's economic profit is π = $20(160) − $2,045 = $1.155. Since this firm is earning an above-normal rate of return, the firm must be in short-run competitive equilibrium.*
d. *Since firms are earning a positive economic profit, new firms will be attracted into this perfectly competitive industry, which will increase market supply and lower the product price to $9. Equating price to marginal cost, the new profit-maximizing level of output is Q = 50 units. Substituting, total cost is TC = $450. Average total cost is ATC = $450/50 = $9. Since P = ATC, the firm must be earning a zero economic profit, that is π = $9(50) − $450 = $0. Since this firm is earning zero economic profit (a normal rate of return), there is no incentive for incumbent firms to enter or exit the industry. The firm is in long-run competitive equilibrium.*

MONOPOLY

Perfectly competitive firms will not earn positive economic profits in the long run because unimpeded entry by new firms and investment into the industry will put downward pressure on price. Perfectly competitive firms will charge a price equal to marginal cost and earn zero economic profit. But, what if entry into an industry is blocked? How are the predictions of the standard model of perfect competition changed when and industry consists of a single firm? In this section we will review the standard model of monopoly, which in terms of the number of firms in an industry is the polar opposite of perfect competition.

A **monopoly** is an industry consisting of a single firm that produces a product for which there are no close substitutes. Unlike the output of an individual firm in a perfectly competitive industry, a monopolist's output is synonymous with industry supply. Changes in a monopolist's output will shift the supply curve, which will raise or lower the market-clearing price. For this reason, a monopolist can be described as a **price maker**.

The standard textbook treatment of a monopoly is depicted in Figure 8.7. Since the industry consists of a single firm, the demand for the output of a monopolist is the same thing as the downward-sloping market demand curve. As in the case of all profit-maximizing firms, a monopolist will produce up to the level of output where $MR = MC$. This occurs at point E. The corresponding output level Q^m constitutes the market supply. The monopoly price (P^m) is determined where market supply equals market demand. In the case depicted

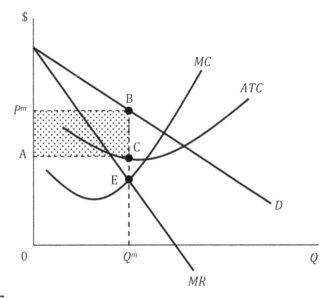

Figure 8.7

in Figure 8.7, price is greater than marginal cost, and the monopolist earns an economic profit equal to the area of shaded rectangle AP^mBC.

If entry into the industry is unimpeded, the existence of economic profits will attract new firms. The resulting increase in the number of close substitutes causes the demand curve for the output of any individual firm to become more elastic (flatter). As prices are pushed lower, the economic profits of individual firms will be squeezed. This process will continue until $P = ATC$ and firms earn zero economic profit, at which point there is no further incentive for new firms to enter the industry. By contrast, if entry by new firms is blocked, the monopolist's privileged position goes unchallenged and long-run positive economic profits become possible.

SOLVED EXERCISE

Suppose that the demand equation for the output of a monopolist is

$$Q = 3,000 - 60P. \tag{8.5}$$

The total cost equation is

$$TC = 100 + 5Q + \frac{Q^2}{480}. \tag{8.6}$$

a. *What are the profit-maximizing price and output?*
b. *What is the monopolist's profit? Is this industry in short- or long-run equilibrium?*

Solution

a. *The inverse demand equation is*

$$P = 50 - \frac{Q}{60}. \tag{8.7}$$

The firm's total revenue equation is

$$TR = \left(50 - \frac{Q}{60}\right)Q = 50Q - \frac{Q^2}{60}. \tag{8.8}$$

From Eq. (8.8), the marginal revenue equation is

$$MR = 50 - \frac{Q}{30}. \tag{8.9}$$

From Eq. (8.6), marginal cost is

$$MC = 5 + \frac{Q}{240}.$$
(8.10)

Total profit is maximized at the output level where MR = MC, that is Q* = 1,200 units. From Eq. (8.5) the monopolist will charge P* = \$30.

b. *The monopolist's profit at P* = \$30 and Q* = 1,200 is π* = TR − TC = \$26,900. Since the entry of new firms into the industry is impossible, this monopolist will continue to earn a positive economic profit. Unlike perfect or monopolistic competition, this industry is in long-run equilibrium because new firms cannot enter and compete away this profit.*

Sources of Monopoly Power

The standard model of monopoly assumes that entry by firms into the industry is blocked, in which case a monopolist can earn economic profits in the long run. There are several examples of entrepreneurs who earned significant economic profits because they were first to market a new good or service. In time, however, these profits were competed away as new firms entered the fray in search of above-normal rates of return. It should be clear that for a firm to continue to earn monopoly profits it must be possible to erect **barriers to entry** that impede or prevent new firms from entering the industry, thereby driving down prices and squeezing profits. In this section we will briefly review several barriers to entry, including government franchises, economies of scale, patents, control of scarce resources, and positive network externalities.

Government Franchise

An important source of monopoly power is when a firm is the exclusive beneficiary of a **government franchise**. Governments often impose restrictions on the entry of new firms into an industry to control market activity. In the fifteenth and sixteenth centuries, for example, governments of some maritime countries granted trading monopolies in exchange for a share of the profits.[1] A more contemporary example is the U.S. Postal Service, which has a monopoly on local mail delivery service. Other examples of government franchises in the private sector include state lotteries, cable television companies, such as Time Warner Cable and Cablevision, and public utilities, such as Consolidated Edison in New York City and Tucson Electric Power, which enjoy regional monopoly status.

In exchange for the exclusive franchise right to market a good or service, the government often retains the right to regulate prices and other activities. An argument in favor of publicly-franchised monopolies is that the government is acting in the best interests of consumers by discouraging behavior that would reduce **net social welfare**.

Natural Monopoly

Government franchised monopolies are sometimes justified on the basis of significant economies of scale. **Economies of scale** exist when a firm's per-unit cost of production declines with a proportional increase in the use of all factors of production. In the case of public utilities, it is more cost efficient for a single large firm to generate and distribute electricity than it is for multiple companies to satisfy market demand. Such a firm is referred to as **natural monopoly**. In principle, these cost savings are passed along to the consumer in the form of lower prices.

In exchange for a government franchise, public utilities are subject to price regulation. Fairness is another reason frequently cited in defense of government regulation. In many states, local telephone service is subject to regulation to ensure that low-income consumers have access to affordable service. Profits earned by telephone companies from its business customers are used to subsidize private household service, which is often priced below marginal cost.

A natural monopoly may also arise from **economies of scope**, which occur when the total cost of producing two or more goods together is less than producing these goods separately. Firms that enjoy economies of scale and scope tend to be larger than those that do not. Since larger firms are able to extract discounts from suppliers and are better able to obtain lower cost funding to finance capital expansion than to smaller firms, which may serve as an effective barrier to entry. In the extreme, economies of scale result in a natural monopoly.

Another explanation for the emergence of a natural monopoly is **cost complementarities**, which occur when the marginal cost of producing a good or service declines following an increase in the output of some other good or service. Firms that enjoy cost complementarities are able to produce to several goods at lower marginal cost than smaller firms that produce only one good, or which do not also enjoy cost complementarities. As with economies of scale and scope, firms that benefit from cost complementarities also tend to be larger and have bargaining power in financial markets. This may limit the ability of smaller firms to enter the industry.

Patents

A **patent** grants to an inventor the exclusive legal right to a product or process for a limited period of time. Contrary to popular belief, a patent does not confer the right to produce and market an invention. Rather, it a legal barrier to keep others from doing so.[2] In the United States, patent protection is granted by the U.S. Congress for a period of twenty years. Patent protection gives inventors with an incentive to invest in product research, development, and innovation. Without such protection, investors are less apt to incur the financial risks and development costs associated with bringing a new product to market. On the other hand, patent protection discourages competition, which leads to product innovation, more efficient production techniques, and lower prices. It is for these reasons that patents are not granted in perpetuity.

Arguments for and against patents have recently taken center-stage in the debate over the escalating cost of health care in the United States. Pharmaceutical companies have been granted thousands of patents for a wide range of prescription medicines. The resulting high prices place are a financial burden to low-income individuals, particularly the elderly, who rely upon government assistance. Proponents argue that high prices are necessary to compensate pharmaceutical companies for billions of dollars invested in research and development. In fact, some of these prescription medicines are never even brought to the market, or fail to receive approval from the U.S. Food and Drug Administration.

Lawsuits

Industry leaders have sought to protect their market position by filing expensive lawsuits against potential competitors claiming real or bogus patent or copyright infringement. Start-up companies typically need to get their products to market as quickly as possible to generate much needed cash inflows. Regardless of the merits of the lawsuit, cash strapped start-up companies are financially ill prepared to weather such legal challenges. In the end, small or start-up companies may be forced out of business, or may even be acquired by the monopolist.

Control of Essential Resources

Another barrier to entry is exclusive control of an essential raw material. The most famous example of this involved the Aluminum Company of America (Alcoa). In 1945, Alcoa owned or controlled nearly all of the world's known sources of bauxite. This gave Alcoa near total control over the downstream production of aluminum and led to one of the most famous antitrust cases in the post–World War II era. In the United States v. Alcoa, the Supreme Court ruled that Alcoa's control of over the raw ingot market was intended to thwart potential competition and ordered that that the company be broken up.

A contemporary example of a company's ability to keep prices high by controlling raw materials can be found in the global diamond trade. Although DeBeers Consolidated Mines, Ltd. of South Africa has a relatively small equity share of the global diamond market, it has been able to control the flow of most of the world's raw diamonds by means of a global diamond cartel. Unfortunately, high diamond prices have not only resulted in lower **consumer surplus** for jewelry buyers, but have led to serious geopolitical problems from trade in "blood diamonds."[3]

Positive Network Externalities

An interesting source of monopoly power is **positive network externalities**, also called **positive feedback effects**. As will be discussed in greater detail in Chapter 16, a **network** is any system of integrated interconnections sharing a common technical platform. An example of a network is that segment of the telecommunications industry that provides voice and data services using the Internet and the World Wide Web. The idea behind positive network externalities is that the benefits received by members increase exponentially with the number of members. The greater-than-proportional increase in a network's value serves a lure to new members. This viral-like growth creates a significant barrier to entry until a single dominant network emerges. An interesting example of positive network externalities is *Facebook*—the Internet social networking platform that allows its members to create an online nexus of interpersonal relationships. Launched in 2004 for use by Harvard University students, by 2011 *Facebook* had over 600 million subscribers.

Barriers to Entry

Barriers to entry do not guarantee that a monopolist will earn above-normal rates of return. Figure 8.8 depicts a situation in which a monopolist breaks even since $P^m = ATC$ at the profit maximizing level of output. For this monopolist to earn a positive economic profit, it is necessary to reduce cost or increase demand, perhaps by increasing its advertising expenditures.

It is even possible for a monopolist to incur an economic loss. This situation is illustrated by the shaded area in Figure 8.9. Unless it can reduce cost or

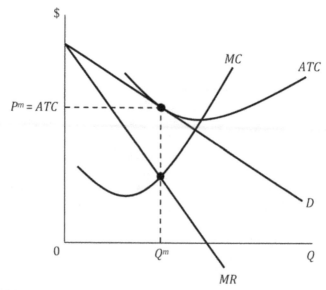

Figure 8.8

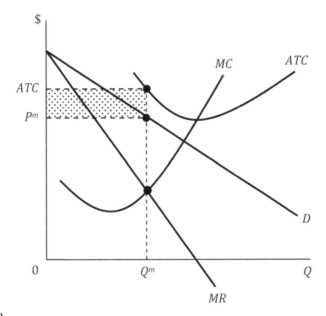

Figure 8.9

increase the demand, a monopolist will eventually shut down. In some cases, however, this may not be possible. Many public are monopolies that perennially run budget deficits. In 2009, New York City subway system, which is operated by the Metropolitan Transportation Authority (MTA), incurred a budget shortfall of $1.2 billion. A public transit system cannot simply go out of business. Since raising subway is politically unpopular, the MTA relies on public subsidies in the form of taxes and tolls from bridges and tunnels to keep the subway system running.

Welfare Implications of Monopoly

It is safe to say that monopolies are viewed with distain by the general public. Monopolies are sometimes condemned as avaricious, unethical, and self-serving with little concern for the welfare of society as a whole. But, is this criticism justified? After all, the objective of managers of both monopolies and perfectly competitive firms is to maximize shareholder value. Viewed in this light, it is difficult to argue that competitive firms are virtuous and that evil resides in the hearts of monopolists.

To evaluate the relative social merits of perfect competition and monopoly, a more objective metric needs to be applied. The concept of net national welfare, which was introduced in Chapter 2, provides such a metric. Recall that net national welfare was defined as the sum of consumer surplus and

producer surplus. Figure 2.9 illustrates net national welfare in a perfectly competitive market. Now, suppose that the firms in this industry are consolidated to form a profit-maximizing monopoly. This new market structure is depicted in Figure 8.10. For ease of exposition, the marginal cost curve is linearly related to output.

The monopolist depicted in Figure 8.10 maximizes profit by producing Q^m units where $MR = MC$ and charging a price of P^m. Unlike firms in long-run competitive equilibrium, this monopolist earns a positive economic profit since $P^m > ATC$. What is more, at Q^m the market price exceeds the marginal cost to society of the resources used it its production. Since $P^m > MC$ the monopolist produces a less-than-socially-desirable level of output. It would be in society's best interest to produce an additional unit since its selling price exceeds marginal cost. As a result, this monopolist produces less output, and charges a higher price, compared with perfect competition. Finally, unlike firms in long-run competitive equilibrium, the firm depicted in Figure 8.10 does not produce at minimum per-unit cost.

As a result of the transformation of the perfectly competitive industry into a monopoly, consumer surplus was reduced by the area $P^{pd}P^mBE$. A portion of this lost consumer surplus ($P^{pd}P^mGB$) has been transferred to the monopolist in the form of higher profits. Overall, net national welfare has declined by

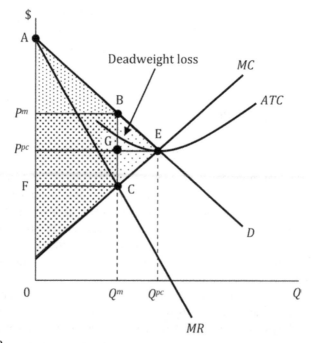

Figure 8.10

the area CBE. This welfare loss is the deadweight loss to society associated with producing less than the perfectly competitive level of output.

It is tempting to conclude from the above analysis that monopoly is an inferior market structure when compared with perfect competition. This judgment must be tempered by the social benefits of research and development expenditures that may only be possible from large scale. As noted earlier, pharmaceutical companies invest billions to bring life-saving pharmaceuticals to market. Patent protection, which is a source of monopoly power, provides an incentive for these socially beneficial investments.

LANDMARK U.S. ANTITRUST LEGISLATION

Although perfect competition provides a framework for evaluating **economic efficiency**, the conditions that define this market structure are rarely satisfied in the real world. The output of rival firms is often differentiated; buyers and sellers rarely have complete information; and entry into and exit from the industry is frequently inhibited. Moreover, industries dominated by large firms frequently engage in anticompetitive practices that stifle competition, resulting in higher prices, and inhibit product innovation and new product development. This exercise of market power leads to market failure in which free markets fail to provide a socially optimal mix of goods and services.

Since 1890, the U.S. Congress has attempted to regulate business practices that restrain competition by promulgating a host of antitrust legislation, the most important of which include the Sherman Act (1890), the Clayton Act (1914), the Federal Trade Commission Act (1914), the Willis-Graham Act (1921), the Robinson-Patman Act (1936), the Wheeler-Lea Act (1938), the Cellar-Kefauver Act (1950), and the Hart-Scott-Rodino Act (1980).

Sherman Act (1890)

The Sherman Act was the first major antitrust legislation designed to prevent the acquisition and exercise of monopoly power. The essence of the Sherman Act is captured in its first two sections:

Section 1. Every contract, combination in the form of trust or otherwise, or conspiracy, in restraint of trade or commerce among the several States, or with foreign nations, is hereby declared illegal . . .

Section 2. Every person who shall monopolize, or attempt to monopolize, or combine or conspire with any other person or persons, to monopolize any part of the trade or commerce among the several States, or with foreign nations, shall be deemed guilty of a misdemeanor, and, on conviction thereof, shall be punished by a fine not exceeding five thousand dollars, or by imprisonment not exceeding one year, or by both said punishments, in the discretion of the court.

The Sherman Act had several shortcomings. To begin with, while the Sherman Act declared monopolistic structures and practices as illegal, it was unclear what specific acts constituted a "restraint of trade." Moreover, there was no specific agency designated to enforce its provisions. This shortcoming was rectified in 1903 with the creation of the Antitrust Division of the U.S. Department of Justice.

In 1911, two major antitrust cases were brought before the Supreme Court. The plaintiffs were the Standard Oil Company, which controlled about 91 percent of the petroleum refining industry, and the American Tobacco Company, which controlled between 75 and 90 percent of the tobacco market (except for cigars). Both companies used ruthless tactics to acquire or drive out of business competing firms. The U.S. Supreme Court found that both companies were guilty of violating Sections 1 and 2 of the Sherman Act and were ordered to divest itself of large holdings in other companies. In its ruling, however, the court indicated that not all practices that appeared to restrain trade violated the Sherman Act. By enunciating its "rule of reason" the court ruled that violations of the Sherman Act included only those actions that were "unreasonable." Thus, it would be possible for a near-monopoly to be in compliance with the Sherman Act so long as it had increased its market share through reasonable means.

In the subsequent decade, the U.S. Justice Department brought antitrust cases under the provisions of the Sherman Act against Eastman Kodak, International Harvester, United Shoe Machinery, and United States Steel. While each of these companies controlled a significant share of their respective markets, all four cases were dismissed on the grounds that there was no evidence of "unreasonable conduct." The "rule of reason," however, did little to clarify the wording of the Sherman Act. This shortcoming was largely rectified with the passage of the Clayton Act.

Clayton Act (1914)

The purpose of the Clayton Act was to strengthen the provisions of the Sherman Act and clarify the "rule of reason." The Clayton Act made a number of specific practices illegal if these practices substantially lessened competition or tended to create a monopoly. These practices included price discrimination, exclusive and tying contracts, intercorporate stockholdings, and interlocking directorates. As defined by the legislation, **price discrimination** is the practice of charging different customers different prices provided that these differences were not the result of grade, quality, or quantity of the product sold, where lower prices resulted from cost differences, or where lower prices were offered to match competitors' prices. An **exclusive contract** forces customers to purchase a product as a precondition for obtaining some other product. A **tying contract** makes the purchase of a product from one firm contingent on the customer's refusal to purchase products from competing firms. **Intercorporate stockholding** results when a corporation acquires an equity stake in a competing corporation. An **interlocking directorate** is when an individual sits on the board of directors of two or more competing corporations.

Federal Trade Commission Act (1914)

The Federal Trade Commission Act created the Federal Trade Commission (FTC), which investigates "the organization, business conduct, practices and management" of companies engaged in interstate commerce. Unfortunately, the Federal Trade Commission Act contributed to uncertainty in antitrust legislation by declaring that "unfair methods of competition in commerce are hereby declared unlawful." The determination of what constituted unfair methods, however, was left to the discretion of the FTC. The FTC was also given the authority to issue "cease-and-desist" orders in cases of violations of the law.

Whereas the Sherman Act emphasized the punishment of violators, the Clayton Act and the Federal Trade Commission Act were designed to prevent abuse. The FTC could proactively safeguard the public from unfair or misleading business practices. Under the Federal Trade Commission Act, the government no longer had to wait for private law suits before prosecuting firms engaged in unfair business practices.

Willis-Graham Act (1921)

The Willis-Graham Act exempted telephone mergers from antitrust review. The reason for this was that the government determined that the telephone industry, which was dominated by the American Telephone & Telegraph Company (AT&T), was a natural monopoly, which may emerge when a firm exhibits substantial economies of scale in production. Because AT&T was able to provide telephone service at lower per-unit cost than a large number of smaller, it was believed to be in the public's best interest to regulate, rather than to break up, the telecommunications giant.

Robinson-Patman Act (1936)

The Robinson-Patman Act (often referred to as the Anti-Chain-Store Act), which amended Section 2 of the Clayton Act, was designed to protect independent retailers and wholesalers from unfair price discrimination by large sellers exercising market power. This legislation was enacted in response to complaints by small grocery store owners that faced stiff competition from large grocery chain stores, such as The Great Atlantic & Pacific Tea Company (A&P), which used their size to extract supplier discounts. The Act outlawed several practices including charging different prices to different customers on identical sales; selling at different prices in different parts of the country "for the purpose of destroying competition or eliminating a competitor"; selling at "unreasonably low prices" to eliminate competition or a competitor; price discrimination; paying brokerage commissions to buyers, or to intermediaries under their control; and granting allowances, services, or other accommodations to sellers by buyers, regardless of whether the services are provided by the buyer or not, which are "not accorded to all purchasers on proportionally equal terms." Because the Robinson-Patman Act was designed to protect competitors, it has had the unintended effect of actually harming consumers by raising product prices.

Wheeler-Lea Act (1938)

This legislation extended the language of the Federal Trade Commission Act to protect consumers against "unfair and deceptive acts or practices" in interstate commerce. The Wheeler-Lea Act gave the FTC authority to prosecute companies engaged in false and deceptive advertising. The act defines "false advertising" as "an advertisement other than labeling which is misleading in a material respect." The Wheeler-Lea Act is significant because it gave consumers an equal footing with producers who may have been materially harmed as a result of unfair competition.

Celler-Kefauver Act (1950)

The Celler-Kefauver Act extended Section 7 of the Clayton Act, which made it illegal for companies to acquire shareholdings in competing corporations. The Clayton Act outlawed *horizontal mergers* (mergers of firms producing the same product). The Celler-Kefauver Act closed this loophole by giving the government the authority to prohibit **vertical integration** and **conglomerate mergers** provided that it can be shown that such mergers substantially reduced competition or tended to result in monopolies. As we discussed in the previous chapter, a horizontal merger is a merger of firms producing the same product. A vertical merger is a merger of firms at various stages of the production process. A conglomerate merger is a merger of firms producing unrelated products.

The purpose of the Celler-Kefauver Act was to maintain and promote competition. This legislation targeted mergers among large firms, or mergers of large firms with small firms. The act was not intended to prevent mergers among small firms that strengthened their competitive position in the market.

Hart-Scott-Rodino Act (1980)

Before the Hart-Scott-Rodino Act, antitrust legislation targeted the business practices of corporations. Many large companies, such as law and accounting firms, however, are not corporations but partnerships. The Hart-Scott-Rodino Act extended antitrust legislation to include proprietorships and partnerships. This act required that proposed mergers of proprietorships and partnerships be reported to the Antitrust Division of the Justice Department.

CONTESTABLE MARKETS

As we have seen, a profit-maximizing monopolist will produce at an output level and charge a price where $MR = MC$. Unlike perfect competitive firms, barriers to entry make it possible for monopolists to price their products above marginal cost and earn positive economics profit in the long run and in the short run. But, is it possible for a firm to sustain its monopoly position even when there are no effective barriers to entry? What are the implications for monopoly pricing?

The requirement that potential competitors actually enter the industry for prices to fall has been criticized as overly restrictive. Baumol, Panzar, and Willig (1982) argued that it is not necessary for new firms to actually enter an industry for incumbent firms with market power to charge lower prices. It is only necessary that the threat of entry exist for this to occur. This is referred to as a **contestable market**. In the absence of significant barriers to entry large companies may choose to price their products at or near marginal cost to eliminate the incentive for potential competitors to enter market in search of above-normal rates of return.

A special case of a contestable market is a *contestable monopoly*. In some cases, it may be socially preferable for an industry to consist of a single firm rather than many small firms. The reason for this is that a monopolist may be able to produce at lower per-unit cost due to economies of scale, economies of scope, and cost complementarities. If the market is contestable, government policies that artificially promote competition may not only be inefficient, but unnecessary.

Several conditions must be satisfied for a market to be considered contestable. For one thing, there exist an unlimited number of potential profit-maximizing competitors that produce a homogeneous product using the same production technology. Moreover, entry into the industry should not involve substantial **sunk costs**. Entry into the industry must be relatively unimpeded. Finally, firms in a contestable market engage in price competition. As we will see in the next chapter, such firms are often referred to as Bertrand competitors.

To make the discussion more concrete, suppose there are two firms, Alpha Company and Beta Company, which produce an identical product. Alpha Company is the incumbent monopolist and Beta Company is the latent challenger. Each firm is capable of satisfying the entire market, sunk costs are negligible, and both firms use the same production technology. Alpha company's total cost equation is

$$TC = 70 + 100Q. \tag{8.11}$$

From Eq. (8.11), Alpha Company's marginal cost is $100. Its average total cost is

$$ATC = \frac{70}{Q} + 100. \tag{8.12}$$

Suppose that the inverse market demand equation is

$$P = 180 - 10Q. \tag{8.13}$$

From Eq. (8.13), Alpha Company's total and marginal revenue equations are

$$TR = PQ = 100Q - 10Q^2; \tag{8.14}$$

$$MR = 100 - 20Q. \tag{8.15}$$

This situation is depicted in Figure 8.11. When entry is impossible, the profit-maximizing price and output are $140 and 4,000 units, respectively. Alpha Company is a natural monopoly because per-unit cost declines throughout the entire range of output. To avoid earning an economic loss, the lowest price that this monopolist can charge occurs where the average total cost curve intersects the demand curve at 7,000 units and a price of $110. From society's perspective, this is a second-best solution. The long-run perfectly competitive price and output level is determined at the intersection of the marginal cost and demand curves, which occurs at a price and output of $100 and 8,000 units, respectively. This price-quantity combination is a first-best solution since it results in zero deadweight loss.

Assume that Alpha Company and Beta Company engage in price competition. Both companies simultaneously announce a price for their products. This price cannot be easily changed once the announcement has been made.

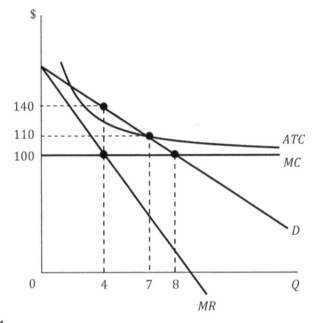

Figure 8.11

Alpha Company knows that if it announces a price that is greater than average total cost, Beta Company will capture the entire market by charging a slightly lower price. Alpha Company has no choice but to set price equal to average total cost to deter entry by Beta Company. In this example, Alpha cannot charge a price equal to marginal cost since this will result in an economic loss, but it will charge the lowest price possible.

The role of sunk cost is critical to our analysis of a contestable monopoly. If Alpha Company charges a price that is greater than average total cost, Beta Company will capture the entire market by charging a slightly lower price. On the other hand, if Beta Company incurs substantial sunk costs by entering the market then it will not be able to contest the market without incurring economic losses. The greater Alpha's sunk cost, the higher Alpha's price and the greater its profit. If sunk costs are sufficiently high, Alpha Company may even be able to engage in monopoly pricing.

CHAPTER EXERCISES

8.1   In the standard model, perfectly competitive firms are ref͡
        price takers. What does this imply for the price and ͡
        of profit-maximizing firms?

8.2   Under what circumstances should a perfectly competitive firm shut down?

8.3   A profit-maximizing firm produces an output level where the price is less than the average total cost. Under what conditions will this firm continue to operate? Under what conditions will this firm shut down?

8.4   In the standard model, a perfectly competitive firm in long-run equilibrium produces at minimum per-unit cost. Explain.

8.5   The perfectly competitive firm's marginal cost curve is also its supply curve. Do you agree with this statement?

8.6   What will likely happen to the market-determined price when that price is greater than average variable cost for a typical firm in a perfectly competitive industry?

8.7   A monopolist's supply curve is the portion of its marginal cost curve that lies above minimum average variable cost. Do you agree?

8.8   Why do monopolists always price their product along the elastic portion of the demand curve for their product?

8.9   Maximizing total revenues the same thing as maximizing total profits?

8.10 Why do governments grant patents and copyrights?

8.11 What do contestable markets imply about government regulation to promote allocative efficiency?

8.12 A firm's total cost equation is

$$TC = 50 + 5Q + 0.025Q^2.$$

The firm can sell all its output for $10 per unit.
a. What is the profit-maximizing output level?
b. What is the firm's maximum profit?

8.13 Suppose that the total cost equation of a perfectly competitive firm is

$$TC = 100 + 0.01Q^2.$$

a. If the market-determined price is $25, what is the firm's profit-maximizing level of output?
b. What is the firm's maximum profit?

8.14 The total cost (*TC*) and inverse demand equations for a monopolist are:

$$TC = 100 + 5Q^2;$$

$$P = 200 - 5Q.$$

a. What is the profit-maximizing quantity?
b. What is the profit-maximizing price?
c. What is the monopolist's maximum profit?

8.15 Bucolic Farms supplies milk to B&Q Food Stores. Bucolic has estimated the following total cost function for its product.

$$TC = 100 + 12Q + 0.06Q^2,$$

where Q is measured in hundreds of gallons.
a. What are the *ATC, AVC, MC,* and *TFC* equations?
b. What is the shut-down quantity and price?
c. What is the break-even quantity and price?
d. Suppose that there are 5,000 nearly identical milk producers in this industry. What is the market supply curve?
e. Suppose that the market demand function is

$$Q = 660,000 - \left(\frac{196,000}{12}\right)P.$$

What are the market equilibrium price and quantity?
f. Determine Bucolic's profit.
g. Assuming that there is no change in demand or costs conditions, how many firms are there if this industry is in long-run competitive equilibrium?

8.16 A monopoly faces the following demand and total cost equations for its product:

$$Q = 30 - \frac{P}{3};$$

$$TC = 100 - 6Q + Q^2.$$

a. What is firm's profit-maximizing price and output level?
b. What is the monopolist's economic profit?

8.17 The demand equation for a product sold by a monopolist is

$$Q = 25 - 0.5P.$$

The firm's total cost equation is

$$TC = 225 + 5Q + 0.25Q^2.$$

a. Calculate the profit-maximizing price and quantity?
b. What is the monopolist's profit?

8.18 The market equation for a product sold by a monopolist is

$$Q = 100 - 4P.$$

The monopolist's total cost equation is

$$TC = 500 + 10Q + 0.5Q^2.$$

a. What are the profit-maximizing price and quantity?
b. What is the firm's maximum profit?

NOTES

1. In 1492, Queen Isabella of Spain financed and granted Christopher Columbus a trading monopoly in exchange for a share of any gold found in the New World. In 1602, the States-General of the Netherlands granted the Dutch East India Company a spice trading monopoly to ensure close relations with its colonial possessions. In 1670, the Hudson Bay Company (HBC) was granted a general trading monopoly by English royal charter in the area around Hudson Bay in Canada. Toronto-based HBC, which today operates retail stores throughout Canada and the United States (including Lord & Taylor and Saks Fifth Avenue), initially functioned as the English monarchy's *de facto* government in North America.

2. Patents, which are granted under Article I, Section 8 of the U.S. Constitution, gives Congress the authority to "promote the progress of science and the useful arts, by securing for limited times to authors and inventors the exclusive right to their respective writings and discoveries."

3. Blood diamonds (also called *conflict diamonds* and *war diamonds*) describes diamonds that are illegally mined and traded to finance insurgencies in such war-torn African countries as Angola, Ivory Coast, and Sierra Leone.

Chapter 9

Imperfect Competition

One of the most important decisions that a manager can make is how to price the firm's product. A firm with **market power** can charge a price that is greater than marginal cost to earn an above-normal rate of return. Market power reflects the nature and degree of competition in an industry. Among other factors, a firm's market power declines with an increase in competition.

A perfectly competitive industry is characterized by a large number of equivalently sized firms producing identical products and where **barriers to entry** by potential rivals are very low. Firms in perfectly competitive industries do not have market power. The prices of their products are determined by the impersonal forces of supply and demand. For this reason, perfectly competitive firms are described as **price takers**. Managers of perfectly competitive firms maximize profit by producing where price equals marginal cost. In the long run, price taking perfectly competitive firms earn zero **economic profit**.

At the other end of the competitive spectrum is pure **monopoly**, which is an industry that consists of a single firm producing a good or service for which there are no close substitutes and where entry by potential competitors is impossible. Pure monopolies are **price makers** that can charge a price that is greater than marginal cost to earn positive economic profits in the long run. In this chapter we will examine the imperfectly competitive **market structures** of oligopoly and monopolistic competition. The analysis will emphasize importance of **strategic behavior** in the managerial decision-making process.

OLIGOPOLY

An **oligopoly** is an industry dominated by a few large firms producing near or perfect substitutes. The automobile industry, for example, is comprised of a few relatively large firms producing similar, but differentiated, products. Although the Honda Accord and the Ford Taurus are mid-sized sedans, consumers do not view these automobiles as perfect substitutes. By contrast, some large firms produce homogenous products, such as USX and Mitsubishi Steel that manufacture high-quality cold-rolled steel. Another example of this is ExxonMobil and Royal Dutch Shell, which refine and market various grades of gasoline.

Oligopolies are characterized by high barriers that make entry by new firms into the industry difficult, which make it possible to earn economic profits in the long run. George Stigler (1968) defined a barrier to entry as any cost that is not borne by incumbents, but that must be paid by potential rivals. According to Joe Bain (1956), legal, economic, and other barriers to entry give incumbent firms a competitive advantage not enjoyed by latent competitors.

Many of the barriers to entry in oligopolies are the same as those found in monopolies, such as patent and copyright protection. Oligopolists have also restricted competition by controlling distribution outlets, or persuading retail chains to carry only its product with the use of selective discounts, long-term supply contracts, and gifts to management. Product guarantees also serve as an effective barrier to entry. New car warranties, for example, inhibit competition by requiring the exclusive use of authorized parts and service.

OLIGOPOLY MODELS

A distinguishing feature of imperfect competition is that a firm's pricing, output, and other decisions affect, and is affected by, the decisions of rival firms. There are many possible ways to model this strategic interaction. Beginning in the early nineteenth century, several models were developed that provide insights into the strategic nature of the decision-making process. In this section, we will review three classic oligopoly models of strategic behavior—the Cournot, Stackelberg, Bertrand and collusion models. In the first three models, strategic interaction is rivalrous. In the case of **collusion**, the firms cooperate by forming a multi-plant coalition to maximize joint profits.

Cournot Model

In the early-nineteenth century, French mathematician Antoine Augustin Cournot (1838) explored strategic interaction in a **duopoly** where two profit-maximizing firms compete by simultaneously, independently, and irrevocably decide how much to produce. In the **Cournot model**, the output of firms 1 and 2 are perfect substitutes and the market price (P) adjusts to clear the market. Barriers to entry prevent new firms from entering the industry. Since there are only two firms serving many consumers, industry supply is the sum of the output of the each firm ($Q_T = Q_1 + Q_2$). The inverse demand equation for the output of this industry is

$$P = f(Q_T) = f(Q_1 + Q_2).\tag{9.1}$$

The objective of each firm is to maximize its profit given the output of its rival. Suppose, for example, that the inverse demand equation for the output of the industry is

$$P = 25 - 0.5Q_T = 25 - 0.5(Q_1 + Q_2),\tag{9.2}$$

where output is measured in thousands of units. The total revenue equations for firms 1 and 2 are given by the equations:

$$TR_1 = 25Q_1 - 0.5Q_1^2 - 0.5Q_2Q_1;\tag{9.3}$$

$$TR_2 = 25Q_2 - 0.5Q_2^2 - 0.5Q_1Q_2.\tag{9.4}$$

Suppose the total cost equations for these firms are:

$$TC_1 = 10Q_1;\tag{9.5}$$

$$TC_2 = 10Q_2.\tag{9.6}$$

The corresponding marginal revenue equations are:

$$MR_1 = 25 - Q_1 - 0.5Q_2;\tag{9.7}$$

$$MR_2 = 25 - Q_2 - 0.5Q_1.\tag{9.8}$$

From Eqs. (9.7) and (9.8), each firm has a marginal cost of $10. Equating marginal revenue and marginal cost, the profit-maximizing level of output for each firm, which is a function of the output of its rival, is given by the equations:

$$Q_1^*(Q_2) = 15 - 0.5Q_2;\tag{9.9}$$

$$Q_2^*(Q_1) = 15 - 0.5Q_1.\tag{9.10}$$

Cournot-Nash Equilibrium

Eqs. (9.9) and (9.10) are the firms' **best-response functions**—also referred to as **reaction functions**. These equations identify each firm's profit-maximizing level of output given the output level of the other firm. Simultaneously solving these reactions functions, the profit-maximizing output level for each firm is $Q_1^*(Q_2^*) = Q_2^*(Q_1^*) = 10$ thousand units. Total industry output is 20 thousand units. This result, which is called a **Cournot-Nash equilibrium**, is depicted in Figure 9.1. From Eq. (9.2), the market-clearing price is $P^* = \$15$. In this example, each firm earns a maximum profit of $\pi^* = TR - TC = (\$15 - \$10)10 = \$50$ thousand.

Stackelberg Model

The **Stackelberg model** (von Stackelberg, 1934) is similar to the Cournot model, but with a critical difference. Unlike the Cournot model in which the firms' output levels are simultaneously and independently determined, in the Stackelberg model output is determined sequentially. The firm that commits to an output strategy first is referred to as the *Stackelberg leader*. This is followed by the output decision of the second firm, which is referred to as the *Stackelberg follower*. Since output decisions are made sequentially, only the Stackelberg follower has a reaction function, which we assume is known by the Stackelberg leader.

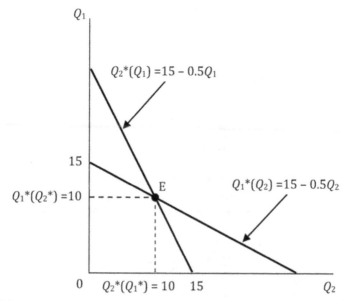

Figure 9.1

To facilitate comparisons with the predictions of the Cournot model, we will assume the same market demand and total cost equations. Firm 1, which is the Stackelberg leader, chooses the output Q_1^* that maximizes profit, which firm 2 incorporates into its reaction function to determine its profit-maximizing level of output $Q_2^*(Q_1^*)$. Only firm 2 has a reaction function, which is given by Eq. (9.10). Whereas equilibrium in the Cournot model is $\{Q_1^*(Q_2^*), Q_2^*(Q_1^*)\}$, equilibrium in the Stackelberg model is $\{Q_1^*, Q_2^*(Q_1^*)\}$.

To determine firm 1's profit-maximizing output, substitute firm 2's reaction function into Eq. (9.3), which yields

$$TR_1 = 17.5Q_1 - 0.25Q_1^2. \tag{9.11}$$

The corresponding marginal revenue equation is

$$MR_1 = 17.5 - 0.5Q_1. \tag{9.12}$$

Equating firm 1's marginal revenue to $MC_1 = \$10$, the profit-maximizing level of output for firm 1 is $Q_1^* = 15$, or 15,000 units per month. Substituting this result into firm 2's best-response function, the profit-maximizing output level is $Q_2^* = 7.5$, or 7,500 units per month. Substituting total industry output of 22.5 thousand units into Eq. (9.2), the market-clearing price is $P^* = \$13.75$. Using these results, the Stackelberg leader and follower earn profits of \$56,250 and \$28,125, respectively. The Stackelberg leader enjoys a **first-mover advantage** because it earns a greater profit than when both firms moved simultaneously in the Cournot model (\$50,000).

Firm 1's ability to commit to an output strategy first may reflect superior management or an R&D program that makes it possible to develop new or improved products to market ahead of its competition. It may also stem from the firm's relationships with suppliers that make it possible to bring its product to market more rapidly than its competition. For these reasons, Stackelberg competition is less likely to be found in industries where consumer tastes are volatile, or where changes in product technology are rapid and unpredictable, such as in the personal computer and telecommunications industries.

Bertrand Model

If you are uncomfortable with the output-setting assumption of the Cournot model, you are not alone. In fact, firms with market power set both prices and quantities. One of the first economists to criticize Cournot's approach was the nineteenth-century French mathematician and economist Joseph Bertrand (1883). While Cournot assumed that firms simultaneously set output levels with prices adjusting to clear the market, the **Bertrand model** assumes that firms simultaneously, independently, and irrevocably set price, and that consumers' purchases clear the market.

Assume that an industry consists of two identical firms producing perfect substitutes at the same constant marginal cost, and consumers who buy from the firm charging the lowest price. More specifically, if $P_1 < P_2$, the demand for the output of firms 1 and 2 are $Q_1 = Q_1(P_1)$ and $Q_2 = 0$, and vice versa for firm 2. If both firms charge the same price ($P_1 = P_2 = P$), they will split the market and $Q_1 = Q_2 = (1/2)Q_T$. For obvious reasons, it is assumed that each firm has sufficient production capacity to satisfy the entire market demand at each price.

Bertrand-Nash Equilibrium

What is the optimal pricing strategy for each firm? Suppose firm 2 charges a price that is greater than the monopoly price ($P_2 > MC$)? In this case, firm 1 should charge the monopoly price ($P_1 = P^m$), sell to the entire market, and earn monopoly profit. If firm 2 charges a price that is less than the monopoly price ($P_2 < P^m$), firm 1 should set its price just below that of firm 2 ($P_1 < P_2$) and recapture the entire market. Finally, if firm 2 charges a price that is less than marginal cost ($P_2 < MC$), firm 1 set price equal ($P_1 = MC$). Although firm 2 will capture the entire market but earn an economic loss, firm 1 produces and sells nothing and earns zero economic profit. When Firm 1's best-response function $P_1 = P_1^*(P_2)$ is depicted in Figure 9.2.

Of course, if firm 2 has the same marginal cost as firm 1, its reaction function will be identical to that of firm 1. For this reason, the firms' reaction functions are symmetrical around a 45-degree line in Figure 9.3. The highest

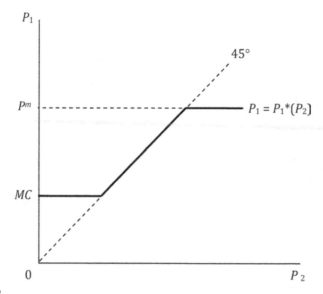

Figure 9.2

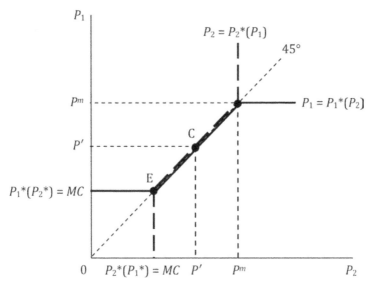

Figure 9.3

price that each firm will charge is P^* and the lowest price that each firm will charge is P^m. Starting at P^m, each firm will undercut its rival until the market-determined price equals marginal cost and will earn a zero economic profit. Thus, the **Bertrand-Nash equilibrium** for this price setting game occurs at point E where $P_1^*(P_2^*) = P_2^*(P_1^*) = MC$.

Is it possible for firms producing perfect substitutes to form a coalition and jointly charge a price $P' > MC$ that constitutes a Bertrand-Nash equilibrium? At this price, each firm would sell to one-half of the market and earn a positive economic profit of $1/2[Q'(P' - MC)]$. This coalition will be unstable, however, since each has an incentive to charge a lower price to capture the entire market. The only price that constitutes a Bertrand-Nash equilibrium is $P_1^*(P_2^*) = P_2^*(P_1) = MC$. When we apply these principles to Eqs. (9.2), (9.5) and (9.6) we obtain a market price of $P^* = MC = \$10$. Substituting this price into Eq. (9.2), industry output is $Q_T = 30$ units per month, with each firm producing $Q_i = 15$ units per month. The economic profit of each firm is $\pi_i = (\$10 - \$10)15 = \$0$.

Bertrand Paradox

The remarkable thing about the Bertrand model is that it predicts that identical firms with market power will practice marginal cost pricing and earn zero economic profit. This prediction is precisely what we would expect in perfectly competitive industries with and many small sellers with no market power. This prediction is known as the **Bertrand paradox**.

The prediction is a paradox because oligopolies that engage in price competition charge prices that are greater than marginal cost and earn positive economic profits. Only when the number of firms in the industry that produce an identical product increases will the market price approach marginal cost. There are at least three explanations why the predictions of the Bertrand model are not observed in the real world, including capacity constraints, differentiated products, and collusion.

Capacity Constraints

The Bertrand paradox assumes that the combined output capacity of competing firms is sufficient to satisfy total market demand at a price equal to marginal cost. If this is not the case, the market-determined price will be greater than marginal cost and each will earn a positive economic profit. To see why, suppose that each firm satisfied one-half of market demand at any market-determined price. Suppose that each firm initially produces $Q_i^M = (1/2)Q^m$. At the combined industry output of Q^m the market determined price is P^m, which is depicted in Figure 9.3. Suppose, however, that each firm has a production capacity of $Q_i' = (1/2)Q'$. Once Bertrand price competition begins, each firm increases output until the price falls to $P' = f(Q_1' + Q_2')$. This price is less than P^m, but greater than $P^* = MC$, which requires a minimum output capacity for each firm of $Q_i^* = (1/2)Q^*$, where $Q^* > Q' > Q^m$. The Bertrand-Nash equilibrium in this occurs at point C in Figure 9.3.

Differentiated Products

The Bertrand paradox can also be explained for firms that produce differentiated products. This condition comes closer what is actually observed in the real world. Examples of industries in which firms produce differentiated products abound, including clothing, soft drinks, beer, cosmetics, computer hardware, computer software, automobiles, petroleum refineries, fast-food franchises, and so on. Fast-food restaurants McDonald's, Wendy's, Carl's Jr., White Castle, Burger King, In-N-Out Burger, Checkers, and Sonic, for example, sell hamburgers that differ in terms of ingredients, taste and appearance. These restaurants also differ in style, motif, atmosphere, customer service, packaging, and so on.

Product differences may be real or imagined. Regular (87-octane) gasoline is the same product at all gas stations. Yet, many consumers willingly pay higher prices charged by ExxonMobil or Texaco because they believe their gasoline is better. Firms producing differentiated products often commit substantial sums to advertising, product placement, and packaging to reinforce real and perceived product differences. The goal is to create and reinforce customer loyalty and brand-name identification, which increases the firm's market power by making the demand for its product more price inelastic.

To illustrate how **product differentiation** helps to explain the Bertrand paradox, consider the following demand equation for the output of firm i, which depends on its price (P_i) and the price charged by firm j (P_j).

$$Q_i = 50 - 2P_i + P_j \qquad (9.13)$$

The positive relationship between Q_i and P_j indicates that goods i and j are substitutes. Suppose that the total cost of firms 1 and 2 are given by Eqs. (9.5) and (9.6). The firms' total profit equation is

$$\pi_i = \left(50 - 2P_i + P_j\right)\left(P_i - 10\right). \qquad (9.14)$$

Proceeding in a manner similar to that used in our analysis of the Cournot model, the Bertrand-Nash equilibrium is $\{P_1{}^*(P_2{}^*),\ P_2{}^*(P_1{}^*)\} = \{\$16.67,$ $\$16.67\}$. At these prices, the profit maximizing level of output for each firm is $Q_1{}^* = Q_2{}^* = 33.33$. Since $P_1 = P_2 > MC$, each firm earns a positive economic profit of $\pi_1{}^* = \pi_2{}^* = (\$16.67 - \$10)33.33 = \$222.31$.

The duopoly models discussed in this chapter have been criticized for the simplicity of their underlying assumptions. As E. H. Chamberlin (1933, p. 46) noted: "When a move by one seller evidently forces the other to make a countermove, he is very stupidly refusing to look further than his nose if he proceeds on the assumption that it will not." Chamberlin realized that mutual interdependence would lead imperfectly competitive firms to form coalitions and price as a monopolist.

Collusion

It turns out that the outcome for the Cournot output-setting model is a less than optimal from an individual firm's perspective. In the Cournot model both firms have an incentive to maximize their individual profit. On the other hand, both firms will be better off by forming a coalition and behaving like a multi-plant monopolist. In this case, the inverse demand and total cost equations are:

$$P = 25 - 0.5Q; \qquad (9.15)$$

$$TC = 10Q, \qquad (9.16)$$

where Q is the combined output of both firms. From Eq. (9.16), the coalition's marginal cost is $MC = \$10$. The total revenue equation for the coalition is

$$TR = 25Q - 0.5Q^2. \tag{9.17}$$

The coalition's marginal revenue is

$$MR = 25 - Q. \tag{9.18}$$

Equating marginal revenue with marginal cost, the profit-maximizing level of output for the entire industry is 15 thousand units, compared with 20 thousand units when the two firms behaved as Cournot competitors. Each firm will produce one-half of that amount, or 7.5 thousand units. Substituting industry output into Eq. (9.15), the market-clearing price is $17.50, compared with $15 previously. Acting as a monopolist, each firm in the coalition earns a profit of $56.25 thousand, compared with $50 thousand as Cournot competitors.

Why wouldn't these firms choose to collude rather than compete? For one thing, **price fixing** is illegal in many countries. Managers would need to weigh risks and returns associated with violating a country's antitrust laws. Another consideration is the **present value** of the future earnings from collusion versus competition, which depends on the prevailing **discount rate**. These issues will be explored in greater detail in the next chapter.

Comparing Oligopoly Models

We will conclude this section by pulling together the results of the Cournot, Stackelberg, Bertrand, and collusion models of duopolists that produce perfect substitutes. Table 9.1 summarizes the results of each of the models for the duopolies characterized by Eqs. (9.2), (9.5) and (9.6).

The first thing to note is that when firms that produce homogeneous products form a coalition and behave as a multi-plant monopolist that industry output is lower, price higher, and industry profits greater than in the more competitive environments of the Cournot, Stackelberg and Bertrand models. As we will see in the next chapter, the viability of this collusive arrangement

Table 9.1

	Collusion	Cournot	Stackelberg	Bertrand
Industry output	15	20	22.5	30
Firm 1	7.5	10	15	15
Firm 2	7.5	10	7.5	15
Price	$17.50	$15	$13.75	$10
Industry profit	$112.50	$100	$84.375	$0
Firm 1	$56.25	$50	$56.250	$0
Firm 2	$56.25	$50	$28.125	$0

depends on several factors. But, if we assume that future cooperation is uncertain, the output strategy profile $\{7.5, 7.5\}$ constitutes a unique equilibrium with each firm earning a profit of \$56.25.

A comparison of the Cournot and Stackelberg models reveals that when both firms produce a homogeneous product, industry output is greater ($22.5 > 20$), price lower ($\$13.75 < \$15$), and industry profits less ($\$84.375 < \$100$) in the Stackelberg model than in the Cournot model. Industry profit is less than if the firms collude. The Stackelberg leader enjoys a first-mover advantage earning a greater profit in the Stackelberg model ($\$56.25 > \$50$) than in the Cournot model. In fact, the Stackelberg leader earns as much profit as when firms collude, and twice as much as the Stackelberg follower. Industry output is greatest ($Q^* = 30$), price lowest ($P^* = MC = \$10$), and industry profits the least ($\pi = \$0$) for Bertrand competitors. Finally, because the firms have identical costs, each accounts for one-half industry output, except for the Stackelberg model in which the leader has a two-thirds share.

MONOPOLISTIC COMPETITION

Edward Chamberlin (1933) and Joan Robinson (1933) were among the first economists to analyze market structures consisting of a large number of intensely competitive firms that exercised market power. Edward Chamberlin first coined the term **monopolistic competition** to describe industries that exhibited characteristics of both perfect competition and monopoly.

Like perfect competition, monopolistically competitive industries consist of a large number of firms with low barriers to entry by new firms. Unlike perfect competition, firms do not produce perfect substitutes. The importance of product differentiation is that consumers make choices based on a variety of factors, including product design, functionality, durability, and quality. Examples of monopolistically competitive industries include clothing, soft drinks, beer, cosmetics, consumer electronics, and Italian restaurants.

Product differentiation can form the basis of a firm's marketing strategy. Firms conscientiously reinforce real and perceived product differences in the minds of consumers by committing substantial sums for advertising. By creating customer loyalty through the use of brand names, trademarks, celebrity endorsements, packaging, and so on, firms endeavor to carve out a market niche, within which it can exercise a limited degree of market power.

Customer loyalty is not always the result of how much a company spends on advertising. It may be the result of fast and courteous service. Dell computer, for example, established its reputation by coupling quality with superior technical support. Successful restaurants are distinguished by its menu, ambience, and friendliness, courtesy and efficiency of its staff. Location also matters. Small retail stores and minimarts often compete successfully with large shopping malls, retail chains, and "big box" outlets because they are within easy reach.

Perfectly competitive firms are price takers that earn zero economic profit in the long run. By contrast, monopolistically competitive firms exercise a limited degree of market power by carving out a market niche. But can they earn economic profits in the long run?

Short-Run Profit-Maximizing Price and Output

The demand for the output of a perfectly-competitive firm is infinitely elastic because it produces a homogeneous product. By contrast, the demand for the output of a monopolistically competitive firm is elastic because of the availability of many close substitutes. This implies that the firm has limited market power. Loyal customers are willing to pay a somewhat higher price, but may switch if the price is too high. Consider the situation depicted in Figure 9.4.

The firm depicted in Figure 9.4 is said to be in short-run monopolistically competitive equilibrium. This firm is maximizing its profit by producing where marginal cost equals marginal revenue and charging a price of P_1. Since price is greater than average total cost, this firm is earning a positive economic profit equal to the area of the rectangle AP_1BC. This happy state of affairs, however, will not last.

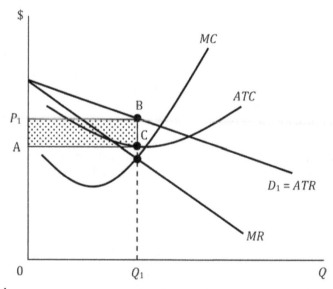

Figure 9.4

Long-Run Profit-Maximizing Price and Output

Attracted by the lure of above-normal rates of return, new firms will enter the industry. Each new firm will offer a similar, albeit slightly different, version of an existing product. This will cause some customers to switch because the new product is more suitable to their particular tastes and preferences. This leads to further market segmentation and smaller market share for incumbent firms. This is illustrated by a left-shift in each firm's demand curve. Moreover, the demand curve becomes more elastic (flatter) because of the increased availability of close substitutes, such as the shift from D_1 to D_2 in Figure 9.5.

As new firms enter the industry, the price charged by an incumbent firm will decline until price equals average total cost, such as point B in Figure 9.5. At this price-quantity combination, total revenue equals total cost and the firm earns zero economic profit, and there is no longer any incentive for new firms to enter the industry. When $P = ATC$, the market is long-run monopolistically competitive equilibrium. This market will remain in long-run monopolistically competitive equilibrium until something disrupts the *status quo*, such as an increase in demand.

This model of monopolistic competition has been criticized since it was first proposed by Edward Chamberlin and Joan Robinson in the early-1930s. The most important of these criticisms is that the model fails to consider the strategic behavior of rival firms. The standard model of monopolistic competition assumes that the price and output decisions rival firms are independent.

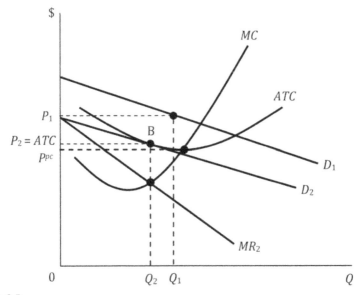

Figure 9.5

But, as we saw with oligopoly, this assumption is unrealistic. Decisions made by rival firms affect, and are affected by, the decisions made by rivals. Strategic behavior is a distinguishing feature of all imperfectly competitive market structures.

Advertising and Product Differentiation

We saw in Chapter 7 that advertising creates, highlights, and reinforces real and perceived differences of a firm's product lines from those of its rivals to segment the market by creating customer loyalty. If successful, the firm may be able to exercise a degree of market power. Analytically, successful advertising is to increase the demand for a firm's product, which is depicted in Figure 9.6 as a right-shift in the demand curve from D_1 to D_2, which increases marginal revenue from MR_1 to MR_2. Since advertising is expensive, the firm's marginal and average total costs have increased from MC_1 to MC_2 and ATC_1 to ATC_2, respectively. Advertising expenditures will be considered money well spent if the resulting increase in unit sales and price results in an increase in profits—in this case from π_1 to π_2.

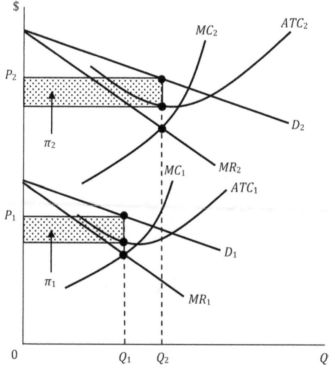

Figure 9.6

How much advertising is optimal? In principle, the optimal level of advertising expenditure maximizes a firm's profits. As a general rule, the firm will maximize its profits from advertising when the marginal revenue from increased sales equals the incremental increase in advertising expenditures. It may be demonstrated that the profit-maximizing advertising-to-sales ratio is

$$\frac{A}{TR} = -\frac{\varepsilon_{x,A}}{\varepsilon_{x,x}}, \tag{9.19}$$

where A is total advertising expenditures, TR is total revenues, $\varepsilon_{x,x}$ is the **price elasticity of demand**, and $\varepsilon_{x,A}$ is the **advertising elasticity of demand**.

Eq. (9.19) suggests several important relationships. To begin with, the more elastic the demand for a firm's product, the less the firm will spend on adverting as a percentage of it total sales. An increase in the availability of close substitutes implies that the demand for a firm's product is more price elastic, which makes it more difficult for a firm to recover advertising expenditures by charging a higher price. In the case of perfect competition where $\varepsilon_{x,x} = -\infty$, the advertising-to-sales ratio is equal to zero. This makes perfect sense since this market structure assumes a very large number of firms producing an identical product. Thus, increase price will result in a total loss of sales as consumers switch their purchases to competing firms.

Eq. (9.19) also suggests that firms facing a downward-sloping demand curve for its product should engage in advertising. This would include monopolists who do not face any immediate competitive pressures. There are at least two reasons why a monopolist would advertise. As we have seen, **informative advertising** provides consumers with information about new and existing goods or services. **Persuasive advertising** attempts to increase sales by getting consumers to purchase a product that they might not otherwise, or to switch their purchases from other firms. Although there are other firms in the industry, the existence of **contestable markets** may justify advertising expenditures to solidify a monopolist's customer base.

Finally, Eq. (9.19) indicates that the greater the advertising elasticity of demand, the greater the profit-maximizing advertising-to-sales ratio. The more sensitive the consumer is to a good sales pitch, the more it will pay for a firm to engage in advertising. For example, advertising is likely to me much more effective when consumer spending is sensitive to peer pressure and fads, such as frequently occur in the toy and fashion industries.

SOLVED EXERCISE

The manager of a monopolistically competitive firm hires a business consultant to identify the optimal level of advertising expenditures. On the basis of *historical data, the business consultant determined that the price and adver-tising elasticities of demand are $\varepsilon_{x,x} = -4.5$ and $\varepsilon_{x,A} = 0.25$, respectively. How much should the firm devote to advertising to maximize profit?*

Solution

Substituting these values into Eq. (9.19) we get

$$\frac{A}{TR} = \frac{0.25}{5} = 0.05. \qquad (9.20)$$

This result suggests that the manager should devote 5 percent of total rev-enues to advertising to maximize the firm's profit.

PRODUCT DIFFERENTIATION AND STRATEGIC BEHAVIOR

Managers of firms in monopolistically competitive industries attempt to gain a competitive advantage in the market place by selling products that are somewhat different from the products sold by rival firms. Product differences can take many of forms, including substance, appearance, packaging, and cus-tomer service. By differentiating its product from those of its competitors, a firm may be able to carve out a market niche that caters to the preferences of a subset of consumers. If successful, the firm becomes a sort of mini-monopolist in that segment of the market. Product differentiation is a strategy that can shed light on the decision-making process in many business situations.

Firms can differentiate their products both horizontally and vertically. **Horizontal differentiation** occurs when a firm alters its product in a way that makes it recognizably different (better or worse) in the eyes of consum-ers than similar products offered for sale by rival firms. Arm & Hammer, for example, horizontally differentiates its toothpaste by adding peroxide and baking soda for extra whitening. While individual buyers may disagree about the value of this enhancement, some consumers are willing to pay a higher price for a brighter smile.

Vertical differentiation refers to changes in a firm's product that makes it recognizably better in the eyes of all consumers relative to similar goods offered for sale by rivals. For example, a new computer with a free service warranty is better for everyone than a new computer in which the buyer must pay for service warranty. One form of vertical differentiation is the location of the seller. A firm's location relative to that of its customers can signifi-cantly affect its bottom line. Other things being equal, customers prefer to purchases goods and service from vendors located nearby to minimize search and travel costs. Moving closer to its customers is a change that is a recogniz-able improvement in the eyes of everyone.

The effect of proximity on sales and revenues can be explained with the help of Figure 9.7, which depicts two mobile hot dog vendors (*West* and *East*), which are initially located at opposite ends of a 5-mile, east-west stretch of beach. *West* is located at the west end and *East* is located at the east end the beach.

Other things being equal, hot dog buyers consider two factors when deciding which concession to patronize—price and location. Assume that both vendors initially charge $2 per hot dog, and that customer travel cost is $0.10 per mile. We will also assume that hot dog buyers are uniformly distributed along the beach.

Because travel is costly, we can predict that *West* and *East* will split the market. Hot dog buyers to the west of mile 2.5 will patronize *West*, and hot dog buyers to the east of mile 2.5 will patronize *East*. Since there is no difference in price, customer C_1 is indifferent between buying from *West* or *East*. In this example, the only factor that differentiates hot dogs is location.

Suppose that *West* lowers its price $1.75, while *East* continues to charge $2. What effect will this have on sales? Consider a hot dog buyer located m miles from *West* and $5 - m$ miles from *East*. The cost of a hot dog from *West* is $1.75 + $0.10m$ and the cost of a hot dog from *East* is $2.00 + $0.10(5 - m)$. Customer C_2, who is located at mile 3.75 is indifferent between buying from *West* or *East* since $1.75 + $0.10(3.75) = $2.00 + $0.10(5 - 3.75) = 2.125. *West* will sell hot dogs to buyers located to the west of mile 3.75 and *East* will sell hot dogs to buyers to the east of mile 3.75.

But, why should *West* charge $1.75 and attract customers to the west of mile 3.75 when it can attract buyers from the entire beach by charging a price of $1.50? If *West* and *East* are Bertrand price-setting competitors, *East* will respond by also charging $1.50. The result is that *West* and *East* return to the *status quo ante* by splitting the market, but earning less profit. If per-unit operating cost is $0.50, *West* and *East* will each earn $1.00 from each hot dog sold.

Since there is nothing to be gained by lowering price, what else can the vendors do to increase sales? One possibility is to relocate. Suppose in Figure 9.7 that 500 hot dog buyers are uniformly distributed along the beach. *West* reasons that it can increase its sales by relocating a little further east. In this way, *West* can expect to sell to all buyers to the west of its location and half the

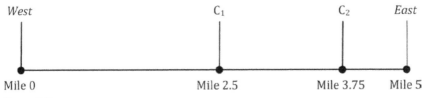

Figure 9.7

buyers between its location and *East*. The best response by *East* is to move a little further west; sell hot dogs to all buyers to the east of its location and half the buyers between its location and *West*. *West* will counter by moving still further east, and so on. Proceeding in this manner, the Nash equilibrium strategy profile is for *West* and *East* to locate at mile 2.5. This analysis helps explain why fast-food restaurants, gasoline stations, and similar retail outlets tend to cluster around at centralized location, such as shopping malls. This strategy appears counterintuitive since they are vying for the same group of customers.

CHAPTER EXERCISES

9.1 Suppose that the inverse demand equation for an industry's output is

$$P = 55 - Q.$$

The industry consists of two profit-maximizing firms with constant average total and marginal cost equal to $5 per unit and no fixed cost. Both firms are Cournot competitors.
  a. Determine the reaction function for each firm.
  b. What is the Cournot-Nash equilibrium?
  c. What is the market price?
  d. What is the profit for each firm?

9.2 Suppose that market demand equation for the output of two firms that are Cournot competitors is

$$P = 100 - 5(Q_1 + Q_2).$$

The total cost equations for the two firms are:

$$TC_1 = 5Q_1;$$

$$TC_2 = 5Q_2.$$

  a. Determine each firm's reaction function.
  b. What is the Cournot-Nash equilibrium?
  c. What is the market price?
  d. What is the profit for each firm?

9.3 Suppose that two firms are Cournot competitors producing a homogeneous product. The market demand and firm cost equations are:

$$P = 200 - 2(Q_1 + Q_2);$$

$$TC_1 = 2Q_1;$$

$$TC_2 = 4Q_2.$$

a. Calculate each firm's reaction function.
b. What is the Cournot-Nash equilibrium?
c. What is the market price?
d. Calculate the profit for each firm.

9.4 Suppose that the demand equation for the output of the industry is

$$P = 145 - 5(Q_1 + Q_2).$$

The total cost equations are:

$$TC_1 = 5Q_1;$$

$$TC_2 = 3Q_2.$$

Suppose that firm 1 is a Stackelberg leader and firm 2 is a Stackelberg follower.
a. What is the output of each firm?
b. What is the market price?
c. What is the profit for each firm?

9.5 Suppose that there are two firms producing an identical product for sale in the same market. The market demand for the product is given by the equation

$$Q = 1,200 - P.$$

Each firm has a marginal cost of $MC = 0$. Neither firm incurs a fixed cost. Firms 1 and 2 have 200 units and 300 units of capacity, respectively.
a. What is the Bertrand-Nash equilibrium?
b. What is each firm's profit?

9.6 Suppose that the manager of Trinity Company wants to increase profits by determining the optimal level of advertising expenditures. The estimated price and advertising elasticities of demand are −4 and 0.1, respectively. How much will the economist recommend that Trinity spend on advertising?

Chapter 10

Thinking Strategically

Many of you who are planning to make a career in business will soon discover in practice what you already suspect in theory. Namely, that decisions by firms affect, and are affected by, the decisions of rivals. In the previous chapter, we examined several formal models of strategic interaction in imperfectly competitive markets. This interaction took the form of **best-response (reaction) functions**. The ability of a manager to correctly anticipate a competitor's response to a change in a market strategy can be critical to a firm's success or failure. To complicate matters, while a manager is trying to anticipate a rival's best response; rival managers are doing the same. The bottom line is that many managerial decisions are not made in a competitive vacuum.

WHAT IS GAME THEORY?

Many of us think of a game as a recreational activity involving two or more players, such as chess, gin rummy, football, or the computer game *Halo*. In business, we often speak of the winning "team" as the company with greatest return on equity or largest market share. Unlike chess, however, success in business may result from cooperation to achieve a mutually advantageous outcome.

Game theory is the formal study of **strategic behavior**, which involves interactive situations of move and countermove.[1] Game theory can deepen our understanding of strategic situations to identify win-win situations when cooperation is possible, but also provides insights as to how to outmaneuver rivals in conflict situations. How well we perform in strategic situations depends on several factors, including a player's strategic skills, understanding of the rules and information about a rival's resources, goals and intentions. Master chess players, for example, do not simply react to moves, but attempt to unravel an opponent's strategy and tactics. It would be shortsighted for a manager to lower price to boost sales without anticipating a competitor's response to lost market share. It would be negligent for a national leader to ignore the potential consequences of a change in foreign policy that encourages terrorism or risks plunging the country into war.

Lexicon of Game Theory

In game theory, a decision maker is referred to as **player**, which includes individuals, groups, companies, and governments. A **payoff** refers to the gains or losses from players' strategy choices. Payoffs may be measured in terms of utility, profits, revenues, market share, and so on.

There are several features common to all games. Games have rules that define the order of play. Moves are based on strategies. A **strategy** is the underlying rationale for a player's moves. In a one-time game (that is, a game in which the players move just once), a player's strategy and a player's move are synonymous. In a game involving multiple moves, a strategy is a player's game plan. Games may involve pure or mixed strategies. A **pure strategy** is a complete and nonrandom game plan. Knowledge of a player's strategy allows us to predict the next move. By contrast, a **mixed strategy** involves randomly mixing pure strategies.

A complete description of the players' strategies is called a **strategy profile**. In static games, strategy profiles are summarized within curly brackets. Suppose, for example, that the managers of rival firms A and B are considering whether to charge a *high price* or a *low price*. This game has four possible strategy profiles: {*High price, High price*}, {*High price, Low price*}, {*Low price, High price*}, and {*Low price, Low price*}. The first entry refers to the strategy adopted by A and the second entry is the strategy adopted by B. Each strategy profile results in payoffs, which will be summarized in parentheses. For example, suppose that each firm earns a profit of $1 million by adopting a *high price strategy*. The payoffs to firm A and firm B are written ($1 million, $1 million).

There are two basic types of games: static and dynamic. In a **static game**, players do not know the moves of other players in each stage until all moves have been made. A **simultaneous-move game** in which all players move at the same time is an example of a static game. In the children's game "rock, paper, scissors," for example, the players simultaneously show a closed fist (rock), an open hand (paper), or a separated index and middle finger (scissors). The winner depends on the combination of moves as rock breaks scissors, scissors cut paper, and paper covers rock. The important thing about static games is that it is not necessary for all players to move at the same time. To see why, suppose that the players are separated. A disinterested referee then asks each player to privately reveal his or her move. The referee then declares a winner. Only then are the players made aware of each other's moves.

By contrast, the players in a **dynamic game** (also called a **sequential-move game**) take turns. Chess is an example of a sequential-move game in which player A (white) moves first, followed by player B (black), followed by player A, and so on. As we will see, white has the advantage of forcing play by moving first. On the other hand, black may learn something useful by observing white's first move.

Games are also defined by the number of times they are played. A **one-time game** is played just once. A **repeated game** is played more than once. If you and a friend agree to play just one game of backgammon, you are playing a one-time game. You are playing a repeated game if the best two out of three wins.

Rational Versus Actual Behavior

In game theory, we generally assume that players behave rationally. By **rational behavior** we mean that players make decisions that are in their own self-interest. In order to make rational choices, however, players must have complete information about payoffs, strategy choices, and the preferences of other players. Even when decision makers have a shared understanding of the strategic environment, preconceptions, misperceptions, and biases influence players' strategy choices.

Herbert Simon (1957) recognized the limitations imposed on purely rational behavior in situations characterized by less-than-complete information and computational complexity. Simon noted that decision-makers act both rationally and emotionally depending on their cognitive limitations and the time available to make decisions. Simon characterized this as *bounded rationality*. So, how useful is game theory for understanding real-world behavior?

While game theory seeks to describe a player's best response to situations involving move and countermove, it does not necessarily explain the way decision makers actually behave. As Thomas Schelling (1960) noted:

> A study of conscious, intelligent, sophisticated conflict behavior—of successful behavior—is like the search for rules of 'correct' behavior in a contest-winning sense. . . . We may wish to understand how participants actually do conduct themselves in conflict situations; an understanding of the 'correct' play may give us a bench mark for the study of actual behavior. (p. 3)

STATIC GAMES

The basic elements of a static game may be illustrated with perhaps the best known and most studied of all game theoretic scenarios—the **prisoner's dilemma**. The prisoner's dilemma is a two-player, one-time, static game in which each player has a **dominant strategy**, which is the same best response regardless of the strategy adopted by another player. Although it is in the players' best interest to cooperate, each player has an incentive to adopt their dominant strategy, which results in a less-than-optimal outcome.

To illustrate the prisoner's dilemma, suppose that two suspects are arrested by the police following a burglary. Although the authorities believe them to be guilty, there is not enough evidence to convict them of the crime. To extract a confession, the suspects are separated and advised of their options. If neither suspect confesses, there is only enough evidence to convict the suspects of a minor offense, which carries a penalty of 6 months in jail. If only one suspect turns state's evidence, that suspect goes free and the other suspect will go to jail for 10 years. If both suspects confess and testify against the other, both will receive 5 year jail sentences. Figure 10.1 summarizes the players, payoffs and strategies. The negative payoffs indicate that less prison time is preferred.

The game depicted in Figure 10.1 has four possible outcomes: {*Confess, Confess*}, {*Confess, Silent*}, {*Silent, Confess*}, {*Silent, Silent*}. The worst outcome is for a suspect to remain silent while the other suspect confesses. In the lower, left-hand cell of the payoff matrix, for example, suspect A confesses and suspect B remains silent. In this case, suspect A goes free while suspect B gets 10 years behind bars.

If both suspects are rational, each will have a strong incentive to confess. To understand why, consider the problem from suspect A's perspective. If suspect B remains silent, it is in suspect A's best interest to confess since this will result in no jail time as opposed to six months in jail by not confessing. On the other hand, if suspect B confesses, it is again in suspect A's best interest to confess since this would result in five years in jail, compared with ten years by remaining silent. In other words, suspect A's best response is

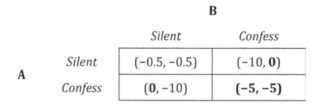

Payoffs: (A, B)

Figure 10.1

to confess, regardless of the decision made by suspect B. Since the payoff matrix is symmetrical, the same is also true for suspect B.

The most likely outcome of the prisoner's dilemma is for both players to confess, even if they agree before being separated to remain silent. The reason for this is that the prosecutor has made trust impossible. Each suspect has a powerful incentive to confess to get a better deal, and neither suspect wants to be left holding the bag by remaining silent.[2] Since each suspect wants to avoid the so-called "sucker's payoff," confess is a dominant strategy. The resulting strategy profile is {*Confess, Confess*} with both suspects going to jail for five years.

Nash Equilibrium

The strategy profile {*Confess, Confess*} in Figure 10.1 is called a **Nash equilibrium** in honor of John Forbes Nash, Jr., who along with John Harsanyi and Reinhard Selten were awarded the 1994 Nobel Prize in economics for their pioneering work in game theory. A game has a Nash equilibrium when all players adopt a strategy that is the best response to the strategies adopted rivals. When a strategy profile is a Nash equilibrium, it is not possible for a player to obtain a better payoff by unilaterally switching strategies.

The prisoners' dilemma provides important insights into strategic business behavior. To see how, suppose that managers at rival firms A and B are considering whether to charge a "high" price or a "low" price for their product. Since they are competing for the same group of customers, each manager recognizes that their firm's payoff depends on the pricing decision of its rival. If A charges a high price and B charges a low price, B will increase its market share at A's expense, and *vice versa*.[3] On the other hand, if both firms cooperate by charging a high price, they will split the market and earn greater profit than if they both charge a low price. This situation is depicted in Figure 10.2 in which payoffs are in millions of dollars.

In this game, both firms have a dominant *low price* strategy. Regardless of the strategy adopted by A, B will charge a low price since it results in a

B

		High price	Low price
	High price	(1, 1)	(0.1, **5**)
A	*Low price*	(**5**, 0.1)	(**0.25, 0.25**)

Payoffs: (A, B)

Figure 10.2

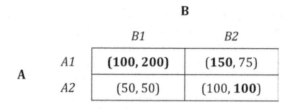

Payoffs: (A, B)

Figure 10.3

larger payoff. Since the payoffs are symmetrical, A has the same dominant *low price* strategy. The strategy profile {*Low price, Low price*} is a Nash equilibrium since neither player can improve its payoff by unilaterally adopting a different strategy.

As we saw earlier, the distinguishing feature of prisoner-dilemma-type games is that rational self-interest produces a less-than-optimal outcome for both players. Even though it is in both firms best interest to charge a high price, cooperation will break down since each firm has an incentive to switch strategies.

Prisoner's-dilemma-type games are frequently encountered in business, which explains the widespread use of contracts to enforce coalitions. A **contract** is a formal agreement that binds two or more players to a specific course of action in exchange for something of value. Failure by either party to adhere to the terms and conditions of the contract can result in legal sanctions involving **restitution damages** and **punitive damages**. Contracts bind players to agreements by changing the payoffs in the event of defection. In the absence of such an enforcement mechanism, players would fail to come to an agreement to realize a mutually beneficial outcome. The prisoner's dilemma also helps to explain why companies form joint ventures instead of entering into informal **strategic alliances**.

In each of the above examples, a Nash equilibrium emerged because both players had a dominant strategy. Yet, it is only necessary for one player to have a dominant strategy for a unique Nash equilibrium to emerge. Consider the game in Figure 10.3 in which only player A has a dominant *A1* strategy. Player B's best response is *B1* since it results in the best payoff. Since neither player can improve its payoff by unilaterally switching strategies, the Nash equilibrium strategy profile for the game is {*A1, B1*}.

Secure Strategy

An essential element of successful game play is to correctly interpret a rival's intentions. We have thus far assumed that the strategy choices of players in static games were based on obtaining the best payoff. But, what if this assumption is incorrect? What if it turns out that a rival's objective is more nefarious? To see how this can adversely affect a player's welfare, consider the game depicted in Figure 10.4, which summarizes strategy choices of two rival firms and where payoffs are millions of dollars.

Suppose initially that larger payoffs are preferred by both firms. The reader should verify firm A does not have a dominant strategy, but expects firm B to adopt its dominant *B2* strategy. The resulting Nash equilibrium strategy profile is {*A2, B2*} with payoffs of $200 million and $100 million, respectively. But, what if firm A incorrectly interprets firm B's intentions. What if the objective of firm B is to cripple firm A's business, perhaps with the ultimate goal of pushing firm A into bankruptcy? To accomplish this, firm B adopts a "bait and switch" strategy by signaling to firm A that its objective is to maximize profit, but instead adopts a *B1* strategy. The payoffs for the resulting {*A2, B1*} strategy profile are −$1,000 million and $95 million, respectively. The reduction in profit to firm B is just $5 million, but firm A suffers a loss of $1 trillion, which was firm B's intention all along.

Given the importance of correctly interpreting a rival's intentions, it may be in a player's best interest to adopt a **secure strategy** that avoids the worst payoff. Identifying a player's secure strategy in a two-player, two-strategy static game is straightforward. A player first identifies the worst possible payoff, and adopts a strategy that avoids this outcome. In the game depicted in Figure 10.4, for example, the worst possible payoff is −$1,000 million, which is only possible if firm A adopts an *A2* strategy. To avoid this outcome, firm A's should adopt its secure *A1* strategy. In games involving more than two strategies, a player first identifies the lowest payoff and eliminates that strategy. Next, identify the worst payoff from among the remaining payoffs and eliminate that strategy. Continue in this manner until there only the secure strategy remains. While a secure strategy might not result in a best payoff, it will always avoid the worst possible outcome.

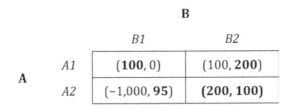

Payoffs: (A, B)

Figure 10.4

SOLVED EXERCISE

Consider the competitive, one-time static game depicted in Figure 10.5 in which larger payoffs are preferred.
a. *Does either player in this game have a dominant strategy?*
b. *Does this game have a Nash equilibrium?*
c. *What is the strategy profile if both players adopt a secure strategy?*

Solution

a. *Neither player has a dominant strategy. If A moves A1, B's best response is B1 because it results in a larger payoff. If A moves A2, B's best response is B2. Since B's strategy depends on the strategy adopted by A, B does not have a dominant strategy. This is also true of player A.*
b. *The game depicted in Figure 10.5 has two Nash equilibrium strategy profiles: {A1, B1} and {A2, B2}.*
c. *If B moves B1, the minimum payoff for A is −100 by moving A2. If B moves B2, the minimum payoff for A is 75 by moving A1. Since 75 > −100, A1 is A's secure strategy. Analogously, if A moves A1, the minimum payoff for B is 65 by moving B2. If A moves A2, the minimum payoff for B is 90 by moving B1. Since 90 > 65, B1 is B's secure strategy. The secure strategy profile is {A1, B1}.*

MIXED STRATEGIES

Not all static games in pure strategies have a unique Nash equilibrium in pure strategies, while others have multiple Nash equilibria. Yet, all static games with a finite number of players and pure strategies have a unique Nash equilibrium in mixed strategies, which involves randomly mixing pure strategies. It is for this reason that a Nash equilibrium is virtually unchallenged as a solution concept in strategic settings.

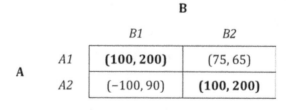

Payoffs: (A, B)

Figure 10.5

An interesting real-world application of a game that does not have a Nash equilibrium in pure strategies involves the **manager-worker principal-agent problem**. One way for managers to get workers to put forth their best efforts is to monitor performance. Constant monitoring, however, is expensive and can negatively affect worker morale and productivity. A more cost efficient alternative is to perform spot checks. For spot checks to be effective, however, they must be random; otherwise workers will know when to work hard and when to shirk. To illustrate the problem, consider the zero-sum game depicted in Figure 10.6.

The payoffs in Figure 10.6 may be interpreted as follows. Managers who *observe* lose (−1) when workers *work* because the firm incurs unnecessary monitoring costs. Workers benefit (1) because their diligence is recognized. Managers who *observe* win (1) when workers who *shirk* are identified (−1) and penalized. Managers who *ignore* win (1) when workers *work* because the firm does not incur monitoring costs. Workers lose (−1) because diligence is not recognized. Finally, managers who *ignore* lose (−1) when workers *shirk* because negligence is not identified. Workers win (1) because they are compensated even though they do not put forth their best efforts.

Neither player has a dominant strategy in Figure 10.6. If managers *observe*, worker *work*. If managers *ignore*, workers *shirk*. Similarly, if workers *work*, managers *ignore*. If workers *shirk*, managers *observe*. In each case, a player's best response depends on the strategy adopted by the other player. As a result, this game does not have a pure-strategy Nash equilibrium.

The solution to the problem is to randomly mix strategies. Denote the manager's mix of strategies as $(\alpha, 1 - \alpha)$, where α is the probability of observing and $1 - \alpha$ is the probability of ignoring. Denote the worker's mixing rule as $(\beta, 1 - \beta)$, where β is the probability of working and $1 - \beta$ is the probability of goofing off. Intuition suggests that the optimal mixing rule for both players is (½, ½). That is, the manager should randomly *observe* and *ignore* by, say, flipping a fair coin. Similarly, the worker should randomly *work* and *shirk* in a similar manner.

Worker

		Work	Shirk
Manager	*Observe*	(−1, **1**)	(**1**, −1)
	Ignore	(**1**, −1)	(−1, **1**)

Payoffs: (Manager, Worker)

Figure 10.6

To see why this mixing rule is a Nash equilibrium, suppose that the manager adopts a (⅓, ⅔) mixing rule. That is, the manager randomly observes one-third of the time and randomly ignores two-thirds of the time. By adopting a pure *shirk* strategy, the worker's expected payoff is ⅓(−1) + ⅔(1) = ⅓ and the manager's expected payoff is −⅓. By contrast, the worker's expected payoff from a pure *shirk* strategy if the manager adopts a (½, ½) mixing rule is ½(−1) + ½(1) = 0. The manager's expected payoff is also 0. The mixing rule (½, ½) is a Nash equilibrium because no other mixing rule will result in a better payoff.

We saw in the monitoring game that it may be possible to improve a player's payoff by mixing strategies, but this does not mean that flipping a fair coin is always the optimal mixing rule. The optimal mixing rule varies with the players' payoffs. Regardless of the optimal mixing rule, player strategies must be randomized since rivals will exploit any systematic and predictable behavior.

COOPERATION

Firms in an industry that recognize that their actions are mutually interdependent might agree to coordinate their actions to achieve a mutually beneficial outcome. Cooperation need not be a formal, explicit agreement, but may take the form of a tacit understanding based on shared interests. **Collusion** is the name that economists use to describe a coalition among firms to enhance their **market power** to earn greater returns. Collusive behavior may include such activities as **price fixing**, bid rigging, production quotas, market segmentation, information sharing, or some other practice that stifles competition.

In our discussion of one-time, static games we observed that when individual self-interests conflict with the best interest of the group that cooperation is inherently unstable. Is it possible, however, for cooperation r to constitute a Nash equilibrium when games are played repeatedly? For this to be the case, the gains from cooperation must outweigh gains from conflict.

Finitely-Repeated Static Games

For decades, Proctor & Gamble (P&G) and Unilever, which are giants in the household-products industry, were locked in intense global competition. In recent years, however, these companies appear to have come to an understanding not to "blind side" each other by unexpectedly changing their marketing strategies. It is not uncommon for companies to have an ongoing strategic relationship, but what would happen if P&G were to violate this tacit understanding? What are the possible consequences for both companies

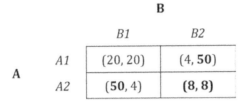

Payoffs: (A, B)

Figure 10.7

from upsetting the status quo? Would P&G's actions provoke a marketing war that ultimately leaves both companies worse off? Is there anything that P&G can prevent Unilever from retaliating? Can Unilever punish P&G for breaking the peace?

One possible explanation may be found in the dynamics of the ongoing relationship between P&G and Unilever. To see what is involved, consider the pure-strategy, static game depicted in Figure 10.7, which is variation of the prisoner's dilemma. Is it possible for the strategy profile {*A1, B1*} to constitute a Nash equilibrium if this game is played repeatedly? What if this game is played, say, two times?

Although both players are better off by moving {*A1, B1*} in both stages, this agreement is not part of a Nash equilibrium. The reason for this is that once the first stage has been played, the second (and final) stage becomes a one-time game in which both players have an incentive to defect. To see why, note that the payoff to each player moving {*A1, B1*} in both stages is 20 + 20 = 40. On the other hand, if one player unilaterally defects, the payoff is 20 + 50 = 70. Since 20 + 50 > 20 + 20, a coalition in which both players move {*A1, B1*} in both stages will break down. But, if both players defect the payoff is 20 + 8 = 28 < 20 + 20. We are left to determine whether the combination of moves {*A1, B1*} in the first stage and {*A2, B2*} in the second stage is a Nash equilibrium strategy.

The combination of moves {*A1, B1*} in stage 1 and {*A2, B2*} in the stage 2 is also not a Nash equilibrium. To see why, suppose that B unilaterally violates the agreement in the stage 1. Since 50 + 8 > 20 + 8, B has an incentive to defect. Because of the symmetry of the payoffs, A has an incentive to defect in stage 1 as well. Since both players have an incentive to defect, the only strategy profile that constitutes a Nash equilibrium in both stages is {*A2, B2*}.

End-of-Game Problem

We have seen that the strategy profile {*A1, B1*} in Figure 10.7 cannot be part of a Nash equilibrium in a two-stage game. What if the game were played three, four, or *n* times? Would an agreement between players A and B to move {*A1, B1*} in any stage of a **finitely-repeated static game** constitute a Nash equilibrium? Suppose that this game were played five times. The payoff to both players from an {*A1, B1*} coalition is 20 + 20 + 20 + 20 + 20 = 100. The payoff to a player who unilaterally defects in stage 5 is 20 + 20 + 20 + 20 + 50 = 130. Since both players have an incentive to defect in the fifth stage, the actual payoff to each player is 20 + 20 + 20 + 20 + 8 = 88.

Is the strategy profile {*A1, B1*} in the first four stages and {*A2, B2*} in the fifth stage part of a Nash equilibrium? By moving {*A2, B2*} in stage 5, stage 4 effectively becomes the last stage. The payoff from unilateral defection in the fourth stage is 20 + 20 + 20 + 50 + 8 = 108. Since both players have an incentive to defect, the actual payoff is 20 + 20 + 20 + 8 + 8 = 68. Stage 3 now becomes the last stage, and so on all the way back to the stage 1. Just as when this game was played twice, the search for a Nash equilibrium reduces to a series of one-time, static games. Thus, the Nash equilibrium strategy for player A is to move *A2,* and for player B to move *B2* in each and every stage of this game. This unraveling of a finitely-repeated static game into a series of one-time static games is called the **end-of-game problem**. How a player move in the last stage determines how that player will move in the first and all subsequent stages.

An interesting real-world example of the end-of-game problem involves a worker who announces on Monday her intention to quit on Tuesday. As a rule, people work hard partly because they fear retribution if caught shirking. In general, workers will work hard if the benefit from diligence is greater than the penalty from negligence. But, will this worker be diligent on Tuesday? Since she will not show up for work on Wednesday, threats made by management for goofing off on Tuesday will not carry much weight. The worker's choice between working hard and shirking on Tuesday is a one-time game in pure strategies. Since management cannot retaliate on Wednesday, a warning of retribution is an empty threat.

Will the employee's attitude toward work on Monday be affected by her decision to leave on Tuesday? Since Tuesday is the last stage of a two-stage game, Monday becomes a one-time game, which suggests that the worker will goof off on Monday as well. The same line of reasoning applies when the worker gives two-week notice. Each day becomes a one-time, static game.

What, if anything, can management do to compel the worker put forth her best effort in the final days of employment? Management could immediately discharge the worker on the spot. This could be counterproductive since the worker could change her strategy from two weeks' notice to quitting at the close of business on the last day. This would make it difficult to find a replacement on short notice without disrupting the firm's operations.

Moreover, firing an employee without cause could lead to morale and legal problems.

A possible solution to this end-of-game problem is to extend the employer-employee relationship beyond the quit date. Management could, for example, offer the employee assistance in identifying new employment opportunities, or provide letters of recommendation to potential future employers. By extending the game into the future, it will be in the worker's best interest to avoid burning bridges by goofing off during her final days on the job.

Tit-For-Tat

There are several examples of companies that had an incentive to violate an agreement, but the coalition endured because of the expected cost of retaliation was unacceptably high. Even when coalitions break down, they were subsequently reformed even though the conditions that led to disintegration still existed. In late-October 2009, for example, Wal-Mart declared war on Amazon.com by slashing prices on 10 highly-anticipated best-selling hardcover books to $10 for online pre-orders—tat! Almost immediately, Amazon, the world's largest online book retailer, fired back by matching Wal-Mart's price cut—tit! Wal-Mart counterattacked by lowering prices further to $9—tat! Before the day was out, Amazon retaliated by again matching Wal-Mart's price cut—tit! Within a week of Wal-Mart's opening salvo, Target entered the fray by adopting its own tit-for-tat pricing strategy for the same reason as Amazon—to remain competitive.

Was Wal-Mart's effort to wrest market share from Amazon a success? Although the Wal-Mart claimed that it was only trying to kick-start its online sales, Wal-Mart exercised poor judgment when it attempted to increase its market share at Amazon's expense. Wal-Mart should have anticipated that Amazon would respond decisively to a direct attack on its core business. Amazon's measured response was not intended to destroy Wal-Mart, but rather to demonstrate it would not be able to increase its market share by cutting prices. In the end, the online book market returned to the *status quo ante*. Market shares remained unaffected and reported earnings from online book sales were significantly lower.

The interaction between Wal-Mart and Amazon is an example of **tit-for-tat**, which is a variation of the eye-for-an-eye rule found in the Bible (Exodus 21:22; Leviticus 24:19-20; Deuteronomy 19:21; Matthew 5:38). It is an enforcement mechanism in which coalition members mimic each other's moves. While rivals will not violate an agreement, neither will they allow defection to go unpunished.

To illustrate the tit-for-tat strategy, consider two neighborhood gas stations (PETROX and GLOMAR), which are located at the same highway intersection. Both have a core of loyal customers who are insensitive to small price differences. There is also a third group of customers that will always buy from the gas station charging the lowest price.

Suppose that each gas station's operating cost, which includes the price of regular gasoline from a local distributor, is $2.80 per gallon, which they resell for $3.00. Since both initially charge the same price, each gas station sells to its loyal customers and splits the sales to the price-sensitive group. Assume that each gas station adopts the following tit-for-tat strategy: If my rival cuts price, I will respond by cutting my price by twice that amount. Since neither gas station wants to lose money, the lowest that either gas station will charge is $2.80 per gallon.

Suppose that PETROX (mistakenly) believes that GLOMAR is about to cut its price by $0.01 to $2.99 per gallon. Acting on this belief, PETROX cuts its price by $0.02 to $2.98 per gallon. Since GLOMAR will not allow this breach to go unpunished, it strikes back by slashing its price by $0.04 to $2.94 per gallon, and so on. This price war continues until each gas station breaks even by charging $2.80 per gallon.

The fundamental problem with a tit-for-tat strategy is that once initiated, the chain reaction of move and countermove will lead to a complete breakdown in the initial tacit agreement to charge $3.00. In its most naive version, a player will react to a real or perceived violation by striking back. At no point does a player quietly accept retaliation. Moreover, there is no mechanism for short-circuiting this downward spiral.

According to Robert Axelrod (1984), tit-for-tat exhibits four general characteristics of an effective strategy. According to Axelrod (1984, p. 54), tit-for-tat is effective because it is a ". . . combination of being nice, retaliatory, forgiving, and clear." Tit-for-tat is nice because it never initiates defection. It is retaliatory because it never lets defection go unpunished. It is forgiving because it does not rule out the possibility of future cooperation. In the gasoline pricing game, for example, PETROX will soon realize that its preemptive price cut has made both firms worse off. Raising its price will be taken as a signal that both firms would be better off returning to the *status quo ante*. In fact, this pattern of behavior is frequently observed in the airline industry where fare cuts by competing carriers are reversed shortly thereafter. Finally, tit-for-tat is clear because it is simple and easy to understand.

One reason why tit-for-tat is so compelling is that performs well against alternative strategies. Axelrod (1984) invited several game theorists to participate in a computer tournament. They were asked to submit strategies for playing finitely-repeated, prisoner-dilemma-type games, which were then pitted against each other. Although tit-for-tat never beat another strategy (although they occasionally resulted in a tie), it won the tournament by accumulating the highest overall score. The reason, according to Axelrod, was that tit-for-tat did not close the doors to future cooperation.

The most severe shortcoming of a tit-for-tat strategy is that a player might misinterpret a rival's actions or intentions. Miscalculations may take one of two forms. Either a player incorrectly observes a rival's action, or correctly observes the action, but misinterprets a rival's motives. A miscalculation will immediately trigger a punishing countermove that will set into motion a cycle of retaliation by both players.

Infinitely-Repeated Static Games

We have seen that a coalition between players A and B in Figure 10.7 is likely to break down since both players have an incentive to defect. Can the strategy profile is {*A1, B1*} constitute is a Nash equilibrium if this game is infinitely repeated? An **infinitely-repeated static game** is a static game that is played over and over without end.

Evaluating Payoffs in Infinitely-Repeated Games

To determine whether the agreement between A and B to move {*A1, B1*} is a Nash equilibrium in an infinitely-repeated game, it is necessary to compare the **present value** of the stream payoffs from defection to the present value of the stream of payoffs from cooperation. It may be demonstrated that the present value of the stream of equal payoffs for the *j*th player in an infinitely-repeated game is

$$PV^j = \frac{\pi^j (1+i)}{i}, \tag{10.1}$$

where i is the interest rate used to discount future payoffs. From this general result, the present value of the stream of Nash equilibrium payoffs (π_N) is

$$PV_N^j = \frac{\pi_N^j (1+i)}{i}. \tag{10.2}$$

Similarly, the present value of the stream of payoffs from a coalition (π_C) is

$$PV_C^j = \frac{\pi_C^j (1+i)}{i}. \tag{10.3}$$

Finally, the present value of the stream of payoffs for player *j* from defection (π_D) is the one-time gain $(\pi_D{}^j - \pi_N{}^j)$ plus the present value of the infinite stream of Nash equilibrium payoffs beginning the next period, which is

$$PV_D^j = \left(\pi_D^j - \pi_N^j\right) + \frac{\pi_N^j(1+i)}{i}. \tag{10.4}$$

In general, it pays for player j to defect whenever the present value of the payoffs from violating the agreement is greater than the present value of the payoffs from cooperation, that is

$$\left(\pi_D^j - \pi_N^j\right) + \frac{\pi_N^j(1+i)}{i} > \frac{\pi_C^j(1+i)}{i}. \tag{10.5}$$

Defection Rule for Infinitely-Repeated Games

This result may be simplified to derive a defection rule for a two-player, infinitely-repeated game. Rearranging Inequality (10.5) we obtain

$$\frac{\pi_C^j - \pi_N^j}{\pi_D^j - \pi_C^j} < i. \tag{10.6}$$

If this inequality is satisfied, it will be in a player's best interest to defect. If the term on the left side of Inequality (10.6) is greater than the interest rate to discount future payoffs, it will pay for the player to cooperate. Finally, if the term on the left equals the interest rate then a player will be indifferent between cooperation and defection.

SOLVED EXERCISE

Consider the game depicted in Figure 10.7. Suppose that the interest rate used to discount future payoffs is 5 percent.

a. *What is the present value of the stream of payoffs if the players do not cooperate?*
b. *What is the present value of the stream of payoffs from a coalition?*
c. *What is the present value of the stream of payoffs from defection?*
d. *Does cooperation constitute a Nash equilibrium?*
e. *For what interest rate will the players be indifferent between cooperation and defection?*

Solution

a. *The present value of the stream of payoffs by not cooperating is*

$$PV_N^j = \frac{\pi_N^j(1+i)}{i} = \frac{8(1.05)}{0.05} = 168. \tag{10.7}$$

b. *The present value of the stream of payoffs from a coalition is*

$$PV_C^j = \frac{\pi_C^j(1+i)}{i} = \frac{20(1.05)}{0.05} = 420. \tag{10.8}$$

c. *The present value of the stream of payoffs from defection is*

$$PV_D^j = \left(\pi_D^j - \pi_N^j\right) + \frac{\pi_N^j(1+i)}{i} = (50-8) + 168 = 210. \tag{10.9}$$

d. *Since $PV_C^j > PV_D^j$, forming a coalition is a Nash equilibrium.*
e. *The players will be indifferent at an interest rate of*

$$\frac{\pi_C^j - \pi_N^j}{\pi_D^j - \pi_C^j} = \frac{20-8}{50-20} = 0.4, \tag{10.10}$$

or 40 percent.

DYNAMIC GAMES

So far we have only considered games in which the players move in each stage without prior knowledge of a rival's move. We will now explore the basic elements of dynamic(sequential-move) games. Unlike static games, the players in dynamic games move in sequence. Except for the very first move, each player observes a rival's countermove, and then uses that information to confirm or revise or confirm a strategy whenever possible.

A diagrammatic representation of a sequential-move game, which is referred to as a **game tree**, is depicted in Figure 10.8. Game trees summarize the players, the information available to the players at each stage, the order

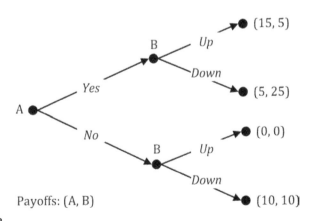

Figure 10.8

of the moves, and the payoffs from alternative strategies. In a dynamic game, a strategy is the complete description of a player's moves at each stage of the game.

A game tree illustrates the strategic interaction of two or more players who alternate moves at branching points. These **decision nodes** are depicted as small closed circles along with the name of the player who moves at that point. A move is represented by an arrow called a **branch**. In the game depicted in Figure 10.8 the first move is made by player A. The initial decision node, which is located at the far left of the game tree, is called the **root of a game tree**. All subsequent decision nodes are referred to as subroots. At the far right of the figure are the "leaves" of the game tree. These small, closed circles are called **terminal nodes**. To the right of the terminal nodes are the players' payoffs. The game ends at the terminal nodes. The first entry in the parenthesis is the payoff to the first mover, in this case player A, and the second entry is the payoff to player B.

In the game depicted in Figure 10.8, the order of play is from left to right. At the root of the game tree, A decides whether to move *yes* or *no*. This is the first stage of the game. In the second stage, B responds by moving *up* or *down*.

The payoffs determine a rational player's strategy. In the game depicted in Figure 10.8, A can only anticipate B's response. B's move, on the other hand, is contingent on how A moves. The ideal order of play for A is to move *yes*, followed by and *up* move by B moving *up* since this results in the best payoff for A, that is (15, 5). By contrast, the ideal order of play for B to for A to move *yes* followed by a down move by B, which results in payoffs of (5, 25). Although it is in both players' for A to move yes, A's opening move will be *no*, which will be followed by a *down* move by B. The resulting payoffs (10, 10) do not represent the best payoffs for either player.

Subgame Perfection

Is there anything that B can do to persuade A to move *yes*? One possibility is for B to threaten to move *up* regardless of A's opening move. If this threat is credible, A's best opening move is *yes* since the resulting payoffs of 15 is preferred to a payoff of 0 by opening with a *no* move. B's threat to move *up* regardless of the opening move by A, however, is not credible. This is because B's payoff is greater with a *down* move regardless of A's opening move.

A *down* move by B following a *yes* move by A is a subgame equilibrium since it is not possible to obtain a better payoff moving *up*. Similarly, a down move by B following a no move by A is also a subgame equilibrium for the same reason. So, which of these subgame equilibria is to most likely outcome for the entire game?

Every decision node is the root of a new **subgame**, which is referred to as a **subroot**. A subgame has the same players as the entire game, although some of these players may not move. This is because the payoffs of all subgames are included among the payoffs for the entire game. A subgame includes the sub-roots, branches, decision nodes, and terminal nodes of all subsequent subgames.

Once a subgame begins, a player must continue to the end. A player cannot turn back or exit in search of an alternative outcome. Each subgame must be treated as complete and self-contained game with its own unique **subgame equilibrium**. There are at least as many subgame equilibria as there are sub-games. With trivial exceptions, a unique equilibrium for the entire game can be found among the complete collection of subgame equilibria. The equilibrium for the entire game is called a **subgame-perfect equilibrium**.

Backward Induction

There is no universally accepted method for finding a subgame-perfect equilibrium. The most commonly used approach, which was developed by Reinhard Selten (1965), is called **backward induction**—also known as the **fold-back method**. The rationale underlying this solution algorithm is simple: Project forward and reason backward. Backward induction involves five steps:

1. Start at the terminal nodes. Trace each branch to its decision node. A *basic decision node* has multiple branches that all lead to terminal nodes. A *trivial decision node* has only one branch that leads to a terminal node. A *complex decision node* has at least one branch leads to another decision node.
2. Compare the payoffs for the player at the decision nodes identified in step 1. The best response leads to the preferred payoff. All other branches should be pruned away.
3. Move backwards to the next decision node. Identify the branches that lead to that player's best payoff. Prune away all other branches from that decision node.
4. Repeat steps 1–3 until the root of the tree has been reached.
5. From the root of the game tree identify which of the remaining branches leads to the best payoff for the first mover. That sequence branches is the subgame-perfect equilibrium.

We will now find the subgame-perfect equilibrium for the game depicted in Figure 10.8 using the backward induction algorithm. Starting at each terminal node, move to the B's decision node, which immediately precedes it. Now consider the B's decision node following a *yes* move by A. Since moving *down* results in the best payoff for B, the *up* branch is pruned from the

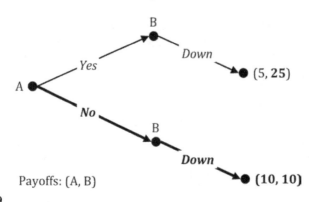

Payoffs: (A, B)

Figure 10.9

game tree. The sequence of moves *yes* followed by *down*, which results in payoffs of (5, 25), is a subgame equilibrium and is depicted in the upper portion of Figure 10.9.

Now consider B's decision node following a *no* move by A. Since the payoff to B by moving *down* results in the best payoff, that *up* branch is also pruned away. The sequence of moves *no* followed by *down*, which results in payoffs of (10, 10), is another subgame equilibrium and is depicted in the lower portion of Figure 10.9.

The subgame-perfect equilibrium for the entire game in Figure 10.9 must be one of these two subgame equilibria. To determine which, identify the sequence of moves that results for the best payoff for A. The payoff to A by moving *yes* is 5. The payoff to A by moving *no* is 10. Since the sequence of moves *no* followed by *down* results in the best payoff for player A, the strategy profile is the subgame-perfect equilibrium. A compact, albeit unconventional, way identify this strategy profile is to list the branches traveled to reach the subgame-perfect equilibrium terminal node, which in this case is {*no* → *down*}. What is remarkable about backward induction is that it will result in a unique subgame perfect equilibrium.[4]

First-Mover Advantage

The reason why backward induction results in a unique subgame-perfect equilibrium is because the moves are sequential. After the initial decision node, each move is a best response. Anyone who plays chess knows that white has an initial advantage since black moves second. This **first-mover advantage** is a feature of sequential-move games. A first-mover is a player who can irrevocably commit to an opening move before any other player. As a result, the payoff to this player can be no worse than the payoff in a static game—and could be better.

The first-mover advantage can be illustrated with the well-known chicken game, which is depicted in Figure 10.10. In this game two teenagers, Dean and Brando, challenge each other to a test of nerves. Each will drive their cars directly at each other. The first driver to swerve loses. If neither swerves they crash, which could result in serious injury and wrecked cars. If both swerve they will be unscathed, except for damaged egos.

This static game has two Nash equilibria in pure strategies: {*Commit, Swerve*} and {*Swerve, Commit*}. The strategy profile {*Commit, Swerve*} is preferred by Dean and the strategy profile {*Swerve, Commit*} is preferred by Brando. Moving first is the key to turning this game to a driver's advantage. To see how, consider the game from Dean's perspective.

Suppose that as they race toward each other, Dean removes out his steering wheel and tosses it out the window for Brando to see. Dean has moved first by making a credible commitment (*commit*) not to swerve. In effect, Dean has transformed a static game into the sequential-move game depicted in Figure 10.11. Using the method of backward induction, the

Brando

		Swerve	Commit
Dean	Swerve	(1, 1)	**(0, 10)**
	Commit	**(10, 0)**	(−10, −10)

Payoffs: (Dean, Brando)

Figure 10.10

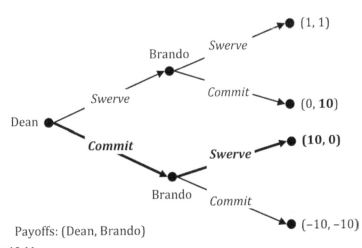

Payoffs: (Dean, Brando)

Figure 10.11

subgame-perfect equilibrium for this game is {*Commit* → *Swerve*}. By making a credible commitment not to swerve, Dean is rewarded with his preferred payoff.

It is sometimes argued that a key to success in business being first to market with a new product or innovation. Amazon.com, Bayer, Coca-Cola, IBM, Intel, Kodak, Microsoft, Standard Oil, and Xerox are well-known examples. Being first, however, does not guarantee success. It is commonly believed that Proctor & Gamble (P&G) was first to introduce the re-sealable, disposable diaper (Pampers) in 1961. In fact, this honor belongs to Kimberly Clark, which introduced the now defunct Chux diapers. P&G succeeded because it offered a lower cost product with wider market appeal. A similar story applies to video recorders, which were first developed in 1956 by California-based Ampex. Twenty years later, this market was dominated by such Japanese companies as Matsushita and Sony.

This pattern of first-mover being outdone by imitators has been repeated time and time again. A study by Tellis and Golder (1996) found that in more than fifty markets, first-movers were industry leaders only 10 percent of the time. Moreover, current industry leaders on average entered the market thirteen years after the first-mover. One explanation for this is that industry leaders have little incentive to risk their market share by bringing an unproven product to market. In general, their dominant strategy is to "follow the pack." IBM, for example, is not known for product innovation, but rather for its ability to standardize technology for mass-market consumption. In fact, most new ideas came from then start-up companies as Sun Microsystems and Apple because risky innovations were their best hope of capturing market share.

There are several possible explanations why first movers failed to maintain their leadership position. Having a first-mover advantage only says that a player who can commit to a strategy first and does not falter will enjoy a payoff that is no worse than if all players moved at the same time. Unfortunately, technically innovative managers are not always good game players. Failure to correctly project forward and reason backward frequently leads to lower profits, disappointed stakeholders, and corporate failure.

CHAPTER EXERCISES

10.1 Suppose that the editors of *Time* and *Newsweek* are trying to decide upon their cover story for the week. There were two major news developments: The leaking of a clandestine CIA officer's identity and a terrorist suicide bombing in Amman, Jordan. It is important that the news weeklies not choose the same cover story since some readers will buy only one magazine when they might otherwise buy both. The choice of cover story depends on newsstand sales. The editors believe that 20 percent of newsstand buyers are interested in the CIA story, while 80 percent are interested in the terrorist bombing. If both news magazines run the same cover story, they will evenly share the market, but if they run different cover stories, each will get that share of the market. This static game is depicted in the following figure.

a. Does either news weekly have a dominant strategy?
b. What is the Nash equilibrium strategy profile for this game?

Newsweek

		CIA	Terrorism
Time	CIA	(10, 10)	(20, 80)
	Terrorism	(80, 20)	(40, 40)

Payoffs: (Time, Newsweek)

10.2 Determine the pure-strategy Nash equilibrium for the following static game.

Guildenstern

		Left	Center	Right
	Left	(5, 4)	(6, 1)	(7, 3)
Rosencrantz	Center	(3, 2)	(8, 5)	(4, 7)
	Right	(4, 1)	(10, 7)	(1, 9)

Payoffs: (Rosencrantz, Guildenstern)

10.3 Consider the competitive, static, one-time game depicted in the following figure.
   a. If larger payoffs are preferred, does either player have a dominant strategy?
   b. If B believes that A will move *A1*, how should B move?
   c. If B believes that A will move *A2*, how should B move?
   d. What is the Nash equilibrium strategy profile if this game is played just once?
   e. What is the strategy profile for this game if both players adopt a secure strategy?
   f. What strategy profile results in the best payoff for both players?
   g. Is cooperation a Nash equilibrium if this game is played three times?

B

	B1	B2
A1	(20, 20)	(5, 25)
A2	(25, 5)	(2, 2)

A (to the left of A1/A2)

Payoffs: (A, B)

10.4 Fly-by-night Airlines and Going-going-gone Airways are considering whether to switch from their current standard fare schedule or implement a frequent-flyer program. The following figure summarizes the monthly profits in thousands of dollars from alternative pricing strategies.
   a. Does this game have a Nash equilibrium?
   b. What is the strategy profile for this game if both air carriers adopt a secure strategy? Is the resulting strategy profile a Nash equilibrium?

Going-going-gone

	Standard	Frequent flyer
Standard	(250, 275)	(210, 350)
Frequent flyer	(325, 190)	(200, 150

Fly-by-night (to the left)

Payoffs: (Fly-by-night, Going-going-gone)

10.5 Two radio stations, KRZY and KRUD, are contemplating three possible broadcast formats: Rock, country, and talk radio. Surveys indicate that the market shares for these formats are 40 percent, 30 percent, and 20 percent, respectively. If both stations choose the same format, they will split that portion of the market. If the stations choose different formats, they will get the total share of that portion of the market. The stations' revenues from the sale of advertising are proportional to their market shares. The following figure summarizes the payoffs to each station from alternative strategy profiles.
   a. Does this game have a Nash equilibrium?
   b. What is the strategy profile if both firms adopt a secure strategy?

KRUD

		Rock	Country	Talk
	Rock	(20, 20)	(40, 30)	(40, 25)
KRZY	Country	(30, 40)	(15, 15)	(30, 20)
	Talk	(25, 40)	(20, 30)	(10, 10)

Payoffs: (KRZY, KRUD)

10.6 Consider the following static game. The numbers in each cell represent the expected profits in thousands of dollars from alternative *aggressive* and *reactive* price strategy profiles.
   a. What is the Nash equilibrium if this game is played just once?
   b. What strategy profile results in the best payoff for both players?
   c. Is cooperation a Nash equilibrium if this game is played twice?
   d. Suppose this game is infinitely repeated. If the interest rate used to discount future payoffs is 7 percent, what is the present value of the stream of payoffs to both companies by not cooperating?
   e. What is the present value of the stream of payoffs from cooperation?
   f. What is the present value to either company defection?
   g. Based on your answers to the above, is a coalition stable?
   h. Suppose the interest rate is 12 percent. Is a coalition stable?

Blue

		Aggressive	Reactive
	Aggressive	(500, 500)	(100, 600)
Orange	Reactive	(600, 100)	(150, 150)

Payoffs: (Orange, Blue)

10.7 Consider the following infinitely-repeated static game.
   a. What strategy profile would result in the best payoff for both players?
   b. Above what interest rate used to discount future values can we expect cooperation to break down?

B

		B1	B2
	A1	(5, 5)	(16, 1)
A	A2	(1, 16)	(6, 6)

Payoffs: (A, B)

10.8 Consider the sequential-move game depicted in the following figure.
   a. How many subgames are there?
   b. What is the subgame-perfect equilibrium?

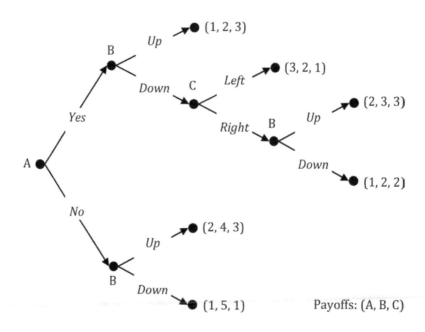

Payoffs: (A, B, C)

10.9 Consider the following static game.
   a. Does either player have a dominant strategy?
   b. Does this game have a unique Nash equilibrium strategy profile?
   c. Suppose that this is a multistage game and player A moves first.
      Illustrate the extensive form of this game.
   d. What is the subgame-perfect equilibrium?

B

		B1	B2	B3
A	A1	(3, 3)	(4, 1)	(5, 4)
	A2	(2, 2)	(3, 1)	(3, 3)
	A3	(2, 2)	(3, 2)	(2, 4)

Payoffs: (A, B)

NOTES

1. The title of this chapter is taken from the best-selling book by Avinash K. Dixit and Barry J. Nalebuff (1991). Students with an interest in game theory are encouraged to add this to their reading list.

2. Numerous experimental trials have confirmed this prediction. In experiments conducted by Cooper, DeJong, Forsythe and Ross (1996), test subjects were asked to play the prisoner's dilemma twenty times against different anonymous rivals. As the players gained experience, the strategy profiles of the players converged toward the predicted Nash equilibrium. In the first five rounds, for example, rivals cooperated 43 percent of the time. This cooperation fell to just 20 percent in the last five rounds.

3. Since firms with market power price their products along the elastic portion of their respective demand curves, charging a lower price will increase total revenues. At constant marginal cost, this implies an increase in total profit.

4. The exception to this occurs when the payoffs to the first mover in two or more subgame equilibria are the same.

Chapter 11

Pricing Strategies

Up to this point we have generally assumed that profit-maximizing firms charge the same price to all customers for each unit sold, that all production takes place in a single location, that firms operate within a well-defined **market structure**, and that managers are blessed with complete and perfect information. In the real world, however, all of these assumptions are rarely, if ever, satisfied.

In this chapter, we will apply the tools of economic analysis developed earlier to formulate optimal pricing strategies for firms with **market power**. Recall that a firm has market power if it can affect the market-clearing price of its product through its output decisions. When a firm has market power, managers can charge a price greater than marginal cost to earn positive **economic profits**. This is characteristic of monopolies and imperfectly competitive firms. By contrast, purely competitive firms, which do not have market power, are said to be **price takers**. For such firms, price is not a decision variable.

STANDARD PRICING RULE

Standard pricing refers to the practice of charging all customers the same per-unit price regardless of the number of units purchased. Recall that a profit-maximizing firm should produce up to the level of output where marginal cost equals marginal revenue. For a purely-competitive firm with no market power $(P = MR)$, this means producing where the market price equals marginal cost and earning zero economic profit in the long run. By contrast, mangers of firms with market power $(P > MR)$ can charge a price that is greater than marginal cost to earn an above-normal rate of return.

Calculating the profit-maximizing price is a reasonably straightforward process when the firm's demand and cost equations are known. Managers of small- and medium-sized firms typically do not have the financial resources or technical expertise to generate quantitative estimates of demand and cost equations. Fortunately, it may still be possible to determine a firm's profit-maximizing price with much less information.

Recall that a useful measure of a firm's market power was given by the **Lerner index**, which was given by Eq. (7.3). Rearranging this equation we obtain Eq. (7.4), which is the standard pricing rule for a profit-maximizing firm. The terms $1/(1 - L)$ and $\varepsilon_{x,x}/(1 + \varepsilon_{x,x})$ tell us how much a manager should mark up the price over the firm's marginal cost to maximize profit when the **price elasticity of demand** for the firm's product is known. For example, suppose that the price elasticity of demand for a firm's product is $\varepsilon_{x,x} = -1.5$. From Eq. (7.4), a profit-maximizing firm with market power should charge a price that is three times its marginal cost.

In some cases, a firm may know its marginal cost, but may know the price elasticity of demand for its product. On the other hand, a manager may have access to publicly available estimates of the price elasticity of demand for the entire industry. If we assume that the firms' output are perfect or near-perfect substitutes, the standard pricing rule for an individual firm becomes

$$P_x = \left(\frac{n\varepsilon_{x,x}^M}{1 + n\varepsilon_{x,x}^M} \right) MC, \tag{11.1}$$

where $\varepsilon_{x,x}^M$ is the price elasticity of demand for the homogeneous output of an industry consisting of n firms. In the case of a **monopoly** ($n = 1$), Eq. (11.1) is equivalent to Eq. (7.8). As the number of firms becomes very large ($n \rightarrow \infty$) we approach the limiting case of pure competition in which each firm to set its price equal to marginal cost.

Interestingly, Eq. (11.1) tells us that the number of firms in an industry that produces perfect substitutes does not have to be very large for pricing to approximate **perfect competition** in the long run. Suppose, for example, that the market price elasticity of demand is $\varepsilon_{x,x}^M = -2$ and the industry consist of two firms. In this case, the profit-maximizing price is $P_x = 2MC$. If the number of firms is just 10 firms, however, the profit-maximizing price is $P_x = 1.05MC$. That is, each firm will charge a price that is just 5 percent above its marginal cost.

EXTRACTING CONSUMER SURPLUS

Thus far, we have assumed that profit-maximizing firms charge the same price to all customers for each unit sold. It may be possible, however, to earn even greater profits by extracting all or part of **consumer surplus**. This may be accomplished by charging different buyers, or different groups of buyers, different prices, or by charging the same buyer a different price for each unit, or blocks of units, sold. Differential pricing of this sort is referred to as **price discrimination**. In this section we will examine three types of price discrimination: first-degree, second-degree, and third-degree price discrimination.

First-Degree Price Discrimination

First-degree price discrimination involves charging the maximum price that each buyer is willing to pay for each unit purchased. The price charged, which is referred to as the **buyer's reservation price**, reflects the willingness to pay for each unit consumed. For example, a thirsty tennis player might be willing to pay a maximum of $5 for the first bottle of water, but only $4 for the second bottle, $3 for the third, and so on. The goal of practicing first-degree price discrimination is to extracting the maximum consumer surplus from each buyer.

While first-degree price discrimination is an interesting concept in theory, it is extremely difficult to practice in reality because of the prohibitive informational requirements, although this may be changing. It wasn't that long ago that the idea of first-degree price discrimination was just a theoretical curiosity. The information needed to practice this form of pricing was simply unavailable. But, to quote songwriter Bob Dylan, "the times they are a-changin'."

Each time you log onto the Internet, "cookies" that are planted in your computer by third parties. A "cookie" is a text file that tracks, monitors, and records your every move as you surf the Internet. Dozens of companies collect, collate, and share your personal information with thousands of vendors. The largest of these is the New York City–based DoubleClick—a subsidiary of the California-based Internet company Google, Inc. DoubleClick's client list includes some of the world's most well-known corporations, including Microsoft, General Motors, Coca-Cola, Apple, Visa, and Nike. Double-Click has agreements with over 11,000 websites to implant cookies to build and maintain information on the personal browsing behavior of well over 100 million users.

Monitoring of the shopper behavior does not stop with the Internet. Credit, store and debit cards leave an electronic footprint. Cell phone calls, and the geographic location of cell users, can be tracked, even when the phone is not being used. Electronic systems for purchasing public-transportation tickets, using road tolls, and accessing public places have spread rapidly. Public and private surveillance and eavesdropping telephone calls, voicemail, e-mail and computer use by employers is easier and more widespread than ever.

To see how *perfect first-degree price discrimination* works, suppose initially that the firm charges the same price to all customers for each unit sold.

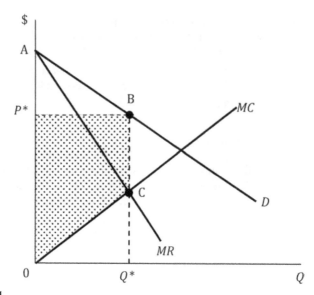

Figure 11.1

This situation is depicted in Figure 11.1 where the produces where $MR = MC$ and charges a price of P^*. The firm's total variable cost is given by area $0CQ^*$. Total revenue is given by the area $0P^*BQ^*$. Thus, the firm's total variable (operating) profit $(TR - TVC)$ is given by the shaded area $0P^*BC$.

Suppose this firm practices first-degree price discrimination by charging each buyer his or her reservation price. This situation is depicted in Figure 11.2. The firm begins by producing Q' units of output where marginal revenue equals average total revenue (ATR). By charging the maximum price that each consumer is willing to pay for each unit consumed, the firm's total revenue is given by the area $0AEQ'$. The firm's total variable cost is $0EQ'$. Thus, the firm's **operating profit** is $0AEQ' - 0EQ' = 0AE$, which is the sum of consumer surplus and **producer surplus**. This operating profit is greater than the situation depicted in Figure 11.1 by the $P^*AB + CBE$.

In general, perfect first-degree price discrimination is not feasible for several reasons. To begin with, units of output are in discrete amounts, which make it impossible to extract the full amount of consumer surplus. A more important obstacle is the prohibitive informational requirements needed to determine the consumer's reservation prices. Of course, a manager could ask each buyer how much he or she is willing to pay for each unit, but this is unlikely to work since many rational buyers have a strong incentive to understate the true value received.

Since perfect first-degree price discrimination impractical, some firms practice *imperfect first-degree price discrimination*, which involves charging

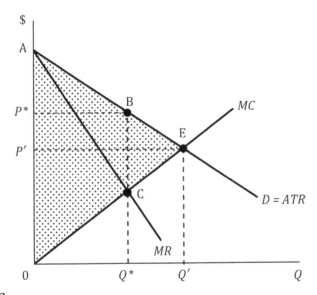

Figure 11.2

higher prices to those who have a greater ability to pay. This form of differential pricing is frequently practiced by doctors, lawyers, certified public
accountants, and other professionals who some understanding of their clients
financial resources. The fee structure of many physicians, for example, is
often based on a patient's income or insurance coverage. Accountants often
set fees based on their clients' tax returns. Financial aid awarded by many
colleges and universities is typically depends on family income or net worth.

SOLVED EXERCISE

Suppose that the inverse demand equation for a firm's product is

$$P = 420 - 10Q. \tag{11.2}$$

The total cost is given by the equation

$$TC = 500 + 20Q^2. \tag{11.3}$$

a. *What are the profit-maximizing price and quantity from a single-price
   strategy?*
b. *Given your answer to part a, what is the firm's total operating profit?*
c. *What is the firm's total operating profit if it engages in perfect first-degree
   price discrimination? What is this firm's total economic profit?*

Solution

a. *The firm's total revenue equation is*

$$TR = 420Q - 10Q^2. \qquad (11.4)$$

Marginal revenue is

$$MR = 420 - 20Q. \qquad (11.5)$$

Marginal cost is

$$MC = 40Q. \qquad (11.6)$$

Total economic profit with a single-price strategy is maximized when MR = MC, which occurs at Q = 7 units. From Eq. (11.2), the firm should charge a price of $350 for each unit sold. This firm's total economic profit equation is

$$\pi = TR - TC = -500 + 420(7) - 30(7)^2 = \$970. \qquad (11.7)$$

b. *Total operating profit is total revenue less total variable cost. Since total fixed cost is $500, the firm's total operating profit is $1,470.*
c. *This firm should produce Q = 8.4 units of output. By charging each buyer his or her reservation price for each unit purchased, the firm's total profit is the sum of consumer and producer surplus. Producer surplus is*

$$PS = 0.5(\$336)8.4 = \$1,411.20. \qquad (11.8)$$

Consumer surplus is

$$CS = 0.5(\$420 - \$336)8.4 = \$352.80. \qquad (11.9)$$

This firm's operating profit is PS + CS = $1,764. Alternatively, the firm's operating profit is TR − TVC = [$336(8.4) + 0.5($420 − $336)8.4] − [$20(8.4)² = $1,764. This firm's economic profit equals its total operating profit less total fixed cost, that is, $1,264, which is $294 greater than under a single-price strategy.

A firm that is first to market with a new product may be in a position to practice a form of first-degree price discrimination called **price skimming**. Until rival firms develop a close substitute, the innovating firm is able to charge a monopoly price. Consumers who willing and able to pay will buy first. The firm then lowers its price somewhat to attract more buyers. This process is repeated until rival firms enter the market. By incrementally lowering prices, the innovating firm is able to extract as much consumer surplus as possible.

Second-Degree Price Discrimination

Second-degree price discrimination—also known as **volume discounting**—differs from first-degree price discrimination in that a firm attempts to extract a portion of consumer surplus by selling its product in "blocks" or "bundles" rather than one unit at a time. Two types of second-degree price discrimination are block pricing and commodity bundling.

Block Pricing

Block pricing is the practice of charging different prices for different amounts or "blocks" of a good or service, such as selling a package of eight frankfurter rolls or a six-pack of beer. The idea behind block pricing is to charge a package price that includes some consumer surplus. To illustrate the ideas behind block pricing, suppose that the manager of a supermarket purchases frankfurter rolls from a distributor for $0.10 each. The inverse demand equation of a typical customer is

$$P = 0.3 - 0.025Q. \tag{11.10}$$

Suppose the manager adopts a one-price strategy. To maximize profit, the manager should charge a price such that $MR = MC$. The supermarket's marginal revenue equation is

$$MR = 0.3 - 0.05Q. \tag{11.11}$$

Since $MC = \$0.10$, the supermarket should charge $P = \$0.20$ per frankfurter roll and sell $Q = 4$ frankfurter rolls per buyer. The supermarket's per customer operating profit is

$$TR - TVC = (\$0.20 - \$0.10)(4) = \$0.40. \tag{11.12}$$

Now, suppose the manager adopts a block pricing strategy by selling multiple frankfurter rolls in a package. How many frankfurter rolls should be included in the package, and at what price? What is the supermarket's per customer operating profit? The answers to these questions are illustrated in Figure 11.3.

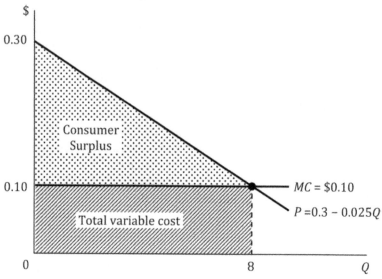

Figure 11.3

To determine the number of frankfurter rolls in each package, equate price in Eq. (11.10) to marginal cost. Solving, the optimal number of frankfurter rolls per package is $Q = 8$. The price charged per package equals the total value received by the buyer, which is given by the shaded area in Figure 11.3, which is equal to the sum of consumer surplus and total variable cost. In this example, the price per package is $TR = 0.5(\$0.30 - \$0.10)8 + (\$0.10)8 = \$1.60$. The supermarket's operating profit equals consumer surplus of $TR - TVC = \$1.60 - \$0.80 = \$0.80$, which is $\$0.40$ greater than the operating profit when selling frankfurter rolls one at a time.

A variation of block pricing occurs when a firm charges a different price for different ranges of quantities. This is typical of the electric utilities that charge a higher rate for the first block of kilowatt hours and a lower rate for the next block of kilowatt hours, and so on. The primary advantage of this pricing scheme is that the firm is able to extract some consumer surplus without any prior knowledge of which buyer places a higher value on smaller amounts of kilowatt hours consumed. Once the utility company posts its sliding rate schedule, consumers will self select according to willingness to pay.

Two-Part Pricing

A computationally close variation of block pricing is **two-part pricing,** which is the practice of charging a fixed fee for the right to purchase a good or service at a per-unit price equal to marginal cost. The per-unit charge covers the firm's operating cost. The fixed fee, which is equal to average consumer surplus, is the firm's per-customer operating profit. The firm's per customer economic profit equals consumer surplus less the customer's share of total fixed cost. Two-part pricing is frequently practiced by health and country clubs that charge an annual dues plus a per-visit user fee.

SOLVED EXERCISE

The average per-family seasonal inverse demand equation for rounds of golf at a local country club is

$$P = 50 - Q. \tag{11.13}$$

where P is the price (greens fee) and Q is the number of rounds of golf played. The per-family cost of maintaining the country club's facilities is

$$TC = 1 + 10Q. \tag{11.14}$$

a. *What is the country club's maximum per-family profit if it only charges greens fees?*
b. *What is the country club's profit if managers adopt a two-part pricing strategy?*

Solution

a. *From Eq. (11.13), the country club's per-family total revenue is equation is*

$$TR(Q) = PQ = 50Q - Q^2. \tag{11.15}$$

The corresponding marginal revenue equation is

$$MR(Q) = 50 - 2Q. \tag{11.16}$$

From Eq. (11.14), MC = 10. Setting MR = MC, the profit-maximizing quantity is Q = 20 rounds of golf per family. From Eq. (11.13), the country club should charge a greens fee of P = \$30 per round. The country club's maximum profit is

$$\pi(Q) = TR(Q) - TC(Q) = -1 + 40(20) - (20)^2 = \$399. \tag{11.17}$$

b. *By adopting a two-part pricing strategy, the optimal greens fee per round is MC = \$10 per round. At this price, the quantity demanded is Q = 40 rounds of golf per family. At this quantity, consumer surplus*

$$CS = 0.5(\$50 - \$10)40 = \$800. \qquad (11.18)$$

Thus, the optimal two-part pricing strategy is for the country club to charge $800 for a seasonal family membership and a per-round fee of $10. Since the greens fees cover the country club's operating cost, the country club's operating profit is $800. I total per family profit is operating profit less fixed cost, that is $800 – $1 = $799.

A variation of two-part pricing is practiced by such "big box" outlets as Costco, BJ's or Sam's Club. These retailers charge shoppers an annual membership fee, but also combine per unit pricing with block pricing. Another interesting variation of two-part pricing is practiced by theme (amusement) parks. Suppose, for example, that the inverse demand equation of an average park guest is

$$P = 8 - \frac{Q}{3}, \qquad (11.19)$$

where P is the price per ride and Q the number of rides demanded. Suppose that the marginal cost of allowing one more rider on, say, a roller coaster is $0. Suppose the amusement park practices single-ride pricing. Setting $MR = MC$ we obtain

$$8 - \left(\frac{2}{3}\right)Q = 0. \qquad (11.20)$$

Solving Eq. (11.20), the theme park will charge a profit-maximizing price is $4 per ride and the average park visitor rides 12 times. The park's operating profit per guest is

$$TR - TVC = (\$4 - \$0)(12) = \$48. \qquad (11.21)$$

If the amusement park adopts a two-part pricing strategy it will charge a one-time admission fee, but allow guests to ride for free, that is $P = MC = \$0$. At this price, the average park guest will ride $Q = 24$ times. At this price and quantity, a typical guest's consumer surplus $CS = 0.5(\$8 - \$0)24 = \$96$. By charging a one-time entry fee of $96, the amusement park doubles its operating profit.

In fact, most amusement parks do not charge all park guests the same one-time entry fee, but charge different prices to different groups. As we will see in our discussion of third-degree price discrimination, an amusement park can earn even greater profits by charging a lower admission fee to students, the elderly, or to those who visit after nightfall by exploiting differences in the price elasticity of demand of each group.

The success of second-degree price depends on the ability of amusement parks to deny access by non-payers. Theme parks such as the Six Flags Great Adventure, Busch Gardens Tampa, and Walt Disney World located away from populated areas. Access is restricted to just a few entry points. The parks' perimeters have high fences that are continually patrolled by security personnel. The ability to deny access by non-payers helps to explain why cable television companies practice two-part pricing by charging a one-time installation fees and a monthly, per television subscription fee. Since it is much more difficult to restrict entry to older amusement parks located in densely populated metropolitan areas, an alternative pricing scheme is to sell identifying bracelets that allow park visitors to ride as often as they like for a limited period of time. This pay-one-price (POP) scheme does not control access to the park, but rather controls access to individual rides.

Ironically, two-part pricing by amusement parks results not only generates greater profits, but is also good public relations. Amusement park guests like the idea of not paying per ride and riding as often as they like. Unfortunately, this results in longer lines for more popular rides, which increases waiting times and rider **opportunity costs**. Thus, while many guests believe their comfort and convenience is of paramount concern to park management, the objective is to extract as much consumer surplus as possible.

Commodity Bundling

Commodity bundling is the practice of selling two or more different products at a single "bundled" price. Like block and two-part pricing, commodity bundling attempts to increase profit by extracting some consumer surplus. An example of commodity bundling is when travel agents offer vacation packages that include airfare fares, hotel accommodations, meals, entertainment, and ground transportation. Another example is insurance companies that bundle life, home and automobile coverage. To understand how commodity bundling works, consider a resort hotel that sells weekly vacation packages, which include room, board, and entertainment. Suppose that the cost to the hotel of providing the package is $1,000 per tourist.

Suppose the hotel knows that there are two types of tourists who value the components of the package differently. Unfortunately, the hotel cannot identify which tourist belongs to what group. Table 11.1 summarizes the maximum amount that a tourist in each group is willing to pay for each component of the package.

Suppose that the hotel charges for each component. For simplicity, assume there are ten tourists in each group. If the hotel charges $2,500

Table 11.1

Group	Room and Board	Entertainment
1	$2,500	$500
2	$1,800	$750

for room and board, it will only sell to the first group for total revenues of 10($2,500) = $25,000. If the hotel charges $1,800, it will sell to both groups and earn revenues of 20($1,800) = $36,000. Similarly, if the hotel charges $750 for entertainment, it will only sell to the second group and earn 10($750) = $7,500. If the hotel charges $500, it will sell to both groups and earn 20($500) = $10,000. If the hotel charges $1,800 for room and board and $500 for entertainment, its total profit is $36,000 + $10,000 − 20($1,000) = $26,000. Thus, it is in the hotels best interest to price each component to attract buyers from both groups.

By charging for each component separately, the hotel earns a total profit of $26,000. The hotel can do even better, however, by charging a package price of $2,550 that includes room, board, and entertainment. To see why, note that the maximum price that the first group will pay for the package is $2,500 + $500 = $3,000. The maximum price that the second group will pay is $1,800 + $750 = $2,550. By charging a price of $2,550, the hotel will sell the package to both groups for a total profit of $2,550(20) − $1,000(20) = $31,000, which is $5,000 more than pricing each component separately. At this package price, the hotel extracts the total consumer surplus from the second group and a portion of consumer from the first group.

Third-Degree Price Discrimination

In some cases, it may be possible to charge different groups different prices for the same good or service. **Third-degree price discrimination** is practiced by theaters, restaurants, amusement parks, and retail outlets that offer senior citizen, student, and youth discounts. The underlying idea is that demand tends to be less price elastic for high-income groups than for low-income groups. This pricing strategy has considerable public relations appeal since it is perceived as public spirited, even though it has the potential for generating even greater profits. Third-degree price discrimination is also practiced in international trade where exporters frequently sell in foreign markets at a lower price where demand is more price elastic than the price charged in their home market—a practice sometimes referred to as "dumping."

The rationale behind third-degree price discrimination is reasonably straightforward. Recall that a profit-maximizing firm produces where $MR = MC$. Different groups, however, have different demand and marginal revenue functions. If we assume the same marginal cost of selling to each group, a profit-maximizing firm should set the price of its product such that $MC = MR_1$, $MC = MR_2$, and so on. To see why, suppose that $MR_1 > MC$. It would pay for the firm to lower the price it charges to group 1 since this will increase profit. The firm should continue to lower the price it charges to this group until $MR_1 = MC$.

So, what price should each group be charged? Suppose that the firm sells an identical product to two groups. The price elasticity of demand for groups 1 and 2 are $e_{x,1}$ and $e_{x,2}$, respectively. Applying Eq. (3.17) we obtain

$$MR_i = P_i \left[1 + \frac{1}{\varepsilon_{x,i}} \right], \tag{11.22}$$

where $i = 1$, 2 and $|e_{x,i}| > 1$ (since a firm with market power will never produce along the inelastic portion of the demand curve for its product). The profit-maximizing prices is determined by equating marginal cost to the firm's marginal revenue from each group, that is $MC = MR_1 = MR_2$. Suppose that $e_{x,1} = e_{x,2}$. This firm will charge each group the same price. On the other hand, this firm will charge a higher price to the group in which demand is less elastic. Theaters offer senior citizen discounts because the demand for movie tickets by senior citizens is more price sensitive than for other groups. Offering senior citizen discounts increases ticket sales and revenues from this group. This situation is depicted Figure 11.4.

For third-degree price discrimination to be effective, a firm must know the price elasticity of demand for each group. It must also be relatively easy to identify members of each group, such as asking for proof of age in the case of senior or junior citizen discounts, or a college ID for student discounts.

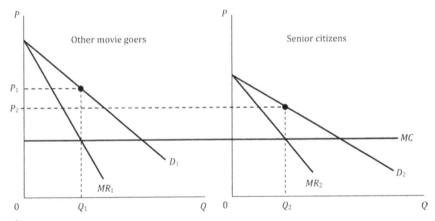

Figure 11.4

Movie theaters owners often offer matinee discounts because demand for during mid-day and mid-week shows is more price elastic. Finally, it must not be possible for the group purchasing at the lower price to resell to the group being charged a higher price. In general, it will not be possible to practice third-degree price discrimination if **transaction costs** are low and there is an active secondary (resale) market.

SOLVED EXERCISE

Red Company sells its product in two separable and identifiable markets. Red Company's marginal cost is $10. What price should Red Company charge in each market if the price elasticity of demand in each market is $\varepsilon_{x,1} = -1.5$ and $\varepsilon_{x,2} = -2$?

Solution

Equating $MC = MR_1 = MR_2$ we obtain

$$P_1\left[1 - \frac{1}{1.5}\right] = P_2\left[1 - \frac{1}{2}\right] = \$10. \tag{11.23}$$

Solving, Red Company should charge prices of $P_1 = \$30$ and $P_2 = \$20$.

So far we assumed that managers are able to distinguish between high price-elasticity of demand customers from low price-elasticity of demand customers. But, what if it is not the case? Third-degree price discrimination may still be possible through **self-selection**—a process known as **indirect price discrimination**. To see how this might work, consider the case of a supermarket that uses coupons to sell items at a discount. High-income customers tend to be less price sensitive when shopping for groceries than are low-income customers. Because time has a greater opportunity cost, high-income customers are less likely to spend their time clipping coupons. In effect, the supermarket is charging customers with a higher price elasticity of demand a lower price. Of course, if too many low price-elasticity of demand customers start clipping coupons then this attempt to extract consumer surplus will fail. The possibility that high-priced sales will be cannibalized by offering low prices to high price-elasticity of demand customers is a potential problem with many indirect pricing schemes.

Another example of indirect price discrimination occurs when a firm offers alternative versions of a product to appeal to different customers types. Consider, for example, the Microsoft Office 2013. The Home and Student edition retails for around $140 while the Professional edition retails for around $400. In this case, the additional features of the high-price Professional edition has greater appeal to businesses even though the marginal cost to Microsoft of including these enhancements is negligible.

SPECIAL PRICING STRATEGIES

In this section we will examine the pricing strategies of profit-maximizing firms with limited production capacity, or that independently or jointly produce multiple products with dependent or independent demands.

Capacity Peak-Load Pricing

In many markets, demand is greater at certain times than at others. The demand for electricity, for example, is higher during the day than at night, and is higher in the summer and winter than in the spring and fall. Toll bridges and commuter railroads are often more heavily congested during "rush hour" than at other times of the day. Airline travel is greater during holidays than during the rest of the year. While charging higher prices during periods of greater demand is not unusual, what these situations have in common is that the firm's production capacity is strained during peak periods, and has surplus capacity during off-peak periods. Capacity limitations during periods of heavy demand often give rise to a practice known as **capacity peak-load pricing**.

Figure 11.5 illustrates peak-load pricing for a profit-maximizing commuter railroad with limited capacity. In this case, the marginal cost of accommodating additional riders is constant until it is no longer possible squeeze any more riders into its railroad cars. At this level of output, the only way to accommodate more passengers is to add more trains and rail lines. For all intents and purposes, the marginal cost of immediately expanding capacity is infinitely great. The same reasoning also applies to building a new bridge or installing a new hydroelectric generator during periods of peak demand after capacity has been reached. For this reason, the marginal cost curve becomes vertical at $Q_{capacity}$.

To maximize profit, the firm depicted in Figure 11.5 may choose to charge different prices during peak and off-peak hours. Since demand is less during off-peak hours, the commuter railroad will charge a lower price during off-peak periods where $MR_{off\text{-}peak} = MC$, which occurs at point A. It will a higher price during peak periods where $MR_{peak} = MC$, which occurs at point B. Peak-load pricing is a way to ration limited capacity by encouraging rail passengers and bridge users to travel during off-peak periods. Paradoxically, some public

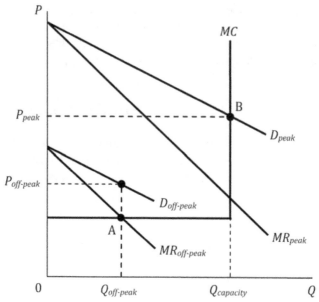

Figure 11.5

agencies often do precisely the opposite by offering volume discounts to rush-hour commuters.

SOLVED EXERCISE

The Gotham Bridge and Tunnel Authority (GBTA) has estimated that the off-peak and peak demand equations for travel on the Frog's Neck Bridge are

$$P_{off-peak} = 5 - 0.02Q_{off-peak}; \tag{11.24}$$

$$P_{peak} = 10 - 0.05Q_{peak}, \tag{11.25}$$

where P is the toll charged for per bridge crossing Q. The marginal cost of accommodating traffic during off-peak periods is \$2.00 per driver. If Frog's Neck Bridge capacity is 80 drivers per minute, how much should GBTA charge for peak and off-peak crossings?

Solution

GBTA should charge an off-peak toll where $MR_{off-peak} = MC$. Total off-peak revenue is

$$TR_{off-peak} = 5Q_{off-peak} - 0.02Q_{off-peak}^2. \tag{11.26}$$

The corresponding marginal off-peak revenue equation is

$$MR_{off-peak} = 5 - 0.04Q_{off-peak}. \tag{11.27}$$

Setting Eq. (11.27) equal to $2.00, the profit-maximizing number of off-peak crossings is $Q_{off-peak}* = 75$. From Eq. (11.24), GBTA should charge an off-peak toll of $P_{off-peak} = \$3.50$. Substituting $Q_{peak} = 80$ into Eq. (11.25), the peak toll is $P_{peak}* = \$6.00$.*

Multiproduct Pricing

We have thus far considered the pricing practices of firms that produce a single product. In this section we will examine **multiproduct pricing**, which involves optimal pricing of two or more goods produced by the same firm. This is a complicated topic since we need to consider whether the goods are complements or substitutes, and whether they are independently or jointly produced. Although a comprehensive discussion of multi-product pricing is beyond the scope of this book, we will examine four scenarios to convey a sense of the issues involved. In particular, we will consider a firm that produces two goods that (1) have independent demands and are independently produced, (2) have independent demands and are jointly produced in fixed proportions, (3) have interdependent demands and are independently produced, and (4) have interdependent demand and are jointly produced.

Independent Demands and Independent Production

Consider the simplest case of multiproduct pricing in which a profit-maximizing firm that produces two unrelated goods (Q_1 and Q_2) that are produced using separate (independent) facilities. Since the goods are unrelated, the **cross-price elasticity of demand** is zero ($\varepsilon_{1,2} = 0$). Since the two goods are produced separately, there are no **cost complementarities**, that is, the marginal cost of good 1 is not reduced by increasing the production of good 2, and vice versa. If this profit-maximizing firm has market power, it will produce where $MR_1(Q_1) = MC_1(Q_1)$ and $MR_2(Q_2) = MC_2(Q_2)$. In this case, there is no conceptual difference between this situation and the pricing and output decisions of two unrelated profit-maximizing firms.

Independent Demands and Joint Production

The next case involves a firm that produces two goods with unrelated demands ($\varepsilon_{1,2} = 0$), but are jointly produced using the same manufacturing facilities.

In this case, the firm may enjoy cost complementarities, such as might occur from the joint production of beef and cowhide from cattle, liquid oxygen and nitrogen from air, and gasoline and fuel oil from petroleum.

Joint production of the two goods may be in fixed or variable proportions. We will confine our discussion to the analytically simpler case of joint production in fixed proportions in which the production of one good automatically determines the output of the other. We can express this fixed relationship as $Q_2 = kQ_1$, where $k > 0$ is the factor of proportionality. For example, if $k = 3$, for each unit of good 1 produced the firm produces 3 units of good 2. In this case, the firm's total cost function may be written

$$TC(Q_1 + Q_2) = TC(Q_1 + kQ_1) = TC(Q_1).\tag{11.28}$$

The market demands for the two goods are unrelated, the firm's total revenue equation becomes

$$TR(Q_1, Q_2) = TR_1(Q_1) + TR_2(kQ_1) = TR(Q_1).\tag{11.29}$$

Since the goods are produced in fixed proportions, the firm's total revenue and total cost equations may be expressed as a function of just good 1. In this case, a profit-maximizing firm with market power should produce where

$$MR_1(Q_1) + MR_2(kQ_1) = MC(Q_1).\tag{11.30}$$

SOLVED EXERCISE

Suppose that a firm produces two units of good 2 for each unit of good 1 using the same manufacturing facilities, that is $Q_2 = 2Q_1$. The demands for the two goods are unrelated. The inverse demand equations for the two goods are

$$P_1 = 20 - 2Q_1;\tag{11.31}$$

$$P_2 = 100 - 5Q_2.\tag{11.32}$$

The firm's total cost equation is

$$TC = 10 + 45Q_1^2,\tag{11.33}$$

where $Q = Q_1 + Q_2$ thousand units.
a. *What are the profit-maximizing output levels and prices of Q_1 and Q_2?*
b. *What is the firm's total profit?*

Solution

a. *The firm's total revenue equation is*

$$TR(Q) = (20 - 2Q_1)Q_1 + (100 - 5Q_2)Q_2. \tag{11.34}$$

Since $Q_2 = 2Q_1$, the firm's total revenue equations is

$$TR(Q) = 220Q_1 - 22Q_1^2. \tag{11.35}$$

The corresponding marginal revenue and marginal cost equations are

$$MR(Q_1) = 220 - 44Q_1; \tag{11.36}$$

$$MC(Q_1) = 90Q_1. \tag{11.37}$$

Setting $MR(Q_1) = MC(Q_1)$, the profit-maximizing output levels are $Q_1^* = 1.64$ thousand and $Q_2^* = 2Q_1^* = 3.28$ thousand units. From Eqs. (11.31) and (11.32), this firm should charge $P_1^* = \$16.72$ and $P_2^* = \$83.60$.

b. *The firm's total profit is $\pi = \$16.72(1.64) + \$83.60(3.28) - \$131.03 = \$170.60$ thousand.*

Interdependent Demands and Independent Production

Many firms produce multiple products that are consumption complements or substitutes. Dell Computer, for example, sells several models of desktop and laptop computers, which are substitute goods. Dell also offers a complete line of complementary "peripherals," such as routers, web-cameras, scanners, gaming keyboards, and so on. Since the goods are related, the inverse demand functions are $P_1 = P_1(Q_1, Q_2)$ and $P_2 = P_2(Q_1, Q_2)$. If we assume that the two goods are produced using separate (independent) production facilities, this firm will maximize profit where

$$MR_1(Q_1, Q_2) = MC_1(Q_1); \tag{11.38}$$

$$MR_2(Q_1, Q_2) = MC_2(Q_2). \tag{11.39}$$

SOLVED EXERCISE

Gizmo Brothers produces two models of yo-yos: the Exterminator and Eliminator. While some yo-yo aficionados are devotees of a particular model, others consider these yo-yos close substitutes. The inverse demand equations of the two models are

$$P_1 = 56 - 5Q_1 + 7Q_2; \tag{11.40}$$

$$P_2 = 48 - 2Q_2 + 4Q_1, \tag{11.41}$$

where Q_1 and Q_2 are thousands Exterminators and the Eliminators, respectively. Since the yo-yo's are independently produced, the total cost equations are

$$TC_1 = 4 + 2Q_1^2; \tag{11.42}$$

$$TC_2 = 8 + 6Q_2^2. \tag{11.43}$$

a. *What is the profit-maximizing price and output for each yo-yo?*
b. *How much is Gizmo's total profit?*

Solution

a. *The total revenue equations are*

$$TR_1 = P_1Q_1 = 56Q_1 - 5Q_1^2 + 7Q_1Q_2; \tag{11.44}$$

$$TR_2 = P_2Q_2 = 48Q_2 - 2Q_2^2 + 4Q_2Q_1. \tag{11.45}$$

The respective marginal revenue equations are

$$MR_1 = 56 - 3Q_1 + 7Q_2; \tag{11.46}$$

$$MR_2 = 48 - 4Q_2 + 4Q_1. \tag{11.47}$$

The marginal costs of producing Exterminators and Eliminators are

$$MC_1 = 4Q_1; \tag{11.48}$$

$$MC_2 = 12Q_2. \tag{11.49}$$

Equating marginal revenue to marginal cost for each yo-yo, the profit maximizing levels of output are $Q_1^* = 6.286$ thousand and $Q_2^* = 4.571$ thousand. From Eqs. (11.41) and (11.42), the profit-maximizing prices are $P_1^* = \$62.14$ and $P_2^* = \$58.$

b. *Gizmo's total profit is $\pi_1 + \pi_2 = (TR_1 - TC_1) + (TR_2 - TC_2) = \$272.57 + \$159.18 = \$431.75$ thousand.*

Interdependent Demands and Joint Production

It can be demonstrated that optimal pricing of two goods jointly produced in fixed proportions with interdependent demands is analytically equivalent to interdependent demands and independent production. If production exhibits cost complementarities, it may also be in the firm's best interest to practice **cross subsidization**, which occurs when the profits generated from the sale of one product is used to subsidize the sales of a complementary product.

An example of cross subsidization is practiced by Adobe Systems Inc., makers of *Adobe Reader* and *Adobe Acrobat*. Adobe Reader allows users to read documents prepared in portable document format (pdf). Adobe Acrobat allows users to create ("write") pdf documents. Even though Adobe Reader is a by-product of Adobe Acrobat, the company could charge for both reader and writer. Instead, Adobe Systems provides Adobe Reader free of charge. By doing so, the company increases the demand for its writer, which it is able to sell at higher price. As a result, Adobe Systems earns greater profits than if the reader and writer are sold separately.

NON-MARGINAL PRICING

We have thus far assumed that managers make pricing decision to maximize profit. In fact, many managers are not. Some managers may be "satisficers" whose objective is to satisfy shareholder expectations (Simon, 1956). Still others focus on market share, return on assets, return on equity, or some predetermined profit margin. Many managers of firms with market power who would like to maximize profit, but lack the cost data to make that possible. For this reason, many managers rely on rules-of-thumb methods for pricing their product.

Cost-Plus Pricing

One of the most popular forms of non-marginal pricing is **cost-plus (mark-up or full-cost) pricing**. This approach involves charging a price that includes a "mark up" over the firm's per-unit (average total) cost of production. Although inconsistent with the goal profit maximization, this pricing strategy is simple to understand and easy to apply. Cost-plus pricing is given by the equation

$$P_x = ATC(1+m), \qquad\qquad (11.50)$$

where P_x is the price of good x, ATC is average total cost, and m is the percentage mark-up. This equation may be rewritten as

$$m = \frac{P_x - ATC}{ATC}. \qquad\qquad (11.51)$$

The numerator may be written as $P_x - AVC - AFC$. The term $P_x - AVC$ is called the firm's *contribution margin per unit*. The mark-up may be viewed as the firm's profit per unit of output minus some allocation to defray per-unit overhead costs.

Cost-plus pricing has several potential shortcomings. To begin with, accounting estimates of average variable and total fixed cost typically exclude **implicit costs**. A more serious shortcoming is that this pricing scheme is insensitive to changes in market demand. We know from Eq. (7.8) that firms with market power charge a price that is greater than marginal cost. This price is sensitive to changes in market demand. By contrast, the mark up in cost-plus pricing is both arbitrary and constant. To overcome these shortcomings, managers should adjust the mark up to reflect the price elasticity of demand for the firm's product. If we assume that that MC is approximately equal to ATC, it may be demonstrated that

$$m = -\frac{1}{1+\varepsilon_{x,x}}. \qquad\qquad (11.52)$$

Eq. (11.52) says that a firm should lower its mark up if demand becomes more price elastic. For example, if $\varepsilon_{x,x} = -2$, the mark-up should be $m = -1/(1-2) = 1$, or 100 percent. If $\varepsilon_{x,x} = -5$, the mark-up should be $m = -1/(1 - 5) = 0.25$, or 25 percent. When demand is perfectly elastic ($\varepsilon_{x,x} = -\infty$), such as in perfectly competitive markets, the mark up should be $m = 0$.

Price Fixing

Another non-marginal pricing strategy is **price fixing**, which occurs when firms form a coalition to fix prices to maximize industry profits. Price fixing coalitions may involve allocating market shares, assigning production quotas, engaging in cooperative price advertising, standardizing credit terms, offering uniform trade-in allowances, and so on. Although such collusive behavior is frequently illegal, the success of a price-fixing strategy depends on several factors, including the number of firms, their relative contribution industry output, and public transparency.

In general, price-fixing agreements are more likely to succeed when the coalition involves a small number of firms with similar interests since compliance is easier to monitor. If there are n price-fixing firms, each firm must monitor compliance of the other $n - 1$ firms. Thus, the total number of monitoring arrangements is $n(n - 1)$. For example, Vienna-based Organization of Petroleum Exporting Countries (OPEC) assigns production quotas to each of its 13 members. To effectively police compliance, $13(13 - 1) = 156$ monitoring arrangements are required. Costly monitoring and the difficulty of imposing sanctions when quotas are violated increases with the size of the coalition. The likelihood that an agreement will disintegrate increases along with the size of the coalition.

When cartels are illegal, firms may engage in tacit or secret collusion. Tacit collusion may emerge from the firms' shared experiences or by observing the past behavior of rivals. This "understanding" may lead to payoffs that are possible with explicit agreements. When tacit collusion is infeasible, firms may enter into a secret, albeit illegal, explicit agreement.

Price Matching

To understand how tacit price collusion might emerge, suppose the managers of "big-box" superstores Home Depot and Lowe's Home Improvement are deciding whether to charge a high price or a low price for a similar product. While both retailers have a core of loyal customers, there is a third group that will always buy from the lowest-price vendor. The profits from alternative pricing strategies are summarized in Figure 11.6.

This one-time, static pricing game is an example of a **prisoner's dilemma**—both firms have a dominant low price strategy, but would be better off by forming a coalition and charging a high price. Although the strategy profile {*High price, High price*} results in a greater payoff, past efforts to capture a larger market share were thwarted by retaliatory price reductions. Since price wars were counterproductive, price matching may introduce an element of stability into tacit price-fixing coalition. **Price matching** occurs

		Loew's	
		Low price	*High price*
Home Depot	*Low price*	**(90, 80)**	**(110,** 50)
	High price	(60, **110**)	(100, 90)

Payoffs: (Home Depot, Loew's)

Figure 11.6

when a firm publicly announces that it will match any lower price offered by a competitor. This pricing strategy is not only good for public relations, but also results in higher prices.

The rationale underlying a price matching strategy was discussed in Chapter 9. Any attempt by one firm to capture market share will be thwarted by offsetting price reductions by rivals. When each firm adopts a price matching strategy, consumers searching for a lower price will be unsuccessful. As a result, each firm maintains its market share and earns greater profits.

The cost of punishing defectors can be quite high. Firms must not only lower the price it charges rivals' customers, but must lower the price that it charges its own customers. While each firm may experience a small increase in unit sales because of the generally lower price, the result is lower revenues and profits for the entire industry. This frequently happens in the airline industry when an air carrier attempts to lure fliers from rivals by offering discounts.

An important aspect of a price-matching strategy is that it does not require firms to monitor a rival's compliance. This costly activity is borne by the consumers who incur search costs. It may also negatively affect good-will since customers are often required to provide proof, such as a newspaper advertisement, of a rival's lower price.

Most-Favored Customer

A variation of price matching is a **most-favored customer** policy. This strategy promises to charge all "most favored" customers the lowest price paid by any other customer. Firms that adopt this pricing strategy are better able to withstand pressures to lower price because they can argue that "I'd really like to offer you a lower price, but if I do it for you, I'll have to do it for everyone else."

Price Leadership

In some cases, a leading firm sets the price for the rest of the industry. Two forms of **price leadership** are barometric price leadership and dominant price leadership. In the case of **barometric price leadership**, an industry leader initiates a price change based on its reading of industry-wide market conditions, such as might occur when Citibank raise its prime interest rate. Rival firms agree with this decision they will follow suit. If they disagree, they will not change price, and the initiating firm will modify its decision until an industry-wide consensus is reached.

Some highly concentrated industries are characterized by a dominant firm and many smaller rivals. In such industries, the dominant firm may set the

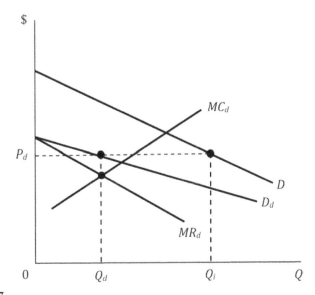

Figure 11.7

price for the rest of the industry. This phenomenon, which is known as **dominant price leadership**, is depicted in Figure 11.7. The demand curve for the industry's output is D, of which the dominant firm supplies D_d. The dominant firm maximizes profit by producing where $MC_d = MR_d$ and charging a price of P_d, which becomes the industry standard. At this price, the industry supplies Q_i units of output. The dominant firm supplies Q_d and the rest of the industry supplies $Q_i - Q_d$.

An interesting aspect of dominant price leadership is that once the industry price is established, the smaller rivals behave as if the industry was purely competitive since, that is, they are price takers. If entry and exit into and from the industry is relatively easy, above-normal profits will attract new firms into the industry, which may weaken the market power of the dominant firm. Whether this occurs partly depends on the circumstances that gave rise to the firm's rise to industry dominance in the first place, and whether those factors are sufficient to maintain the firm's preeminence.

Penetration Pricing

A firm that attempts to gain a foothold in a market by undercutting incumbent firms engages in **penetration pricing**. A variation of penetration pricing is *dumping*, which is defined by the Department of Commerce as a foreign firm selling in the U.S. at below fair market value. U.S. firms may file dumping charges against foreign competitors to obtain relief from unfair competition, such as import higher tariffs. Domestic companies frequently claim that dumping is an attempt by foreign firms to take over the domestic market. While this argument may seem compelling, *predatory dumping* is difficult to prove since the practice is typically an international form of third-degree price discrimination.

TRANSFER PRICING

Our analysis has thus far focused on optimal pricing strategies a firm's final product. In this section, we will briefly examine the subject of **transfer pricing**, which involves the internal pricing of components produced by an "upstream" division that are used to produce the output of the "downstream" division of the same company. Consider, for example, a telescope company that uses lenses produced by another division of the same company. What price should the upstream lens division charge the downstream telescope division to maximize company profits?

Transfer pricing is important in situations where managers are deciding whether to organize upstream and downstream divisions into semiautonomous **profit centers** since this gives rise to **double marginalization**, which occurs when each division sets $MC = MR$ to maximize individual division profits. The problem is that the combined maximum profits of the two divisions may be less than when the company is operated as an integrated whole. This is because the profit of the lens division is added to its "transfer" price, which raises the marginal cost of the telescope division. As a result, the downstream division charges a higher price, sells fewer telescopes, and earns less profit. Since both divisions are trying to extract a profit from the sale of telescopes, company profits suffer. In fact, double marginalization is a variation of the principal-agent problem discussed in Chapter 5. There is an inherent conflict between profit-maximizing divisions (agents) and the profit-maximizing firm (principal).

Transfer pricing is a complicated topic that encompasses a wide range of market situations. To develop a basic understanding of the issues involved, we will consider just two versions of the transfer pricing problem. We will begin by assuming that the upstream division produces a specialized component for which there are no close substitutes available in the external market. This will be followed by a discussion of the upstream production of a standardized component for which there exists a perfectly competitive external market. In both cases, the solution to the transfer pricing problem is to transform the upstream division from a profit center to a cost center, which is rewarded not on the basis of how much profit they earn, but on how much they reduce production costs.

No External Market

Suppose that a company consists of an upstream division that supplies specialized component Q_u for which there is external demand to a downstream division that produces Q_d for final sale. To simplify the analysis, assume that one unit of Q_u is used to produce one unit of Q_d. This situation is depicted in Figure 11.8. To maximize the company's profit, the downstream division should produce where $MR_d = MC_d$. The marginal cost of producing Q_d includes the marginal cost of producing the upstream component. To maximize profit, the downstream division's produces Q_d^* units and charges a price of P_d^*.

The transfer price (P_T) charged by the upstream division is equal to the marginal cost of producing Q_u at the profit-maximizing level of output Q_d^*. At this price, the upstream division earns zero economic profit since $P_u^* = P_T = MC_u$. Suppose, however, that the upstream division charges the downstream division $P_u > MC_u$ to maximize its individual profit. This increases the marginal cost of producing the downstream product from MC_d to $MC_d + (P_u - P_T)$, which results in a less-than-optimal level of output $(Q_d' < Q_d^*)$ and a higher price $(P_d' > P_u^*)$.

SOLVED EXERCISE

Suppose that the Parallax Corporation manufactures microscopes. Because of the rapid growth of the company in the 1990s, Parallax management

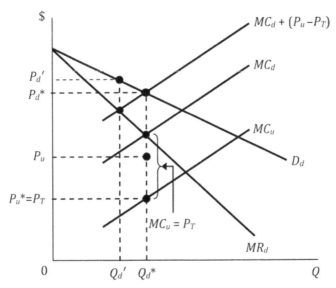

Figure 11.8

decided to reorganize the company into a microscope division and a lens division to control production costs. The inverse demand equation for Parallax microscopes is

$$P_M = 909 - 0.5Q_M. \tag{11.53}$$

The total cost of producing microscopes is

$$TC_M = 100 + 0.005Q_M^2. \tag{11.54}$$

   Although Parallax procures most of its components from outside vendors, each microscope requires three highly polished lenses that are manufactured by the company's lens division. Since these lenses must meet precise specifications, there is no external market for Parallax lenses. The total cost equation for producing Parallax lenses is

$$TC_L = 2,000 + 0.0025Q_L^2. \tag{11.55}$$

a. *What is the profit-maximizing price and quantity for Parallax microscopes?*
b. *What is Parallax's total profit?*
c. *What transfer price should the lens division charge the microscope division for its lenses?*

Solution

a. *The total revenue equation for Parallax microscopes is*

$$TR_M = (909 - 0.5Q_M)Q_M = 909Q_M - 0.5Q_M^2. \tag{11.56}$$

The marginal revenue from microscope sales is

$$MR_M = 909 - Q_M. \tag{11.57}$$

The marginal cost of producing microscopes is

$$MC_M = 0.01Q_M. \tag{11.58}$$

After setting $MR_M = MC_M$, the profit-maximizing output is $Q_M^* = 900$ microscopes. From Eq. (11.53), the profit-maximizing price is $P_M^* = \$459$.
b. *Parallax's profit at this level of output is*

$$\pi_M = \$459(900) - \left[100 + 0.005(900)^2\right] = \$408,950. \tag{11.59}$$

c. *Since each microscope requires three lenses then $Q_L = 3Q_M$. Thus, the marginal cost of producing lenses is*

$$MC_L = 0.005Q_L = 0.005(3Q_M) = 0.015Q_M. \qquad (11.60)$$

At the profit-maximizing level of microscope production, Parallax will produce 3(900) = 2,700 lenses. To maximize Parallax profits, the lens division should charge the microscope division a transfer price of $P_T = MC_L = 0.015(900) = \$13.50$ per lens.

Perfectly Competitive External Market

Suppose, instead, that the upstream division produces a standardized component for which there exists is a perfectly competitive external market. This situation is depicted in Figure 11.9. Suppose that the market-determined price of Q_u is P_u^*. As before, the downstream division should produce where $MR_d = MC_d$, which includes the marginal cost of producing the upstream component at that level of output. The downstream division produces Q_d^* units of output and charges a price of P_d^*. The upstream division, however, should produce Q_u^* units of output at the market-determined price of P_u^*. Since $Q_u^* > Q_d^*$, $Q_u = Q_d^*$ will be "sold" to the downstream division at a price of $P_T = MC_u$. The surplus production of the upstream division $(Q_u^* - Q_u)$ should then be sold in the external market at a price of P_u^*. Short-run profits

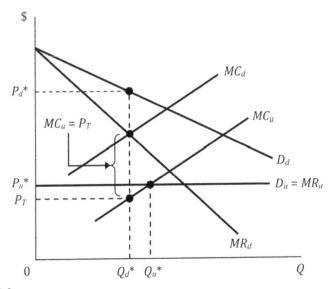

Figure 11.9

earned from the sale of the intermediate good in the external market supple-
ment the profits earned from the sale of the downstream product.

What should the company do if the market-determined price of the
upstream good is less than the transfer price? In the absence of some other
compelling reason for producing the intermediate good internally, such as
significantly lower transaction costs, the upstream division should discon-
tinue operation. The downstream division should purchase the intermediate
good in the external market, and the resources of the upstream division transferred to the company's core business.

SOLVED EXERCISE

*Suppose in the above Solved Exercise that there is a perfectly competitive
market for the lenses produced by the upstream division of Parallax Corporation and that market-determined price of a lens is $18.55.*
a. *What is the profit-maximizing price and quantity for Parallax microscopes?*
b. *What transfer price should the lens division charge the microscope
division?*
c. *Will the lens division's level of output satisfy the requirements of the
microscope division?*

Solution

a. *The profit maximizing price ($P_M* = \$459$) and output ($Q_M* = 900$) of
microscopes is unaffected by the existence of a purely competitive external
market for the lenses.*
b. *The transfer price of lenses remains unchanged at $P_T = \$13.50$.*
c. *The marginal cost of producing lenses is given by Eq. (11.60). Marginal
revenue from lens sales is the market-determined price of $P_L* = \$18.55$.
Setting MC = MR, the firm will produce $Q_L* = 3,710$ lenses, of which
$3(885) = 2,655$ lenses will be sold to the downstream microscope division
at the transfer price. The remaining 1,077 lenses will be sold in the external market at the market-determined price.*

ENTRY DETERRENCE

We have thus far examined several pricing strategies of firms that operate in
an imperfectly competitive business environment. At some point, however,
an incumbent industry leader may be confronted with the threat of lower
prices and reduced profits as new firms enter the industry and compete for

market share. Is there a pricing strategy that the incumbent firm can adopt to turn back this challenge? One possibility is for the incumbent firm to engage in **predatory pricing** by slashing prices to deter entry by the challenger. Once the upstart firm has been driven from the market, the incumbent recoups its losses by restoring price to its pre-challenge level. To highlight the issues involved, consider the situation depicted in Figure 11.10.

Suppose that David is a start-up company and Goliath is the established industry leader. David has developed a more efficient operating system that industry analysts believe challenges Goliath's preeminence in the market. The strategy choices facing David are to *enter* or *stay out* of the market. If David enters the market and Goliath adopts a *competitive* pricing strategy, the **present value** of David's future operating profits is $500,000, although the present value of Goliath's operating profits decline from $5 million to $2 million. If Goliath adopts a *predatory* pricing strategy, the David's incurs an operating loss of −$500,000 and Goliath's operating profit plummets to $500,000. Should David take Goliath's threat to slash prices seriously?

It turns out that predatory pricing by Goliath is an empty threat. To see why, suppose that David enters the market. Goliath's payoff from a predatory pricing strategy is $500,000 and $2 million by pricing competitively. Using **backward induction**, the **subgame-perfect equilibrium** is for David to enter the market, and for Goliath to price competitively.

Analytically, the problem for Goliath is that David has a **first-mover advantage**. If Goliath can reverse these roles, it may be possible to keep David from entering the market. Suppose that Goliath's CEO circulates an internal memo indicating that the legal department is prepared to file a lawsuit claiming copyright infringement should David enter the market. The present value of the lawsuit for each company is $1 million in legal fees. What is the effect of the lawsuit if the contents of the memo are intentionally leaked to David's senior managers?

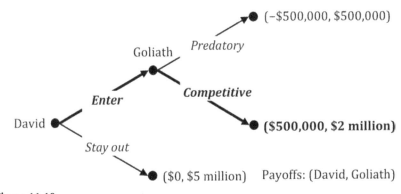

Figure 11.10

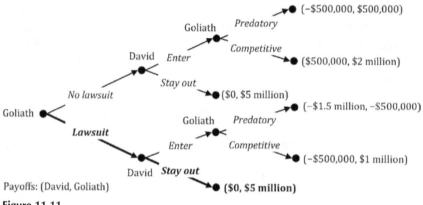

Payoffs: (David, Goliath)

Figure 11.11

Start-up companies typically need to get their product to market quickly to generate much-needed cash flows. Even if David's lawyers are dubious of the merits of the lawsuit, the company will not be able to weather this legal challenge. The effects of Goliath's preemptive lawsuit strategy are depicted in Figure 11.11. By seizing the first-mover advantage, the subgame-perfect equilibrium is for Goliath to file a lawsuit, and for David to stay out of the market.

According to a study by Oster and Strong (2001), predation is frequently practiced by airlines that use their near-monopoly status at hub airports to drive out potential competitors. The study cited twelve instances in which a new entrant attempted to enter a market dominated by a major carrier by offering low fares. In every case, the incumbent adopted a predatory-pricing strategy. Within two years, half the challengers had been forced out of the market, while most incumbents were able to recoup their losses by subsequently raising prices.

Limit Pricing

A variation of predation is **limit pricing**, which occurs when a monopolist, or a coalition of firms, attempts to prevent the entry of new firms into the industry. This pricing strategy, which is illegal in the U.S. and elsewhere, attempts to discourage competition by keeping prices at or near the coalition's per-unit production cost. It does this by producing at a sufficiently high level of output such that any addition to industry supply will guarantee that the challenger will incur a loss.

The strategic problem with limit pricing is an increase in industry supply could result in negative profits for coalition members as well. In other words, the coalitions output may no longer constitute a best-response strategy since it would be forced to reduce output to salvage its own (and the challenger's) bottom line. Thus, in order for limit pricing to be effective, the coalition's threat must be credible. The coalition must be able to irrevocably commit itself to a level of output to discourage entry, such as by signing long-term collective bargaining agreement in which the coalition agrees to employ a large number of workers, or by undertaking a capital expansion project to increase production capacity.

CHAPTER EXERCISES

11.1 The manager of a retail computer equipment outlet uses the company's standard 100 percent mark-up and charges $200 for its most popular model of motherboards. The manager recently read in an economic journal that the price elasticity of demand for motherboards is –3.5. Is this manager optimally pricing this product? If not, what price should the manager charge to maximize the outlet's profit on the sale of motherboards?

11.2 An industry consists of five, Cournot output-setting firms producing a homogeneous product. The market price elasticity of demand is –2.5. If the market price is $64.20, what is the firm's marginal cost?

11.3 An amusement park has estimated the following demand equation for the average park guest

$$Q = 16 - 2P,$$

where Q represents the number or rides per guest, and P the price per ride. The total cost of providing a ride is

$$TC = 2 + 0.5Q.$$

a. How much should it charge per ride basis if the park wishes to maximize its profit? What is the park's per guest profit?

b. What admission fee should the park charge if it wants to maximize profit? What is the park's profit per guest?

11.4 Blotto Brothers Lumber Supply sells lumber to local construction companies. Blotto has estimated that the demand for plywood by home contractors is given by the equation

$$Q = 51 - \frac{1}{10}P.$$

Blotto's total cost of procuring and packaging plywood for delivery to its customers is

$$TC = 10Q.$$

a. If Blotto engages in standard pricing, what is the profit-maximizing price and quantity?
b. Given you answer to part a, what is Blotto's per customer profit?
c. If Blotto practices block pricing, how many sheets of plywood should the company include in a bundle?
d. What price should it charge for a bundle of plywood?
e. What is Blotto's per customer variable profit?

11.5 A car dealership is offering a GPS system, DVD player and UBS audio interface in all its new models. The manager of the dealership believes that its customers fall into three groups, and there are 100 buyers each group. The manager does not know which buyer belongs to what group. Suppose that it costs the dealership $25, $50, and $400 to install the GPS, DVD, and UBS, respectively.
a. What price should the dealership charge for each option to maximize its profit?
b. How much should the dealership charge for a package of options to maximize profit?

Group	GPS	DVD	UBS
A	$150	$70	$500
B	$50	$100	$1,000
C	$370	$90	$750

11.6 A firm sells its product in two separable and identifiable markets. The firm's total cost of production is

$$TC = 5 + 5Q.$$

The demand equations for these products are

$$Q_1 = 10 - 0.5P_1;$$
$$Q_2 = 20 - 0.2P_2,$$

where $Q = Q_1 + Q_2$.
a. Calculate the firm's profit-maximizing price and output level in each market.
b. Verify that the demand is less elastic in the market with the higher price.
c. What is the firm's total profit?

11.7 Jacob Grimm sells barrels of Skull & Bones Ale to the isolated villages of Forlorn and Dismal. Because Forlorn and Dismal are separated by a high mountain range populated by werewolves and vampires, it is not possible to resell in Dismal the ale that was purchased in Forlorn, and *vice versa*. The respective demand equations in Forlorn and Dismal are

$$Q_F = 50 - \frac{P_F}{4.5};$$

$$Q_D = 75 - \frac{P_D}{7.5}.$$

Jacob's total cost equation is

$$TC = 10 + 0.5Q^2,$$

where $Q = Q_F + Q_D$.
a. What is the profit-maximizing price and output level in each village?
b. Verify that the demand for Skull & Bones Ale is less elastic in the market in which Jacob charges the higher price.
c. Calculate Jacob's total profit.

11.8 Suppose that a company has estimated the average variable cost of producing its product to be $10. The firms total fixed cost is $100,000.
a. If the company produces 1,000 units and its standard pricing strategy is to add a 35 percent markup, what price should the company charge?
b. Verify that the this price represents a 35 percent mark-up over the estimated average cost of production.

11.9 What is the estimated percentage mark-up over the fully-allocated per-unit cost of production when the price elasticities of demand are −10, −6, −3, −2.3, and −1.8?

11.10 Suppose that a company produces an intermediate good that is used in the production of a good for final sale. The demand equation the final good is

$$Q_f = 1,500 - 15P_f.$$

The total cost of producing the final good is

$$TC_f = 100 + 2Q_f^2.$$

The total cost of producing the intermediate good is

$$TC_i = 50 + 0.02Q_i^2.$$

There is no external market for the firm's intermediate good.

a. What is the profit-maximizing price and quantity the final good?
b. What is the transfer price of the intermediate good?
c. What is the company's maximum profit?

11.11 The Interboro Rapid Transit Authority (IRTA) has estimated the following peak and off-peak demand equations for its commuter rail service:

$$Q_p = 50 - 2P_p;$$

$$Q_{op} = 20 - 4P_{op},$$

where Q is measured in thousands of passenger miles. IRTA's marginal cost of providing commuter rail service is constant at \$3 per passenger mile. IRTA's capacity is 20 thousand passenger miles, which it reaches during peak, rush hours. What fare should IRTA charge during peak and off-peak hours?

Chapter 12

Bargaining

Whether in business, politics, law, international relations, or everyday life, bargaining is an important aspect of everyday life. Whether negotiating with your boss for a pay raise, haggling over the price of a used car, hammering out an agreement with suppliers over the prices of raw materials, bargaining is a feature of almost all commercial activities.

It is useful to think of bargaining as a process whereby rivals negotiate over the division of something of value. In general, there are two questions that must be answered when analyzing bargaining scenarios. First, what are the bargaining rules? Second, what happens if the players fail to reach an agreement? In most retail establishments, for example, the seller posts a fixed asking price. The customer must decide whether to accept or reject this price. This is an example of a take-it-or-leave-it bargaining rule. In the case of collective bargaining, union representatives propose a wage and benefit package. Management may accept the offer, reject the offer and wait for the union to modify its proposal, or reject the proposal and make a counteroffer. In some cases, the order of play is determined by custom or law. In other cases, strategic considerations may determine the sequencing of the bargaining process.

In this chapter, we will apply the principles of **game theory** developed in earlier chapters to deepen our understanding of the dynamics of the bargaining process. Although much of the analyses proceeds on the basis of rather simplistic assumptions, an understanding these principles is fundamental when formulating optimal negotiating strategies.

THE BARGAINING PROBLEM

Trade is the process whereby individuals exchange goods, services. If these transactions are voluntary, both parties benefit. All market transactions involve implicit or explicit contracts. **Bargaining** is the process by negotiating the terms of a **contract**. If either is not satisfied, the transaction will not take place. The bargaining problem is to determine how the gains from trade will be distributed between the buyer and seller.

All bargaining problems involve two basic features. The first is a complete description of the possible payoffs to all participants from a successful negotiation. The second is to identify the payoffs if the players fail to come to an agreement. The bargaining problem is for both players to agree on the transaction price. An efficient bargaining outcome maximizes the sum of the players' payoffs. The players in bargaining games negotiate over the distribution of the **bargaining surplus**, which is the difference between the lowest price that a seller is willing to accept and the highest price that a buyer is willing to pay.

NASH BARGAINING

Nash bargaining is a **static game** in which risk-averse rivals simultaneously bid for a share of a monetary pie of known value. If the sum of the bids is less than the size of the pie, the players receive their proposed share. If the sum of the bids is greater than the size of the pie then each bidder receive nothing, in which case the players submit a revised bid.

Although detailed analysis of Nash bargaining is beyond the scope of this book, consider the following simple bargaining scenario involving two risk-neutral bidders. Under the terms of a collective bargaining agreement, Matrix Corporation and labor union leaders enter into negotiations over the distribution of company's profits in excess of depreciation allowances. Matrix's accountants have determined that these excess profits amounted to $200 per worker at the end of the last fiscal year. By the terms of the collective bargaining agreement, each side submits a one-time, sealed bid for a share of these profits. To ensure fairness, both sides agree to employ the services of an independent auditor to monitor the bargaining proceedings.

To simplify the analysis, suppose that all bids must be in $50 per worker increments. If the sum of the bids equals $200, the bidders receive their proposed distribution and negotiations end. If the sum of the bids is less than $200, the bidders receive their proposed distribution and the remainder is distributed to Matrix shareholders. If the sum of the bids exceeds $200, each side must resubmit their bids. To avoid the possibility that this game will be infinitely repeated, each side is penalized $5 per worker to defray monitoring costs. This static bargaining game is depicted in Figure 12.1.

Consider the Nash bargaining game from management's perspective. If management bids $200, an agreement is possible only if the union bids $0. The strategy profile {*$150, $50*}, for example, is a **Nash equilibrium** strategy profile since neither player can improve its payoff by switching bids given the strategy of the other bidder. It is unlikely, however, that union representatives will be so altruistic. Similarly, the strategy profile {*$0, $200*} also constitutes a Nash equilibrium, but this outcome is even more unlikely. It should be obvious that it is in the best interest of both sides to submit bids of $100. The Nash equilibrium strategy profile for this game is {*$100, $100*}.

The game depicted in Figure 12.1 offers clues as to why it is often negotiations can be difficult and protracted. Ten of the twenty five strategy profiles involve payoffs that are less than the amount of excess profits available for distribution. Ten strategy profiles involve combined bids that exceed the value of the monetary pie. Fortunately, experimental and anecdotal evidence demonstrate that participants in bargaining games tend to accept an equitable split as "fair," even in the presence of multiple Nash equilibria.

The game depicted in Figure 12.1 can also be used to illustrate the **first-mover advantage**. Of the five possible Nash equilibria in this bargaining game, the strategy profiles {*200, 0*} and {*150, 50*} favor management and the strategy profiles {*50, 150*} and {*0, 200*} favor the union. It is clearly in both sides best interest to irrevocably commit to a negotiating position first. It is unlikely that the union would ever accept a {*200, 0*} collective bargaining agreement. It is equally unlikely that management would ever accept a {*0, 200*} collective bargaining agreement. On the other hand, if management can convince the union that it will take a hard line in negotiations, a {*150, 50*} collective bargaining agreement may be possible. Similarly, a {*50, 150*} collective bargaining agreement is possible if the union has the first-mover advantage.

		Union				
		$0	*$50*	*$100*	*$150*	*$200*
	$0	(0, 0)	(0, 100)	(0, 120)	(0, 150)	**(0, 200)**
	$50	(50, 0)	(50, 50)	(50, 100)	**(50, 150)**	(−5, −5)
Management	*$100*	(100, 0)	(100, 50)	**(100, 100)**	(−5, −5)	(−5, −5)
	$150	(150, 0)	**(150, 50)**	(−5, −5)	(−5, −5)	(−5, −5)
	$200	**(200, 0)**	(−5, −5)	(−5, −5)	(−5, −5)	(−5, −5)

Payoffs: (Management, Union)

Figure 12.1

RUBINSTEIN BARGAINING

We often think of bargaining as a sequential-move process. That is, one party makes an offer, which is followed by a counteroffer from the other party. In this section we will discuss **Rubinstein bargaining**, which refers to a general class of sequential-move (dynamic) bargaining games involving a potentially infinite number of offers and counteroffers in which the players have complete information about strategies and payoffs. While unrealistic, this assumption makes it easier to identify optimal bidding strategies in more realistic bargaining scenarios.

Before considering sequential-move bargaining games with an infinite time horizon, we will examine situations with a finite number of offers and counteroffers. For example, suppose that Boris wants to buy Sarah's car. Sarah knows that Boris is willing to pay up to $1,000; Boris knows that Sarah will not accept anything less than $500. The maximum price that Boris is willing to pay is called the **buyer's reservation price**. The minimum price that Sarah is willing to accept is called the **seller's reservation price**. If Boris and Sarah come to an agreement, the gain to both will add up to bargaining surplus, which is the difference between the buyer's and the seller's reservation prices. In the used-car bargaining game, the bargaining surplus $500.

The used-car bargaining game is depicted in Figure 12.2. To keep things simple, assume that this bargaining game has only three stages—an offer, a counteroffer, and an accept/reject decision. As buyer, Boris makes the first move by offer Sarah a price of P_B. Sarah can either accept, or reject, Boris's offer. If the offer is accepted, the game ends and the payoffs to Boris and Sarah are ($1,000 – P_B$, P_B – $500). If the offer is rejected, Sarah can make a

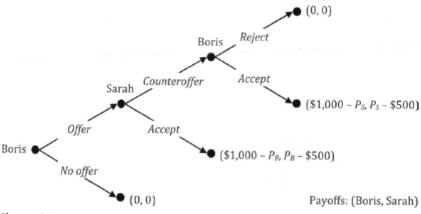

Figure 12.2

counteroffer of P_S, where $P_S > P_B$. If the counteroffer is accepted, the payoffs to Boris and Sarah are ($1,000 - P_S$, $P_S - 500). If Boris rejects Sarah's counteroffer, the game ends and the payoffs are (0, 0).

Suppose, for example, that Boris makes an offer of $800. If Sarah accepts Boris's offer, the game ends and the payoffs are $1,000 - $800 = $200 and $800 - $500 = $300, respectively. The sum of the bargaining surpluses received by Boris and Sarah is $200 + $300 = $500. Suppose that Sarah does not accept Boris's offer and makes a counteroffer of $900. If Boris accepts Sarah's counteroffer, the game ends. The payoffs to Boris and Sarah are $1,000 - $900 = $100 and $900 - $500 = $400, respectively. Once again, the sum of the bargaining surpluses is $100 + $400 = $500. This version of the used-car bargaining game is depicted in Figure 12.3.

Using the method of **backward induction**, the **subgame-perfect equilibrium** for the game in Figure 12.3 is for Sarah to reject Boris's offer of $800 and for Boris to accept Sarah's counteroffer of $900. Boris will receive $100 of the $500 bargaining surplus and Sarah will get the other $400.

As it turns out, Sarah's counteroffer of $900 is not optimal. Sarah can do better by making an even larger counteroffer. To see why, suppose Boris's offer remains $200, but Sarah's counteroffer is $950. As before, Sarah will reject Boris's offer, and Boris will accept Sarah's counteroffer. The resulting payoffs are ($50, $450). In fact, Sarah will reject any offer made by Boris that is less than $1,000, and Boris will accept any counteroffer made by Sarah up to, but not greater than, $1,000. Boris will accept this counteroffer because this is how much he values Sarah's car. Thus, the Nash equilibrium strategy profile for this game is {*Offer* → *Counteroffer* → *Accept*} with payoffs of (0, $1,000).

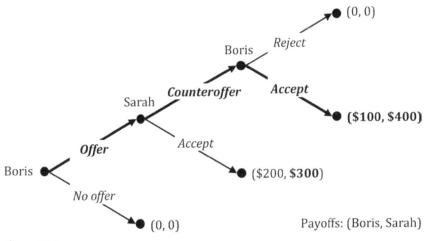

Figure 12.3

Last-Mover Advantage

The subgame-perfect equilibrium for the used-car bargaining game is for Sarah to reject any offer that is less than his reservation price, and for Boris to accept any counteroffer up to and including Sarah's reservation price. Sarah's ability to extract the entire surplus of $500 regardless of Boris's initial offer is referred to as a **last-mover advantage**.

As we shall see, the above example suggests that the final outcome of bargaining games depends on who makes the first offer, and on the number of offers and counteroffers. In the game depicted in Figure 12.3, Boris made the first offer. Since there is an even number of offers and counteroffers, Sarah had the last-mover advantage. On the other hand, if there had been an odd number of offers and counteroffers, Boris would have had the last-mover advantage, in which case he would have extracted the entire $500 surplus.

Symmetric Impatience

In this section, we will extend our analysis of bargaining games by assuming multiple rounds of offers and counteroffers. Assume that the players incur **opportunity costs** by not immediately reaching an agreement. Over time, these opportunity costs lower the **present value** of the bargaining surplus. In this section it will be demonstrated that the interest rate used to determine the present value of payoffs and the number of offers and counteroffers determines the division of the bargaining surplus.

The used-car bargaining game in Figure 12.3 involved just two offers and counteroffers. In fact, negotiations may drag on for days, weeks, months, or even years. Depending on the time value of money, a failure to quickly reach an agreement may impose considerable opportunity costs on the negotiating parties. To see how, suppose that the used-car bargaining game involved thirty rounds of offers and counteroffers. As before, Boris makes the first offer.

Since there is an even number of offers and counteroffers, Sarah will make the last offer. Will Sarah still enjoy a last-mover-advantage, and if so, how great will that advantage be? To keep things simple, assume that each negotiating round takes one period, and that any delay in reaching an agreement reduces the gains to both players by $i = 0.05$, or an interest rate of 5 percent per period. Thus, the **discount rate** for each player is $\delta = 1/(1 + i) = 1/(1.05)$. Since the discount rate is the same for both players, the players are said to have **symmetric impatience**. The greater the discount rate, the more impatient a player is to reach an agreement.

As before, we will assume that the players complete and perfect information. Each player is fully aware of the opportunity costs associated with failing quickly to come to an agreement. With 30 rounds of offers and counteroffers, it is impractical to illustrate the bargaining process in extensive form. For that reason, consider the information summarized in Table 12.1.

Table 12.1 Symmetric Impatience with $i = 0.05$

Round	Player	Offer	Sarah's surplus	Boris's surplus
30	Seller	$1,000.00	$500.00	$0.00
29	Buyer	976.19	476.19	23.81
28	Seller	977.32	477.32	22.68
27	Buyer	954.59	454.59	45.41
26	Seller	956.75	456.75	43.45
⋮	⋮	⋮	⋮	⋮
5	Buyer	819.93	319.93	184.07
4	Seller	824.70	324.70	175.30
3	Buyer	809.24	309.24	190.76
2	Seller	818.32	318.32	181.68
1	Buyer	803.16	303.16	196.84

In the table, Sarah is the seller and Boris is the buyer. Boris makes the first offer in round 1 and Sarah makes the final counteroffer in round 30.

Because Sarah has the last-mover advantage, he will sell his car for $1,000.00 and extract the entire surplus of $500. Since the present value of $500 in the twenty-ninth round is $500/1.05 = $476.19, it makes sense for Boris to offer Sarah $976.19 in the twenty-ninth round. If this offer is accepted, Boris will realize a surplus of $500 – $476.19 = $23.81. Of course, this is not the end of the story.

Sarah knows that any delay in reaching an agreement will reduce Boris's surplus by 5 percent per round. The present value of Boris's surplus of $23.81 in the twenty-ninth round $23.81/1.05 = $22.68 in the twenty-eighth round. Thus, Sarah should make a counteroffer of $977.32. This will increase Sarah's surplus to $477.32. Using backward induction, Boris's best offer in the first round is $803.16, which Sarah will accept. Sarah and Boris will enjoy a surplus of $303.16 and $196.84, respectively. This result differs from the bargaining game in which Sarah extracted the entire surplus of $500. The reason for this was that we implicitly assumed a zero discount rate. Since there are not opportunity costs, neither player was penalized for failing to immediately come to an agreement.

Asymmetric Impatience

Suppose that Boris is more anxious to come to an agreement than Sarah. This increased anxiety is reflected in a greater opportunity cost. The more impatient player will have a larger discount rate. This new bargaining game is characterized by **asymmetric impatience**. In this section we will show that while the last mover still enjoys a greater share of the bargaining surplus and the more impatient a player, the smaller is that player's share of the bargaining surplus.[1]

How will symmetric impatience affect the outcome of the used-car bargaining game? Suppose that the interest rate used to determine Boris's interest rate is 10 percent, and the interest rate used to determine Sarah's discount remains unchanged at 5 percent. The results of these negotiations are summarized in Table 12.2.

Using backward induction, Boris's best offer in the first round offer is $843.02. This will give Sarah a bargaining surplus of $343.02, which is more than double the gain enjoyed by Boris and almost $40 more than in Table 12.1. These results demonstrate that a more patient last-mover will enjoy a greater share of the bargaining surplus. If Boris is more patient than Sarah, Sarah will still have a last-mover advantage, but will enjoy a smaller bargaining surplus.

The more impatient the player (the higher the discount rate) the smaller will be that players share of the bargaining surplus. Ariel Rubinstein (1982) demonstrated that there exists a unique subgame-perfect equilibrium in sequential-move bargaining games with an infinite number of moves and countermoves.[2] Suppose that a buyer and seller are bargaining over the division of a surplus; the buyer makes the first offer; there is a (potentially) infinite number of offers and counteroffers; both players accept an offer when indifferent between accepting and rejecting. If we denote the buyer's discount rate as $\delta_B = 1/(1 + i_B)$ and the seller's discount rate as $\delta_S = 1/(1 + i_S)$, the share of the bargaining surplus going to the buyer (ω_B) is

$$\omega_B = \frac{1-\delta_S}{1-\delta_B\delta_S} = 1-\omega_S. \tag{12.1}$$

The share of the bargaining surplus going to the seller (ω_S) is

$$\omega_S = \frac{\delta_S(1-\delta_B)}{1-\delta_B\delta_S} = 1-\omega_B. \tag{12.2}$$

Suppose the game summarized in Table 12.2 is (potentially) infinitely repeated. The share of the bargaining surplus going to the buyer is

Table 12.2 Asymmetric Impatience with i_B = 0.10 and i_S = 0.05

Round	Player	Offer	Sarah's surplus	Boris's surplus
30	Seller	$1,000.00	$500.00	$0.00
29	Buyer	976.19	476.19	23.81
28	Seller	978.35	478.35	21.65
27	Buyer	955.57	455.57	44.43
26	Seller	959.61	459.61	40.39
⋮	⋮	⋮	⋮	⋮
5	Buyer	849.85	349.85	150.15
4	Seller	863.50	363.50	136.50
3	Buyer	846.19	346.19	153.81
2	Seller	860.17	360.17	139.83
1	Buyer	843.02	343.02	156.98

$$\omega_B = \frac{1 - 0.9524}{1 - (0.9524)(0.9091)} = 0.35. \qquad (12.3)$$

The share of the bargaining surplus going to the seller is

$$\omega_S = \frac{0.9524(1 - 0.9091)}{1 - (0.9524)(0.9091)} = 0.65. \qquad (12.4)$$

The amounts of the surplus going to the buyer and seller are 0.35($500) = $175 and 0.65($500) = $325, respectively. Thus, the buyer should offer the seller $500 + $325 = $825 in the first round, and the seller should accept.

SOLVED EXERCISE

Briana and Steve are bargaining over the price of a service contract. The highest price that Briana is willing to pay is $250. The lowest price that Steve is willing to accept is $100. Suppose that the interest rates used to determine Briana's and Steve's degree of impatience is $i_B = i_S = 0.06$.

a. *What price should Briana offer Steve for the service contract in the first round? What portion of the surplus will each player receive?*
b. *Suppose that $i_B = 0.08$ and $i_S = 0.06$. What price should Briana offer Steve for the contract in the first round? What portion of the bargaining surplus will each player receive?*

Solution

a. *The bargaining surplus in this bargaining game is $250 − $100 = $150. The corresponding discount rates are $\delta_B = \delta_S = 1/(1.06) = 0.943$. From Eq. (12.1), the fraction this surplus going to Briana is*

$$\omega_B = \frac{1 - \delta_S}{1 - \delta_B \delta_S} = \frac{1 - 0.934}{1 - (0.943)(0.943)} = 0.515. \qquad (12.5)$$

Thus, the amount of the surplus going to Briana is 0.515($150) = $77.25. The fraction of this surplus going to Steve is

$$\omega_S = \frac{\delta_S(1 - \delta_B)}{1 - \delta_B \delta_S} = \frac{0.943(1 - 0.943)}{1 - (0.943)(0.943)} = 0.485. \qquad (12.6)$$

The amount of the bargaining surplus going to Steve is 0.485($150) = $72.75. The sum of the players' surpluses is $72.75 + $77.25 = $150.

Thus, Briana should offer Steve $100 + $72.75 = $172.75 in the first round for the service contract.

b. *The discount rate for Briana is $\delta_B = 1/(1.08) = 0.926$. The fraction this surplus going to Briana is*

$$\omega_B = \frac{1-0.94}{1-(0.943)(0.926)} = 0.45. \qquad (12.7)$$

Thus, the amount of the surplus going to Briana is 0.45($150) = $67.50. The fraction of the surplus going to Steve is

$$\omega_S = \frac{0.943(1-0.926)}{1-(0.943)(0.926)} = 0.55. \qquad (12.8)$$

The amount of the surplus going to Steve is 0.45($150) = $82.50. A more impatient Steve receives a smaller share of the bargaining surplus. The sum of the players' surpluses is $67.50 + $82.50 = $150. Briana should offer Steve $182.50 in the first round for the service contract and a more impatient Steve should accept.

CHAPTER EXERCISES

12.1   Suppose that two individuals are bargaining over the distribution of $1,000. Each player submits a one-time bid, which must be in increments of $1. If the sum of the bids is less than or equal to $1,000, each player receives their bid and the game ends. If the sum of the bids is greater than $1,000, the game ends and the players go home empty-handed.
a. Does this game have a Nash equilibrium?
b. What is the most likely Nash equilibrium strategy profile for this game?

12.2   Two individuals are bargaining over the distribution of $100 in which payoffs must be in increments of $5. Each player must submit a one-time bid. If the sum of the bids is less than or equal to $100, each player gets the amount of the bid and the game ends. If the sum of the bids is greater than $100, the game ends and the players get nothing.
a. Does this game have a Nash equilibrium?
b. What is the most likely equilibrium strategy profile for this game?

12.3   Suppose that Benny wants to purchase a boat from Sylvia. Benny is willing to pay up to $18,000, while Sylvia will not part with the boat for anything less than $15,000.

a. Suppose that the interest rates used to determine Benny's and Sylvia's degree of impatience are $i_B = i_S = 0.05$. If there are an infinite number of bargaining rounds, what portion of the bargaining surplus will Benny and Sylvia receive?

b. How much should Benny offer Sylvia?

c. Suppose that the interest rates are $i_B = 0.15$ and $i_S = 0.20$. What portion of the bargaining surplus will Benny and Sylvia receive?

d. At these interest rates, how much should Benny offer Sylvia?

12.4 Suppose that Betty wants to purchase Spike's car. Betty is prepared to pay a maximum of $2,000. Spike will not accept any amount less than $1,000.

a. Suppose that the interest rates used to determine Betty's and Spike's degree of impatience is $i_B = i_S = 0.10$. If there are an infinite number of bargaining rounds, what portion of the bargaining surplus will Betty and Spike receive?

b. How much should Betty offer Spike?

c. Suppose that Spike's interest rate is $i_B = 0.10$, but Betty's interest rate is $i_B = 0.20$, what portion of the bargaining surplus will Betty and Spike receive?

d. At these interest rates, how much should Betty offer Spike?

NOTES

1. Among other interpretations, a player with a lower discount rate may be a more skilled negotiator.

2. The proof of this result is rather difficult. A reader-friendly explanation can be found in Binmore (1992) and Osborne and Rubinstein (1994).

Chapter 13

Economics of Information

We have thus far assumed that managers make decisions with known and measurable outcomes. In the real world, however, decisions are frequently made under a cloud of uncertainty. Managers must deal with the uncertainty of public reaction to new product lines, business cycle fluctuations, shifting consumer tastes, disruptions in flow of essential raw materials, price volatility, labor unrest, and political instability—all of which affect sales, revenues, and profits. Experience, economic and political analysis, and market research can reduce, but never completely eliminate, the uncertainty associated with running a successful business.

   This chapter introduces the reader to the **economics of information**, which involves decision making under conditions of risk and uncertainty. We begin by distinguishing between the often confused concepts of risk and uncertainty. We will then ask why a manager would choose to undertake one risky project, but not another. Alternatively, why would a manager invest in a risky project, while another manager would not? The answer often reflects their respective attitudes towards risk.

RISK AND UNCERTAINTY

The concepts of **risk** and **uncertainty** are frequently confused. Both risk and uncertainty refer to the variability of expected payoffs. In the case of risk, the probability distribution of alternative outcomes is known, perhaps on the basis of historical data, whereas uncertainty is subjective (Knight, 1921). We might estimate the variability of rates of return on alternative investments, but can only speculate as to the winner of the next Barclay's Premier League championship. The phrase "decision making under conditions of uncertainty" is frequently used to describe the probability distribution of multiple out-comes, whether or not these probabilities have any real meaning.

When comparing alternative payoffs, a decision maker will balance expected payoffs with the volatility of those payoffs over alternative states of nature. In general, a manager must be compensated with a greater expected return if a high-risk project is to be preferred over a low-risk project. How much additional compensation is required depends on the manager's attitude toward risk. We will begin our discussion of the economics of information by introducing the most commonly used statistical measures of expected return and risk.

Mean

The standard summary measure of the return from alternative outcomes is the **mean**, which is also referred to as the **expected value**. These random payoffs may refer to profits, capital gains, prices, unit sales, and so on. The mean is a weighted average of all possible outcomes (x_i), with the weights being the probabilities (p_i) of each outcome. More formally, the expected value of a discrete random outcome is

$$E(x) = \mu = p_1 x_1 + p_2 x_2 + \cdots + p_n x_n \qquad (13.1)$$

where $p_1 + p_2 + \ldots + p_n = 1$. When the probability of each outcome is the same, the expected value is the sum of the outcomes divided by the number of observations.

Variance

By itself, expected values say nothing about the riskiness of a decision. Alternative decisions may have the same expected payoff, but they may not have the same risk. In general, if two projects have the same expected payoff, but the first project is less risky than the second, then the first will be preferred. Consider, for example, a manager who must choose between investing in project A or project B. The success of the projects depends on whether the economy enters a period of prosperity or recession, either of which is equally likely. The payoff from project A in the event of prosperity is $101,000 and $99,000 in the event of a recession. The expected payoff is 0.5($101,000) + 0.5($99,000) = $100,000. By contrast, the payoff from project B in the event of prosperity is $200,000 and $0 in the event of a recession. As with project A, the expected payoff is 0.5($200,000) + 0.5($0) = $100,000. Although both projects have the same expected payoff, project B is riskier because the payoffs are more volatile.

In the above example, risk was defined in terms of the volatility of payoffs. A common measure of this volatility is the **variance**, which is calculated as the sum of the squared deviations of each payoff from its mean multiplied by probability of its occurrence.

$$Var(x) = \sigma^2 = p_1(x_1 - \mu)^2 + p_2(x_2 - \mu)^2 + \cdots + p_n(x_n - \mu)^2. \qquad (13.2)$$

When the probability of each outcome is the same, the variance is the sum of the squared deviations of each payoff from its mean divided by the number of outcomes. In our example, the variance for project A is $\sigma_A^2 = [(\$101,000 - \$100,000)^2 + (\$99,000 - \$100,000)^2]/2 = \$1,000,000$. The variance for project B is $\sigma_B^2 = [(\$200,000 - \$100,000)^2 + (0 - \$100)^2]/2 = \$10,000,000,000$. Since $\sigma_B^2 > \sigma_A^2$, project B is riskier than project A.

Standard Deviation

The most popular statistical measure of risk is the **standard deviation**, which is the square root of the variance, that is $\sigma = \sqrt{\sigma^2}$. The standard deviation is generally preferred to the variance because it can be interpreted as having the same units of measurement as x and μ. In our example, the expected payoff from both projects was $\mu = \$100,000$. The variance of the payoffs for project A is $\sigma_A^2 = \$1,000,000$ and the variance for project B is $\sigma_B^2 = \$10,000,000,000$! By contrast, the standard deviation of the payoffs are $\sigma_A = \$1,000$ and $\sigma_B = \$100,000$, which much closer in magnitude to the original data.

SOLVED EXERCISE

Suppose that for a payment of $3.50, Bob agrees to pay Nabob the dollar value of any roll of a fair die. For example, if Nabob rolls 1, Bob will pay him $1. If Nabob rolls a 6, Bob will pay him $6.

a. *How much can Nabob expect to win if he accepts Bob's offer?*
b. *Calculate the variance and standard deviation of the payoffs.*

Solution

a. *The probability of any number between 1 and 6 is 1/6. Thus, Nabob can expect to win $E(x) = (1 + 2 + 3 + 4 + 5 + 6)/6 = \$3.50$. Since it will cost $3.50 to accept Bob's offer, Nob's expected payoff is $E(x) - \$3.50 = \$0$.*
b. *The variance is $\sigma^2 = [(1 - 3.5)^2 + (2 - 3.5)^2 + (3 - 3.5)^2 + (4 - 3.5)^2 + (5 - 3.5)^2 + (6 - 3.5)^2]/6 = \$2.92$. The standard deviation is $\sigma = \sqrt{\$2.92} = \$1.71$.*

STATIC GAMES WITH UNCERTAIN PAYOFFS

Before considering the important role that risk plays in the decision-making process, consider the oil-drilling game depicted in Figure 13.1. In this **static game**, two oil companies, PETROX and GLOMAR, must decide whether or not to drill for oil. To underscore the issues involved, we will initially assume that the managers' decisions are based only on expected payoffs. The riskiness of each project is assumed to play no role in the decision-making process. In other words, the managers are said to be risk neutral, which will be discussed in greater detail below.

The game depicted in Figure 13.1 begins when the Global Mining and Recovery (GLOMAR) Corporation purchases a two-year lease on land, which it believes lies directly above a two-million-barrel crude oil deposit with an estimated market value of $200 million, or $100 per barrel. The price per barrel of crude oil is not expected to change in the foreseeable future. In order to extract the oil, GLOMAR has the option of drilling a wide well (*W*) or a narrow well (*N*). GLOMAR's main rival in the project is the Petroleum Exploration (PETROX) Company, which has purchased a two-year lease on land adjacent to the land leased by GLOMAR. The land leased by PETROX also lies above the same crude oil deposit.

The game on the left summarizes the payoffs to each company from alternative drilling strategies if oil is present. If both companies drill the same sized wells, for example, each company will extract half of the total crude oil reserve. If GLOMAR and PETROX drill wide wells, each company will extract one million barrels in six months and will earn profits of $24 million. On the other hand, if each company drills narrow wells, it will take one year to extract the oil, although each will earn profits of $52 million since it is less

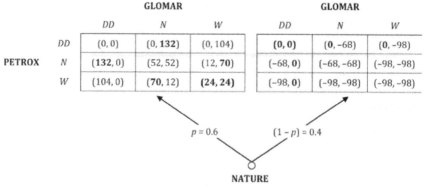

Payoffs: (PETROX, GLOMAR)

Figure 13.1

expensive to drill a narrow well than it is to drill a wide well. If both companies adopt a "don't drill" strategy (*DD*), the payoff to each is $0. The remaining cells summarize the payoffs to each company from alternative strategy profiles. The reader should verify that if oil is present, the **Nash equilibrium** strategy profile is for both companies to drill wide wells, that is {*W, W*}.

On the other hand, the game on the right summarizes the payoffs to each company if no oil is present. In this case, the Nash equilibrium is for both companies not to drill, that is {*DD, DD*}. The problem for both companies is that it is not known for certain whether seismic testing has detected the presence of oil or water (a "dry" well). Although the presence of oil is not known with certainty, the companies' geologists believe that there is a 60 percent chance of striking oil and a 40 percent chance of finding water, that is, a "dry" well.

One way to incorporate this uncertainty into the decision-making process is to introduce a third player, which we will refer to as Nature (Harsanyi, 1968). Nature has no vested interest in the outcome of the game, but moves first by randomly determining states of nature with fixed probabilities that are common knowledge. Nature is not a strategic player in the sense that it receives a payoff at the end of the game. Nature's **decision node** in Figure 13.1 is depicted by a small open circle, which is referred to as **chance node**. A chance node is a decision node at which the probability of a random event is determined.

The game depicted in Figure 13.1 is referred to as a **static Bayesian game** since it is characterized by **incomplete information** since the payoffs are not known with certainty. The oil companies do not know for certain whether they are playing the game on the left or the right. They only know the respective probabilities determined by Nature. Since the managers are assumed to be risk neutral, however, the decision to drill or not drill will be based on expected payoffs. The expected payoff from a {*W, W*} strategy profile, for example, is $0.6(24) + 0.4(-98) = -\$24.8$ million for each company. The expected payoffs from alternative drilling strategies are summarized in Figure 13.2. The unique **Bayesian Nash equilibrium** strategy profile for this game is for both companies to drill narrow wells, that is {*N, N*}.

GLOMAR

		Don't drill	Narrow	Wide
	Don't drill	(0, 0)	(0, **52**)	(**0**, 23.2)
PETROX	Narrow	(**52**, 0)	(**4, 4**)	(−20, 2.8)
	Wide	(23.2, **0**)	(2.8, −20)	(−24.8, −24.8)

Payoffs: (PETROX, GLOMAR)

Figure 13.2

Although expected payoffs have been used to identify the **pure strategy** Nash equilibrium strategy, this should not be confused with the actual pay-offs, which are realized only after the wells have been drilled. If oil is found, the payoff to each company is $52 million, which is the best payoff if both companies cooperate, compared with $24 million when the decisions are made with compete information. If no oil is found, each company will lose $68 million.

ATTITUDES TOWARD RISK

In the oil-drilling game in Figure 13.2, the players were assumed to be risk neutral. The volatility of payoffs played no role in the oil companies' drilling strategies. Unfortunately, the decision to drill when oil is not present could result in substantial losses. A player's attitude toward risk is an important element in the decision-making process. The decision to drill depends on the expected payoff and the company's attitude towards risk. Since uncertainty is inevitable, it must be dealt with systematically if managers are to make optimal decisions.

We will begin our discussion of a player's attitude towards risk by con-sidering the situation depicted in Figure 13.3. Suppose, for example, that A is asked to choose option 1 or 2. Choosing option 1 will result in a certain payoff of $950. The payoff from choosing option 2 depends on the flip a "fair" coin. If the coin comes up "heads," A will receive $2,000. If the coin comes up "tails," A gets nothing. Option 2 can be described as a *lottery* with an expected payoff of 0.5($2,000) + 0.5($0) = $1,000. Which option will A choose? The answer depends on A's attitude towards risk.

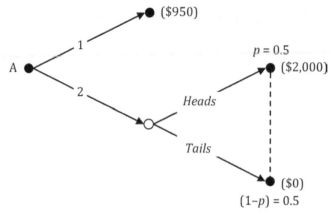

Figure 13.3

The choice of option 1 or 2 depends on how much satisfaction (utility) is received by A. In general, a player's utility (U) is an increasing function of the amount of money (M) received. There is an infinite number of utility functions for which an increase in the amount of money received will yield greater utility, such as $U(M) = M$, $U(M) = M/50$, $U(M) = 100M^{0.5}$, and so on. Since more money is preferred to less, it is safe to assume that $U(\$0) = U(\$950) = U(\$2,000)$.

Depending on A's attitude towards risk, the utility received from option 1 is $U(M) = U(\$950)$. The utility received from option 2 is $0.5U(\$0) + 0.5U(\$2,000)$. Option 1 will be strictly preferred if

$$U(\$950) > (0.5)U(\$0) + (0.5)U(\$2,000). \tag{13.3}$$

Option 2 is strictly preferred if the opposite is true.

Will A prefer a certain payoff of $950, or an expected payoff of $1,000? To answer this question, suppose that A's utility function is given by the equation $U(M) = 100M^{0.5}$. Since

$$100(\$950)^{0.5} > (0.5)\left[100(\$0)^{0.5}\right] + (0.5)\left[100(\$2,000)^{0.5}\right], \tag{13.4}$$

A prefers option 1 with a certain payoff of $950 to option 2 with an expected payoff of $1,000.

Risk Aversion

The idea of risk-averse behavior was identified by the eighteenth-century Swiss mathematician Daniel Bernoulli (1738). Bernoulli speculated that most individuals will not accept a **fair gamble** because it exhibits diminishing marginal utility of money. A gamble is a random event with a payoff associated with each outcome. A gamble is said to be fair if the expected payoff from accepting the gamble is zero. Suppose, for example, that player A is offered the following fair gamble. Player A flips a fair coin. If the coin comes up "heads," player A wins $1,000. If the coin comes up "tails," player A loses $1,000. Since there is an equal chance of a fair coin coming up heads or tails, the expected payoff is zero.[1] Alternatively, suppose that the payoff if the coin comes up "tails" is zero, but it costs $500 to play. Once again, the expected payoff is zero, which makes this a fair gamble.

Returning to our first example, suppose that player A has an amount of money $M = \$50,000$, from which she receives $U = 100(50,000)^{0.5} = 22,361$ units of satisfaction. If player A flips "heads," her total utility increases to $U = 100(51,000)^{0.5} = 22,583$, or a gain of 222 units of satisfaction. If player A flips "tails," her total utility declines to $U = 100(49,000)^{0.5} = 22,136$, or a loss of 225 units of satisfaction. If player A is risk averse, the regret from losing $1,000 is greater than the elation from winning $1,000. Player A's expected utility from this fair gamble is $0.5[100(49,000)^{0.5}] + 0.5[100(51,000)^{0.5}]$ = 22,359.50 units of satisfaction, which is less than $U(M) = 22,361$ by refusing to play. This situation is depicted in Figure 13.4.

Player A in our example is said to be **risk averse** because she prefers a sure payoff of zero by refusing to play than an expected payoff of the same amount by accepting a fair gamble. In general, a risk-averse individual will not accept a fair gamble since $U(M) > E[U(M)]$.

Is there any way to persuade player A to accept this fair gamble? One approach would be to offer a **risk premium**, which is an amount required to make player A indifferent between a certain payoff and an expected payoff of the same amount. The amount of the risk premium depends on the degree of risk aversion. The greater the degree of risk aversion, the greater is the required risk premium. In Figure 13.5, player A must be paid $6.70 to make her indifferent between accepting and rejecting this fair gamble.

The more risk averse an individual, the more concave (bowed out) the utility function, and the greater the required risk premium. A **risk neutral** person is indifferent between a certain payoff and a risky prospect with the same expected payoff. In this case, a risk premium would not be required to induce a risk neutral individual to accept a fair gamble. Different degrees of risk aversion, and their associated risk premiums, are depicted in Figure 13.6.[1]

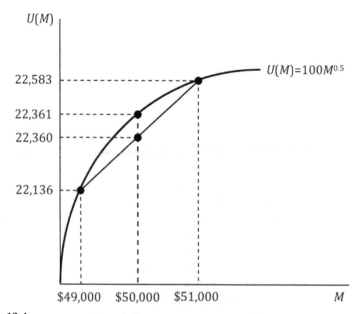

Figure 13.4

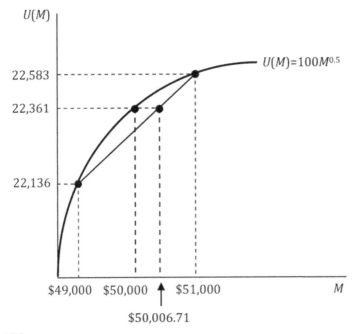

Figure 13.5

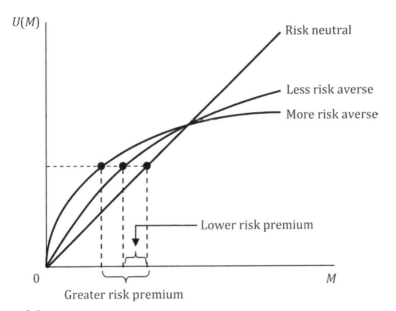

Figure 13.6

SOLVED EXERCISE

Adam is offered the following fair gamble. If the flip of a fair coin comes up "heads," Player A will win $1,000. If the coin comes up "tails," player A will lose $1,000. Suppose that Adam's total utility of money equation is

$$U(M) = M^{1.1}, \tag{13.5}$$

where M represents Adam's initial money holdings. If M = $50,000, should Adam accept this fair gamble?

Solution

When M > $50,000, Adam's total utility is U = ($50,000)$^{1.1}$ = 147,525.47 units of satisfaction. If Adam wins $1,000, his total utility becomes U = ($51,000)$^{1.1}$ = 150,774.26, for a gain of 3,248.79 units of satisfaction. If Adam loses $1,000, his total utility becomes U = ($49,000)$^{1.1}$ = 144,283.17, for a loss of 3,242.30 units of satisfaction. The expected change in total utility by accepting the offer is

$$E(\Delta U) = (3,248.79)0.5 + (-3,241.70)0.5 = 3.55. \tag{13.6}$$

Since the expected change in utility is positive, Adam will accept this fair gamble. Alternatively, Adam's expected utility by accepting this fair gamble is E(U) = 0.5(49,000)$^{1.1}$ + 0.5(51,000)$^{1.1}$ = 147, 528.72, which is greater than the 147,525.47 units of satisfaction that Adam receives by not accepting the offer.

Since Adam receives greater satisfaction from accepting the offer than by not accepting the offer, Adam may be described as **risk loving** *because he prefers a risky gamble with a relatively low expected payoff. Adam receives positive utility from risky situations. Unlike the concave utility functions depicted in Figure 13.6, Adam's utility function has a convex (bowed in) shape.*

Understanding Risk-Averse Behavior

Understanding of risk-averse behavior is useful when making optimal business decisions. To see how, suppose that a company is considering adding toothpaste to its product line. How can the marketing managers of this company apply their understanding of risk aversion to persuade consumers to switch to its new brand of toothpaste? Other things being equal, consumers will prefer to stay with established brands rather than switch to a new product of uncertain quality.

Risk-averse consumer behavior suggests at least two possible marketing strategies. One possibility would be to offer its new brand of toothpaste at a low, introductory price (risk premium) to compensate for consumer uncertainty to establish a foothold in the market. Alternatively, the firm could launch an advertising campaign to convince consumers that its brand of toothpaste is superior. Both approaches are designed to raise consumers' expected net benefit from sampling the new brand.

Another example of the consequences of risk-averse behavior relates to the advantage enjoyed by chain stores and franchise operations over independently owned and operated retail outlets. A risk-averse American tourist visiting a foreign country for the first time, for example, is more likely to have his or her first meal at a local McDonald's rather than sample the native cuisine at a local bistro. A risk-averse tourist may initially prefer a familiar meal of predictable quality to more exotic fare of unpredictable quality. This response to product uncertainty also helps to explain why large retail chain stores or franchise operations are typically located in urban centers where there are a relatively large number of out-of-town visitors.

Risk aversion also plays a prominent role in the managerial decision-making process. Strategies involving product pricing, new product development, advertising, capital investment, and so on all involve an element of risk. Consider, for example, a firm that is contemplating two or more capital investment projects. Typically, managers begin by comparing the **present values** of the stream of net income for each project for the life of each investment using the equation

$$NPV = \frac{R_1 - O_1}{(1+k)^1} + \frac{R_2 - O_2}{(1+k)^2} + \cdots + \frac{R_n - O_n}{(1+k)^n} \qquad (13.7)$$

where R_t is the projected cash inflows (revenues) and O_t the projected cash outflows (expenditures) for each period. If these cash flows are known with certainty then the assessment process is relatively straightforward. On the other hand, most such decisions are made under a cloud of uncertainty, in which it is necessary to incorporate the manager's attitude towards risk into decision-making process.

Figure 13.7 depicts the risk-return tradeoffs of three managers for the same investment. Risk, which is calculated as the standard deviation (σ) of the expected returns, is measured along the horizontal axis. The expected rate of return (k) is measured along the vertical axis. The combinations of risk and return for which the managers are indifferent are called **investor indifference curves**.

Figure 13.7 can also be used to be used to illustrate the risk premium, which is the additional return required to make a risk-averse investor indifferent

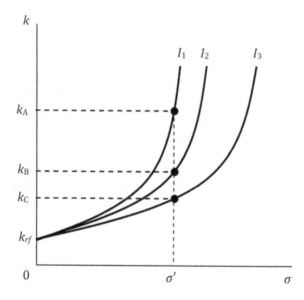

Figure 13.7

between a risky ($\sigma > 0$) and a risk-free ($\sigma = 0$) investment. The size of the risk premium depends on the shape of the indifference curve. Suppose, for example, that investor B is contemplating an investment with risk σ'. This investor would require a minimum risk premium of ($k_B - k_{rf}$), where k_{rf} is the rate of return on a risk-free investment. By contrast, investor A, who is more risk averse, requires a greater risk premium ($k_A - k_{rf}$) > ($k^B - k_{rf}$). Investor B, who is less risk averse, requires a smaller risk premium ($k^C - k_{rf}$) < ($k^B - k_{rf}$).

Investor indifference curve may be used to evaluate **mutually exclusive investments** and **independent investments**. A collection of investments are said to be mutually exclusive if acceptance of one means rejection of all others. Investments are independent if the returns from alternative investments are unrelated and acceptance of one does not rule out investment in another. Figure 13.8 illustrates an investor's indifference curve and three mutually exclusive and equally risky investments.

When choosing from among two or more mutually exclusive investments of equivalent risk, a risk-averse investor will choose the investment with the greatest acceptable expected rate of return. In Figure 13.8, only those investments in the shaded region will be considered. If the projects are mutually exclusive, only projects A and B will be considered. From these, project A will be selected since $k_A > k_B$. The rate of return k_B is the rate of return required to make this investor indifferent between investment B and a risk-free investment. Project C will be rejected out of hand because the expected rate of return (k_C) is not sufficient to compensate the investor for the

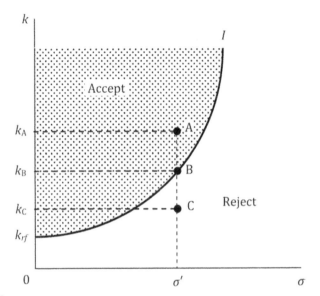

Figure 13.8

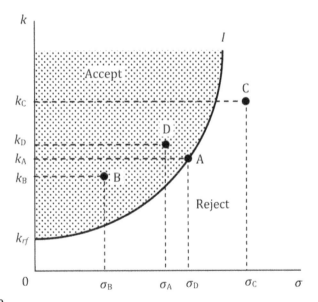

Figure 13.9

risk incurred. If the three investments are independent, the investor will invest projects A, may also invest in project B, but will reject project C.

Figure 13.9 illustrates the more complicated situation in which the expected rates of return and risk are different for each capital investment project.

The expected rate of return from investment C is greater than for investment D, but it is also considerably riskier. So risk, in fact, that it is rejected outright. If these investments are independent, this investor will choose projects B and D, and may choose A. If the projects are mutually exclusive, will choose between project B or D, but which one, and why?

MANAGING RISK

As the preceding discussion has demonstrated, most consumer and business decisions involve some degree of risk. It seems logical to infer from this that risk-averse individuals should be willing to pay some amount to reduce the negative consequences of risky decisions. In fact, this is precisely the case. In this section we will examine three common methods for reducing risk—insurance, diversification, and the use of options contracts.

Insurance

Each year, millions of risk-averse individuals purchase insurance protection against the possibility of catastrophic loss. Consumers purchase life insurance, automobile insurance, and health insurance. Property owners buy flood insurance, tornado insurance, and earthquake insurance. Concert violinists buy insurance in the event of they lose the use of their hands. Professional athletes insure themselves against career-ending injuries. Surgeons and other health-care professionals purchase medical malpractice insurance. Businesses purchase product-liability insurance. Indeed, it is possible to purchase insurance for every imaginable type of risk. The reason why a risk-averse individual would purchase insurance can be explained using Figure 13.10.

Suppose that an automobile owner has an income of $51,000 and there is a 50 percent chance of having an accident that will cost $2,000 in repairs. Without insurance, this person's utility is 22,192 from an expected income of $50,000, which is the average utility of $51,000 without an accident and $49,000 in the event of an accident. This person would clearly be better off purchasing actuarially **fair insurance** of $1,000. Insurance is said to be fair when the expected value of a calamitous event is equal to what the insurer pays out in claims. The reason for this is that in the event of an accident the insurance company will pay $2,000 in repairs and the driver will continue to receive utility from a guaranteed income of $50,000. With insurance, this person's utility is 22,361.

The problem is that no insurance company would ever sell fair insurance. The reason for this is that insurance companies' operating costs include not just claim payouts, but also the administrative costs of handling a claim.

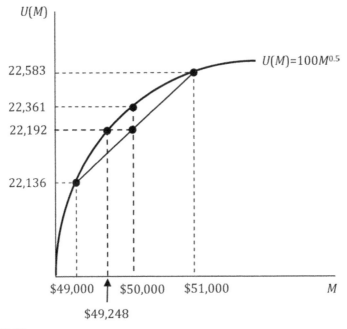

Figure 13.10

Because of this, the driver in our example can expect to pay something more than the actuarially fair premium of $1,000. Insurance is said to be unfair when the expected value of a calamitous event is greater than what the insurer pays out in claims. In the situation depicted in Figure 13.10, this person would be willing to pay up to $51,000 − $49,248 = $1,752 since this amount yields the same utility from being uninsured. If the insurance company charges a premium greater than $1,752, it will be in the driver's best interest to self insure by risking an accident. In short, risk-averse individuals will buy insurance against risky outcomes provided the insurance premiums are less than or equal to the expected loss.

One way to avoid unfair insurance associated with small risks is the use of a *deductible*, which is a common feature of automobile insurance. The deductible provision of an automobile insurance policy requires the insured to pay, say, the first $500 to repair damages from a collision, with the insurance company paying the balance. The purpose of the deductible is to deter insured drivers from filing small claims to fix scratches and other minor repairs. The reason for this is that administrative costs of handling claims are about the same regardless of size. Because administrative costs are a high percentage of the value of small claims, insurance against small losses tend to be actuarially unfair.

Some risks are uninsurable. There are several reasons for this. To begin with, it must be possible to assess risk to determine actuarially fair premiums. This may not be possible in unique cases, such as providing flood insurance in connection with the Mayan end-of-the-world prediction on December 21, 2012. Since there is no precedent for estimating premiums, most insurers would refrain from such coverage.

Another reason why insurers might refrain from offering coverage relates to problems of **asymmetric information**. Individuals who buy insurance coverage have more or better information about the likelihood incurring a loss than does the insurer. If it is not possible to identify high risk from low risk individuals, the premiums charged will reflect the average level of risk. High-risk individuals will be more than happy to pay the lower (for them) average premium, while low risk individuals will not want to pay the higher (for them) average premium. As a result, low-risk individuals will drop out of the insurance market, which then becomes crowded with high-risk individuals—a situation known as **adverse selection**. Unless the insurance company can identify and control who buys insurance, no insurance will be provided even though there are individuals who want to buy insurance at the right price. Two possible methods of accomplishing this is *screening* and *signaling*, which will be discussed later in this chapter.

Another problem stemming from asymmetric information that may limit the availability of insurance coverage is **moral hazard**, which refers to the risk (hazard) that an individual will engage in riskier (immoral) behavior once insured. For example, an insured driver may not drive as carefully knowing that the insurance company will cover damages in the event of an accident. As a result, insured individuals tend to incur greater losses than those who are uninsured. Problems adverse selection and moral hazard associated with asymmetric information will be discussed a greater detail later in this chapter.

Diversification

Buying insurance is not the only way for and individual to reducing risk. Another method is **diversification**, which refers to reducing nonsystematic risk by undertaking a variety of investments or investing in a variety of assets. By spreading risk, it may be possible for an individual to increase utility above that obtainable by focusing on a single activity. To see how this is possible, consider the situation depicted in Figure 13.11 in which an individual with an income of $51,000 decides how to invest $2,000 in shares of common stock.

Suppose that this individual is considering purchasing shares of stock in company A or company B. Each company's share price is $1. This individual believes that if either company "succeeds" then its share price will increase

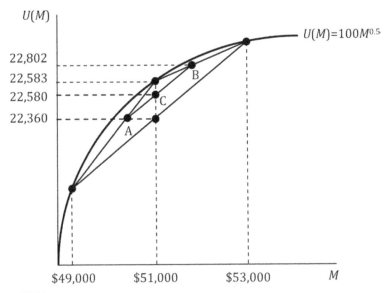

Figure 13.11

to $2 by the end of the year. If either company "fails" then its share price will fall to $0. Suppose that the probability of either outcome is 50 percent. How should this individual invest her $2,000?

Given the symmetry of the choices, it might seem that it does not matter whether this person invests the entire $2,000 in company A, or company B, or both. But, if the performances of the companies are unrelated, this person's will be able to reduce risk by investing in both companies. To see why, suppose that this investor purchases 2,000 shares of company A. The expected payoff from this undiversified investment strategy is 0.5($49,000) + 0.5 ($53,000) = $51,000, which will yield total utility of 22,576. On the other hand, suppose that this person invests $1,000 in both companies. This diversified investment strategy has four possible payoffs, which are summarized in Figure 13.12.

Since these outcomes are equally likely, the expected payoff from a diversified investment strategy is 0.25($49,000) + 0.5($51,000) + 0.25($53,000) = $51,000, which is the same expected payoff from an undiversified investment strategy. So what is the benefit to this investor from diversification?

In Figure 13.11, point A represents the expected utility from an undiversified investment strategy should the company fail, which in our example is 22,360 units of satisfaction. Thus, point A is the risk associated with an undiversified investment strategy. Point B represents the expected utility from an undiversified investment strategy in the event that the company succeeds, or

B

		Fail	Succeed
A	*Fail*	$49,000	$51,000
	Succeed	$51,000	$53,000

Figure 13.12

22,802 units of satisfaction. Point C represents the expected utility associated with a diversified investment strategy, which yields or 22,580 units of satisfaction. In other words, a diversified investment strategy is preferable to an undiversified investment strategy since it increases utility by reduces this individuals risk of losing all or part of her investment.

Options Contracts

Another method for reducing risk is through the use of an **options contract**, which grants the buyer of the option the right, but not the obligation, to buy or sell something of value at a future date at a previously agreed upon price. Although options contract are most often associated with financial market transactions (such as an options contract to purchase corporate equities), in fact this approach to managing risk is frequently encountered in everyday life. Since this privilege is desirable, we would expect that options contracts have market-determined prices.

The interesting thing about is that they fall into a class of assets known as derivatives. A **financial derivative** is a contract that derives its market value from the underlying **financial instrument** or commodity. To illustrate, suppose that Adam is in the market for a used car. He has identified two individuals, Dick and Jane, who are selling cars that appear to satisfy his precise specifications. Although the asking price in both cases is $1,000, this transaction is characterized by asymmetric information since only the sellers know for certain whether the cars are in good working order. But, there is a difference. Dick's offer is final. If Adam buys from Dick, the car is his, warts and all. By contrast, Jane offers Adam a 30-day, no-questions-asked, money-back guarantee. If for any reason Adam is unsatisfied with the car, for the next month Jane will repurchase the car at the original price. It doesn't take an Albert Einstein to figure out whose car Adam will purchase. Jane's guarantee gives Adam the right, but not the obligation, to resell the car to Jane. This option reduces the uncertainty associated with purchasing Jane's car. By purchasing from Jane, Adam receives value in excess of $1,000.

Features of an Options Contract

In the above example, Jane offers Adam with a money-back guarantee free of charge. Suppose, on the other hand, that Jane offers to sell Adam the option to resell. How much would Adam be willing to pay to reduce the risk associated with purchasing a used car that is not worth $1,000? Determining the value of an option can be difficult because the conditions that need to be satisfied before the option can be exercised can be complex. There are conceivably as many different types of options contracts as there are transactions. In spite of this, all options contracts have three features in common, including a *description of the underlying transaction*, the *exercise period*, and the *option price*.

The value of an option is "derived" from the underlying transaction. For this reason, an option must include a complete description of details of the asset, its price, and any other relevant features. In the used-car example, the conditions of the resale might have included a provision relating to vehicle depreciation and damage. Options contracts must also specify the time period during which it may be exercised. In the used-car example, the exercise period was 30 days.

In some cases, the price of the option is explicit. For example, the prices of options contracts to purchase or sell corporate equity shares at a specified price are published in newspapers and on the Internet. In other cases, the price of an option is part of the transaction price. Suppose, for example, that Adam values the resale option at $100. In this case, Adam would be willing to pay a price of $1,100 for the used car. The value of the option is included in the asking price for the car.

How Does the Value of the Underlying Transaction Affect the Value of an Options Contract?

Because an option is exercised in the future, its value is uncertain at the time it is issued. Although Adam purchases Jane's used car for $1,000, what will it be worth tomorrow, or in 30 days? If the used car performs as expected, its future value is approximately equal to what Adam paid for it, in which case the option to resell has little or no value. On the other hand, if Adam discovers that he has purchased a lemon that is not worth $1,000, the option to resell at the purchase price has considerable value.

To illustrate this last point, suppose that after a week Adam discovers that the used car has a rotten transmission, which can be replaced at a cost of $800. Since Adam now owns a used car that is only worth $1,000 − $800 = $200, the option to resell is worth $800. In general, the lower the realized value of the used car, the more valuable is the option to resell. By the same token, if Adam discovers that he has purchased a plum worth $1,400 then Adam will not exercise his option to resell, in which case the option has no value.

In addition to the realized value of the underlying transaction, the volatility of the expected value of the underlying transaction also affects the value of an option. In general, the greater the expected value of the transaction, the more valuable will be the option. To see why, suppose that there is a 50 percent probability that the used car has a faulty transmission that can be repaired for $400 and a 50 percent probability that the used car is in good working order. Since the value of the lemon is $600, Adam can realize a gain of $400 by exercising the option. If the used car performs as expected and is worth $1,000, Adam breaks even by exercising the option. In this case, the expected value of the option to resell is $0.5(\$400) + 0.5(\$0) = \$200$. By contrast, suppose that the transmission cannot be repaired, but must be replaced at a cost of $800. In this case, the expected value of the option is $0.5(\$800) + 0.5(\$0) = \$400$.

The volatility of expected value can also affect the value of the option. In general, the greater the volatility, the more valuable is the option. To see why, consider two different transactions. In the first transaction there is a 50 percent probability that Adam purchased a lemon that needs its transmission repaired at a cost of $400. In this case, Adam owns a used car that is only worth $600. Exercising the option yields Adam $400. On the other hand, suppose Adam owns a used car that does not need to be repaired and is worth $1,000. In this case, Adam does not realize any gain from exercising the option. Thus, the expected value of this transaction is $0.5(\$0) + 0.5(\$400) = \$200$.

In the second transaction, suppose that there is a 50 percent probability that Adam purchased a lemon with a rotten transmission that can be replaced for $800. Since Adam owns a used car that is only worth $200, he can realize a gain of $800 by exercising the option. On the other hand, suppose that there is also a 50 percent probability that Adam purchased a plum worth $1,400. In this case, Adam will lose $400 by exercising the option. In this case, the expected value of this transaction is $0.5(\$800) + 0.5(-\$400) = \$200$.

Although both transactions have an expected value of $200, the second transaction is riskier than the first because $\sigma_2 = \$600 > \sigma_1 = \$200$. Because of this, the option to resell is more valuable in the second transaction. The reason for this is that the option to resell does not have to be exercised. Adam can wait to see how his purchase works out. To see why, recall that there is a 50 percent probability that the used car with a faulty transmission worth $600 and a 50 percent probability that the used car in perfect working order is worth $1,000. The expected value of the option once the condition of the used car is determined is $200. In the second transaction, there is a 50 percent probability that the used car with a rotten transmission is worth $200 and a 50 probability that the used car is a plum worth $1,400. Since Adam will not exercise the option if the used car is a plum, the expected value of the option once the condition of the used cars is 0.5($800) + 0.5($0) = $400. Thus, the greater volatility of the second transaction results in a more valuable option. In this case, the value of the plum matters when determining the expected value the uncertainty is resolved, but plays no role in determining the value of the option once the value of the used car has been determined.

How Does the Exercise Period Affect the Value of an Options Contract?

The value of an option increases with the exercise period. This is because a person with a longer time to exercise an option is more likely to do so. A related consideration has to do with the time value of money. An increase in the interest rate might delay the execution of a buy option since surplus funds can be invested for the exercise period. This is especially true of buy options with a greater exercise period. By contrast, an increase in the interest might accelerate execution of a sell option since the proceeds can be similarly invested at the prevailing interest rate.

Black-Scholes-Merton Model

Option contracts are used to reduce the risk associated with investing in such financial instruments as stocks and bonds, and when speculating in such assets as commodities and foreign exchange. An option to sell a stock at a specified ("strike") price is called a "put". An option to buy a stock at its strike price is called a "call". Determining the value of a put or call is somewhat similar to determining the resell option in the used-car example. To see how, suppose that Amazon.com is currently trading at $P = \$225$ per share. A call option gives an investor the right, but not the obligation, to purchase shares of Amazon.com in 30 days at a strike price of $P_s = \$230$ per share. This option has value if the investor believes that the price of Amazon.com shares will rise to $240 on the execution date. The question is: How much is this call option worth?

One way to approach this problem is to identify the value of an alternative investment that is equivalent to owning a call option. Suppose, for example, that there is a 50-50 probability that Amazon.com shares will sell for either a low price of $P_{LP} = \$200$ or a high price a high price of $P_{HP} = \$240$ in 30 days, that is $p_{LP} = p_{HP} = 0.5$. If the shares sell for $200 then the call option is worthless. If the shares sell for $240, the call option is worth $10. How can we duplicate these payoffs by purchasing a portfolio of Amazon.com shares?

Suppose that an investor borrows and amount L to finance the purchase θ fraction of Amazon.com for $225 per share. For simplicity, assume an interest rate on the loan of zero percent. In 30 days, the call option will be is executed, the shares sold, and the loan repaid. If Amazon.com shares sell for $200, the values of L and θ must satisfy the equation

$$\theta P_{LP} - L = \$0. \tag{13.8}$$

If Amazon.com shares sell for $240, these values must satisfy the equation

$$\theta[\beta P_{HP}] - L = \beta[P_{HP}] - P_S. \tag{13.9}$$

where $\beta = p_{HP}/p_{LP}$. Solving Eqs. (13.8) and (13.9) $L = \$50$ and $\theta = 0.25$. This investor should borrow $50 to purchase a 0.25 share of Amazon.com at the current price P. Thus, the price of the option (P_O) is

$$P_O = \theta P - L = 0.25(\$225) - \$50 = \$6.25. \tag{13.10}$$

Borrowing $50 to purchase a 0.25 share of Amazon.com at a price $225 is equivalent to purchasing a call option for $6.25. Combining Eqs. (13.8) to (13.10), the price of this simple call option is

$$P_O = \frac{(P - P_{LP})(P_S - \beta P_{HP})}{P_{LP} - \beta P_{HP}}. \tag{13.11}$$

The above example masks the fact that valuing options contracts in the real world can be quite difficult. Fortunately, a useful model for pricing European options, which was developed by Fischer Black and Myron Scholes (1973), and expanded upon by Robert Merton (1973), provides a good approximation of European call options.[2] The rationale underlying the Black-Scholes-Merton model (or more commonly the Black-Scholes model) is not dissimilar from the example presented above. By buying shares of stock and simultaneously selling call options, an investor can create a risk-free investment position where gains from the stock are offset by losses from the option. This risk-free "hedge" earns a rate of return equal to the option price. As a result of their work in pricing options contracts, Myron Scholes and Robert Merton were awarded the Nobel Prize in Economics in 1997. Although Fischer Black did not share in the prize because of his passing in 1995, he was mentioned by the Royal Swedish Academy of Sciences for his contributions.

UNCERTAINTY AND SEARCH COSTS

We have so far assumed that consumers know with certainty the prices of goods and services, and firms know with certainty the prices of inputs. In fact, this is rarely the case, which complicates our analysis of the behavior of buyers and sellers. In this section we will consider situations in which consumers and producers do not know the prices charges by different sellers of the same good, service or input. Given that search costs are nontrivial, under what circumstances does it pay to stop "window shopping"?

To keep the analysis simple, suppose that it costs a fixed amount (c) to obtain the price charged by a given vendor. This price may involve the cost of travel, the time it takes to obtain and reviewing a catalog, or may simply involve a making a phone call. Suppose further, that 80 percent of all vendors charge a price of $100 and 20 percent charge a price of $50. Suppose the buyer randomly contacts a vendor who charges a price of $100. Given that shopping around is expensive, should he or she buy or continue looking?

In analyzing this search problem, we will make two critical assumptions. First, there is no penalty should a buyer decide to return to a vendor and pay the original offer price. Second, that shopping around does not cause sellers to change their prices. Given these assumptions, 20 percent of the time the buyer will save $100 − $50 = $50 and will save nothing 80 percent of the time. Thus, the buyer's expected saving $E(S)$ from searching for a lower price is $E(S) = (\$100 - \$50)0.2 + (0)0.8 = \$10$. In general, the buyer should continue to search for a lower price as long as the expected saving is greater than search costs. This decision rule is depicted in Figure 13.13. If search costs are greater than the expected savings ($c > E(S)$), the buyer will pay the asking price. On the other hand, if expected savings are greater than search cost ($E(S) > c$), the buyer will reject the asking price and keep looking. The **buyer's reservation price** (R) is the price at which the buyer is indifferent between accepting and rejecting the asking price.

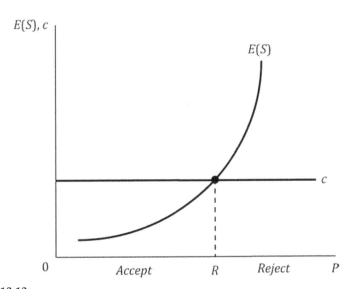

Figure 13.13

In Figure 13.13, an increase in search costs would be illustrated as an up-shift of the horizontal line labeled *c* (not shown). This would result in an increase in a buyer's reservation price. A reduction in search costs would have the opposite effect. This suggests that managers carefully consider search costs when setting the price of their products. When search costs are low buyers will engage in comparison shopping to a much greater extent than when search costs are high. Thus, to increase the chances of making a sale, managers should charge a lower price when search costs are low than when search costs are high.

DYNAMIC GAMES WITH UNCERTAIN PAYOFFS

We have used **game trees** to analyze multistage games involving certain outcomes. In this section, we will search for subgame perfect equilibria in games involving risky outcomes. Consider the multistage, complete-information pricing game depicted in Figure 13.14. Firm A moves first and must decide whether to charge a *high price* or a *low price*. Using **backward induction**, the **subgame-perfect equilibrium** is {*Low price → Low price*} with payoffs of $250,000 for both firms.

The first entries in the parentheses at the **terminal nodes** are the *expected* payoffs to firm A. The second entry, however, is the *certain* payoff to firm B. The subgame equilibrium strategy profiles for this game are {*High price → Low price*} and {*Low price → Low price*}. Regardless of the strategy adopted by firm A, firm B will charge a low price. Firm A's strategy choice, on the other hand, depends on the expected payoff. Firm A's expected payoff from a high

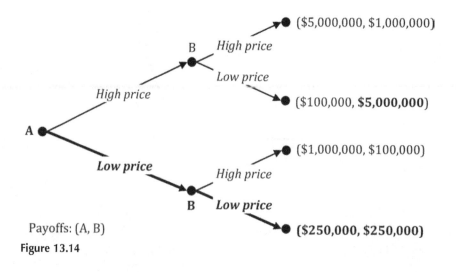

Payoffs: (A, B)

Figure 13.14

price strategy is $E(\pi_{HP}) = 0.4(\$5,000,000) + 0.6(\$100,000) = \$2,060,000$. If firm A charges a low price the expected payoff is $E(\pi_{LP}) = 0.8(\$1,000,000) + 0.2(\$250,000) = \$850,000$. If firm A's move is based on the highest expected payoff, the subgame-perfect equilibrium for this game is {*High price → Low price*}, with actual payoffs are ($100,000, $5,000,000). Recall that with certain payoffs, the subgame-perfect equilibrium was {*Low price → Low price*} with payoffs of $250,000 for both firms.

We will now modify the game in Figure 13.14 by introducing uncertainty into the decision-making process. We will assume that both firms are risk neutral, so that strategy choices are based only on expected payoffs. Suppose that firm A believes that by charging high price there is a 40 percent chance that firm B will charge a high price and a 60 percent chance that it will charge a low price. Similarly, if firm A charges a low price, there is an 80 percent chance that firm B will charge a high price and a 20 percent chance of charging a low price. The resulting extensive pricing game with expected payoffs is depicted in Figure 13.15.

The first entry in the parentheses at the terminal nodes is the *expected* payoff to firm A, while the second entry is the *certain* payoff to firm B. The reason for this is that as the first mover, firm A is uncertain about the pricing strategy of firm B. In this game, regardless of the strategy adopted by firm A, firm B will charge a low price. By contrast, firm A's optimal strategy is based on expected payoffs. If firm A charges a high price, its expected payoff is $E(\pi_{HP}) = 0.4(\$5,000,000) + 0.6(\$100,000) = \$2,060,000$. If firm A charges a low price, its expected payoff is $E(\pi_{LP}) = 0.8(\$1,000,000)$

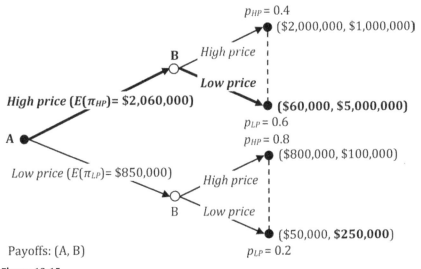

Payoffs: (A, B)

Figure 13.15

+ 0.2($250,000) = $650,000. Thus, if firm A is risk neutral, the subgame-perfect equilibrium is {*High price* → *Low price*}, with actual payoffs are ($100,000, $5,000,000). Recall that with certain payoffs, the subgame-perfect equilibrium was {*Low price* → *Low price*} with payoffs of $250,000 for both firms.

Suppose, however, that firm A is risk averse. In this case, its choice of pricing strategy will also depend on the volatility of the payoffs. The standard deviation of firm A's expected payoff from a *high price* strategy is $\sigma_{HP} = \$2,400,000$. The standard deviation of firm A's expected payoff from a *low price* strategy is $\sigma_{LP} = \$300,000$. A high price strategy has a greater expected return, but is also riskier. If the greater expected payoff is insufficient to compensate the firm for the increased volatility, risk-averse firm A will charge a low price.

SOLVED EXERCISE

Consider the extensive form game in Figure 13.15. If firm A charges a high price, there is a 5 percent chance that firm B will charge a high price and a 95 percent chance that it will charge a low price. If firm A charges a low price, there is a 25 percent chance that firm B will charge a high price and a 75 percent chance that it will charge a low price.

a. *What is the subgame-perfect equilibrium if firm A is risk neutral?*
b. *What can you say about the outcome of this game if firm A is risk averse?*

Solution

a. *The extensive form of this game is depicted in Figure 13.16. The optimal strategy for firm B is to charge a low price regardless of the strategy adopted by firm A. If firm A charges a high price, the expected payoff is $E(\pi_{HP}) = 0.05(\$5,000,000) + 0.95(\$100,000) = \$345,000$. If firm A charges a low price, the expected payoff is $E(\pi_{LP}) = 0.25(\$1,000,000) + 0.75(\$250,000) = \$437,500$. If firm A is risk neutral, the subgame-perfect equilibrium strategy profile for this game is {Low price → Low price}, with payoffs of ($100,000, $5,000,000).*

b. *The standard deviation of firm A's payoffs a high price strategy is $\sigma_{HP} = \$1,067,930$. The standard deviation of firm A's payoffs from a low price strategy is $\sigma_{LP} = \$324,760$.*

The expected payoff from a low price strategy is not only greater, but less risky. Regardless of whether firm A is risk neutral or risk averse, the subgame-perfect equilibrium for this game is {Low price → Low price} with actual payoffs of payoffs of ($250,000, $250,000).

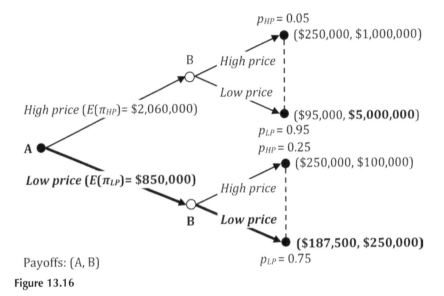

Payoffs: (A, B)

Figure 13.16

Bayesian Updating

In **dynamic games** with incomplete information, players possess private information but are ignorant or ill informed about the information possessed by rivals. Games with incomplete information might be transformed into games with complete but imperfect information using a Harsanyi transformation. Unfortunately, Harsanyi transformations are of limited usefulness when analyzing dynamic games in which the players possess private information.

In games involving incomplete information, players cannot distinguish decision nodes. When this happens, players do not know for certain their position in the game tree. One way to deal with this problem is for players to form conditional expectations about payoffs from alternative strategies, and to update these expectations as more and better information is received—a procedure known as **Bayesian updating**. Expected payoffs are determined using conditional probabilities, which may be calculated using Bayes' theorem.[3] Since this topic is beyond the scope of this book, we will describe the procedure for finding Nash equilibria when strategy choices are based on conditional probabilities.

In dynamic games with imperfect information, players are unaware of their positions in the game tree. When analyzing dynamic games in which the players possess private information, however, it is essential that we keep track of what the players know and when. *Information sets* allow us to keep track of decision nodes that appear the same to the player, but that are, in fact, different. In games involving multiple information sets, the collection

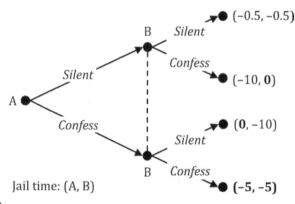

Figure 13.17

of information sets constitutes an **information partition**. Since a player's knowledge is the same at each decision nodes within an information set, a player will make the same move at each decision node. The information sets in Figure 13.17 are referred to as **valid information sets** because a player cannot distinguish between decision nodes. The validity of an information set depends on the assumption of **total (perfect) recall** in which a player remembers everything ever learned about a game, including prior moves made by rivals.

The idea of a valid information set is not a new concept. In fact, we have been dealing with valid information sets throughout most of this text. Recall the **prisoner's dilemma** in Figure 10.1, which is reproduced as the extensive form game Figure 13.17. This game highlights the fact that in static games, players move with complete, but imperfect, information.

In dynamic games with incomplete information, prior moves may reveal private information to other players, who will incorporate this new information into future decisions. To illustrate Bayesian updating, consider the relationship between GLOMAR and Nature in the oil-drilling game. Assume that independent geological surveys suggest that there is a 20 percent chance that oil is present. Since that GLOMAR decides to conduct additional seismic surveys before deciding whether or not to drill. Unfortunately, seismic testing is not foolproof. The test can produce a *false positive* (that oil exists when it does not) or a *false negative* (that oil does not exist when it does). Based on the results of further seismic testing, should GLOMAR drill? The extensive form of this game is depicted in Figure 13.18.

In Figure 13.18, Nature moves first by assigning probabilities to the results of the independent geological surveys, which are 20 percent and 80 percent, respectively. Nature then moves by assigning probabilities to determine the results of seismic testing. Applying Bayes' theorem, the conditional

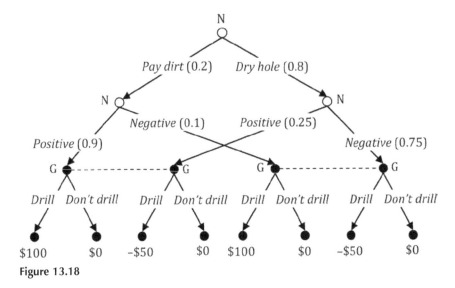

Figure 13.18

probability of a false positive is 25 percent and the conditional probability of a false negative is 10 percent. This assignment of probabilities is referred to as a players' **belief profile**. A **perfect Bayesian equilibrium** a subgame-perfect equilibrium that is consistent with the probability distribution of states of nature and player beliefs. A player must be able to calculate the expected payoffs associated with a move from any given information set. Since these beliefs are likely to change during the course of game play, it must also be possible for players to revise their strategies and expected payoffs using Bayesian updating whenever possible. Should GLOMAR drill or not drill?

If GLOMAR drills and hits oil, the company will earn $100 million. If GLOMAR drills and does not hit oil, the company will lose $50 million. The expected payoff from drilling without seismic testing is 0.20($100) + 0.80($50) = –$20. Since the payoff from not drilling is $0, a risk-neutral GLOMAR will choose not to drill. How will seismic testing affect this decision? To answer this question, we must ask how seismic testing changes the probabilities used to estimate the expected payoff from drilling.

Bayes' theorem allows us to update the probability of an event (B_i) after learning that some other event (A) has occurred.[2] Denote the unconditional probability that oil is present as $P(B_i)$. Since this probability comes first, this is referred to as the *prior probability*. The probability that oil exists will be revised once GLOMAR receives the results of its seismic testing (A). This is referred to as the *posterior probability*. The revised probability that oil exists given the results of seismic testing is $P(B_i|A)$. This process of Bayesian updating involves replacing prior probabilities with posterior probabilities once prior moves have been observed.

According to Bayes' theorem, if the seismic test is positive then there is a 47 percent probability that GLOMAR will strike oil and a 53 percent probability of not finding oil. Using these posterior probabilities, the expected payoff of finding oil is $0.47(\$100) + 0.53(-\$50) = \$20.5$. Since the expected payoff from not drilling is $0, a risk-neutral GLOMAR will *drill*. By using Bayes' theorem and updating the prior probability of finding oil using seismic testing, the expected value of finding oil has increased from –$20 million to +$20.5 million.

Conditional probabilities are very sensitive to changes in prior probabilities. To see this, suppose that the prior probability of finding oil is 10 percent instead of 20 percent. It is left as an exercise for the reader to show that the revised (posterior) probability of finding oil is only 28.6 percent. Using this result, the expected payoff of finding oil is –$7.1 million. Risk neutral and rational GLOMAR would choose not to drill. This result is somewhat surprising given that seismic testing in this example is highly accurate. It is left as an exercise for the reader to demonstrate that a less accurate test will result in an even larger expected loss from drilling.

ASYMMETRIC INFORMATION

There are many market situations in which some participants have more or better information about a good or service being transacted than other market participants. This problem of asymmetric information may lead to problems of adverse selection and moral hazard. If not resolved, these problems could lead to inefficient markets or no market at all.

Adverse Selection

Adverse selection an *ex ante* problem because it is a problem that may arise before the transaction takes place. Nobel laureate George Akerlof (1970) identified the problem of adverse selection in the used-car market. Professor Akerlof began by identifying two types of used cars: good used cars (peaches) and bad used cars (lemons). In this market, transactions take place directly between the buyers and sellers of used cars. Buyers of used cars are willing to pay a "high" price for peaches, but a "low" price for lemons. The problem is that the sellers of used cars know if they own peaches or lemons and the buyers do not.

Since buyers are unable to distinguish between peaches and lemons, the market price will reflect the average quality of used cars. Owners of lemons are more than happy to sell at the average (higher) price because it overstates the value of their used cars. Owners of peaches will not want to sell at the average (lower) price because it understates the value of their used cars. Thus, some owners of peaches will withdraw from the market and the market for used cars will become crowded with lemons. Since buyers of used cars know this, few used cars will be purchased. If the problem of asymmetric information is severe enough, the used-car market could disappear entirely.

The lemons problem has multiple applications. In the market for financial securities, for example, sellers of stocks and bonds have better information about a company's underlying financial strengths or weaknesses than buyers. Buyers of corporate equities, for example, are less able to distinguish high-earnings, low-risk companies from low-earnings, high-risk companies. As in the case of the used-car market, share prices tend to reflect the average financial strength of similar companies. Sellers of low-quality stocks are happy to receive the average (higher) price. Sellers of high-quality stocks will not be happy to receive the average (lower) price.

In a similar manner, buyers of corporate bonds may be unable distinguish high-default-risk companies from low-default-risk companies. Because of the lemons problem, the interest rate paid will tend to reflect average default risk. Sellers of high-default-risk bonds will be more than happy to pay the average (lower) interest rate, while sellers of low-default-risk bonds will not be happy to borrow at the (higher) average interest rate. Once again, asymmetric information could result in inefficient equity and bond markets—or no securities markets at all. Of course, used-car, equity, and bond markets do exist, which means remedies have been devised to overcome adverse selection problems arising from asymmetric information.

Banks frequently fall victim to adverse selection when making loans. Since bad credit risks are most likely to apply for loans, banks typically request copious amounts of financial information to evaluate an applicant's ability and willingness to nominally service outstanding debt obligations. Bad credit risks, however, are more likely to withhold or alter their financial profile to obtain a loan at a lower interest rate and more favorable payment terms. An example of this is when business owner inflates company earnings to demonstrate its ability to nominally service its debt obligations. The bank has made an adverse selection if it makes the loan on the basis of based on the falsified financial information.

Moral Hazard

In contrast to adverse selection, moral hazard is an *ex post* problem because it occurs after the transaction takes place. An example of moral hazard is when the owner of a company obtains a private loan to finance a capital investment project. The lender's decision may be based on the belief that the investment will generate sufficient returns to repay the loan. Once the loan is made, however, the borrower has an incentive to use the loan for some other, riskier, investment. Because moral hazard lowers the probability that the loan will be repaid, the bank may decide not to make the loan.

To illustrate the problem of moral hazard in lending, suppose an individual is considering a $500 investment with an 80 percent probability of a $1,000 payoff and a 20 percent probability of a $0 payoff. A bank is considering financing the investment with a $500 fair loan at an interest rate of 25 percent. If the investment pays off, the bank receives $500 + $125 = $625, otherwise it receives nothing. Thus, the bank's expected payoff is 0.8($500 + $125) + 0.2($0) = $500. The borrower's expected payoff is 0.8($1,000 – $500 – $125) + 0.2($0) = $300.

Suppose that after receiving the loan the borrower identifies a riskier $500 investment with an 8 percent probability of a $10,000 payoff and a 92 percent probability of a $0 payoff. In this case, the borrower's share of the expected payoff jumps to 0.08($10,000 – $500 – $125) + 0.92($0) = $750, while the bank's share of the expected payoff drops to 0.08($500 + $125) + 0.92($0) = $50. If the bank cannot control the borrower's behavior then it may decide not to make the loan. In practice, there are a number of ways that a can bank protect itself against moral hazard, such as requiring collateral or including restrictive covenants in the loan contract to ensure that the loan is used for the intended purposes.

Signaling

Signaling is a possible solution to the problem of adverse selection. Signaling occurs when an informed individual sends a credible and irreproducible signal to convey important information that is otherwise not directly observable. For example, companies often use signals to convey information about the benefits of a good or service to potential customers. Since the benefits are not realized until the firm's product is actually consumed, the signal is designed to convince potential customers to give the product a try.

In many cases, the signals involve a "try-it-and-you'll-like-it" approach. These signals include money-back guarantees, free trial periods, and so on. In some cases, signals are linked to a firm's reputation. These "you know me so you can trust me" signals often entail packaging that prominently displays the company's logo. If the firm has been around for a long time, signaling can be as simple as a neighborhood storefront that displays the year in which the company was founded.

Signaling is characteristic of the labor market. Prospective employers typically require job applicants to submit supporting documentation, such as letters of recommendation, college transcripts, résumés, etc. Résumé transmit signals to the employer about the applicant's potential value to the firm.

These signals include work experience, internships, educational background, schools attended, degrees earned, extracurricular activities, professional certifications, licenses, grade point average, professional and academic awards, fraternal and academic honor societies, community service and so forth. Each of these signals is intended to convince the prospective employer that the job applicant will positively contribute to the firm's "bottom line."

For a signal to be effective, it must be observable, reliable, and not easily mimicked. Consider the case of a potential employer who plans to hire a worker from a pool of applicants. To keep things simple, suppose that the employer believes that there are only two types of prospective employees: Unproductive workers who will contribute nothing to the firm's revenues, and productive workers who will contribute $100,000. This contribution is referred to as the value of the workers marginal product. In this example, there is a problem of asymmetric information. The applicant knows whether he or she is productive, but the employer does not.

Suppose that the employer believes that there is a 50–50 chance of hiring a productive worker. This information can be used to calculate the expected value of a worker's marginal product, which in this case is 0.5($0) + 0.5($100,000) = $50,000. If the prospective employer is risk neutral, the most that the firm will offer the applicant is a salary of $50,000. This creates the same kind of lemons problem that we observed in the used-car market. Unproductive workers will be more than happy to accept a salary offer of $50,000, while productive workers will not, but what about productive workers?

Suppose that productive workers have a choice. They can either accept the $50,000 offer, or start their own businesses and earn, say, $75,000. Productive workers will refuse the offer and start their own businesses. Unless the problem of asymmetric information can be overcome, the pool of applicants will become crowded with unproductive workers. Unless the problem of asymmetric information is resolved, an optimal strategy of prospective employers is not to hire anyone.

Since productive workers are harmed by employers' inability to distinguish between worker types, it will be in the best interest of productive workers to signal their productivity. One way to do this is to simply tell employers that they are productive. The problem with this approach is that unproductive workers will say the same thing. What productive workers need to do is transmit credible signals that cannot be reproduced by unproductive workers. If successful, employers are more likely to offer salaries that are commensurate with worker productivity.

At one time, having an undergraduate college degree was an effective signal of worker productivity, such as was a high-school diploma century earlier. Employers believed that only productive workers could earn a college degree. Having a college degree was an effective signal because a worker either graduated from college or did not. As college degrees became increasing the norm, employers began to revise their expected value of workers with college degrees. Suppose, for example, that employers believe that there is a 90 percent probability that a worker with a college degree is productive. In this case, the expected value of workers with college degrees is no longer $100,000 but 0.1($0) + 0.9($100,000) = $90,000.

As the market became flooded with productive and unproductive college graduates, employers began to look for different signals of worker productivity. These productivity signals include degrees from prestigious universities, high grade point averages, applicants with graduate degrees from accredited professional programs, and so on. The employer will use these and other signals to weed out unproductive workers from the pool of job applicants.

Separating and Pooling Strategies

Signaling games often have multiple Nash equilibria. In searching for these equilibria, we will investigate how a firm might use education as a productivity signal. There are two ways to proceed with this investigation. The first is to assume that high-productivity types attend college and low-productivity types do not go beyond high school. A strategy that distinguishes (separates) high-productivity from low-productivity types is called a **separating strategy**. A firm that adopts a separating strategy will use transmitted signals to differentiate player types. The Bayesian Nash equilibrium that results when a different strategy is adopted for different player types is referred to as a **separating equilibrium**.

Alternatively, the firm can assume that education provides no information about a worker's productivity. In this case, the firm lumps all productivity types into the same pool regardless of education. This is referred to as a **pooling strategy**. Since a worker's education is assumed to reveal no information about a worker's productivity, a pooling strategy that does not use transmitted signals to differentiate player types. The firm assumes that the probability distribution of productivity types for the population also applies to players with different levels of education.

Finding a Bayesian Nash equilibrium in signaling games involving pooling strategies proceeds along the same lines as the oil-drilling game discussed earlier. Using a Harsanyi transformation, Nature determines the probability distribution of productive and unproductive workers. The resulting perfect Bayesian equilibrium is referred to as a **pooling equilibrium**.

It may be somewhat disturbing that a perfect Bayesian equilibrium depends on the employers prior beliefs about worker productivity types. Unfortunately, this unhappy state of affairs is true of almost all signaling games.

Because signaling games involve less than complete information, the search for a perfect Bayesian equilibrium is extremely difficult. In fact, a unique Nash equilibrium in signaling games is the exception rather than the rule.

Screening

A strategy that is similar to signaling is **screening**, which attempts to sort player types according to well-defined criteria. In the loan market, for example, the problem of adverse selection makes it necessary for lenders to screen out bad credit risks. When an individual applies for a mortgage loan, for example, the bank or mortgage broker requests copious information, including proof of income, income tax returns, checking and savings account balances, financial assets, real assets (such as automobiles and real estate), credit history, employment history, and so on. If the prospective borrower is a business, the lender will require financial statements (income statements and balance sheets), feasibility studies, and so on. It is the responsibility of the lending officer to assess credit risk and decide whether the loan should be made. Some banks may even specialize in the types of loans that they make, such as lending to small businesses, or to firms in specific industries or geographic regions. By specializing, banks develop the expertise necessary to assess the creditworthiness of prospective borrowers.

Screening is used by prospective employers to sort job applicants according to productivity characteristics. One type of screening mechanism is **self-selection**. Job applicants are informed by the prospective employer that there are prerequisites to employment, such minimum level of education, minimum grade point average, specific kinds of work experience, etc. Those workers possessing these characteristics will continue the application process.

To illustrate how screening works, suppose that Adam is considering applying for a management position that pays $50,000 or a sales position that pays $40,000. Adam knows that he has terrible organizational skills and would not make a very good manager. Because of this, he would add only $30,000 of value to the firm as a manager. On the other hand, Adam has terrific interpersonal skills, which would add $60,000 of value to the firm as a salesperson. Although Adam knows that he would make a better salesperson, he would prefer to be a manager because of the greater payoff. Unfortunately, the personnel officer does not know Adam well enough to know whether to offer him a position as a manager or a salesperson. What, if anything, can the personal officer do to overcome this problem of asymmetric information?

Suppose that the personnel officer comes up with the following scheme: Offer Adam his choice of either job at a guaranteed annual salary of $20,000, plus a $5,000 bonus for each $10,000 of value added to the firm. With this compensation scheme, Adam can earn $20,000 + $5,000 ($30,000/$10,000) = $35,000 as a manager, but $40,000 as a salesperson. If income is the deciding factor, Adam will choose to go into sales. Thus, even though the personnel officer has incomplete information, this self-selection mechanism has directed Adam to the job yields the greatest monetary benefits to both players.

CHAPTER EXERCISES

13.1 Greater volatility of payoffs must be compensated by a higher expected payoff. Do you agree with this statement? For what type of person is this statement likely to be true?

13.2 What is the standard statistical measure of risk? What does it measure? If two payoffs have the same expected value, why is the payoff with the large standard deviation considered riskier than the payoff with a small standard deviation?

13.3 Many risk-averse people play government-sponsored lotteries even though they are unfair gambles. How would you explain this? Would a government ever sponsor a fair lottery?

13.4 Explain how a Harsanyi transformation transforms a static game with incomplete information into a static game with imperfect information. Is it possible to find a perfect Bayesian equilibrium for such static games? Why?

13.5 What is the market for lemons? In what way do you think used-car dealers help reduce the problem of adverse selection? How might the lemons problem manifest itself in the labor market?

13.6 Would you be more or less willing to make a business loan to a friend who had invested his or her life savings in a business?

13.7 Do you think that the lemons problem is more or less severe for financial securities traded in the New York Stock Exchange or in the market for financial derivatives?

13.8 Explain why graduates of Ivy League universities receive higher starting salaries than do graduates from less prestigious institutions. How is this related to the problem of adverse selection? Do you believe that this is fair?

13.9 In your opinion, what is a better signal for worker productivity: A so-so grade point average from a prestigious research university, or a high grade point average from a mediocre private or public college or university? What other signals do you believe would improve a job seeker's chances of employment?

13.10 Rosie Hemlock offers Robin Nightshade the following wager. For a payment of $10, Rosie will pay Robin the dollar value of any card drawn from a standard 52-card deck. For example, for an ace of any suite, Rosie will pay Robin $1. For an 8 of any suit, Rosie will pay Robin $8. A ten or picture card of any suit is worth $10.
   a. What is the expected value of Rosie's offer?
   b. Will risk-neutral Rosie accept this offer?

13.11 Suppose that capital investment project X has an expected value of $\mu_X = \$1,000$ and a standard deviation of $\sigma_X = \$500$. Suppose that capital investment project Y has an expected value of $\mu_Y = \$1,500$ and a standard deviation of $\sigma_Y = \$750$. What is the relatively riskier project?

13.12 Senior management of Rubicon & Styx is trying to decide whether to advertise its world-famous hot sauce "Sergeant Garcia's Revenge" on television (campaign A) or in magazines (campaign B). The marketing department of Rubicon & Styx has estimated the probabilities of alternative sales revenues (net of advertising costs) using each of the two media outlets, which are summarized in the following table.
   a. Calculate the expected revenues from each advertising campaign.

Television Sales	Probability	Magazine Sales	Probability
$5,000	0.20	$6,000	0.15
$8,000	0.30	$8,000	0.35
$11,000	0.30	$10,000	0.35
$14,000	0.20	$12,000	0.15

   b. Calculate the standard deviation of sales revenues from each advertising campaign.

13.13 Suppose that there is a 50–50 chance that a risk-averse individual will have an automobile accident and suffer a loss of $100,000.
   a. Calculate the cost of actuarially fair insurance if this individual's current income is $200,000. Illustrate your answer and show that this individual prefers to fair insurance to self insuring.
   b. Suppose that two types of insurance policies are available. Policy 1 is fair insurance covering complete loss. Policy 2 is fair insurance covering half of the loss incurred. Demonstrate that this individual will prefer policy 1 to policy 2.
   c. Suppose that individuals who purchase policy 2 are likely to be more careful drivers, which reduces the cost of an accident to $70,000. In this case, what is the cost of policy2? Explain how some individuals might now prefer policy 2.

13.14 Sally purchases a dozen eggs. Although the cost of transporting the eggs is zero, Sally knows that there is still a 50 percent probability that she will break all of the eggs before she gets home. Knowing this, Sally considers two transportation strategies. The first strategy involves carrying all the eggs home in one trip. The second strategy involves carrying six eggs in each of two trips.
   a. How many eggs are expected to survive using each strategy?
   b. Suppose that Sally is risk averse. Illustrate Sally's strategy options.
   c. If the cost of transporting eggs is zero, which strategy should Sally choose? Is it possible for Sally in increase her utility by increasing the number of trips? How might your answer be different if transporting eggs is costly?

13.15 A share of stock in MagnumOpus, Inc. is $54 per share. It is equally probable that MagnumOpus shares will sell for $50 or $62 per share in 30 days.
   a. Suppose that the strike price on a 30-day call option is $55. What is the price of a call option if the cost of borrowing (interest rate) to finance the purchase is zero?
   b. How is the price of a call option affected if the strike price increases to $56?
   c. Suppose the strike price is $56. How will the price of a call option be affected if it is equally likely that MagnumOpus shares sell for $48 or $65 in 30 days?
   d. How is your answer to part c affected if the interest rate is 5 percent?
   e. Consider the situation in part b. What is the price of the call option if the probability of a low price after 30 days is $p_L = 0.4$ and the probability of a high price after 30 days is $p_H = 0.6$?

13.16 Using investor indifference curves, illustrate three investment in which the expected rates of return are $k_C > k_A > k_B$, and the risks associated with each project are $\sigma_C > \sigma_A > \sigma_B$. Draw an indifference curve corresponding to each investment.

13.17 Using investor indifference curves, illustrate three investment in which the expected rates of return are $k_A > k_B > k_C$, and the risks associated with each project are $\sigma_C > \sigma_A > \sigma_B$. Draw an indifference curve for each investment.

13.18 Ted Sillywalk offers Wally Wobble the fair gamble of receiving $500 of the flip of a fair coin showing heads, and losing $500 if the coin comes up tails. Suppose that Wally's total utility of money function is

$$U = M^{1.2}.$$

   a. For some positive level of money income, what is Wally's attitude toward risk?
   b. If $M = \$5,000$, will Wally accept Ted's offer? Explain.

13.19 Consider the static oil-drilling games depicted in Figures 13.1 and 13.2. What is the Nash equilibrium strategy profile if PETROX and GLOMAR are risk neutral and there is a 50–50 chance of finding oil?

NOTES

   1. The curvature of the utility function can be determined by examining its first and second derivatives. The utility function is concave, which is characteristic of risk-averse behavior, if the second derivative is negative. Denoting the first and second derivatives as $U'(M)$ and $U''(M)$, a well-known measure of risk aversion developed by Kenneth Arrow (1970) and John Pratt (1964) is given by $-MU''(M)/U'(M)$. Suppose, for example, that $U(M) = M\beta$. The corresponding first and second derivatives are $U'(M) = \beta M^{\beta-1}$ and $U''(M) = \beta(\beta - 1)M^{\beta-2}$. The *Arrow-Pratt measure of relative risk aversion* is $-MU''(M)/U'(M) = 1 - \beta$. If $\beta = 1$, this measure of risk aversion is 0, which indicates risk neutral behavior and a linear utility function. One the other hand, if $0 < \beta < 1$, this measure of risk aversion is a positive fraction, which indicates risk-averse behavior and a concave utility function. The closer this value is to zero, the greater the degree of risk aversion.
   2. European call options are executed on the exercise date. American call options can be exercised any time up to the exercise date.
   3. Bayes' theorem allows a player to update the probability that an event (B_i) will occur after observing that that some other event (A) has occurred. Let B_i be the ith of k mutually exclusive and collectively exhaustive events with a nonzero probability. If event A has a nonzero probability, the probability that event B_i occurs, which is conditional on event A occurring is

$$P(B_i|A) = \frac{P(A|B_i) \cdot P(B_i)}{\sum_{i=1}^{k} P(A|B_i) \cdot P(B_i)}.$$

Chapter 14

Contracts

In the previous chapter we examined the several key concepts related to the bargaining process, including value creation and division, bargaining with symmetric and asymmetric impatience, and the last-mover's advantage. In many business settings, once negotiations are completed, it is time to prepare a contract.

The **contract** is a defining characteristic of many business and economic relationships. It is a formal agreement that obligates the parties to perform, or refrain from performing, a specified act in exchange for something of value. Labor contracts summarize negotiations between firms and workers over wages, health benefits, work assignments, and so on. Loan contracts between lenders and borrowers specify interest rates, debt service payments, collateral requirements, and restrictive covenants. Contracts between firms and resource suppliers stipulate input prices, raw materials and components specifications, and delivery schedules. Homeowners sign service contracts with landscapers, building contractors, personal and property security providers, and insurance companies. Nations sign bilateral and multilateral treaties that define tariffs, intellectual property rights, human rights, laws of the sea, environmental regulations, military cooperation, and international security agreements.

Contracts are important because they reduce uncertainty by clearly specifying the obligations of the contracting parties. Contracts are necessary because many business relationships resemble prisoner's-dilemma-type games—each player benefits from cooperation, but each has an incentive to violate the terms of the agreement. If this were not the case, legally binding written contracts would be replaced with verbal agreement and a handshake.[1] A contract can transform an unstable coalition into a **Nash equilibrium** by changing the payoffs in the event of a breach.

Explicit and implicit contracts lie at the heart of virtually all market transactions. For this reason, contract law is among the most important areas of
jurisprudence. Since contract law is extremely complex, anything approach-
ing a detailed discussion of its intricacies is beyond the scope of this book
and the expertise of the author. The purpose of this chapter is to illustrate how
game theory can be used to enhance our understanding of elements that are
common to all contracts.

CONTRACTING ENVIRONMENT

The **contracting environment** refers to those factors that directly or indirectly affect interaction between and among the contracting parties. This
interaction may be referred to as the parties' **contractual relationship**. The
contracting environment may include participation of third parties, such as
the judges, mediators and arbitrators, in the event of a breach by either party.
These third parties may be considered players that have the authority to take
actions that can affect the outcome by changing the payoffs.

Contractual relationships can be conceptually divided into two phases.
The *contracting phase* refers to negotiations and other interactions between
the parties that come to define the terms of the contract. This is followed
by the *implementation phase* in which the contract is executed and enforced.
There are two fundamental ways in which a contract may be enforced. A contract is *self-enforced* if it is in the players' individual interest to abide by the
terms of the contract. A contract is said to be *externally enforced* if it requires
the intervention of a third party to enforce compliance.

CONTRACTING PHASE

During the contracting phase of a contractual relationship, the players negotiate terms, obligations and payoffs. The result may be an explicit, written
agreement, such as an international trade treaty between countries or a formal
document that defines management-labor relations. A contract may also be
less formal tacit or verbal understanding, such as might define the obligations of family members. In addition to defining the obligations and payoffs
of the contracting parties, contract negotiations must also take into account
the dynamics of the bargaining process, which were discussed in the previous
chapter.

To illustrate the basic elements of a contractual relationship, consider the
following example of a simple loan contract, which is depicted in Figure 14.1.
In this game, player 1 (the lender) decides to *lend* or *not lend* an amount (L)
in exchange for a promise by player 2 (the borrower) to *repay L* plus simple

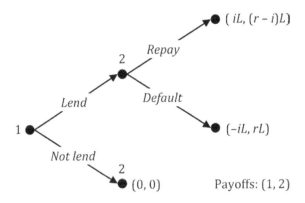

Figure 14.1

interest (iL) in one year. Player 2 promises to use the loan to finance a capital investment with an expected rate of return of r. To guarantee repayment of principal, the loan is fully collateralized.

In the lending game depicted in Figure 14.1, we assume that the borrower has the ability to repay the loan with interest, but may not have the willingness to do so. In the literature dealing with asymmetric information, this is a **moral hazard** problem, which is the risk (hazard) that the borrower will engage in an activity (default) that is undesirable (immoral) from the lender's perspective. We also assume that the players are risk averse and that a dollar received yields the same marginal utility to both players.

The game begins when player 1 decides to *lend* or *not lend*. If player 1 does not lend, the game ends and the payoff to both players is $0. If player 1 lends, player 2 decides whether to *repay* or *default* in the second stage. If the loan is nominally serviced, player 1 earns iL and player 2's earns $(r - i)$ $L > 0$. If player 2 defaults, player 1 loses interest earnings ($-iL$), but does not lose principal because the loan is collateralized. The payoff to player 2 is rL, which is the return on the investment.

IMPLEMENTATION PHASE

Once the terms of the contract are negotiated and specified in the contract is written, the next step is execution and enforcement. In this section, we will examine two basic methods of enforcement in our loan contract example: Self-enforcement and external enforcement.

Self-enforcement

A contract is self-enforced if it is in both players best interest to abide by the terms of the contract. In the lending game depicted in Figure 14.1, the

contract will be self-enforced provided that the strategy profile {*lend* →
repay} is a **subgame-perfect equilibrium**, which is possible if and only if

$$(r - i)L \geq rL. \tag{14.1}$$

Unfortunately, condition (14.1) can only be satisfied when the lender
charges a zero or negative interest rate! In other words, the contract is self-
enforcing only if the lender subsidizes the borrower's investment. For any
positive interest rate, it will be in the borrower's best interest to default. For
any positive interest rate, the subgame-perfect equilibrium is {*not lend*}, in
which case a profitable investment opportunity is lost.

To make the lending game more concrete, suppose that player 2 wants to
borrow $100 at 5 percent simple interest to finance an investment that prom-
ises a 10 percent rate return. This lending game is depicted in Figure 14.2.
Based on the payoffs, it is in the borrower's best interest to default if the loan
is made. Thus, it is in the lenders best interest not to lend. The subgame-
perfect equilibrium for this game is {*Not lend*}.

External Enforcement

In the game depicted in Figure 14.1, self-enforcement will be ineffective
unless the lender subsidizes the borrower's investment. What role can the
courts play in the enforcement of the loan contract? One thing that the court
can do is to step in and compel one party to pay the other party damages in the
event of a default. In this case, the court will remedy the situation by requiring the borrower to transfer an amount (α) to the lender. This revised lending
game is depicted in Figure 14.3.

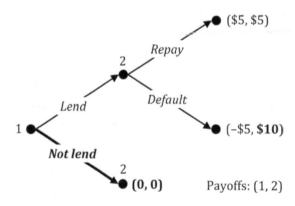

Figure 14.2

Depending on the amount of the transfer, external enforcement changes the outcome by altering the payoffs. To keep the lender from defaulting, the court-ordered transfer must satisfy the condition

$$\alpha \geq iL. \qquad (14.2)$$

Suppose, for example, that it is known to both players that the court will order the borrower to pay the lender $\alpha = \$6$ in the event of default. In this case, the payoff to the borrower is $rL - \alpha = \$4$. This new situation is depicted in Figure 14.4. The reader should verify that the subgame-perfect equilibrium is $\{Lend \rightarrow Repay\}$. By altering the payoffs, the threat of a court-imposed transfer has made self-enforcement desirable. Note that in this game, the size of the transfer was set to alter the borrower's behavior—not to protect the lender. In the unlikely event of default, the transfer does not protect the borrower from incurring **opportunity costs**.

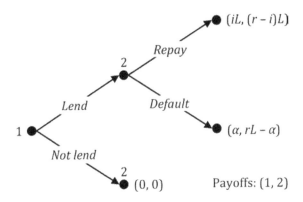

Figure 14.3

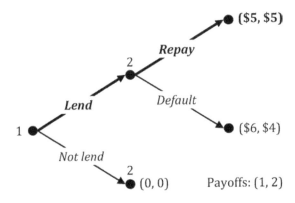

Figure 14.4

In reality, intervention by the court does not always lead to a transfer between contracting parties since high legal costs impose a transfer on both players. As a result, litigants frequently negotiate an out-of-court settlement that produces an economically inefficient outcome.

SOLVED EXERCISE

Several years ago the U.S. Army requested proposals from its top contractors to develop the Hell Cat armored helicopter gunship. Although Sikorsky Aircraft was expected to win the competition, the contract was eventually awarded to a joint venture between Dynamic Diesel and Sea-Air Systems. The joint venture was unusual because of the fierce competitive rivalry that existed between these two companies over the past five decades. After the contract with the U.S. Army was signed, each company simultaneously, and independently, decides to fully invest (FI) or under-invest (UI) in the project. The normal form for this one-time, noncooperative static game is depicted in Figure 14.5. Assume that payoffs are in millions of dollars and that transfers between players are possible.

a. *What conditions must be satisfied for the value of this joint venture to be maximized?*
b. *Under what conditions would this contract be self-enforced?*
c. *Suppose that the U.S. Army relied upon the courts to enforce this contract. What conditions must be satisfied with respect to the size of court-enforced transfers to produce an economically efficient outcome?*

Solution

a. *For the value of the joint venture to be maximized, it must be the case that $a + b > c + d$, $a + b > e + f$, and $a + b > 0$.*
b. *This contract will be self-enforced if it is in the players' best interest to play the Nash equilibrium strategy profile is {FI, FI}. For this to happen,*

Sea-Air Systems

		FI	UI
Dynamic Diesel	FI	(a, b)	(e, f)
	UI	(c, d)	$(0, 0)$

Payoffs: (Dynamic Diesel, Sea-Air Systems)

Figure 14.5

it must be the case that $a \geq c$ and $b \geq f$. If these conditions are not satisfied, enforcement by a third party, such as the courts, may be required.

c. *The players in the contract game depicted in Figure 14.5 have an incentive to defect if $c > a$ and $f > b$, in which case the Nash equilibrium strategy profile is {UI, UI}. Now, consider the revised contract game depicted in Figure 14.6 in which α and β represent the values of court-order transfers. In order for the external enforcement to induce the economically efficient outcome {FI, FI}, the court-ordered transfers must satisfy the conditions $\alpha \geq c - a$ and $\beta \geq f - b$.*

Complete Contracts with Full Verifiability

We will now change the nature of the game depicted in Figure 14.3 by allowing the parties to incorporate the size and type of transfer in the contract. Whereas external enforcement relies on the court to both specify and enforce the amount of the transfer, a complete contract only requires the court to enforce a transfer previously agreed to by the players. We will assume that the court has complete information regarding the details of the loan transaction, the players, strategies, payoffs, and the transfer. This informational requirement, which is referred to as *full verifiability*, means that the court has the evidence it requires to enforce the transfer provision of the contract.

An example of a complete contract is a mortgage in which property purchased with the proceeds of the loan is used as collateral in the event of default. Typically, the size of the loan is less than the value of the property put up as collateral. In the event of default, the lender seizes the collateral, which is then sold to repay the loan. Provided that the loan is not "underwater," the lender will sell the collateral to pay off the outstanding balance.[2] If the proceeds from the sale of collateral is greater than the loan, the difference is returned to the borrower.

Suppose that in our example, the transfer specified in the loan contract is $\alpha = iL = \$5$. This new game is depicted in Figure 14.7. Unlike the situation

Sea-Air Systems

		FI	UI
Dynamic Diesel	FI	(a, b)	$(e + \beta, f - \beta)$
	UI	$(c - \alpha, d + \alpha)$	$(-\alpha, -\beta)$

Payoffs: (Dynamic Diesel, Sea-Air Systems)

Figure 14.6

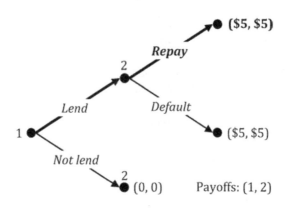

Figure 14.7

depicted in Figure 14.4, the negotiated transfer not only encourages self-enforcement, but in the unlikely event of default, the lender is fully protected.

Complete Contracts with Limited Verifiability

Unfortunately, in some cases the court may not have complete information regarding the underlying loan transaction. For example, the court may not have the expertise necessary to assess the market value of the collateral, verify the expected return on the investment (r), or determine whether the borrower used the loan proceeds as intended (a moral hazard problem). This condition of **incomplete information** is referred to as *limited verifiability*.

In the case of limited verifiability, it is difficult for the court to accurately determine a transfer amount that will result in an efficient outcome. One solution is for the players to allow the court to impose a transfer based upon the limited information that it is able to verify. Unfortunately, this makes it difficult for the players to write a contract that guarantees an efficient outcome.

BREACH REMEDIES

We have thus far assumed that contracts are complete in that they fully reflect deliberate negotiations between the contracting parties and account for every possible contingency. In many real world situations, however, contracts are incomplete in the sense that they only reflect how the players intend to behave. Preparing a contract is time consuming, and costly. Since it may be difficult or impossible to anticipate every possible outcome, the contracting parties frequently rely on the courts to clarify grey areas in the event of a **breach of contract**, which occurs when a party to a contract fails to perform, or refuses to perform, a specified obligation.

In the event of a breach, the injured party, or *plaintiff*, may seek court-ordered **damages** from the injurer, or *defendant*. Once the court has established **liability**, it may then impose a **breach remedy**, which may take the form of a transfer of money or some other form of compensation from the defendant to the plaintiff. Since it may be difficult in incomplete contracts to fully verify damages, the court may provide the defendant with relief based of certain legal principles, such as expectation damages, reliance damages, and restitution damages.[3]

Expectation Damages

Breach remedies based on the legal principle of **expectation damages** attempt to compensate the plaintiff by ordering the defendant to pay damages equivalent to the amount that the plaintiff would have received had the contract been fulfilled. This is the situation depicted in Figure 14.3 where the transfer is $\alpha = iL$. If expectation damages are correctly specified, the borrower will not have an incentive to breach the contract.

Expectation damages will likely result in the same efficient outcome as when the contract is completely specified. This is because the borrower is indifferent between the *repay* and *default* payoffs. It is unlikely, however, that the courts will have sufficient information to correctly specify expectation damages. If this information had been available, the players would have written a complete contract. The court not only has to determine who was responsible for the breach, the precise value of the resulting payoffs, and what the payoffs would have been had the contract not been breached.

Reliance Damages

An alternative to expectation damages as a breach remedy is **reliance damages**, which is a court-ordered transfer designed to restore the plaintiff to a condition that would have prevailed in the absence of a contract. Reliance damages include any expenses that may have been incurred by the plaintiff who did not anticipate a breach of contract.

Determining the amount of reliance can be problematic since it involves the determining the value of the plaintiff's next best alternative activity had the contract not been signed. Moreover, reliance damages must be sensitive to the problem at hand. The amount of the transfer must be sufficiently large to encourage subgame perfection.

Restitution Damages

Another example of a breach remedy is **restitution damages**, which is designed to negate undue enrichment by the defendant resulting from the breach relative to what would have prevailed in the absence of a contract. In terms of Figure 14.1, the restitution damages imply a transfer in the lending game of $\alpha = rL$. As in the case of reliance damages, efficient restitution damages assumes that in the event of a breach the courts are able to accurately determine the plaintiff's expenditures, the value of the plaintiff's foregone opportunities, and the value of the defendant's undue enrichment.

CHAPTER EXERCISES

14.1 Explain the difference between a contractual relationship and a contracting environment.

14.2 Legally enforceable contracts are always necessary for a market transaction to take place. Do you agree with this statement? Explain.

14.3 Under what circumstances will a contract be self-enforced? When is it necessary to externally enforce a contract?

14.4 What is the role of the courts when enforcing a complete contract that is fully verifiable?

14.5 What problems are confronted by the courts when attempting to enforce a complete contract with limited verifiability?

14.6 When the parties to a contract are reasonably certain that the victim of a breach has legal recourse to recover damages, it is possible to structure a contract that gives players an incentive to adopt strategies that are mutually and socially beneficial. Why?

14.7 When it is difficult to fully verify damages, the court-imposed breach remedies may be based on legal principles. Name three such legal principles, and explain how they differ.

14.8 Consider the lending game depicted in Figure 14.1. Suppose that the payoff to the borrower in the event of default is $rL - R$, where R represents the present value of the borrower's reputation in credit markets. Loss of reputation increases the borrower's future financing costs. For what values of R will the loan contract be self-enforcing?

14.9 A lender has to decide whether to extend a $1,000 loan in exchange for a promise by the borrower to repay the loan and 10 percent simple interest in one year. The borrower plans to invest the proceeds of the loan with a certain 25 percent rate of return. The lender believes there is a 90 percent chance that the loan will be repaid. What is the subgame-perfect equilibrium for this lending game?

14.10 Consider the game depicted in following figure. Suppose that two companies (Firm 1 and Firm 2) form a joint venture to develop a new product. The parties write a contract that obligates both parties to fully invest in the project. When the contract is implemented, each company simultaneously, and independently, decides to fully invest (*FI*) or under-invest (*UI*).

   a. Is this game self-enforcing? Why?
   b. What is the normal form of this game if the court imposes breach remedies under the legal principle of expectation damages?
   c. Suppose that the companies write a complete contract with limited verifiability in which the court can only determine whether under-investment has occurred, but not which company has underinvested. Is there a contract that will result in an efficient outcome?

Firm 2

		FI	UI
	FI	(10, 12)	(4, 13)
Firm 1			
	UI	(11, 4)	(4, 4)

Payoffs: (Firm 1, Firm 2)

14.11 Consider the game depicted in the following figure. Two companies (Firm 1 and Firm 2) form a joint venture to develop a new product. The players write a contract that obligates both parties to fully invest in the project, which relies on the courts to impose a remedy in the event of a breach. At the outset of the game, each company simultaneously, and independently, decides to fully invest (*FI*) or under-invest (*UI*).

   a. What is the normal form of this game with court-imposed *expectation damages* that encourages the strategy profile {*FI*, *FI*}? Explain.
   b. What is the normal form of this game with court-imposed *reliance damages* that encourages the strategy profile {*FI*, *FI*}? Explain.
   c. What is the normal form of this game with court-imposed *restitution damages* that encourages the strategy profile {*FI*, *FI*}? Explain.
   d. Suppose that each player incurs court costs (c) in the event of litigation following a breach of contract. What is the normal form of this game if the court imposes expectation damages?
   e. What values for c will the plaintiff have an incentive to sue?

Firm 2

		FI	UI
	FI	(10, 10)	(2, 19)
Firm 1			
	UI	(8, 2)	(6, 6)

Payoffs: (Firm 1, Firm 2)

NOTES

1. Samuel Goldwyn (1882–1974), founder of Metro-Goldwyn-Mayer, is reported to have quipped: "A verbal agreement isn't worth the paper it's written on."

2. A mortgage is said to be "underwater" when the outstanding balance on the loan is greater than the value of the collateral.

3. See Steven Shavell (1980) for an analysis of the breach remedies examined in this section.

Chapter 15

Auctions

Bargaining involves two or more parties negotiating over the terms of a contract. In an **auction**, buyers and sellers compete in a public forum for the right to purchase or sell something of value. Auctions have been around for pretty much all of recorded history. The ancient Greek historian Herodotus described bride auctions in Babylonia two and a half millennia ago. Slave auctions were legal and commonplace in the United States for over 250 years until the mid-nineteenth century, and trafficking in human bondage still exists in almost every corner of the world.

Today, auctions in trade and commerce are ubiquitous. Auctions are used to sell U.S. Treasury securities, corporate equities in initial public offerings, tobacco, construction contracts, off-shore drilling licenses, airport landing rights, pollution emission rights, raw materials and spare parts, service and repair contracts, and a multitude of other goods and services. In this chapter, we will examine several types of auctions and discuss optimal bidding strategies for the most common types of auctions.[1]

AUCTIONS AND THE INTERNET

One of the most remarkable developments in recent years has been the dramatic growth in Internet auction sites. Online auctions have dramatically altered the way businesses acquire productive resources used to manufacture goods and services and the manner in final products are priced and marketed. The Internet lowers **transaction costs** by reducing the time and expense of locating input suppliers and product outlets. Farmers, for example, use online auctions to procure seed, feed, and fertilizer to lower cultivation, harvesting, and processing costs. Farmers have also been able to obtain higher prices by

selling into a global marketplace. Online consumer auctions, such as eBay and
Yahoo! Auctions, sell everything from fish sticks to plastic surgery. Priceline.
com allows travelers submit price bids, which can be accepted or rejected
by airlines and hotels. While online auction sites may not be appropriate for
every transaction, the Internet has transformed the global marketplace.

Perhaps the best known and most popular on-line auction site is eBay,
which has proven to be fertile ground for economists, game theorists, and
market researchers seeking to uncover underlying patterns in auction processes. The basic rules of an eBay auction are quite simple. A seller offers an
item for sale and prospective buyers submit on-line bids. The bidder submitting the highest bid when time expires wins the auction.

A feature of eBay auctions that has received a great deal scrutiny is the
effectiveness of "sniping" in which bidders wait until just before the close
of the auction to avoid being outbid. Although many eBay bidders swear by
the practice, the evidence suggests that snipers in situations involving standardized merchandise, such as consumer electronics, and a large number of
bidders, do not do outperform other bidders in terms of their success rate or
price paid. Sniping does, however, appear to be a successful when there are
few bidders and the value of specialized merchandise is difficult to determine.
Researchers have also focused on the effectiveness of "secret reserves" in
which sellers have the option of rejecting bids that are lower than an unde-
clared minimum price. The evidence suggests that secret reserves dissuade
fewer bidders from participating, which results in lower prices.

TYPES OF AUCTIONS

There are two basic types of auctions: standard and procurement auctions. In
a **standard auction**, multiple buyers compete in public for right to purchase
an object of value. In a **procurement (reverse) auction**, multiple sellers compete for the right to sell something of value to a buyer. The specific features of
an auction are defined by its rules and the characteristics of the participants.

Auction rules refer to the formal procedures that govern the bidding process, including who may bid, which bids are acceptable, the manner in which
bids are submitted, the information available to the players during the bidding
process, when the auction ends, how the winner is determined, and the price
paid. An **auction environment** refers to the characteristics of bidders, including attitudes towards risk, information structure, the private valuations of the
object being auctioned, and whether these private valuations are correlated
or uncorrelated.

Auctions may be open-bid or closed-bid. In an **open-bid auction**, anyone may participate. In a **closed-bid auction**, participation is by invitation.

Bidders may be licensed, required to pay a nonrefundable entry fee, or post a **performance bond** to ensure timely payment. An auction may also have a reserve price. In a standard auction, a **seller's reservation price** is the seller's minimum acceptable price. The seller's reservation price is frequently the opening price announced by an **auctioneer**. In the case of a secret reserve, an auction will be cancelled if the highest bid is less than the seller's reservation price. Reservation prices are used to prevent bidder collusion ("bidding rings") or when the number of bidders is small since this could result in a winning bid that is less than the value placed on the object by the seller.

An auction may be sealed-bid or oral. In a **sealed-bid auction**, secret bids are submitted and a winner subsequently declared. Sealed-bid auctions are typical of many government auctions, such as the sale of timber harvesting rights on public lands or off-shore oil drilling rights. There are two types of sealed-bid auctions. In a **sealed-bid, first-price auction**, the winner submits, and pays, the highest sealed bid. In a **sealed-bid, second-price auction**, the winner submits the highest bid, but pays the price submitted by the second-highest bidder. Seal-bid, second price auctions are called **Vickrey auctions** in honor of Nobel laureate William Vickrey, who showed that bidders have an incentive to submit bids that reflect their true valuations of the object being auctioned.

Bids in an **oral auction** are public. Oral auctions differ from sealed-bid auctions in that the bidders' identities are known at the moment they submitted, which may convey important information to rival bidders. Suppose, for example, that a wealthy collector bids on an oil painting. The amount of the bid may cause rival bidders modify their private valuations and bidding strategies resulting in a higher price. As a result, bidders often employ the services of surrogates, or may submit bids by telephone or secure Internet connection to conceal their identities. Even when the bidders' identities are unknown, intense bidding activity may also cause rivals to adopt more bidding strategies.

There are two main types of oral auctions. In a standard, **English (open-ascending-bid) auction**, the auctioneer opens the bidding with a low asking price. As prices are incrementally increased bidders who value the object least drop out. This process is repeated until there is only one bidder remains, who is declared the winner. In a standard, **Dutch (open descending-bid) auction**, the auctioneer begins by announcing a very high opening price, which is incrementally lowered.[2] The first bidder to accept the announced price is declared the winner. Since the winner in this auction is the bidder who values the object most, Dutch and sealed-bid, first-price auctions are strategically equivalent.

A variation of the Dutch auction is the **multiple-item Dutch auction** in which bidders submit offers for blocks of an identical item. The seller accepts the lowest price that will dispose of the entire amount being auctioned with each successful bidder paying the same price. Multiple-item Dutch auctions are frequently used to sell financial securities, such as U.S. Treasury bills, notes, bonds, and other debt instruments to institutional and individual investors. Multiple-item Dutch auctions have also been used to sell equity shares in initial public offerings.

INFORMATION STRUCTURES

Optimal bidding strategies depend on the auction rules and the information available to bidders, including the bidder's private valuation of the object being auctions, and whether a bidder's private valuation affects, and is affected by, the valuations of rival bidders.

The term **information structure** refers to the degree to which bidders' private valuations of the object being auctions are common knowledge. In a **complete-information auction** bidders' private valuations are common knowledge. We would expect, however, that auctions are characterized by **asymmetric information** in which the bidders know their own private valuations, but not the private value estimates of others. This is referred to as an **incomplete-information auction**.

INCOMPLETE-INFORMATION AUCTIONS WITH INDEPENDENT PRIVATE VALUES

In an incomplete-information auction, bidders' private valuations may be independent or correlated. Bidders are said to have **independent private values** if their valuation of the object being auctioned is determined by individual tastes and preferences. Independent private valuations are unaffected by the value placed on the object by rival bidders. On the other hand, **correlated value estimates** describes an auction environment in which bidders' private valuations affect, and are affected by, the private value estimates of other bidders. For example, suppose that a previously unknown drawing by Leonardo da Vinci is being sold at auction. Bidders initially disagree about the about drawing's authenticity. Value estimates are correlated if the bidders revise upwards their value estimates when an acknowledged da Vinci expert submits a high bid.

Sealed-Bid, First-Price Auction

Recall that in a complete-information, sealed-bid, first-price auction the winner is the bidder who values the object most, and submits a bid that is higher by the bidding increment than the private valuation of the next-highest bidder. When information is incomplete, however, each player has an incentive to submit a bid that is less somewhat than what he or she believes the object is worth. While a higher bid increases the likelihood of winning, it also lowers the expected payoff, and vice versa. So what is the bidder's optimal strategy when private valuations are not common knowledge? The answer depends on the number and distribution of the bidders' private valuations.

Although private valuations are not common knowledge, we will assume that private valuations are independent, random, and uniformly distributed, where L is the lowest possible private valuation and H is the highest possible valuation. It has been demonstrated (McAfee and McMillan, 1987) that this auction has a unique, pure-strategy **Nash equilibrium** in which the optimal strategy of a risk-neutral bidder is

$$b_i^*(V_i) = V_i - \frac{1}{n}(V_i - L), \tag{15.1}$$

where b_i^* is bidder i's the optimal bid, V_i is bidder i's private valuation of the object and n is the number of bidders.

Eq. (15.1) says that a risk-neutral bidder in an incomplete-information, sealed-bid, first-price auction should make an offer that is less than his or her private valuation. How much less depends on the number of bidders. As the number of bidders increases, optimal bids approach a bidder's private valuation. Moreover, as the distribution of private valuations becomes denser, the highest and next-highest valuations converge.

Optimal bidding strategy in an incomplete-information, sealed-bid, first-price auction with independent private values: A bidder should submit a bid that is less than his or her private valuation. This bid approaches the bidder's private valuation with an increase in the number of bidders.

As an illustration, suppose that Consider, for example, a sealed-bid, first-price auction which Zoe and Jacob compete for the right to purchase an antique pocket watch. Suppose that Zoe's reservation price is $562 and Jacob's reservation price is $442. That is, the maximum that Zoe and Jacob are willing to pay for the pocket watch is $562 and $442, respectively. The winner of this auction submits, and pays, the highest bid. Suppose further that private valuations are of the pocket watch are independent, random, and uniformly distributed between $L = \$200$ and $H = \$800$. This information may be arrived at in several ways, such by canvassing antique pocket watch experts, surveying Internet sites to identify high and low selling prices, and so on. Applying Eq. (15.1), Zoe's optimal bid is $b_Z^*(V_Z) = \$381$. Jacob's optimal bid is $b_J^*(V_J) = \$321$.

In this example, Zoe and Jacob submit bids that are strictly less than their private value estimates. Suppose that a third bidder, Luke, enters the auction. Luke's private valuation of the pocket watch is $V_L = \$386$. According to Eq. (15.1), the bidders' optimal bids are $b_Z^* = \$441.33$, $b_J^* = \$361.33$ and $b_L^* = \$321.00$. If there are 20 bidders, these optimal bids become $b_Z^* = \$543.90$, $b_J^* = \$429.90$ and $b_L^* = \$376.70$, and so on. As the number of bidders increases, the optimal bids approach the bidders' private valuations.

Sealed-Bid, Second-Price Auction

In a sealed-bid, second-price auction, the winner submits the highest bid, but pays the bid submitted by the next-highest bidder. In a complete-information auction environment, the bidder with the highest private valuation should submit any bid that is greater than the private valuation of the next-highest bidder. How does this bidding strategy change in an incomplete-information auction environment with independent private values? Since bidder with the highest private valuation is unknown, each bidder should offer his or her private valuation. There is no incentive for any bidder (including the unknown bidder with the highest valuation) to submit a higher bid.

> *Optimal bidding strategy in an incomplete-information, sealed-bid, second-price auction with independent private values: A bidder should submit a bid that is equal to his or her private valuation. All other bids are strictly dominated.*

It is easy to see why this is an optimal bidding strategy. Suppose that Zoe submits a bid that is greater than her valuation and Jacob submits a bid that is equal to his valuation. Zoe's wins the auction and pays Jacob's bid. In this case, Zoe earns a positive surplus. On the other hand, suppose that Zoe outbids Jacob, who submits a bid greater than his private value estimate. Zoe wins the auction and pays Jacobs bid, which may be greater than her private valuation, in which case she suffers a loss. Submitting a bid that is lower than a bidder's private valuation reduces the chance of winning without increasing the payoff. Submitting a higher bid increases the chance of winning, on the other hand, but could result in a negative payoff.

English Auction

What effect does the assumption of independent private valuations have on optimal bidding strategies in English auction? No effect at all. Recall that in an English auction, prices are announced in ascending order. Bidders should continue to bid until the announced price exceeds his or her **dropout price**. As bidders drop out, they reveal their approximate private value estimates. Because these estimates are independent, this does not provide information about the dropout prices of the remaining bidders, although the price paid by the winner converges to his or her private valuation. Thus, the optimal strategy in an incomplete-information English auction with independent private values is strategically equivalent to a sealed-bid, second price auction under the same condition.

Optimal bidding strategy in an incomplete-information English auction with independent private values: An incomplete-information English auction with independent private values is strategically equivalent to a complete-information, sealed-bid, second-price auction.

Dutch Auction

We saw that the optimal bidding strategy in a complete-information Dutch auction is strategically equivalent to a sealed-bid, first-price auction. The winner with the highest valuation accepts a price that is marginally higher than the valuation of the next-highest bidder. In an incomplete-information auction with independent private valuations, a bidder's optimal strategy is to accept a price that is less than his or her private valuation. If these private valuations are independent, random, and uniformly distributed, the optimal bidding strategy is given by Eq. (15.1).

Optimal bidding strategy in an incomplete-information Dutch auction with independent private values: An incomplete-information Dutch auction with independent private values is strategically equivalent to an incomplete-information, sealed-bid, first-price auction with independent private values.

In a multiple-item Dutch auction bidders submit sealed offers for blocks of an identical item. The seller accepts the highest price that will dispose of the entire offering, with all bidders paying that price. Multiple-item Dutch auctions are frequently used to sell financial securities, such as U.S. Treasury bills and equity shares in initial public offerings. The optimal bidding strategy in a multiple-item Dutch auction is strategically equivalent to a standard Dutch auction. To illustrate, suppose that XYZ company announces that it will accept block bids on 1 million shares using a multiple item Dutch auction. The highest bids and the number of shares desired are summarized in Table 15.1.

The lowest bidder for whom shares are available is investor E who makes an offer to purchase 100,000 shares at $25 per share. Every investor who offers more than $25 receives the number of shares requested, but pays the

Table 15.1   Multiple-Item Dutch Auction

Investor	Bid per share	Shares	Shares remaining
A	$10,000	1,000	999,000
B	$100	250,000	749,000
C	$50	150,000	599,000
D	$30	500,000	99,000
E	$25	100,000	−1,000
F	$24.99	50,000	0
⋮	⋮	⋮	⋮

bid submitted by investor E. Once these requests are satisfied, however, there are only 99,000 shares remaining, which will be allocated to investor E. While bidding high will guarantee that an offer will be accepted, bidding too low runs the risk of not receiving the desired number of shares, or not receiving any shares at all. This was the fate with investor F who bid just 1 cent below the bid submitted by investor E.

Even though everyone pays the lowest bid that disposes the entire offering, submitting a high price does not constitutes an optimal strategy. If it did, even the lowest bidder would submit a very high price, which could result in substantial losses for everyone once the shares are sold in the secondary market. This is one reason by sellers frequently specify a price range for acceptable bids. This price range should reflect the sentiments of the market. If the private valuations of a large number of bidders are independent, random, and uniformly distributed, the lowest bid should approximate the lower end of this price range.

Expected Revenues from Incomplete-Information Auctions with Independent Private Values

With incomplete-information auctions and independent private values, bidders do not learn anything about the private valuations of rival bidders. In each of the auctions examined, the winner has the highest private valuation. In the antique pocket watch example, Zoe pays $381 in a sealed-bid, first-price auction, $442 in a sealed-bid, second-price and English auctions, and $562 in a Dutch auction. As the number of bidders increase, the private valuation of the next-highest bidder approaches the private valuation of the highest bidder. In the limit, Zoe pays her private valuation of $562 in each of these auctions.

> *Revenue-equivalence for incomplete-information auctions with independent private values: The expected price paid in incomplete-information, first- and second-sealed-bid, second-price, English and Dutch auctions, with independent private values is the winners private value estimate.*

INCOMPLETE-INFORMATION AUCTIONS
WITH CORRELATED VALUE ESTIMATES

In an auction characterized by correlated value estimates, a bidder's private valuation affect, and is affected by, the private valuations of the other bidders. For example, Zoe may value the antique pocket watch more if she believes that Jacob values it highly. In other words, Zoe derives value from owning something that others want.

What kind of information would cause Zoe to raise or lower her private valuation? Zoe might acquire information from the bidding process itself. Zoe might interpret a rival's high bid as reflecting of superior information about the quality of the pocket watch. In an English auction, intense bidding activity may be as signal that the pocket watch is worth more Zoe initially believed. Alternatively, lackluster bidding activity might lead Zoe to downgrade her private value estimate.

How are bidding strategies affected when bids are correlated, or when bidders are uncertain about the true value of the object being auctioned? The answer depends upon the type of auction, and whether the bidders can act on new information. Information received once the auction ends has little or no value.

Common-Value Auctions and the Winner's Curse

A special case of correlated value estimates is a **common-value auction** in which bidders have different private estimates of the true, but unknown, value of the object being auctioned. Suppose, for example, that the U.S. Department of the Interior announces its intention to sell oil-drilling rights in Yosemite National Park using a sealed-bid, first-price auction. The problem is that the actual value of these oil reserves is unknown until the oil is extracted. This leads to a phenomenon called the **winner's curse**, which occurs when the bidder with the most optimistic private value estimate wins, but pays a price that is greater than the true value of the object.

To illustrate the winner's curse, suppose that twenty oil companies submit sealed, first-price bids for the right to on public land. Before bidding, each company conducts independent seismic and geological tests to assess the size and value of the oil reserve. Suppose that these private value estimates are independent, random, and uniformly distributed. In a sealed-bid, first-price auction, the company with the most optimistic estimate submits the highest bid and wins the oil-drilling rights. The problem is that the other nineteen companies believe that the oil is worth less than the winning bid. This means that the winner probably paid too much.

How might the oil companies mitigate the winner's curse? Suppose, for example, that a company's senior geologist estimates that the crude oil reserve is worth $100 million. The lowest possible value is $0 in the event of a "dry hole" (water instead of oil) and a maximum possible value of $150 million for "light sweet crude" (oil with low-sulfur content). Rather than submit a bid equal to this estimate, the company uses Eq. (15.1) to submit a bid of $100 − 0.05($100 − $0) = $95 million to mitigate the winners curse. The optimal bidding strategy in a common-value auction is to submit a bid that is less than its private value estimate.

> **Optimal bidding strategy in a common-value auction:** *A bidder should submit a bid that is less than his or her private value estimate.*

The winner's curse is most pronounced in sealed-bid, first-price auctions because it is not possible to learn anything about the other bidders' private valuations until after the bids have been submitted. By contrast, players may be able to infer something about their rivals' private value estimates during the course of a multistage auction. In an English auction, for example, the player's optimal strategy is to participate until the price exceeds the bidder's private value estimate, which may be raised or lowered based information gleaned during the bidding process.

Depending on the auction rules, the winner's curve may even prevent a transaction for occurring. Consider the following variation of the winner's curse discussed by Max Bazerman and William Samuelson (1983). Suppose that the owner of a company plans to make a take-it-or-leave-it offer for a privately-held company that produces a related product. Both the buyer and seller believe that the merger will increase the target company's value by 50 percent. The problem is asymmetric information. The value of the company is known only to the seller.

To make this example more concrete, suppose that the buyer believes that the company is worth between $20 and $100 million. The seller knows the value the company is worth $50 million. The **expected value** of the company to the buyer is 1.5[($20 + $100)/2] = $90 million. What is the buyer's best one-time offer?

The seller will accept any offer that is greater than or equal to $50 million. The seller, for example, will accept an offer of $90 million. At that price, however, the buyer reasons that the company is worth $90/1.5 = $60 million. At that price, however, the buyer's expected loss of $30 million. At a revised price of $60 million, the company is worth $60/1.5 = $40 million for an expected loss of $20 million. The only offer that the buyer can make to avoid the winner's curse is $20 million, which the seller will reject. The example underscores the importance of a properly structured auction that takes into consideration player incentives and bidders to act on revised strategies as new information becomes available.

INCOMPLETE-INFORMATION AUCTIONS
AND RISK AVERSION

We have thus far assumed that the bidders are risk neutral. In what way are bidding strategies affect affected if bidders are risk averse? It turns out that a bidder's attitude toward risk will affect some bidding strategies, but not others. In the case of an English auction, attitudes toward risk play no role. A bidder will continue to participate until the announced price exceeds his or her private value of the object. There is also no change in bidding strategies with a sealed-bid, second-price auction since a bidder will submit a bid that is equal to his or her private valuation.

By contrast, in a sealed-bid, first-price with independent private values, a risk-averse player will submit a bid that is lower than the bid submitted by a risk-neutral bidder according to Eq. (15.1). How much lower depends on the degree of risk aversion. While this lower bid increases the possibility of losing the auction, it also increases the expected payoff. What about auctions involving correlated value estimates? Recall that in these auctions the information revealed during an English auction reduces the winner's curse. Because of this, risk-averse bidders will submit bids that are somewhat higher than in a second-price auction.

CHAPTER EXERCISES

15.1   Is there any difference in optimal bidding strategies in auctions that involve independent private value estimates and correlated value estimates?

15.2   In a sealed-bid, first-price auction with independent private values, risk-neutral bidders will submit bids that are higher than their private values of the object. Do you agree? Explain.

15.3   In a sealed-bid, first-price auction with independent private values, as the number of risk-neutral bidders increases, each bid will be lowered, eventually converging to the next-highest bidder's valuation of the object being auctioned. Explain.

15.4   Why would a company going public using a multiple-item Dutch auction begin by specifying a price range for investor bids?

15.5   The U.S. Department of the Interior has announced its intention to use a sealed-bid, first-price auction to sell petroleum-drilling rights on public land in Alaska. Four oil companies have indicated their intention to participate in this auction. The problem is that the actual value of the oil reserves is unknown with certainty. Before submitting their bids, each oil company conducted independent seismic and geological tests to obtain an estimate of the quality and quantity of the petroleum reserves. The petroleum-deposit value estimates in millions of dollars of the four companies are $V_1 = \$250$, $V_2 = \$170$, $V_3 = \$320$ and $V_4 = \$265$. Although the companies do not know their rivals' estimates, they believe that these valuations are independent and randomly distributed between a low value of $L = \$100$ and a high possible price of $H = \$400$.

a. What is the optimal bid of each oil company?

b. Who will win the auction and what price will the winner pay for the drilling rights?

c. Do you believe that the winner of this auction paid too much for the drilling rights? Why?

15.6   Consider a sealed-bid, first-price auction in which the players have independent private values. The general consensus is that the true value of the object being sold is uniformly distributed between $1 and $10.

a. If the true value of a risk-neutral player is $2, what is this player's optimal bidding strategy if there are only two bidders?

b. If this is a Dutch auction, what is the player's optimal bidding strategy if there are three bidders?

c. If this is a sealed-bid, second-price auction, what is a player's optimal bidding strategy?

15.7   Consider an independent private value auction with twenty risk-neutral players. The players' valuations are generally believed to be uniformly distributed between $0 and $50,000. Suppose that the true private value of one player is $40,000. For each of the following auction formats, what is the player's optimal bidding strategy?

a. Sealed-bid, first-price

b. Sealed-bid, second-price

c. English

d. Dutch

NOTES

1. Public interest in the analysis and design of auctions was intensified in 1994 when the U.S. Federal Communications Commission (FCC) auctioned ten nationwide licenses for "narrow-band" frequencies used by cellular phones, pagers, and other personal communication service (PCS) devices (McMillan, 1994). After consulting game theorists and auction experts, the FCC devised a multiple-round auction in which four telecommunications companies paid $3.5 million for the right to submit bids for up to three of ten licenses. The auction raised more than $600 million, which

was 10 times greater than the most optimistic prediction. The FCC has since used similar auctions to allocate regional broadband licenses for more advanced PCS devices, which sold for more than $8 billion.

2. Dutch auctions, which date back to the nineteenth century, were named after the system of selling tulip bulbs in Holland.

3. One of the most well celebrated initial public offering (IPO) using multiple-item Dutch auction occurred on August 19, 2004 when Google, the Internet search engine company, sold 111.6 million shares at $85 per share, which raised $1.67 billion. Google's decision to go public using a multiple-item Dutch auction was meant to bypass traditional IPOs in which an investment bank estimates the market value of a company, determines investor interest at a recommended share price, and organizes underwriters. Classic IPOs tend to short-change company owners and make big winners of investment bankers and privileged underwriters who get rich by flipping shares on the first day of public trading.

Chapter 16

Networks

Our analysis of decision making in interactive settings involving move and countermove assumed that managers exhibit purely **rational behavior**. By this we mean that a player's strategy choices are based on self-interested outcomes that are in his or her own self interest. Even the most ardent proponents of pure rationality have come to recognize that in some situations a player's strategy choices are guided less by reason than by instinct, which is the by-product of repeated responses to specific external stimuli over extended periods of time.

EVOLUTIONARY GAME THEORY

Beginning with Charles Darwin (1859), theories of evolution have provided insights into the physical and mental development of all living creatures. John Maynard Smith's (1982) pioneering work in **evolutionary game theory** explained animal behavior in terms of instinctual strategies that are genetically passed along from generation to generation. New survival strategies arise from mutations. If unsuccessful, survival rates decline and the mutation is not passed along to future generations. If successful, they will come to define a species' behavior.

Reproductive Success

The population-dynamic aspect of evolutionary game theory is significant because it does not depend on a player's purely rational choices, but on the much weaker assumption of **reproductive success** in which successful strategies replace unsuccessful strategies over time. The idea of reproductive success can be traced to the application of **game theory** to problems in

381

evolutionary biology (see John Maynard Smith, 1982; Josef Hofbauer and Karl Sigmund, 1998).

Animals in the wild are frequently involved in situations involving strategy choices. Stephen and Melinda Pruett-Jones (1994), for example, applied the principles of game theory to analyze the nesting behavior of bowerbirds. Male bowerbirds construct elaborate nests, or bowers, to attract female bowerbirds. Once built, the male bowerbird leaves his nest to destroy neighboring bowers. While marauding, however, his nest is destroyed. The time devoted to destroying and repairing bowers would be better spent foraging and mating. So, what explains this strange behavior?

In evolutionary game theory, animal behavior is "programmed" into its DNA. Genes that comprise strands of DNA "compete" in the sense that they are passed along to future generations in varying proportions. Animals that are successful in the battle for survival tend to have more offspring. As a result, the proportion of animals with genes encoded with a genetically superior survival strategy will come to dominate the population. An evolutionarily stable strategy is one in which the population is resistant to genes encoded with a mutant strategy.

Evolutionary Equilibrium

The Pruett-Joneses (1994) explain the behavior of male bowerbirds by assuming two strategies: *Maraud* and *guard*. A male that marauds spends all his time destroying the nests of rivals. A male that guards spends all his time protecting his nest. The reproductive success of a male bowerbird depends not only on his strategy, but on the strategy adopted by rival bowerbirds. The Pruett-Joneses found that *maraud* strictly dominates *guard*, even though it is in the best interest of male bowerbirds to guard their nests. Since it is not possible for birds to form a coalition (with the possible exception of Alfred Hitchcock film classic *The Birds*), this behavior is passed along to future generations until marauding bowerbirds dominate the population. Marauding by bowerbirds constitutes an **evolutionary equilibrium**.

NETWORKS

The ideas underlying the notion of an evolutionary equilibrium have economic and business applications. In business, the word **network** refers to any system of integrated interconnections sharing a common technical platform. The telecommunications industry, for example, provides voice and data services using the Internet and the World Wide Web. Airlines, railroads, and shipping companies transport people and products using a hub-and-spoke network.

The transportation sector provides a platform for networks of delivery services, such as the U.S. Postal Service and FedEx. Financial sector networks include on-site securities exchanges, such as the New York Stock Exchange, electronic over-the-counter markets, such as NASDAQ, B2B (business-to-business) and B2C (business-to-consumer) exchanges, credit and debit card networks, and automated banking networks, such as automated teller machines (ATMs).

Many of the features of traditional networks can also apply to a **virtual network**, which is a linked computer network involving servers, terminals, software applications, and so on. Examples of virtual networks include eBay, the Internet auction site, Facebook, the social networking Internet site, and Twitter, the on-line blackboard messaging site.

Firms and households that are part of, utilize, or are organized around a network may enjoy lower cost or receive greater benefits than using different or segregated technologies. Businesses that pool resources, manpower, supplies, and facilities to avoid redundancies, for example, may be able to reduce or eliminate fixed costs, exploit economies of scale and avoid **diseconomies of scale**. In a **unidirectional (one-way) network**, for example, data (goods, services and information) flow in one direction. Examples include public utilities that provide electricity, gas, or water to businesses and households. These networks generate significant scale economies and helps explain why companies such as Con Edison have an exclusive **government franchise** in specific geographic regions.

In a **reciprocal (two-way) network**, data flows in two directions. Consider, for example, the hub-and-spoke network depicted in Figure 16.1. In the telecommunications industry, for example, users A and B are connected by a switching station at the center (hub) of the network.

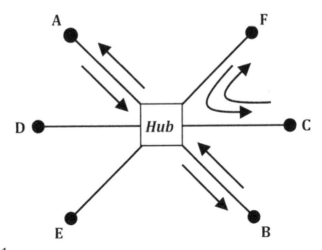

Figure 16.1

Another example of a hub-and spoke network is the airline industry links hundreds of cities to provide cost-effective long-distance transportation. Consider a trip from New York City's LaGuardia Airport to Tucson International Airport aboard Delta Airlines. A passenger must first fly along the spoke from New York to Delta's hub in Atlanta, and then along the spoke from Atlanta to Tucson. Other familiar examples of hub-and-spoke networks include parcel and mail delivery by the U.S. Postal service, parcel delivery by UPS, DHL, and FedEx, physical check clearing and electronic funds transfer operations performed by the Federal Reserve System.

Positive Feedback Effects

An interesting economic application of reproductive success involves two-way networks, which exhibit **positive feedback effects**, also known as **positive network externalities**. An email or telephone network with only one user is worthless, but becomes exponentially more valuable as the number of users increases. Consider, for example, *Facebook*—the social networking platform that allows its members to create an online nexus of interpersonal relationships. Members of social networks are linked by shared interests, experiences, and backgrounds. *Facebook* makes it possible for different social networks to expand and subsume each other, much like the growth of separate colonies of bacteria in a Petri dish. In a similar fashion, the benefits to individual members of a social network increases exponentially with its viral-like growth. In the limit, the resulting evolutionary equilibrium is a single, all-inclusive social network that dominates the population.

A numerical example illustrates how positive network externalities can lead to an evolutionary equilibrium. Suppose that the value of membership in a network is proportional to the number of members according to the expression $n(n-1) = n^2 - n$. If the value of an individual member of a network is 1, the value of the network is $1^2 - 1 = 0$. The value of the network with two members is $2^2 - 2 = 2$. The value of the network when $n = 10$ is $10^2 - 10 = 90$. If membership increases tenfold to 100 members, the value of the network explodes to $100^2 - 100 = 9,900$, or a 110-fold increase! The greater-than-proportional increase in a network's value lures new members until a single dominant network emerges.

Does an evolutionary equilibrium only exist when all players belong to the same network? Not necessarily. For one thing, different networks must be near-perfect substitutes for each other. Moreover, it must not be possible for members of one network to interface with members of another network. At one time, positive feedback effects existed for e-mail networks because members of different networks could not communicate with each other. This ended when software was developed that made communication across different e-mail networks possible. As a result, an evolutionary equilibrium was replaced with multiple network equilibria.

Another example of multiple network equilibria is the competition between broadband technologies. At present, there are two main broadband technologies in use by American households and businesses. Digital subscriber lines (DSL) utilize a copper wire infrastructure that was originally developed to provide home and office telephone service. A coaxial cable infrastructure was originally created to provide pay television service.

DSL and cable provide similar Internet services, including teleconferencing, interactive entertainment, and distance learning. Will competition eventually lead to a dominant Internet technology, or will multiple equilibria emerge consisting of several, or totally different, broadband technologies?

For a single technology to dominate the market, certain conditions must be satisfied, such as economies of scale, positive feedback effects, or a strong consumer preference for a particular technology. While economies of scale appear to exist in satellite and cable broadband distribution, it does not appear that either broadband technology has a distinct competitive advantage. Moreover, consumers do not appear to have a strong consumer preference for a particular broadband technology. Finally, significant positive feedback effects do not exist with any of these broadband technologies.

Although neither DSL nor cable has a distinct competitive advantage at present, the demand for broadband services is sensitive to advances in information technology. While an evolutionary equilibrium in broadband technology does not currently exist, there is no guarantee that this situation will prevail into the future.

Network Game

Positive feedback effects make it difficult for challengers to undermine the competitive advantage of first movers, even when the new network has a superior technology, especially when the incumbent network has a large number of users. This can be illustrated using the two-way network depicted in Figure 16.2 involving users A and B and a single network provider, H_1. Suppose that the value of this two-way network is $n(n-1) = 2^2 - 2 = 2$.

Suppose that a second network provider enters with a technology that is twice as efficient enters the market. The value of network H_2 to A and B is $2n(n-1) = 4$. The two networks are exclusive in the sense that they do not

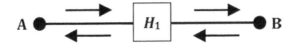

Figure 16.2

communicate with each other. A and B must use either H_1 or H_2. This new situation is depicted in Figure 16.3.

The reason why it is difficult for the new network to enter the market is depicted in Figure 16.4. This one-time, static game has two **Nash equilibrium** strategy profiles: $\{H_1, H_1\}$ and $\{H_2, H_2\}$. The network users are initially at $\{H_1, H_1\}$, each receiving value of 2. Although H_2 is superior, neither user has an incentive to switch.

Does the situation depicted in Figure 16.4 suggest that a first-mover network, such as *Facebook*, will enjoy its **monopoly** status in perpetuity? Although it is difficult to dislodge an incumbent network, evolutionary game theory suggests that the status-quo will continue until a more successful mutation is introduced into the population. The emergence of *Facebook* usurped instant messaging. What new network technology will replace *Facebook*?

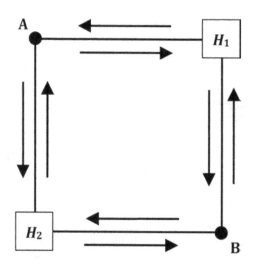

Figure 16.3

	B	
	H_1	H_2
A H_1	(2, 2)	(0, 0)
H_2	(0, 0)	(4, 4)

Payoffs: (A, B)

Figure 16.4

Implications

Positive feedback effects have several interesting implications for **market structure** and pricing, including a reversal of the law of demand, economies of scale, winner-take-all effects, and increased industrial concentration (Nicholas Economides, 2006; Stan Liebowitz, 2006). Positive feedback effects may result in a reversal of the **law of demand**, which states that the quantity demanded of a good or service is inversely related to its price. In the presence of positive network externalities the reverse may be true. Network users may actually be willing to pay more for an additional unit of service given the exponentially increasing value of a larger network. At some price a network demand curve may begin to slope upward.

Economies of scale exist when per-unit costs decline with an increase in the firm's scale of operations. This phenomenon is typically associated with manufacturing industries that produce goods requiring substantial physical capital outlays. An example of this is an automobile company that incurs substantial start-up costs to design a new model, and to create dies and build assembly facilities for its production.

Research intensive high-technology industries that form the backbone of the Internet also exhibit significant economies of scale. While the research and development cost of developing computer software can be substantial, the marginal cost of duplicating, servicing, handling, and delivering the product to consumers is relatively insignificant. The impact of economies of scale on the growth of networks is similar, and may be more important, than positive feedback effects.

Positive network externalities and economies of scale combine to give large, incumbent firms a significant competitive advantage over smaller firms and startup companies attempting to penetrate the market. Larger networks have greater positive feedback effects than do smaller networks. Other things being equal, consumers will be willing to pay more to become members of the larger network, which will enhance the large company's profits and competitive edge. This advantage is reinforced by economies of scale that enable large firms to produce at lower per-unit cost.

The combined effects of positive network externalities and economies of scale can result in a **winner-take-all** outcome in which a single firm dominates the market, as would seem to be the case with, for example, *Facebook*. The winner-take-all effect can give a pioneering company a significant and insurmountable **first-mover advantage**. This is especially pronounced in industries where competing firms provide nearly identical goods and services. This outcome is less certain when competing firms that produce differentiate products segment the market, such as the competition between DSL and cable in the market for broadband technology.

Easy entry by new firms leads to increased competition, lower prices, and a tendency to zero **economic profit** in the long run. This does not appear to be the case with network industries. Even when there are low barriers to entry, significant network feedback effects and economies of scale tend to lead to increased **industrial concentration**. In general, firms in highly concentrated industries have **market power**, which the ability to charge prices that are greater than marginal cost to earn above-normal returns in the long run. This presents a challenge to government anti-trust regulators whose mandate is to protect consumers by promoting competition. Because the winner-take-all effect is characteristic of network industries, superimposing a competitive market structure may be futile at best; counterproductive at worst.

RESTRAINT OF TRADE IN NETWORK INDUSTRIES

There are several features of network industries that give rise are conducive to restraint of trade issues that have been, or may be, the subject antitrust legislation. These features involve, among other things, network bottlenecks, technical standards, and B2B exchanges.

Bottlenecks

A problem that frequently arises in many in network industries is when a segment of the network that is critical to the efficient flow of data is under the exclusive control of a single company. This situation is referred to as a **bottleneck**. An example of a *one-sided bottleneck* is depicted in Figure 16.5. In this case, the link between users A and B is controlled by company H_1. An example of this is when several railroads from points A and B converge to a single track to complete the route, or when several highways converge to a single toll bridge. A frequently cited example of a one-sided network

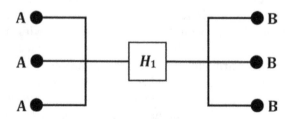

Figure 16.5

bottleneck occurs when local telephone subscribers must use a single switch to complete long-distance calls. Since the company that controls the switch is a monopoly, the result is high prices to send and receive calls. This is what occurred after the breakup of AT&T in 1984 when Regional Bell Operating Companies, also known as "Baby Bells," controlled these local switches.

The anticompetitive implications of the situation depicted in Figure 16.5 are obvious. After the breakup of AT&T, U.S. government dealt with the problem of local switch monopolies by enacting the Telecommunications Act (1996), which attempted to resolve the problem of monopolies at key points of a telecommunications network. This revision of the Clayton Act (1934) mandated the interconnection of all public switched communications. This Act also imposed several rules to prevent anticompetitive business practices, including the mandatory resale of services and prohibiting **price discrimination**. In spite of this, several issues dealing with technical standards were left unresolved.

In the *two-sided bottleneck*, such as the one depicted in Figure 16.6, firm H_1 monopolizes one of two bottlenecks between users A and B, while firm H_2 monopolizes the other link. Each firm must go through the bottleneck controlled by the other firm to deliver its service. An example of this is when two telephone companies with different subscribers require each other's network to complete a call. In this case, firms H_1 and H_2 must pay an *access termination* fee to each other. If each firm sells services to users A and B, then each must pay both access termination and *access origination* fees.

As in the case of one-way bottlenecks, the control of bottlenecks has resulted in high prices. Governments have dealt with this problem by regulating access origination and termination fees, although prices have remained high. The Telecommunication Act imposes cost-based reciprocal fees, which effectively eliminates these charges for equivalently-sized networks. The possibility still exists, however, that a large network will attempt to impose high termination fees on a small network, in which case the small network will only be able to provide within network service. As a result, small networks

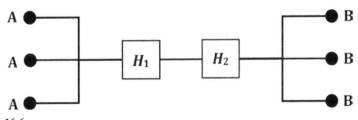

Figure 16.6

might cease to exist since large networks are able to provide its users with greater value. The increase in market share by large networks can result in an increase in market power and higher prices.

Technical Standards

Suppose that firm H_1 dominates a network industry and insists firm H_2, which produces a complementary product, not make these products available to rivals of H_1. An example of this occurred in the mid-1980s when the then dominant virtual game system manufacturer, Nintendo, refused to do business with third-party software producers unless they agree not to write similar games for other platforms, such as Atari and Sega. Although the purpose of this strategy was to increase Nintendo's market value, it had a stifling effect on new product development by reducing revenues of third-party software manufactures. Nintendo eventually abandoned this practice in response to legal challenges claiming restraint of trade.

Technical restrictions by the dominant network platform can significantly lower earnings of third-party producers that are required to meet precise technical standards. In the extreme, these third-party manufacturers might even be forced out of business because they cannot cover substantial development costs, which is typical of high-technology industries.

Another avenue for manipulating technical standards in network industries to reduce competition involves complementary products. Suppose that the product of firm H_1 is complementary, but incompatible, with the product of H_2, but compatible with the product of H_3. Alternatively, suppose the upstream division of H_1 produces the same good that is produced by H_2. By making its product incompatible with H_2, H_1 has increased its market power, resulting in higher prices and reduced product innovation. The solution, of course, would be for the government to standardize upstream components, although this is typically beyond the ken of antitrust authorities.

B2B Exchanges

Many business to business (B2B) exchanges are organized and operated by firms that trade on those very same exchanges. One of the most infamous examples of this was the energy exchange organized and run by Enron. This creates an opportunity for the organizer of the exchange to benefit from information generated from these transactions. Such an arrangement is strictly prohibited in financial and commodity exchanges, but is permitted in B2B exchanges. While B2B exchanges have the potential to consolidate trades, increase market liquidity, promote standardization, and reduce **transaction costs**, they also raise serious antitrust questions.

CHAPTER EXERCISES

16.1 QWERTY keyboards were invented in 1878 to minimize typewriter keys from jamming. This arrangement of letters has long been recognized as inefficient and confusing. Although jamming is no longer an issue with modern computer keyboards, QWERTY continues to dominate the market.
   a. Would you consider QWERTY a network?
   b. Why has QWERTY been resistant to a more efficient arrangement of letters on a keyboard?

16.2 Linux is generally considered to be superior to Microsoft's Windows and Apple's Macintosh operating systems.
   a. Do Windows and Macintosh constitute networks?
   b. Does this explain why Linux has been unable to establish a significant foothold in the computer software market?

16.3 The Internet auction site eBay is an example a hub-and-spoke network that connects multiple buyers and sellers. Explain how first-mover and positive feedback effects enabled eBay to dominate the on-line auction market.

16.4 How would you describe local cable television networks? What effect has this kind of network had on prices paid by cable television subscribers?

16.5 *Twitter* is a real-time, on-line communication service that allows users to simultaneously share information with every other user. Is *Twitter* a network, a bulletin board, or both? Diagram and explain.

16.6 Discuss the difference between a one-way and a two-way bottleneck.

16.7 What are the potential antitrust issues associated with bottlenecks in network industries?

16.8 The Pruett-Joneses have argued that marauding is an evolutionary stable strategy among bowerbirds. Suppose initially that the population is evenly divided between *guarding* and *marauding* bowerbirds. There are four strategy profiles: {*Guard, Guard*}, {*Guard, Maraud*}, {*Maraud, Guard*}, and {*Maraud, Maraud*}. The respective payoffs for are (2, 2), (3, 0), (0, 3), and (1, 1). What is the evolutionary equilibrium for this game?

16.9 Suppose that a two-way network initially involves two groups of users (A and B) and a single provider (H_1). Suppose that H_2 and H_3 enter the market with superior network technologies. This one-time, static game is depicted in the following figure.
   a. What is the Nash equilibrium in this one-time game?

b. If this game is infinitely repeated, is there any interest rate for which existing users will defect to a superior technology?

c. If this game is infinitely repeated, is there any amount that H_2 and H_3 can pay users of H_1 to switch technologies?

B

		H_1	H_2	H_3
	H_1	(2, 2)	(0, 0)	(0, 0)
A	H_2	(0, 0)	(4, 4)	(0, 0)
	H_3	(0, 0)	(0, 0)	(8, 8)

Payoffs: (A, B)

Appendix

Regression Analysis

Throughout this text we assume that managers know the precise functional relationships that form the basis of a firm's strategic decisions. In our discussion of demand, for example, it is not enough for a manager to know the theoretical relationship between a change in the firm's price or advertising expenditures and its unit sales. What are needed are quantitative estimates of these relationships to formulate optimal pricing, advertising, and other business strategies. The purpose of this appendix is to introduce the student to the basics of **ordinary least-squares (OLS) regression analysis**, which is a standard statistical technique for estimating the intercept and slope coefficients of functional relationships that are linear in parameters on the basis of historical data. Despite their many limitations and shortcomings, many spreadsheet programs, such as Microsoft Excel, make the process of estimating regression equations a relatively straightforward process.

There are generally six steps involved in regression analysis. Step 1 involves formulating a preliminary hypothesis about the nature of the relationship between the dependent variable and one or more independent (explanatory) variables. An example of this is the hypothesized demand relationship in Eq. (1.1). Step 2 entails collecting reliable historical data of the variables in our hypothesized relationship. Step 3 involves specifying the nature of the functional relationship. An example of this is the linear relationship in Eq. 2.1. In Step 4 we use OLS or some other statistical methodology to derive numerical estimates of the parameters in our hypothesized relationship, such as the values of $\beta_0, \beta_x, \beta_M$, and β_y in Eq. 2.1. Step 5 is the diagnostics phase, which involves assessing the statistical significance of the individual parameter estimates and the equation as a whole. Step 6 involves evaluation of the regression results for completeness and robustness. If one or more of the estimated parameters are statistically insignificant, or if the estimated

equation is misspecified, this step involves respecify the hypothesized relationship and repeating Steps 1–6. The remainder of this appendix will focus
on estimation, diagnostics, and evaluation.

ESTIMATION

Regression analysis is one of several statistical techniques that constitute a
branch of economics known as **econometrics**, which is the statistical analysis
of economic and business relationships. The results of this analysis may
be used by managers to make optimal business decisions. To understand
the basic ideas underlying regression analysis, consider the scatter diagram
depicted in Figure A.1, which summarizes the observed relationships between
values of the dependent variable Y and the independent (explanatory) variables X. For example, the values of Y might represent a firm's unit sales of a
good or service and its market price X. The scatter of data points suggests that
higher values of Y tend to be associated with lower values of X, and vice versa.

A cursory examination of Figure A.1 suggests that the relationship between
Y and X is not precise. The objective of regression analysis is to estimate an
equation that does the best possible job at approximating the underlying relationship between the values of Y and X. Since this relationship is not precise,
we should expect to find that the predicted value of the dependent variable $\hat{Y}_i$
will deviate by somewhat from its actual value. Thus, the mathematically true
relationship may be written

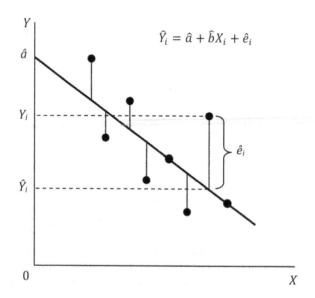

$$\hat{Y}_i = \hat{a} + \hat{b}X_i + \hat{e}_i$$

Figure A.1

$$Y_i = \hat{a} + \hat{b}X_i + \hat{e}_i, \tag{A.1}$$

where Y_i and X_i are observed values of the respective dependent and explanatory variables, $\hat{a}$ is the estimated value of "y-intercept", $\hat{b}$ is the estimated value of the slope coefficient, and $\hat{e}_i$ is an error term. The error term in Eq. (A.1) is the difference between the actual and predicted value of the dependent variable. Since $Y_i - \hat{Y}_i = \hat{e}_i$, Eq. (A.1) may be rewritten as

$$\hat{Y}_i = \hat{a} + \hat{b}X_i. \tag{A.2}$$

Eq. (A.2) may be used to predict values of Y_i on the basis of observed values of X_i. The estimated values $\hat{a}$ and $\hat{b}$ generate the regression line in Figure A.1, which is the best fit of the historical data. Mathematically, this was accomplished by minimizing the sum of the squared errors terms $\hat{e}_i$.

Spreadsheet software packages, such as Microsoft Excel, make the process of estimating the values of a and b in Eq. (A.2) relatively simple and straightforward. As an illustration, suppose that we have conducted a random survey of students from 25 colleges during a given month. The results of this survey were compiled in a Microsoft Excel spreadsheet, which is reproduced in Table A.1.

The data collected in our survey include the average monthly consumption of hamburgers (Q_x), the price of a hamburger (P_x), average annual college tuition (T), and the average price of a soft drink (P_y). The particular explanatory variables where chosen on the basis of intuition and economic theory. By the law of demand, we would expect a negative relationship between the price and quantity demanded of hamburgers. Since hamburgers and soft drinks are complements, we would also expect an inverse relationship. Finally, we would expect that an increase in college tuition will affect the demand for hamburgers by wealth and income constrained students. The nature of this relationship is uncertain since it depends on whether college students consider hamburgers a normal or inferior good.

We begin by estimating a simple bivariate relationship between the quantity demanded of hamburgers and the price of hamburgers. The regression toolbar in Microsoft Excel generates the regression results summarized in rows 28–43 in Table A.2. Cell 42-B tells us that the estimated value of the intercept is $\hat{a} = 28.259$. According to cell 43-B, the estimated slope coefficient is $\hat{b} = -8.268$. Thus, the estimated regression equation that best fits the data is

$$\hat{Q}_x = 28.259 - 8.268 P_x. \tag{A.3}$$

Eq. (A.3) appears to confirm our belief that an increase in the price of hamburgers results in a decrease in the quantity demanded of hamburgers. More specifically, Eq. (A.3) tells us that a $1 increase in the price leads to

Table A.1   Survey Data

	A	B	C	D	E
	College	Q_x	P_X	T	P_Y
1	1	10	2.00	24	1.50
2	2	12	2.00	26	1.45
3	3	13	1.90	18	1.50
4	4	14	1.95	17	1.40
5	5	9	2.10	21	1.50
6	6	8	2.25	15	1.50
7	7	4	2.25	22	1.75
8	8	3	2.50	20	2.00
9	9	15	1.80	28	1.50
10	10	12	1.80	22	1.40
11	11	13	1.90	16	1.30
12	12	14	2.00	15	1.25
13	13	12	2.00	22	1.50
14	14	10	2.10	20	1.75
15	15	10	2.25	24	1.80
16	16	12	2.10	25	1.30
17	17	11	2.50	26	1.40
18	18	12	2.00	22	1.45
19	19	10	2.50	22	1.50
20	20	8	2.50	20	1.40
21	21	9	2.50	23	1.45
22	22	10	2.25	25	1.50
23	23	11	2.25	26	1.45
24	24	12	2.00	27	1.50
25	25	13	1.75	20	1.50

Table A.2   Bivariate Regression Results

	A	B	C	D	E	F	G
28	Regression Statistics						
29	Multiple R	0.693					
30	R Square	0.480					
31	Adj. R Sq.	0.458					
32	Std. Error	2.091					
33	Obs.	25					
34							
35	Analysis of Variance						
36		df	SS	MS	F-Stat	Sig. F	
37	Regression	1	92.913	92.913	21.258	0.0001	
38	Residual	23	100.527	4.371			
39	Total	24	193.440				
40							
41		Coeff	se	t-Stat	p-value	L-95%	U-95%
42	Intercept	28.259	3.836	7.368	1.71E-07	20.325	36.193
43	Price (P_X)	−8.268	1.793	−4.611	0.0001	−11.978	−4.559

an 8.27 decline in the average monthly quantity demanded of hamburgers. Caution, however, is advised. Given a sufficient number of observations, OLS will generate parameter estimates. The question is whether a statistically significant linear relationship does, in fact, exist between the price and the quantity demanded of hamburgers? To help answer this question we need to move on to diagnostics phase.

DIAGNOSTICS

Table A.2 also provides information that can be uses to evaluate the statistical significance and explanatory power of Eq. (A.3). In particular, we want to assess the statistical significance of our estimated parameters and how much of our linear regression equation explains the quantity demanded of hamburgers.

Recall that the data presented in Table A.1 was drawn from a random survey of college students. A different pool of survey respondents would have generated different parameter estimates. To make matters worse, survey data can be unreliable and subject to measurement errors. How reliable, therefore, is our estimated equation? Does our estimated equation confirm the hypothesized inverse relationship between the price and quantity demanded of hamburgers? To answer these questions we need to examine several of the other statistics generated by the regression procedure.

Standard Error

The **standard error** (*se*) is the **standard deviation** of an estimated coefficient. When the value of this statistic is "small," we can be reasonably confident that the estimated coefficient does not differ significantly from its true value. The standard errors for the intercept ($se_{\hat{a}}$ = 3.836) and slope ($se_{\hat{b}}$ = 1.793) can be found in cells C-42 and C-43 of Table A.2, respectively.

Confidence Intervals

If the errors terms have a zero mean and are independent, identical, and normally distributed, the standard errors can be used to **confidence intervals** to test hypotheses about the estimated parameters true value. The greater is this interval, the more difficult it will be to reject hypotheses about a parameter's true value, although this increases the possibility of accepting a false hypothesis. Alternatively, we can reduce the possibility of accepting a false hypothesis by narrowing this confidence interval, but this increases the possibility of rejecting a true hypothesis. A standard rule of thumb in regression analysis is to test hypotheses about the true value of the parameter estimate by constructing a 95 percent confidence interval. These confidence intervals for the estimated parameters in Eq. (A.2) are

$$\hat{a} \pm 2se_{\hat{a}}; \tag{A.4}$$

$$\hat{b} \pm 2se_{\hat{b}}. \tag{A.5}$$

Using the standard error from cell C-43 of Table A.2, the confidence interval for the slope coefficient in Eq. (A.3) is

$$-8.268 \pm 2(1.793). \tag{A.6}$$

This confidence interval tells us that we can be 95 percent confident that the true value of b lies somewhere between -4.682 and -11.854. Fortunately, it is not necessary to perform these calculations. Precise estimates of the lower (L-95%) and upper (U-95%) bounds are presented in Table A.2. The confidence interval for $\hat{a} = 28.259$ are located in cells F-42 and G-42. The precise confidence interval for $\hat{b} = -8.268$ can be found in cells F-43 and G-43.

To illustrate the usefulness of confidence intervals, suppose that we want to test the hypothesis that the true value of coefficient b is -10. Since this value lies within the confidence interval, we cannot reject this hypothesis at the 95 percent confidence level. Suppose, on the other hand, that we are merely interested in determining whether the price of hamburgers is statistically significant in explaining hamburger purchases. This is equivalent to testing the hypothesis that true value of the slope coefficient is $b = 0$. Since this value does not lie within our confidence interval, we would have to reject the hypothesis that price is not statistically significant in explaining hamburger purchases. The confidence interval supports our belief that price is a statistically significant explanatory variable.

t-Statistic

An alternative to confidence intervals for testing the statistical significance of the estimated parameters is to use *t*-statistics, which are routinely reported in the regression output. The **t-statistic** is calculated as the ratio of the parameter estimate to its standard error. Thus, the *t*-statistics for $\hat{a}$ and $\hat{b}$ are

$$t_{\hat{a}} = \frac{\hat{a}}{se_{\hat{a}}}; \tag{A.7}$$

$$t_{\hat{b}} = \frac{\hat{b}}{se_{\hat{b}}}. \tag{A.8}$$

Since the standard error is always positive, the sign of the t-statistic is always the same as the sign of the estimated parameter. Since "small" standard errors are preferred, we would like to see "large" t-statistics.

It was noted earlier that confidence intervals may be used for testing any hypothesis about the true value of the estimated parameter. This includes testing the hypothesis that a relationship does not exist between the dependent and explanatory variable. This is equivalent to testing the hypothesis that the true value of the estimated parameter is zero. The t-statistic is particularly well suited to this task.

A useful rule of thumb is to reject the hypothesis that a relationship does not exist at 95 percent confidence level whenever the absolute value of the t-statistic is greater than or equal to 2. Consider the t-statistic for the estimated value of b, which can be found in cell D-43 of Table A.2. Since $|-4.611| > 2$, we can be at least 95 percent confident that the price of hamburgers is statistically significant in explaining the quantity demanded of hamburgers.

p-Value

A more precise measure of the degree of statistical significance of the estimated parameter is given by the **p-value**, which for $\hat{b}$ can be found in cell E-43 of Table A.2, which is 0.0001. This p-value means that we can be $1 - 0.0001 = 0.9999$, or 99.99 percent confident that the price of hamburgers is statistically significant. Consistent with our rule of thumb in our application of the t-statistic, p-values equal to or less than 0.05 are preferred in empirical research.

A word of caution regarding the diagnostic statistics thus far discussed. The rules of thumb discussed for evaluating the statistical significance of the estimated parameters are only valid if the assumption that the error terms are independent, identical and normally distributed with a zero mean are satisfied. Unfortunately, this assumption is frequently violated, in which case remedial measures may be required. A discussion of this problem and the possible remedies, however, is well beyond the scope of the present discussion.

Coefficient of Determination

After testing the statistical significance of the estimated parameters, the next step is to determine how much of the variation in the value of the dependent variable is explained by our regression equation. The **coefficient of determination (R^2)** is a measure of how well the estimated linear regression line fits the data. It is calculated as the ratio of the sum of the squared deviations of the predicted values of the dependent variable from its mean to the sum of the squared deviations of the actual values of the dependent variable from its mean, that is

$$R^2 = \frac{\sum(\hat{Y}_i - \bar{Y}_i)^2}{\sum(Y_i - \bar{Y}_i)^2} = \frac{SS_{Regression}}{SS_{Total}}. \tag{A.9}$$

The value of R^2 ranges in value from 0 to 1. The closer the coefficient of determination is to 1, the better the regression equation "fits" the data. In the unlikely event that all of the data points lie on the regression line then $R^2 = 1$. In the equally unlikely event that $R^2 = 0$, the data points in the scatter diagram exhibit absolutely no discernable pattern.

How well does Eq. (A.3) explain the demand for hamburgers on the 25 college campuses sampled? The components of Eq. (A.9) can be found in cells C-38 and C-39 in Table A.2. The value of R^2 (0.48), which is located in cell B-30, tells us that Eq. (A.3) explains 48 percent of the total variation of hamburger sales in our sample. Is this good, or bad? The short answer is neither. The coefficient of determination is a purely descriptive statistic. In some studies, a "small" coefficient of determination may be quite acceptable. This is especially true in when the study involves the use of **cross-section data**, which are observations at a given point in time. Table A.1 is an example of cross-section data. At other times, a "large" R^2 may reflect a violation or our assumptions regarding the error terms. This can be a serious problem when dealing with **time-series data**, which involves observations at different points in time. The coefficient of determination may also be telling us that the regression equation is not specified correctly in that important explanatory variables are missing, such as when a low R^2 is accompanied by a statistically significant intercept ($\hat{a}$), which has no economic interpretation.

The danger in empirical research is to confuse a large value of R^2 with robust regression results. Failure to heed this warning often leads to "kitchen-sink" models. This is where the researcher throws everything into the model—including the kitchen sink. Loading up a regression equation with explanatory variables will result in a higher R^2. This is because statistically insignificant explanatory can randomly "explain" some of the variation in the value of the dependent variable.

The value of the coefficient of determination is inversely related the number of *residual degrees of freedom* (*df*), which is equal to the number of observations (*n*) minus the number of estimated parameters (*k*). In our hamburger example, we have two estimated parameters—$\hat{a}$ and $\hat{b}$. Thus, the number of residual degrees of freedom, which can be found in cell B-38 of Table A.2, is $(n - k) = 25 - 2 = 23$. Increasing the number of explanatory variables increases the number of estimated parameters and reduces the number of residual degrees of freedom, which will increase the value of the

coefficient of determination. Building regression models with the sole purpose of increasing the value of R^2 can result in estimated equations that have
very little predictive value.

Adjusted Coefficient of Determination

Because of the temptation to build kitchen sink models, many researchers use
the **adjusted coefficient of determination** (*adj.R²*) as a measure of goodness
of fit. This statistic is superior to R^2 because it penalizes the researcher for
loading up the regression equation with junk. The equation for the adjusted
coefficient of determination is

$$adj.R^2 = 1 - (1 - R^2)\frac{(n-1)}{(n-k)}. \tag{A.10}$$

Eq. (A.10) tells us that adding additional statistically insignificant explanatory variables without a corresponding increase in observations reduces the
adjusted coefficient of determination. In fact, a very low number of degrees of
freedom might actually result in a negative value for *adj.R²*. In our example,
since there is only one explanatory variable, there is little difference between
adj.R², which is located in cell B-31 of Table A.2, and R^2.

F-Statistic

Another diagnostic tool for evaluating the overall statistical significance of
the regression equation is the **F-statistic**, which is especially useful in some
situations where our assumptions about the error terms are violated. When
this occurs, the estimated parameters may appear to be statistically insignificant because of low *t*-statistics, but which are, in fact, statistically significant.
A clue that this may be a problem comes from an examination of the *F*-statistic.

In our hamburger example, the value of the *F*-statistic (21.258) is located
in cell E-37 of Table A.2. Based on the statistical properties of the *F*-statistic,
cell F-37 tells us that the estimated regression equation is statistically significant at the $1 - 0.0001 = 0.9999$, or 99.99 percent confidence level. As with
t-statistics, larger *F*-statistics are preferred. Unlike the *t*-statistic, however,
there is no convenient rule of thumb that can be applied to quickly determine
the statistical significance of a regression equation.

RESPECIFYING THE REGRESSION EQUATION

So far, we have accomplished quite a lot in terms of explaining the demand
for hamburgers based on the price and consumptions statistics in Table A.1.
The reason that Eq. (A.3) is statistically significant in explaining hamburger

consumption based on the estimated F-statistic is because our only explanatory variable (price) is statistically significant according to the estimated t-statistic. Unfortunately, Eq. (A.3) only explains about 48 percent of hamburger consumption. Can we do better?

Table A.3 summarizes the multivariate regression results after including two additional explanatory variables: average annual college tuition (T) and the average price of a soft drink (P_y). The respecified estimated regression equation is

$$\hat{Q}_X = 35.351 - 6.476P_X + 0.116T - 9.102P_y. \qquad (A.11)$$

A superficial examination of Eq. (A.11) appears to verify the inverse relationship between the price and quantity demand of hamburgers, although the inclusion of the additional explanatory variables has reduced the value of the estimated coefficient from –8.268 to –6.476. This suggests that at least part of the effect of tuition in Eq. (A.3) may be captured by changes in the price of hamburgers and the statistically significant intercept.

Eq. (A.11) suggests that a $1,000 increase in college tuition results in a 0.166 increase in average hamburger monthly consumption. Interpreting this result is a bit more difficult. One possible interpretation is that higher tuition leads some students to increase their consumption of relatively less expensive foods, such as hamburgers. Finally, Eq. (A.11) tells us that soft drinks and

Table A.3 Multivariate Regression Results

	A	B	C	D	E	F	G
28	Regression Statistics						
29	Multiple R	0.865					
30	R Square	0.748					
31	Adj. R Sq.	0.712					
32	Std. Error	1.524					
33	Obs.	25					
34							
35	Analysis of Variance						
36		df	SS	MS	F-Stat	Sig. F	
37	Regression	3	144.639	48.213	20.747	0.0000	
38	Residual	21	48.801	2.324			
39	Total	24	193.440				
40							
41		Coeff	se	t-Stat	p-value	L-95%	U-95%
42	Intercept	35.591	3.766	9.451	5.16E-09	27.759	43.422
43	Price (P_x)	-6.476	1.379	-4.695	0.0001	-9.345	-3.607
44	Tuition (T)	0.116	0.085	1.365	0.1867	-0.061	0.292
45	Drink (P_y)	-9.102	1.982	-4.592	0.0001	-13.223	-4.980

hamburgers are complements since a $1 increase in the price of soft drinks results in a 9.102 decline in average monthly hamburger consumption.

How reliable is Eq. (A.11) in explaining the demand for hamburgers by students in our survey? The increase in the value of the coefficient of determination in cell B-30 of Table A.3 from 0.480 to 0.748 suggests that the explanatory power of our estimated equation has increased by nearly 27 percent. On the other hand, a low t-statistic suggests that tuition is statistically insignificant in explaining hamburger consumption. For this reason, tuition should be removed and the regression model reestimated. Our final multivariate regression results are presented in Table A.4. The revised estimated regression equation is

$$\hat{Q}_X = 35.351 - 6.338 P_X - 8.933 P_y. \qquad (A.12)$$

The reader should verify that the estimated parameters for the explanatory variables in Eq. (A.11) are statistically significant at the 99.98 percent confidence level as measured by the t-statistic. What is more, the values of the estimated parameters and R^2 are essentially unchanged, which supports our belief that tuition plays little or no role in explaining hamburger consumption.

Are the regression results presented in Table A.4 the end of the story? Probably not. Although our regression equation is statistically significant as measured by the F-statistic, we have only explained about 70 percent of the variation in hamburger consumption. It may be possible to find to improve

Table A.4   Revised Multivariate Regression Results

	A	B	C	D	E	F	G
28	Regression Statistics						
29	Multiple R	0.852					
30	R Square	0.725					
31	Adj. R Sq.	0.700					
32	Std. Error	1.554					
33	Obs.	25					
34							
35	Analysis of Variance						
36		df	SS	MS	F-Stat	Sig. F	
37	Regression	2	140.309	70.154	29.049	0.0000	
38	Residual	22	53.131	2.415			
39	Total	24	193.44				
40							
41		Coeff	se	t-Stat	p-value	L-95%	U-95%
42	Intercept	37.572	3.542	10.606	4.09E-10	30.226	44.919
43	Price (P_x)	−6.338	1.402	−4.519	0.0002	−9.246	−3.429
44	Soda (P_y)	−8.933	2.016	−4.430	0.0002	−13.115	−4.751

our regression results by including additional explanatory variables, such as family income or the prices of substitute goods, such a pizza. Unfortunately, the search for additional explanatory variables can be both tedious and time consuming, especially in cases when data on statistically significant explanatory variables, such as tastes and preferences, does not exist.

The analysis of the demand for hamburgers presented in this appendix underscores several important points about the use of regression analysis when attempting to quantify suspected functional relationships. In spite of the ease of computation made possible by the ready availability of spreadsheet software programs, such as Microsoft Excel, the process is not nearly as simple and as straightforward as might appear at first glance. Our regression results are only as valid as our assumptions regarding the error terms. We also have to be concerned about the underlying relationship between the dependent and complete set of explanatory variables. We have assumed in our hamburger example that this relationship is linear. If this assumption is incorrect then our assumptions about the error terms will be violated. This may cast a long shadow on the reliability of our estimated parameters and regression equation. The lesson to be learned is that regression analysis is much science as an art form.

Glossary

Accounting cost—see explicit cost.

Accounting profit—the difference between total revenue and total explicit cost.

Adjusted coefficient of determination—the coefficient of determination always increases as additional explanatory variables, whether they are statistically significant or not. The adjusted coefficient of determination increases only when statistically significant explanatory variables are added to the regression equation.

Adverse selection—an *ex ante* asymmetric information problem in which the market becomes crowded with individuals or products having undesirable characteristics.

Advertising elasticity of demand—the percentage change in unit sales given a percent change in advertising expenditures.

Agency costs—the loss of shareholder value resulting from the principal-agent problem.

Allocating function of prices—the process whereby productive resources are reallocated from low-value to high-value use in response to changes in the prices of final goods and services.

Arc price elasticity of demand—the price elasticity of demand calculated using the mid-point formula.

Asymmetric impatience—when players in a dynamic bargaining game use the different discount rates to evaluate the present value of their share of the bargaining surplus.

Asymmetric information—when one party to a transaction has more, or better, information than the other party to the same transaction.

Auction—a public forum in which buyers and sellers compete for the right to purchase or sell something of value.

Auctioneer—the seller's agent in a standard auction and the buyer's agent in a procurement auction.

Auction environment—the characteristics of bidders in an auction.

Auction rules—the formal procedures that govern the bidding process in an auction.

Average fixed cost—per-unit total fixed cost of production.

Average total cost—per-unit total cost of production.

Average variable cost—per-unit total variable cost of production.

Backward induction—a method for finding a subgame-perfect equilibria in which players project forward and reason backward.

Bargaining—the process of negotiating the terms of a contract.

Bargaining surplus—the difference between the combined payoffs from an agreement and the combined payoffs from a failure to agree.

Barometric price leadership—when an industry leader initiates a price change based on industry-wide market conditions and rival firms follow suit.

Barriers to entry—factors that prevent the entry of new firms into an industry.

Bayesian Nash equilibrium—a Nash equilibrium for a static Bayesian game.

Bayesian updating—the process of revising conditional expectations about payoffs as more and better information become available.

Belief profile—a player's assignment of probabilities to alternative outcomes.

Bertrand model—a static model of strategic behavior in which profit-maximizing oligopolies simultaneously, independently, and irrevocably set the prices of their products.

Bertrand-Nash equilibrium—equilibrium in the Bertrand price-setting model.

Bertrand paradox—the prediction of the Bertrand model that firms with market power charge a price equal to marginal cost.

Best-response function—a strategy that describes the best response to decisions made by rivals.

Block pricing—charging different prices for different amounts or "blocks" of a product.

Bond—a debt instrument that promises periodic interest payments for a specific period of time and principal repayment upon maturity.

Bottleneck—when a segment of the network that is critical to the efficient flow of data is under the exclusive control of a single company.

Branch—a possible move at a decision node.

Breach of contract—when a party to a contract fails to perform, or refuses to perform, a specified obligation.

Breach remedy—court-ordered compensation in the event of a breach of contract.

Buyer's reservation price—the maximum price that a buyer is willing to pay for each unit purchased.

Capacity peak-load pricing—charging higher prices when demand is high and capacity fully utilized, and charging lower prices when demand is low and there is excess capacity.

Ceteris paribus—all else remaining unchanged.

Chain of command—a managerial hierarchy in which the authority and accountability flows from senior to junior echelons within an organization.

Chance node—a decision node where the probabilities of random events are determined.

Closed-bid auction—an auction in which participation is by invitation only.

Cobb-Douglas production function—a production function for which inputs may be imperfectly substitutable.

Coefficient of determination—this statistic measures the proportion of the variation in the data that is explained by the estimated regression equation.

Collusion—a coalition of firms to restrict competition to increase market power and profits.

Commodity bundling—the practice of selling two or more different products at a single "bundled" price.

Common stock—a share of equity ownership in a corporation that confers voting privileges and entitles holders to a pro-rated claim on future earnings (dividends).

Common-value auction—when bidders have different private estimates of the true, but unknown, value of the object being auctioned.

Complements in consumption—when the change in the demand of a good or service is negatively related to a change in the price of a related good or service.

Complements in production—the simultaneous production of two or more goods and services using the same production facilities.

Complete-information auction—an auction in which bidders' private valuations are common knowledge.

Concentration ratio—the proportion of the dollar value of total shipments in an industry that is accounted for by the largest n firms.

Confidence interval—a range of values that may be used to test the statistical significance of an estimated parameter.

Conglomerate—a firm that operates two or more unrelated businesses.

Conglomerate merger—the merger of two or more firms from links in different supply chains. It is the joining of two or more firms from unrelated industries.

Constant returns to scale—when total output increases in the same proportion as an equiproportional increase in all inputs.

Consumer surplus—the value consumers receive from the purchase of a good and service in excess of the amount paid.

Contestable market—an industry in which the threat of entry by new firms is sufficient to prevent incumbent firms with market power from charging high prices.

Contract—a legally binding agreement that obligates buyer and seller perform, or refrain from performing, a specified act in exchange for something of value.

Contracting environment—factors that directly or indirectly affect interaction between and among the contracting parties.

Contractual network—an organizational structure in which a company outsources any activity that can be performed more efficiently by independent contractors.

Contractual relationship—the interaction between contracting parties.

Coordination and control—managing information flows between departments and the allocation of decision-making authority within the organization.

Corporate culture—a company's shared values, beliefs, traditions, philosophy, and norms of behavior.

Correlated value estimates—when a bidder's estimated value of an object being auctioned affects, and is affected by, the value estimates of rival bidders.

Cost complementarities—when a firm's marginal cost of producing a good declines with an increase in the production of a related good.

Cost-plus pricing—charging a price that adds a "mark-up" to the firm's per-unit cost of production.

Cournot model—a model of strategic behavior in which profit-maximizing oligopolies simultaneously, independently, and irrevocably decide how much to produce.

Cournot-Nash equilibrium—profit-maximizing equilibrium strategy profile in the Cournot output-setting model.

Cross-price elasticity of demand—the percent change in the demand for a good or a service given a percent change in the price of a related good or service.

Cross-section data—observations at a given point in time.

Cross subsidization—when profits from the sale of one product are used to subsidize the sale of a related product. This term is also used to describe the practice of charging one group of consumers' higher prices to subsidize lower prices charged to another group of consumers.

Damages—court-ordered monetary compensation to offset losses suffered by an individual as a result of a wrongful act or negligence by another individual.

Decreasing returns to scale—when total output increases by a lesser proportion than an equal proportional increase in all inputs.

Decision node—the point in a game tree where the designated player decides how to move.

Dedicated asset—a general investment in plant and equipment that is required to satisfy a specific order.

Departmentalization—the division of labor into groups and subgroups according to some organizing principle, such as by function, product lines, location, or time.

Discount rate—the rate used to determine the present value of future cash flows.

Diseconomies of scale—when per-unit cost at fixed factor prices increases following an equiproportional increase in all factors of production.

Diversification—reducing nonsystematic risk by undertaking a variety of investments or investing in a variety of assets.

Dominant price leadership—when a dominant firm sets the price for the rest of the industry.

Dominant strategy—the same best response regardless of the strategy adopted by another player.

Double marginalization—when upstream managers set price to maximize division profits at the expense of company profits.

Dropout price—the price at which a player drops out of an English auction.

Duopoly—an industry that consists of two firms.

Dutch auction—an auction in which an auctioneer incrementally lowers an initially very high price. The first bidder to accept the announced price wins the auction.

Dynamic game—a game in which players alternate moves.

Econometrics—the statistical analysis of economic and business relationships.

Economic efficiency—when all resources are employed in their highest valued uses.

Economic profit—the difference between total revenue and total economic cost.

Economics—the study of how individuals, institutions and societies choose to allocate scarce resources among competing uses.

Economics of information—the study of decision making under conditions of risk and uncertainty.

Economies of scale—when a firm's per-unit cost of production at fixed factor prices declines following an equiproportional increase in all factors of production.

Economies of scope—when the total cost of producing two or more goods together is less than the total cost of producing each good separately.

Elasticity—the percent change in the value of a dependent variable given a percent change in the value of an explanatory variable.

End-of-game problem—a finitely-repeated static game is a collection of one-time, static games. A player's dominant strategy for the entire game is the dominant strategy for each stage.

English auction—an auction in which the auctioneer opens the bidding with a low asking price. As prices are incrementally increased bidders who value the object least drop out. The last bidder remaining wins.

Evolutionary equilibrium—a population-dynamic equilibrium strategy profile that is resistant to change.

Evolutionary game theory—a branch of game theory that explains animal behavior in terms of reproductive success.

Exclusive contract—a contract in which a seller agrees to sell all of its product to a particular buyer, or a buyer agrees to purchase all of the product of a particular seller.

Expectation damages—a court-ordered breach remedy that is equivalent to an amount that the plaintiff would have received had the contract been fulfilled.

Expected value—the weighted average of random outcomes, where the weights are the probabilities of each outcome.

Explicit cost—payments made workers and other suppliers of productive resources.

Externalities—third-party effects in market transactions.

Fair gamble—a wager in which the cost to play is the same as its expected payoff.

Fair insurance—when the expected value of a calamitous event is equal to what the insurer pays out in claims.

Financial derivative—a contract that derives its market value from the underlying financial instrument or commodity.

Financial instrument—a tradable claim on the issuer's future income or assets, such as bonds and common stock.

Finitely-repeated static game—a static game that is repeated a finite number of times.

Firm architecture—A firm's organizational structure and culture.

First-degree price discrimination—charging the maximum price that each buyer is willing to pay for each for each unit purchased.

First-mover advantage—a player who can commit to a strategy first enjoys a payoff that is no worse than if all players move simultaneously.

F-statistic—a statistic that can be used to test overall statistical significance of a regression equation.

Full-cost pricing—see cost-plus pricing.

Functional form—see unitary form.

Futures contract—an agreement to buy or sell real or financial assets at a predetermined price for future delivery.

Game theory—the formal study of strategic behavior.

Game tree—a diagrammatic representation of a sequential-move game.

Government franchise—a publicly sanctioned monopoly.

Herfindahl-Hirschman Index—a measure of industrial concentration that gives a greater weight to the market share of larger firms.

Hold-up problem—see opportunism.

Horizontal differentiation—when a firm alters its product in a way that makes it recognizably different in the eyes of consumers than the product of a rival firm.

Horizontal integration—the merger of two or more firms from the same link in the supply chain. It is the side-to-side combination of two or more competing firms producing near or perfect substitutes.

Hostile takeover—an attempted takeover that is resisted by the board of directors of the target company.

Implicit cost—the value of resources used for which no direct payment is made.

Incentive contract—a formal agreement that links a manager's compensation to the company's performance.

Income effect—a change in the demand for a good or service resulting from a change in real purchasing power caused by a change in price.

Income elasticity of demand—the percent change in the demand for of a good or a service given a percent change in money income.

Incomplete information—games in which payoffs are not known with certainty.

Incomplete-information auction—an auction in which bidders know their own private valuations, but not the private valuations of rival bidders.

Increasing returns to scale—when total output increases by a greater proportion than the equal proportional increase in all inputs.

Incremental cost—the additional cost arising from the implementation of a managerial decision.

Independent investments—when returns from alternative investments are unrelated and acceptance of one investment does not preclude acceptance of other investments.

Independent private values—bidders' private valuations of an object being auctioned are determined by individual tastes and preferences and are unaffected by the valuations of rival bidders.

Indirect price discrimination—a form of third-degree price discrimination in which buyers self select.

Industrial concentration—the degree to which total industry sales is accounted for by the largest firms.

Inferior good—when the demand for a good or service varies inversely with a change in a buyer's money income, *ceteris paribus*.

Infinitely-repeated static game—a static game that is played over and over without end.

Information partition—a collection of information sets.

Information structure—the availability of bidders' private valuations of an object being auctioned.

Informative advertising—when a firm attempts to boost sales by providing consumers with information about the physical attributes of its product.

Intercorporate stockholding—when a corporation acquires an equity stake in a competing corporation.

Interest rate—the price paid for the use of borrowed funds.

Interlocking directorate—when an individual sits on the board of directors of two or more competing corporations.

Isocost line—a diagram that summarizes all of the input combinations that a firm can purchase or hire at the same total cost and fixed factor prices.

Isoquant—a diagram that summarizes all of the input combinations required to produce a given level of output.

Isoquant map—a representative collection of isoquants.

Investor indifference curve—a curve that summarizes the combinations of risk and expected returns for which an investor is indifferent.

Joint venture—when two or more firms create, and jointly operate, an entirely new business.

Last-mover advantage—when a player in a bargaining game with a finite number of negotiating rounds is able to dictate the final terms of a negotiated agreement.

Law of demand—the quantity demanded of a good or service is inversely related to its price, *ceteris paribus*.

Law of diminishing returns—when incremental additions to total output decline as more of a variable input is combined with fixed inputs.

Law of supply—the quantity supplied of a good or service is directly related to its market price, *ceteris paribus*.

Lerner Index—a measure of market power, it is the ratio of the mark-up over marginal cost to the price of the product.

Learning curve effect—the reduction in per-unit cost as a firm gains experience producing a good or service.

Leontief production function—a production function for which inputs are perfect complements.

Liability—legal responsibility for an act of commission or omission.

Limit pricing—when a monopolist or coalition of incumbent firms set price at, or near, per-unit cost of production to discourage competition.

Linear production function—a production function for which inputs are perfect substitutes.

Long-run average total cost curve—the "envelope" of firm's short-run average total cost curves.

Long-run production function—a production function in which all inputs are variable.

Luxury good—when the percent change in demand is greater than the percent change in money income.

Macroeconomic policy—monetary, fiscal and commercial policies to promote full employment, price stability, and economic growth.

Managerial economics—the application of economic principles to topics of concern to managers.

Manager-worker principal-agent problem—when workers do not put forth their best efforts for managers because compensation is not directly linked to the company's performance.

Marginal cost—the change in total cost from a unit increase in total output.

Marginal rate of technical substitution—the rate at which one variable input must be substituted for another variable input to maintain a constant level of output.

Marginal resource cost of labor—the rental price of an additional unit of labor.

Marginal resource cost of capital—the rental price of an additional unit of capital.

Marginal revenue—the change in total revenue from a change in the number of units sold.

Market—any arrangement that brings together buyers and sellers.

Market demand curve—the horizontal summation of individual consumer demand curves.

Market equilibrium—when at some price the quantity demanded equals the quantity supplied.

Market power—the ability of a firm to charge a price greater than marginal cost to earn a positive economic profit.

Market structure—the nature and degree of competition in an industry.

Mark-up pricing—see cost-plus pricing.

Matrix structure—an organizational structure that organizes workers according to function and project.

Mean—see expected value.

M-form—see multidivisional form.

Microeconomic policy—the use of government regulations to alter the composition of output and consumption to achieve socially desirable goals.

Midpoint formula—an equation for calculating the price elasticity of demand using two data points on a demand curve.

Minimum efficient scale of production—the output level minimizes the firm's long-run per-unit cost.

Mixed strategy—randomly mixing pure strategies.

Monopolistic competition—a market structure characterized by many buyers and sellers of a differentiated product in which entry by new firms into the industry is unimpeded.

Monopoly—an industry consisting of a single firm producing a unique good for which there are no close substitutes and entry by new firms into the industry is impossible.

Monopsony—a market that consists of a single buyer.

Moral hazard—an *ex post* asymmetric information problem in which the risk (hazard) that a party to a transaction engages in activities that are undesirable (immoral) from the perspective of the other party to the same transaction.

Most-favored customer—when a firm guarantees that a lower price received by any customer will be offered to all most-favored customers.

Multidivisional form—an organizational structure that consists of two or more quasi-independent divisions with their own functional structure.

Multiple-item Dutch auction—an auction in which bidders submit bids for blocks of an identical item. The seller accepts the lowest price that will dispose of the entire offering.

Multiproduct cost function—an equation that summarizes the cost of efficiently producing two or more products using the same production facilities.

Multiproduct pricing—optimal pricing of two or more goods produced by the same firm.

Mutually exclusive investments—a collection of investments in which acceptance of one requires rejection of all others.

Nash bargaining—a static game in which the players submit bids to determine distribution of a divisible object of known value.

Nash equilibrium—when each player adopts a strategy that is the best response to the strategies adopted by rivals, and no player can obtain a better payoff by unilaterally switching strategies.

Natural monopoly—when a single firm can satisfy total market demand at lower per-unit cost than an industry consisting of two or more firms.

Necessity—a good for which the income elasticity of demand is between zero and one.

Net present value—the difference between the present value of cash inflows and cash outflows.

Net social welfare—the sum of consumer surplus and producer surplus.

Network—a system of interconnections sharing a common technology in which groups of individuals incur lower costs and greater benefits than when these individuals or groups use different technologies.

Normal good—when the demand for a good or service varies directly with a change a buyer's money income, *ceteris paribus*.

Normal profit—the minimum rate of return necessary to satisfy shareholders.

Normal rate of return—see normal profit.

Oligopoly—an industry dominated by a few large firms producing near or close substitutes.

Oligopsony—a market that consists of a few buyers.

One-time game—a game that is played just once.

One-way network—see unidirectional network.

Open-ascending-bid auction—see English auction.

Open-bid auction—an auction in which anyone may participate.

Open-descending-bid auction—see Dutch auction.

Operating profit—the difference between total revenue and total operating cost.

Opportunism—also known as the hold-up problem, this occurs when one party to a transaction takes advantage of the sunk costs of a specialized investment incurred by the other party.

Opportunity cost—the highest-valued alternative foregone whenever a choice is made.

Options contract—a financial derivative that grants the buyer of the right, but not the obligation, to buy or sell something of value at a future date at an agreed upon price.

Oral auction—an auction in which bids are announced publicly.

Ordinary least-squares regression analysis—a statistical technique for estimating the intercept and slope coefficients of functional relationships that are linear in parameters using quantitative and qualitative data.

Organizational structure—the manner in which a company organizes its human resources.

Owner-manager principal-agent problem—when managers do not act in the best interests of the shareholders because compensation is not directly linked to the company's performance.

Patent—the exclusive right granted by government to market a product or process.

Payoff—the gain or loss resulting from a player's strategy choices.

Penetration pricing—the practice of charging a price that is below that charged by incumbent firms to gain a foothold in the market.

Perfect Bayesian equilibrium—a subgame perfect equilibrium that is consistent with the probability distribution of states of nature and player beliefs.

Perfect competition—a market structure characterized by a large number of small buyers and sellers of an identical product in which entry into, and exit from, the industry is relatively easy.

Perfect recall—see total recall.

Performance bond—*a* bond issued by an insurance company or a bank that guarantees the satisfactory completion of an obligation by a third party.

Performance bonus—compensation in addition to nominal wages or salaries for performance exceeding company expectations to increase productivity.

Persuasive advertising—when a firm attempts to boost sales by creating an image that may have little or nothing to do with the product's physical characteristics.

Physical-asset-specific specialized investment—expenditures incurred by input-supplying firm to meet precise specifications of the output-producing firm.

Piece work—a worker compensation linked to the number of units produced, usually at the expense of quality.

Player—a decision maker in a game.

Point price elasticity of demand—the price elasticity of demand at a single data point on the demand curve.

Pooling equilibrium—a perfect Bayesian equilibrium that results when the same strategy is used for players of different types.

Pooling strategy—a strategy that does not use transmitted signals to differentiate player types.

Positive network externalities—when the value of network membership increases faster than the size of the network.

Predatory pricing—the practice of charging a price that is less than marginal cost to deter competition.

Present value—the value today of some future amount.

Price ceiling—the legal maximum that a supplier can charge for its product.

Price discrimination—the practice of charging different buyers, or different groups of buyers, different prices for the same good or service, or charging the same buyer a different price for each unit, or different blocks of units.

Price elastic demand—when the percentage change in the quantity demanded for a good or service is greater than the percentage change in its price.

Price elasticity of demand—the percent change in the quantity demanded of a good or a service given a percent change in its price.

Price fixing—when firms form a coalition to fix prices to maximize industry profits.

Price floor—the legal minimum price that a supplier can expect for its product.

Price inelastic demand—when the percentage change in the quantity demanded for a good or service is less than the percentage change in its price.

Price leadership—when a leading firm sets the price for the rest of the industry.

Price maker—a firm that exercises market power to earn an above-normal profit in the long run.

Price matching—when a firm promises to match any lower price offered by a competitor.

Price skimming—the practice of initially charging a high price for a new product to extract as much consumer surplus as possible and lowering price as rivals develop close substitutes.

Price taker—a firm with no market power.

Principal-agent problem—when one group (agents) does not act in the best interests of another group (principals) that it represents because their interests are not properly aligned.

Prisoner's dilemma—a static game in which it is in the best interest of players to cooperate, but each has an incentive to adopt a dominant strategy that results in a less-than-optimal outcome.

Procurement auction—a public forum in which multiple sellers compete for the right to sell something of value.

Producer surplus—revenues earned from the sale of a good or service in excess of the minimum required for its production.

Product differentiation—real or perceived differences between a firm's product and those of rival firms.

Production function—the process whereby productive inputs are efficiently transformed into outputs of goods and services.

Profit center—a semiautonomous company unit in which managers exercise decision-making authority over revenues, costs, and who are ultimately held accountable for profits or losses.

Profit sharing—an arrangement in which employees received a share of company profits to increase productivity.

Punitive damages—court-ordered damages meant to punish the defendant in the event of a breach of contract.

Pure strategy—a player's complete and non-random game strategy.

p-**value**—the probability that an estimated parameter in a regression equation is greater than or equal to a parameter value observed by chance.

Quasi-fixed cost—cost that does not change with the level of output, but are only incurred once the firm begins to produce.

Queuing—a non-price rationing mechanism in which buyers wait in line to obtain goods that are in short supply.

Rational behavior—when players make choices that are in their self-interest.

Rationing function of prices—the process whereby price changes eliminate market shortages and surpluses.

Relationship-specific exchange—when a specialized investment creates a long-term relationship between a buyer and seller.

Reciprocal network—a network in which data flows in two directions.

Reliance damages—a court-ordered breach remedy designed to restore the plaintiff to a condition that would have prevailed in the absence of a contract.

Repeated game—a game that is played more than once.

Reproductive success—a weaker assumption than pure rationality in which successful strategies replaces unsuccessful strategies over time.

Research and development—the creation of new knowledge and its practical applications.

Restitution damages—a court-ordered breach remedy designed to negate undue enrichment by the defendant resulting from the breach relative to what would have prevailed in the absence of a contract.

Returns to scale—the proportional increase in total output when all inputs are increased in the same proportion.

Reverse auction—see procurement auction.

Risk—variability of expected payoffs with known probabilities.

Risk averse—when a person prefers a certain payoff to a risky prospect with the same expected payoff.

Risk loving—when a person who prefers a risky gamble with a relatively low expected payoff.

Risk neutral—when a person is indifferent between a certain payoff and a risky prospect with the same expected payoff.

Risk premium—the additional return required to make an investor indifferent between a risky and a risk-free investment.

Root of a game tree—the initial decision node of a game tree.

Rothschild Index—a measure of market power, it is the ratio of the price elasticity of demand for the output of an entire industry to the price elasticity of demand for the output of an individual firm.

Rubenstein bargaining—a general class of dynamic bargaining games that involves a potentially infinite number of offers and counteroffers.

Salvage value—the market value of capital equipment at the end of its life.

Scarcity—the idea that the output of goods and services is limited because the supply of productive inputs and other resources is finite.

Screening—an attempt to sort player types according to well-defined criteria.

Sealed-bid auction—an auction in which bids are submitted in secret.

Sealed-bid, first-price auction—an auction in which the winner submits, and pays, the highest sealed bid.

Sealed-bid, second-price auction—the winner submits the highest sealed bid, but pays the price submitted by the second-highest bidder.

Second-degree price discrimination—selling a product in "blocks" or "bundles" rather than one unit at a time.

Secure strategy—a strategy that avoids the worst payoff.

Self-selection—when players voluntarily sort themselves into different groups according to well-defined criteria.

Seller's reservation price—the minimum price that a seller is willing to accept.

Separating equilibrium—a perfect Bayesian equilibrium that results when a different strategy is adopted for players of different types.

Separating strategy—a strategy that uses transmitted signals to differentiate player types.

Sequential-move game—see dynamic game.

Short-run production function—a production function in which at least one input is fixed.

Short-run total cost—the sum of total fixed and total variable cost.

Shareholder revolt—when the owners of a corporation form a coalition, usually my means of a proxy fight, to ouster senior managers, or to nullify or alter decisions made by senior management.

Signaling—when an informed individual sends a credible and irreproducible signal to convey important information that is otherwise not directly observable.

Simultaneous-move game—when all players move at the same time.

Site-specific specialized investment—when buyer and seller locate near each other to reduce transactions costs.

Specialized investment—an expenditure that must be incurred by either the output-producing or the input-supplying firm before a transaction can take place.

Spot exchange—an off-the-shelf purchase in which there is no legally binding relationship between buyer and seller.

Stackelberg model—an output-setting model in which the Stackelberg leader exploits the best-response of a Stackelberg follower to maximize profits.

Standard auction—is a public forum in which multiple buyers compete for the right to purchase something of value.

Standard deviation—the square root of the variance and a common measure of risk.

Standard error—is the standard deviation of an estimated coefficient. When the value of this statistic is "small," we can be reasonably confident that the estimated coefficient does not differ significantly from its true value.

Static Bayesian game—a static game with incomplete information.

Static game—when players do not know the moves of other players until all moves have been made.

Stock options—a benefit in which an employee has a restricted right, but not the obligation, to purchase company shares at a predetermined price to increase productivity.

Strategic alliance—a formal relationship between two or more companies that share information and resources for mutual benefit, but remain autonomous organizations.

Strategic behavior—when decisions made by individuals or groups affect, and are affected by, the decisions made by other individuals and groups.

Strategy—a complete description of a player's decisions at each stage of a game.

Strategy profile—a complete description of all players' strategies.

Subgame—a subset of subroots, branches, decision nodes and terminal nodes in a game tree.

Subgame equilibrium—is the equilibrium of a subgame.

Subgame-perfect equilibrium—is the equilibrium for the entire game, which is found among the complete set of subgame equilibria.

Subroot—the root of a subgame.

Substitutes in consumption—when the demand for a good or service is positively related to a change in the price of a related good or service.

Substitutes in production—when the supply of a good or service is negatively related to a change in the price of another good or service.

Substitution effect—holding real income unchanged, when buyers shift their purchases into relatively less expensive goods and services following a price increase, and *vice versa*.

Sunk cost—an expenditure that cannot be recovered once incurred.

Supply chain—the process whereby production moves from the procurement of raw materials and components to the distribution and sale of the final good or service.

Symmetric impatience—when players in a dynamic bargaining game use the same discount rate to evaluate the present value of their share of the bargaining surplus.

Synergy—when the interaction of two or more activities produces a result that is greater than the sum of their individual efforts.

Tapered integration—describes a situation in which a firm purchases inputs from an external supplier and produces the input internally.

Terminal node—the summary of payoffs at the end of a sequential-move game.

Third-degree price discrimination—the practice of charging different groups different prices for the same good or service.

Time-series data—observations at different points in time.

Tit-for-tat—when coalition members mimic each other's behavior in the event of defection.

Total economic cost—the sum of total explicit and total implicit cost.

Total fixed cost—cost that does not change with the level of output.

Total operating cost—includes only those expenses relating to a firm's ongoing operations.

Total product of labor—the total output as a function of variable labor and fixed capital.

Total product of capital—the total output as a function of variable capital and fixed labor.

Total recall—when a player remembers everything ever learned about a game, including prior moves made by rivals.

Total revenue—price times the number of units sold.

Total variable cost—costs that vary directly with the firm's total output.

Transaction costs—opportunity costs in excess of the transaction price.

Transfer pricing—the internal pricing of components produced by an "upstream" division that are used to produce the output of the "downstream" division of the same company.

t-**statistic**—is a statistic that is used to test of the significance of an estimated parameter in a regression equation. It is calculated as the ratio of the parameter estimate to its standard error.

Two-part pricing—charging a fixed fee for the right to purchase a good or service, plus an amount for each unit purchased.

Two-way network—see reciprocal network.

Tying contract—a contract that gives a buyer access to a sellers product contingent on an agreement to purchase other products by the same seller.

U-form—see unitary form.

U-form/M-form hybrid—is an organizational structure that combines elements of the U-form and M-form to exploit the advantages of both.

Uncertainty—variability of expected payoffs in which the probability distribution is unknown, meaningless, or subjective.

Unidirectional network—a network in which data flows in one direction.

Unitary form—is a centralized multifunctional organizational structure in which individual departments perform well-defined functions.

Unit elastic demand—when the percentage change in the quantity demanded for a good or service equals the percentage change in its price.

Valid information set—a collection of decision nodes for the same player where no decision node precedes any other decision node in the same information set.

Value marginal product of labor—the extra revenue earned from the sale of the increased output from additional labor employed.

Value marginal product of capital—the extra revenue earned from the sale of the increased output from additional capital employed.

Variance—a measure of the volatility of random outcomes.

Vertical differentiation—when a firm changes its product in a way that makes recognizably better in the eyes of all consumers relative to similar goods offered for sale by rivals.

Vertical integration—the merger of two or more firms from different links in the supply chain. It is the up-and-down combination of two or more stages of production.

Vickrey auction—see sealed-bid, second-price auction.

Virtual network—a linked computer network involving servers, terminals, software applications, and so on.

Volume discounting—see second-degree price discrimination.

Winner's curse—when the bidder with the most optimistic private value estimate wins a common-value auction, but pays a price that is greater than the object's true value.

Winner-take-all—a phenomenon in networks in which the combined effects of positive network externalities and economies of scale results in a single firm dominating the market.

Yield to maturity—the interest rate that equates future payments received from a debt instrument with its value today.

References

Akerlof, George A. "The Market for 'Lemons': Quality, Uncertainty, and the Market Mechanism." *Quarterly Journal of Economics* 84 (1970): 488–500.

Arrow, Kenneth J. *Essays in the Theory of Risk Bearing*. Chicago: Markham, 1970.

Axelrod, Robert. *The Evolution of Cooperation*. New York: Basic Books, 1984.

Bain, Joe S. *Barriers to New Competition: Their Character and Consequences in Manufacturing Industries*. Cambridge, MA: Harvard University Press, 1956.

Baumol, William J., John C. Panzar and Robert D. Willig. *Contestable Markets and the Theory of Industry Structure*. New York: Harcourt, Brace, Jovanovich, 1982.

Bazerman, Max H. and William F. Samuelson. "I Won the Auction but Don't Want the Prize." *Journal of Conflict Resolution* 27 (1983): 618–34.

Bernoulli, Daniel. "Specimen Theoriae Novae de Mensura Sortis." *Commentarii Academiae Scientiarum Imperialis Petropolitannae* (1738). Translated by Louise Sommer as "Exposition of a New Theory on the Measurement of Risk." *Econometrica* 22 (1954): 23–36.

Bertrand, Joseph L. F. "Théorie Mathématique de la Richesse Sociale." *Journal des Savants* 67 (1883): 499–508.

Binmore, Kenneth G. *Fun and Games: A Text on Game Theory*. Lexington, MA: D. C. Heath, 1992.

Black, Fischer and Myron Scholes. "The Pricing of Options and Corporate Liabilities." *Journal of Political Economy* 81 (1973): 637–54.

Brandenburger, Adam M. and Barry J. Nalebuff. *Co-Opetition*. New York: Doubleday, 1997.

Brush, Thomas H. "Predicted Change in Operational Synergy and Post-Acquisition Performance of Acquired Businesses." *Strategic Management Journal* 17 (1996): 1–24.

Chamberlin, Edward H. *The Theory of Monopolistic Competition*. Cambridge, MA: Harvard University Press, 1933.

Chandler, Alfred D. *Strategy and Structure*. Cambridge, MA: Harvard University Press, 1962.

————. *The Visible Hand*. Cambridge, MA: Harvard University Press, 1977.

Cooper, Russell, Douglas V. DeJong, Robert Forsythe and Thomas W. Ross. "Cooperation without Reputation: Experimental Evidence from Prisoner's Dilemma Games." *Games and Economic Behavior* 12 (1996): 187–218.

Cournot, Antoine Augustin. *Recherches sur les Principes Mathématiques de la Théorie des Richesses*, Paris: Hachette, 1838. Translated by Nathaniel T. Bacon as *Researches into the Mathematical Principles of the Theory of Wealth*. New York: Macmillan, 1897.

Darwin, Charles. *On the Origin of Species by Means of Natural Selection*. London: John Murray, 1859.

Datar, S. M., D. A. Garvin and P. G. Cullen. *Rethinking the MBA: Business Education at a Crossroads*. Boston, MA: Harvard Business Press, 2010.

Dixit, Avinash K. and Barry. J. Nalebuff. *Thinking Strategically: The Competitive Edge in Business, Politics, and Everyday Life*. New York: W. W. Norton, 1991.

Economides, Nicholas. "Competition Policy in Network Industries: An Introduction." In *The New Economy and Beyond: Past. Present and Future*, edited by D. W. Jansen. Northampton, MA: Edward Elgar Publishing, 2006.

Frederickson, J. W. "The Straategic Decision Process and Organizational Structure." *Academy of Management Review* 11 (1986): 280–97.

Friedman, Milton. *Capitalism and Freedom*. Chicago: University of Chicago Press, 1962.

Galbraith, John Kenneth. *American Capitalism: The Concept of Countervailing Power*. Boston, MA: Houghton Mifflin, 1952.

Harsanyi, John C. "Games with Incomplete Information Played by 'Bayesian' Players. Parts I–III." *Management Science* 14 (1968): 159–82, 320–34, and 486–502.

Hofbauer, Josef and Karl Sigmund. *Evolutionary Games and Population Dynamics*. Cambridge: Cambridge University Press, 1998.

Knight, Frank H. *Risk, Uncertainty and Profit*. New York: Houghton Mifflin, 1921.

————. *Freedom and Reform*. New York: Harper & Brothers, 1947.

Liebowitz, Stan. "Network Meltdown: The Legacy of Bad Economics." In *The New Economy and Beyond: Past. Present and Future*, edited by D. W. Jansen. Northampton, MA: Edward Elgar Publishing, 2006.

McAfee, R. Preston and John McMillan. "Auctions and Bidding." *Journal of Economic Literature* 25 (1987): 699–783.

McMillan, John. "Selling Spectrum Rights." *Journal of Economic Perspectives* 8 (1994): 145–62.

Merton, Robert C. "Theory of Rational Option Pricing." *Bell Journal of Economics and Management Science* 4 (1973): 141–83.

Nathanson, Daniel and James Cassano. "Organization, Diversity, and Performance." *The Wharton Magazine* 6 (1982): 19–26.

North, Douglass C. "Transactions Costs in History." *Journal of European Economic History* 14 (1985): 557–76.

OECD. *Science, Technology and Industry Scoreboard 1999: Benchmarking Knowledge-Based Economies*, Annex 1. Paris: OECD, 1999.

OECD. *Science, Technology and Industry Scoreboard 2001: Towards a Knowledge-Based Economy*, Annex 1.1. Paris: OECD, 2001.

Osborne, Martin J. and Ariel Rubinstein. *A Course in Game Theory*. Cambridge, MA: MIT Press, 1994.

Oster, Clinton V. and John S. Strong. Predatory Practices in the U.S. Airline Industry (January 15, 2001), http://ntl.bts.gov/lib/17000/17600/17602/PB2001102478.pdf.

Penrose, Edith T. *The Theory of the Growth of the Firm*. New York: John Wiley, 1959.

Porter, Michael E. *Competitive Strategy*. New York: Free Press, 1980.

Prahalad, C. K. and Richard A. Bettis. "The Dominant Logic: A New Linkage between Diversity and Performance." *Strategic Management Journal* 7 (1986): 485–501.

Pratt, John W. "Risk Aversion in the Small and in the Large." *Econometrica* 32 (1964): 122–36.

Pruett-Jones, Stephen and Melinda Pruett-Jones. "Sexual Competition and Courtship Disruptions: Why Do Bowerbirds Destroy Each Other's Bowers?" *Animal Behavior* 47 (1994): 607–20.

Robinson, Joan. *The Economics of Imperfect Competition*. London: Macmillan, 1933.

Rubinstein, Ariel. "Perfect Equilibrium in a Bargaining Model." *Econometrica* 61 (1982): 97–101.

Schelling, Thomas C. *The Strategy of Conflict*. London: Oxford University Press, 1960.

Schumpeter, Joseph Alois. *Capitalism, Socialism and Democracy*. New York: Harper and Brothers, 1942.

Selten, Reinhard. "Spieltheoretische Behandlung eines Oligopolmodells mit Nachfragetragheit." *Zeitschrift fur die Gesamte Staatswissenschaft* 121 (1965): 301–24.

Shavell, Steven. "Damage Measures for Breach of Contract." *Bell Journal of Economics* 11 (1980): 466–90.

Simon, Herbert A. "Rational Choice and the Structure of the Environment." *Psychological Review* 63 (1956): 129–38.

———. "A Behavioral Model of Rational Choice." *Quarterly Journal of Economics* 69 (1957): 99–118.

Smith, Adam. *The Wealth of Nations* (1776). New York: Modern Library, 2000.

Smith, John Maynard. *Evolution and the Theory of Games*. Cambridge: Cambridge University Press, 1982.

Stein, Jeremy C. "Agency, Information and Corporate Investment." In *Handbook of the Economics of Finance*, edited by George M. Constantinides, M. Harris and Rene M. Stultz. Amsterdam: North-Holland, 2003.

Stigler, George J. *The Organization of Industry*. Homewood, IL: Richard D. Irwin, 1968.

Tellis, Gerard J. and Peter N. Golder. "First to Market, First to Fail: Real Causes of Enduring Market Leadership." *Sloan Management Review* 37 (1996): 65–75.

von Stackelberg, Heinrich F. *Marktform und Gleichgewicht*, Vienna: Julius Springer, 1934.

Williamson, Oliver E. "Hierarchical Control and Optimal Firm Size." *Journal of Political Economy* 75 (1975): 123–38.

———. *Markets and Hierarchies: Analysis and Antitrust Implications*. New York: Free Press, 1967.

Index

About the Author

Thomas J. Webster is a professor of economics in the Department of Finance and Economics of Pace University's Lubin School of Business in New York City. Before joining the faculty at Pace University, Dr. Webster held positions as an international economist with the Central Intelligence Agency, the U.S. Department of Defense, Manufacturers Hanover Trust Company, and Continental Illinois National Bank and Trust Company. Dr. Webster has served as graduate and undergraduate finance program chair, and as faculty advisor to Beta Gamma Sigma, the international honor society for collegiate schools of business. He is the recipient of the Lubin School of Business Scholarly Research Award for Basic Scholarship, the Lubin School of Business Outstanding Faculty Service Award, the Pace University Award for Distinguished Service, and the Beta Gamma Sigma Commitment to Excellence Award. Dr. Webster received his BA from the School of International Service of the American University in Washington D.C., and his MA, MPhil, and PhD from the City University of New York.

CPSIA information can be obtained
at www.ICGtesting.com
Printed in the USA
BVHW070821210621
609998BV00002B/115